The Inherence of Human Dignity

The Inherence of Human Dignity

Law and Religious Liberty, Volume 2

Edited by
Barry W. Bussey
Angus J. L. Menuge

ANTHEM PRESS

Anthem Press
An imprint of Wimbledon Publishing Company
www.anthempress.com

This edition first published in UK and USA 2021
by ANTHEM PRESS
75–76 Blackfriars Road, London SE1 8HA, UK
or PO Box 9779, London SW19 7ZG, UK
and
244 Madison Ave #116, New York, NY 10016, USA

British Library Cataloguing-in-Publication Data
A catalogue record for this book is available from the British Library.

Library of Congress Control Number: 2020952918

ISBN-13: 978-1-78527-652-1 (Hbk)
ISBN-10: 1-78527-652-2 (Hbk)
ISBN-13: 978-1-78527-655-2 (Pbk)
ISBN-10: 1-78527-655-7 (Pbk)

Cover image: Photograph by Angus J. L. Menuge

This title is also available as an e-book.

To

John Warwick Montgomery
for his pioneering contributing work Human Rights and Human Dignity *(1986) wherein he reminded us:*

The Bible leaves no doubt that the panoply of human rights derive from man's status as creature of God, made in His image. The sun shines and the rain falls on the just and the unjust (Matt. 5:45): believers have no more human rights over against unbelievers than the latter have over against them.

To

Vicki Menuge
for a life of sacrificial service, raising fine children and caring for her mother

To

LaVonna Bussey
for her unselfish commitment and dedication to her children, grandchildren, parents and parents-in-law

CONTENTS

FOREWORD

Human rights are 'inalienable' rights. They do not follow the contractarian logic of give and take; nor do they function as useful bargaining chips, which people might exchange for political promises of individual welfare or collective security. The insight into the ultimate 'inalienability' of certain elementary rights marks a historic breakthrough. These rights henceforth define a fundamental status position, which people cannot give up without thereby betraying their own humanity, as it were. The term symbolizing this crucial insight is 'human dignity'. It is thus no coincidence that the 1948 Universal Declaration of Human Rights (UDHR), the 'mother document' of international human rights protection, explicitly links the dignity of all human beings to the inalienability of their fundamental rights. The preamble sets in by professing 'recognition of the inherent dignity and of the equal and inalienable rights of all members of the human family'.

The powerful moral connotation that the term 'human dignity' carries points beyond the sphere of positive human rights law. Human dignity is not just a legal or moral right besides other rights. It precedes any positive legal claims or titles by defining their raison d'être. Prior to any national or international legislation, human rights find their ultimate moral justification in the necessity to respect everyone's status as a bearer of dignity, which marks the non-negotiable precondition of any meaningful interaction between human beings whatsoever. Given the unconditional nature of that due respect, human dignity cannot exist in different degrees; nor can it depend on personal skills or faculties, which some individuals may fail to possess. The term 'human dignity' only makes sense when employed in an all-inclusive and egalitarian manner, as exemplified in the just-cited introductory words of the UDHR.

Human dignity undergirds the whole system of human rights, both its general principles and its specific legal titles. All human rights – from the right to life and the freedom of expression to habeas corpus guarantees and rights of political participation and so on – specify the foundational respect that human beings owe to each other as well as to themselves. Freedom of religion or belief is no exception in this regard. It recognizes an important dimension of human life and society, namely the fact that human beings can profess profound and existential convictions, which to a large degree define their personal identity, their understanding of meaning in life and their sense of belonging. Accordingly, freedom of religion or belief also covers the various practical manifestations of people's religious (and non-religious) identity-shaping convictions in private and in public.

In addition, freedom of religion or belief plays an important role in keeping the whole system of human rights open for a diversity of beliefs and orientations. This also has a bearing on the understanding of human dignity. While the term 'dignity' strongly resonates in different religious (or non-religious) traditions, none of these can provide the binding interpretation of dignity, which everyone else would have to adopt. The 'secular' formulation of human dignity, as enshrined in various international human rights documents starting with the UDHR, thus facilitates a diversity of images, metaphors or conceptualizations of a notion, which ultimately remains inexhaustible.

I would like to thank the editors of this book for their kind invitation to provide a short foreword. I hope the book will attract a broad readership and stimulate profound reflections and wide discussions. The current crisis of multilateralism and international law seriously affects the legitimacy and effectiveness of the global human rights infrastructure. In the face of growing political cynicism, new waves of populism and worrying signs of human rights fatigue, it has become more obvious than ever that a mere legalistic and positivistic administration of existing standards will not suffice. What we urgently need is a renewed awareness of the ultimate foundations of human rights, in order to remind ourselves of how much is at stake.

Heiner Bielefeldt
Former UN Special Rapporteur on Freedom of Religion or Belief

TABLE OF CASES

INTRODUCTION

Barry W. Bussey

Making Dignity a Practical Legal Reality

The chapters presented in this volume build on those in the first volume. Almost all of these chapters were presented at the IVR Congress in Lucerne, July 2019. Less than a year after we congregated on the shores of beautiful Lake Lucerne, at the base of Mount Pilatus, we found ourselves facing the practical implications of how we understand and interpret the concept of human dignity as the world gropes its way through the COVID-19 pandemic. The crisis confronts us with the ramifications of society's response to protect the dignity of the vulnerable. We wrestle, as did previous generations, with balancing the need to protect human life from disease – in our situation, by isolation and physical distancing – alongside the requirements of a functioning, healthy society which defends and depends upon basic freedoms and the well-being of citizens in all aspects, from employment to education. Throughout the pandemic, medical personnel, scientists and politicians have been forced to struggle with the life-and-death implications of their decisions and policies. Undergirding these tensions is the presupposition that human beings have inherent dignity: no matter how old, how compromised by illness, they deserve protection from the COVID-19 virus even at high costs to the economy (Koop 2020). And, in the context of this global suffering and uncertainty, additional trauma has been ignited (and exposed) by the brutal killing, at the hands of the Minneapolis Police, of Mr George Floyd, a black man. The ensuing civil unrest and calls for social justice have yet again raised the issue of human dignity for all people, regardless of race.

These current events illustrate the practical complexities of applying the concept of human dignity to real life: a task or goal which may, at times, appear to be as elusive as an artist nailing an aesthetic display of Jell-O to a wall. There is no guarantee that an abstract construction with theoretical validity will meet the requirements of reality in its implementation. In his introduction to the first volume of this two-volume set, my esteemed co-editor, Angus Menuge, aptly describes the struggle to articulate the concept of 'inherent human dignity' used in international instruments like the 1948 Universal Declaration of Human Rights (UDHR). First, dignity claims have been trivialized such that we no longer understand the vision of the UDHR drafters. Second, the word 'dignity' is ambiguous, making it difficult to have a wide, shared understanding. Third, assuming we have a clear understanding of the term, we must ground it in objective reality.

Professor and distinguished Israeli jurist Aharon Barak (2015) points out that as a concept, 'human dignity is a contextually dependent value. It is a changing value in a changing world' (6). Being a 'relative concept', it is 'dependent upon historical, cultural, religious, social and political contexts' (ibid.). These are the social antecedents that shed light on what values (and thus rights) mean. He maintains that human dignity developed as a social value 'based upon different theological and philosophical approaches' (7). Over time the constitutional value and constitutional right became part of the intellectual history of human dignity. Barak explains that 'all of the meanings of human dignity – the theological, philosophical and constitutional meanings – deal with human dignity within society' (8). It does not exist in a void but is a relational concept.

Barak thereby recognizes the interplay between the metaphysical and the practical reality of human dignity. It does not stand alone. The law is tasked with the application of metaphysical conceptualizations of the 'ought' to practical realities. It is one thing to have an abstract understanding of justice. It is quite another to apply that understanding to a case in the courtroom. It is here justice is seen to be done by a public that expects principles of law to apply equally to all citizens with no regard to personal status. Thereby the peace and security of the polis is assured.

Underlying this volume is the notion that protecting religious freedom is an integral part of human dignity. Western philosophical tradition since the Enlightenment has accepted the Kantian idea that it is wrong to treat a person as a thing or a means to some end. A person has a conscience, free will and reason, and on the basis of those faculties, he or she has the innate right to endorse or reject a religious view about the ultimate meaning of life. Therefore, it is wrong to treat a person as a mere thing; an automaton that must passively comply with prevailing cultural and political ideologies even when they directly conflict with that person's religious convictions. We disrespect the dignity of people when we act as if they had no conscientious and rational commitments of their own – as if they were merely clay to be shaped into a form preferred by the state. Thus, almost all people would feel their dignity had been violated if they were required to carry a placard supporting any number of despicable dictators. Similarly, it is a violation of dignity to require people who conscientiously object to abortion or the intentional killing of another person to participate in either of these procedures. This is also why it is wrong to disqualify individuals from serving as judges because of their religious convictions.

The present volume is divided into two parts: first, 'Dignity as Foundation of Law', and second, 'Religious Liberty and Human Dignity'. As will be evident, it was important to distinguish the first six chapters of Part I as they deal primarily with the legal concept of human dignity. In other words, we explore the law's assessment and use of the term 'human dignity'. Understanding that context allows us to narrow the focus in the second part of the volume to the issue of religious liberty. There we delve into the case law addressing religious dignity claims.

Summary of Part I: Dignity as Foundation of Law

We start the first section with Clint Curle's piece that follows the pilgrimage of the legal phrase 'barbarous acts which have outraged the conscience of humankind'. Curle's examination of the terms 'acts of barbarity' which 'shock the conscience' explains the abhorrence humankind has towards senseless violence that has been so evident in our experience. Curle points out that justification of the terms is framed within a positivist approach but the reference to 'conscience' requires something more. While international law does not require a commitment to natural law in reference to conscience, it nevertheless has a 'hint of natural law'. Yet Curle concludes that human rights require 'a moral centre'. 'Without such a centre', says Curle, 'the tendency is to drift towards either a rigid legal positivism or an ever-expanding set of human rights claims that is incapable of distinguishing schoolyard bullying from Buchenwald' (24). In other words, it is a grave error to eliminate the nexus between human dignity and the religious freedom to follow one's conscience. It removes the moral centre of the human rights project that we can ill afford to lose.

Iain T. Benson speaks to our cultural moment of confusion of who we are and argues that the essence of our being is 'not race, sex or religion', but our humanity. Jürgen Habermas saw culture as divided between 'systems' (law and politics) and 'life-worlds' where the systems 'colonize' and 'parasitize' the lived associational life of the 'life-worlds'. Benson likewise worries that de-contextualized abstractions (such as 'equality', 'inclusion' or 'values') allow systems to expand their jurisdiction into the associational life. They make null and void the contextualized differences and specificity of life-worlds in general. This is particularly acute for religious associations.

It is on that basis that human dignity needs to be understood. Our essence as rational, moral beings includes the ability to believe differently and act on those beliefs even in the face of state power that obfuscates its force using the language of 'equality', 'diversity' and 'inclusivity'. Law has failed, according to Benson, to appreciate the diversity of humanness by its insistence that religious communities conform to the majority's feelings and the personal interpretation of such feelings by judges in their decisions. This approach disrespects the diversity of our humanity. And it is due, in no small part, to the inability of the law to comprehend the areas of human essence covered by religion. Yet, the law imposes its will on religious communities that refuse the ideology of the legal elites. Law ends up subjugating human dignity by denying diverse religious expression.

Perhaps the failure of law to appreciate diversity, as noted by Benson, can be mitigated by having in place the constitutional protection of human dignity as Katya Kozicki and William Pugliese argue. They suggest that the constitutional entrenchment of 'human dignity' is essential for contemporary law to appreciate and treat all people well. They see human dignity as an indispensable principle to interpret national and international law, and it is imperative that it be included in every constitution. The explicit protection of human dignity in a constitution makes it work as an interpretative criterion for all the other provisions in the constitution. As a constitutional principle, and as a fundamental right, human dignity's universal character allows it to be invoked in almost any legal case. Kozicki and Pugliese argue this is the strength of 'human dignity' because its enforcement in a wide 'array of cases should result in a coherent system of protection' (53).

Kozicki and Pugliese's argument of the importance of 'human dignity' as a constitutional term forms an excellent backdrop for Andrea Pin's piece that focuses on the role 'dignity' plays in the case law of the Court of Justice of the European Union (CJEU) and its reliance on the Advocate General (AG). The AG is not a judge, but a member of the EU judiciary assigned the role as an intervener that advises the judges on how to rule in the EU's independent interest. Pin observes that understanding the CJEU judgements requires the reading of AG opinions. He notes that the CJEU has used 'dignity' in a variety of meanings and functions as it is applied in the multinational EU context – from the old meaning of 'dignity' as status, ranking and reputation, to 'dignity' referencing fundamental human interests. Understanding human dignity as a 'right' substantiates 'social cohesion and solidarity', requiring individuals be given basic means to a decent life, although the CJEU has ruled it does not mean human dignity is an equalizer where all EU welfare systems have to be the same. The CJEU is flexible in recognizing that the interpretation of dignity changes over time as society seeks to protect vulnerabilities such as equal treatment for men and women and for those with different sexual orientations.

The AG's influence has meant that the CJEU opinions include in-depth discussions of theoretical analyses of dignity using Kantian and European theories. However, the CJEU has strayed into other streams of thought, including Ronald Dworkin's emphasis on dignity and equality. From Pin's perspective, the AGs' theorizations of dignity have given ambivalent CJEU results as different AGs provide different understandings; some give the post–World War II understanding and others draw on contemporary philosophical debates. In the end, Pin observes that dignity is a springboard for further exploration and a good vehicle for legal change.

Pin's observation on the philosophical role in defining dignity in the European context is given some balance with Angus Menuge's work in tracking the nature and origins of the 'new' notion of dignity at work in US Supreme Court decisions such as *Obergefell v. Hodges* and other recent rulings, to its philosophical precursors in the works of Rousseau, Kant (allegedly), Nietzsche, Sartre and postmodern thought. The core idea is that the state should recognize the self-realization projects of each 'inner self', provided only that these projects do no harm to others. By appropriate acts of legislation, the state can confer or remove, and heal or injure, human dignity. Menuge then argues that the resulting account is an unacceptable basis for jurisprudence because it promotes legal decisions that are unintelligible, arbitrary, inconsistent, unstable and untrustworthy. This leads to a decline in the perceived legitimacy of rulings made in accordance with new dignity principles, and since these principles can be used to advance both sides of controversial issues, Menuge argues that they are also a recipe for intractable social and legal conflict.

While Menuge looks to the philosophical issues that create conflict, Dwight Newman's piece considers the importance of ensuring that the term 'dignity' is not commandeered for applications for which it was never intended. He expresses reservations about human rights instruments that attribute dignity not just to the inherent worth of individuals (Newman refers to this as the 'rigorous concept' of dignity) but to groups. For example, the United Nations Declaration on the Rights of Indigenous Peoples attributes dignity to Indigenous *peoples* and individuals.

Newman does not share Jeremy Waldron's enthusiasm for this development as there remains a problem of conceptual drift. He fears that attributing dignity to groups to promote justice is headed for long-term corrosive effects, as it tends to conflict with, and undermine, the rigorous concept of dignity. For there to be 'group dignity' there must be an extension to entities that do not have the same kind of inherent worth as the irreplaceable human person. Further, Newman suggests it takes away from the assumption of an objective moral truth of 'dignity' which asserts that there is a worth beyond human construction. The conceptual non-malleability of the term is compromised if variants can be constructed according to the needs of group justice. Finally, it is anti-egalitarian as not all individuals are members of the group and, therefore, not equal with those who are.

Summary of Part II: Religious Liberty and Human Dignity

Having examined the law's approach to the concept of dignity in both historic and contemporary contexts, the second part of the volume takes a more concrete turn as it focuses specifically on the interrelationships between law, dignity and religious freedom.

Religious freedom once attracted a largely reverent academic enquiry due, perhaps, to the respect shown to non-conformists who faced intolerant scorn from the majority in the context of the Protestant Reformation. The struggles in the early to mid-twentieth century over religion exhibited in communist countries and various European dictatorships also elicited some sympathy.

In the twenty-first century, however, religious freedom is more likely to receive academia's cold shoulder. There is a growing view that a claim for religious freedom is an unnecessary claim for a 'right to discriminate'. Religious freedom is on the defensive in the court rooms and in the law faculties[1] of the Western world. It is ironic, given the historical and philosophical discussions in the first part of this volume, that religious freedom is viewed as a threat to dignity, especially in cases involving sexual identity claims, rather than dignity being seen as the basis or grounds for protecting religious freedom. In short, the selective application of 'dignity' has now shifted towards undermining rather than upholding religious freedom as a fundamental right.

As an example of the criticism that religious freedom now faces, Harvard Law professor Mark Tushnet (2002) argues that the 'free exercise' of religion is a redundant constitutional protection. He also proclaimed in 2016 that the emphasis on religious freedom was 'a new front in the culture wars', which had already been lost by conservatives, whose position has 'no normative pull at all'. Hence, 'for liberals, the question now is how to deal with the losers in the culture wars'. Tushnet (2016) opines that 'it might have made sense to try to be accommodating after a local victory, because other related fights were going on, and a hard line might have stiffened the opposition in those fights. But the war's over, and we won'.

Tushnet is not alone in calling into question the emphasis on religious freedom. Other scholars argue religion is nothing special (Schwartzman 2012); still others say that exercising such a right is a source of intolerance (Nehushtan 2015). Indeed, some scholars argue that religious freedom is an outdated constitutional protection to discriminate (Gasper 2015),[2] and therefore, no moral or legal imperative exists to constitutionally protect religion in the first place (Leiter 2013).

---

[1] Indeed, some scholars suggest that advocates of religious freedom have become 'anti-liberal' in their quest for toleration of religious freedom. See Schragger and Schwartzman (2020).

[2] See an opposing view in Sandberg (2011).

Within such an unsympathetic legal context, this volume seeks to continue the conversation on the fundamental right of religious freedom as part of human dignity. It is not meant to be polemical but, rather, presents a serious exploration of the legal practicality of the human dignity concept in the area of religious freedom. For, as Benson and others have observed, 'dignity' is increasingly used in opposition to religious freedom. While claims on issues like abortion, medical assistance in dying (MAiD) and sexual orientation frequently appeal to the dignity of individuals, they generally fail to recognize the dignity of the religious believer. Rather than clarifying 'dignity', these appeals distort its application. This is evident in popular discourse, in the courts and throughout the legal profession. This volume seeks to be part of the discussion that nudges us back to the 'rigorous concept' that Newman addressed.

To begin this section, we include (with his permission) a reprint of Robert P. George's article 'Religious Liberty and the Human Good'. In this chapter, the government's obligation to recognize and protect religious liberty as a fundamental constituent of human dignity is grounded in the contribution that liberty makes to human well-being and fulfilment. George maintains that the value and limits of religious liberty, clearly articulated in Catholic teaching, may be demonstrated by reason and therefore should be upheld by the state.

Just as George argues that religious liberty contributes to the natural good of human beings, the following chapter, written by Barry W. Bussey, contends that communal religious freedom is a necessary part of recognizing the dignity and autonomy of the individual. Much of today's criticism of religious freedom involves the claim of religious communities to maintain their unique identity based on their religious beliefs and practices. This causes some consternation if the principles and practices of the religious institutions differ from the mainstream. Most Western states accommodate such religious bodies but, as noted earlier, that is coming under academic fire as giving a license to discriminate. Bussey's chapter argues that the right of religious communities to maintain their diversity is justified on the basis of individual human dignity. He acknowledges Newman's concern about the attribution of 'dignity' to a group or community. He argues that the law does not have the jurisdiction to interfere with the internal life of a religious community that has committed no unlawful act. Religious community forms part of an individual's inherent worth and dignity and must be respected as such. Indeed, the dual nature of human beings – that is, individual and communal – forms who we are, and when we respect the communal aspect of humanity, we respect the inherent worth and dignity of each individual. Religious community, Bussey argues, is the practical manifestation of an individual's right to be a part of that which is bigger than herself and yet remain free to choose.

Moving from a national to a global law perspective, the Honourable Justice Dallas K. Miller, who has done a great deal of liaison work with judicial colleagues in other countries, observes that many of the world's rule of law programmes view the work of North American and British academics and jurists as a source of models to emulate. For example, Senior Law Lord Tom Bingham's work *The Rule of Law* (2010) continues to have impact. Bingham suggests eight principles that form the base for a nation to operate under the rule of law. They provide practical ways that laws and policies can be enacted to give life to a fair and just legal system within an appropriate constitutional order. However, Miller observes that Bingham's principles could have been enriched by a more nuanced and thorough analysis of religious freedom – a topic about which Bingham appears 'noticeably uncomfortable'. It is Miller's view that basic to any rule of law model is the protection of personal liberties so as to constrain the unjustifiable intrusion of the state into a zone of belief, conscience and practice into which the 'law' or 'state' may not or should not go. Miller points out that freedom of religion pre-existed the nation state in the same way that the legal right to bodily security, property and contract pre-existed the state.

Matteo Frau and Vito Breda focus on cases in the United Kingdom and Italy that also involve a clash of dignity claims. First, the prerogative to manifest one's identity-based claims, for example, to obtain the right to same-sex marriage; and, second, the prerogative to refuse the messaging or reproduction of such identity-based claims by a service provider because it goes against one's conscience. Frau and Breda argue that the normative and pragmatic implications of these positions should be assessed within a deliberative arena such as parliament and regional assemblies and not the courts. Courts are not the place to deal with the practical implications of the opposing sides. This is because the two claims cannot be constructed in absolute terms. Further, balancing these claims has the effect of limiting private initiatives. Finally, the level of protection against the discrimination of minorities is contextually dependent.

While suggesting a different resolution than that recommended by Frau and Breda, the following chapter provides another illustration of the apparent tensions between identity-based claims and religious freedom claims, particularly within the courts. Greg Walsh, a scholar who has developed a considerable body of literature on the rights of religious schools, focuses in his chapter on the conflicts between the beliefs and practices of religious schools and universities with the convictions of others in society. He takes an in-depth look at the Supreme Court of Canada's (SCC) decisions on Trinity Western University's (TWU) proposed law school. TWU required students to sign an agreement that included an obligation for all students to refrain from sexual activity outside of a heterosexual marriage. The SCC relied on the concepts of equality, dignity and diversity in justifying its decision. Walsh argues that the court adopted a superficial approach that failed to engage with a range of complexities concerning these concepts, especially how they could be used to support a decision in favour of approving the proposed law school.

Michael Quinlan provides another practical example of the problem with the notion of dignity. What happens when two opposing notions of dignity are seeking the support of the law? Quinlan addresses the growing number of Australian states and territories that have introduced exclusion zones around clinics which terminate pregnancies. Legislatures justify these exclusion zones on the basis of 'dignitary harm' said to be suffered by workers and visitors to such sites when they are exposed to prohibited communications and conduct. Quinlan reviews the evidence of such harm and contrasts that with the harm to the dignity of those motivated by religious faith or conscience to provide 'sidewalk counselling'; and the harm to those who wish to pray in such zones. Quinlan also raises the harm to the dignity of those who terminate their pregnancies and suffer deleterious health consequences as a result and who would have accepted assistance if provided to them within a zone. Quinlan argues for the reversal of the exclusion zone trend and for the amendment of existing exclusion zone laws to narrow the scope of the proscribed conduct and give greater recognition to the dignity of those adversely impacted by such laws.

Finally, Neil Foster addresses the harm to dignity when religious organizations face litigation and courts are invited to decide what is a 'valid' or 'correct' religious doctrine. Foster continues the long discussion in Western law that highlights the incompetence of courts in determining religious doctrine. He does, however, make room for courts to become more involved in religious teaching when enforcing a private law right, such as under a charitable trust for the advancement of religion, or an employment contract. In other words, the courts must ensure that deserving parties are not without a valid remedy. He suggests a presumption that courts have a hands-off approach to religious doctrine generally, but that this presumption may be rebutted where there is a civil dispute involving private parties, who have chosen to subject themselves to a specific religious regime. In those circumstances, the court has an obligation to resolve the dispute between the parties, even if that resolution may incidentally involve a consideration of religious doctrine. His chapter does great work in reviewing the judicial approaches in the United States, the United Kingdom and Australia.

Acknowledgements

Over the past several years, I have become more of an academic in my legal pursuits than a practicing lawyer who is in court every day. It has several blessings (and a few drawbacks), including the fact that I get to dig deep into the intellectual challenges that affect everyday life and do what I enjoy most – writing. However, writing can be challenging for one's spouse, who has to deal with copious amounts of opened books strewn hither and yon. It takes a special person to put up with the disarray and the intensity of meeting deadlines. That special person in my life is my amazing wife LaVonna, who had no idea what she was getting into when she married this bibliophile. At least we can laugh about it all. It was so much fun to be able to go to Lucerne in 2019 and enjoy a tremendous journey of walking the lake front; conversing with fellow academics (many of whom are now published in this volume) from around the world as we sampled the various restaurants along the river Reuss; and spending a day on Mount Pilatus with Angus and Vicki Menuge and Mariéle Wulf. It was a privilege to have LaVonna experience that with me.

I had a tremendous time co-chairing our special workshop with Angus Menuge. We had spoken many times on the phone but getting to fellowship with him and Vicki made the experience truly valuable. Working with an outstanding steering committee – Angus Menuge, Andrew Bennett, Dallas Miller, Dwight Newman and Ray Pennings – made our work in Lucerne very productive and fruitful, as these two volumes attest. I thank Dallas, a long-time friend, who encouraged me to get engaged with this group in the first place. I am sorry that I could not get involved sooner but such a great privilege is mine in having done so now. Dwight is an inspiration for his amazing body of work, and his friendship and discussions have been most helpful. Ray is one who is known to get things done, as is Andrew, whose dedication to religious freedom is unwavering.

What a privilege to work with each of the contributors to this volume. Thank you for participating with such intellectual distinction, deep reflection and commitment to the importance of maintaining the protection of humanity from the abuses that have caused such trauma throughout history!

The Australian crew made tremendous contributions to our project. Indeed, there was a large contingent present in Lucerne from 'down under'. Michael Quinlan, Keith Thompson, Iain T. Benson, Greg Walsh, Neil Foster and Nicholas Aroney were among those who travelled far to be at this event, and they contributed much to our success.

Getting these materials ready would not have been as smooth as it was without the brilliant and efficient work of my writing assistant, Amy Ross. Amy has worked for me on a number of projects, and she is such a tremendous help, as all who benefited from her assistance in these volumes will agree.

It was a great pleasure during the IVR Congress to meet up with Heiner Bielefeldt, former United Nations Special Rapporteur on Freedom of Religion or Belief. I had first met Bielefeldt when I served as the UN representative for the Seventh-day Adventist Church some years ago in New York. We are deeply honoured that he was so gracious as to contribute the Foreword to this volume.

Finally, another big thanks to Megan Grieving and her team at Anthem Press, who showed great patience with me in getting this volume together. It has been a very strange time with the COVID-19 crisis, which made it difficult to stay as focused as one might have otherwise.

Again, Angus Menuge and I cannot say enough to express our deep gratitude for the generous support we received through CARDUS, an independent, faith-based, Canadian think tank devoted to the support of human flourishing and religious freedom. This support made our initial special workshop possible and also assisted in the publication process.

References

Barak, Aharon. 2015. *Human Dignity: The Constitutional Value and the Constitutional Right*. Cambridge: Cambridge University Press.

Bingham, Tom. 2010. *The Rule of Law*. London: Allen Lane.

Gasper, Travis. 2015. 'A Religious Right to Discriminate: *Hobby Lobby* and "Religious Freedom" as a Threat to the LGBT Community'. *Texas A&M Law Review* 3, no. 2: 395–417.

Koop, Chacour. 2020. '"Sacrifice the Weak" and "Give Me Liberty": Signs at Coronavirus Protests across US'. *Charlotte Observer*. https://www.charlotteobserver.com/news/coronavirus/article242182796.html.

Leiter, Brian. 2013. *Why Tolerate Religion?* Princeton, NJ: Princeton University Press.

Nehushtan, Yossi. 2015. *Intolerant Religion in a Tolerant-Liberal Democracy*. Oxford: Hart.

Sandberg, Russell. 2011. 'The Right to Discriminate'. *Ecclesiastical Law Journal* 13, no. 2: 157–81.

Schragger, Richard, and Micah Schwartzman. 2020. 'Religious Antiliberalism and the First Amendment'. *Minneapolis Law Review* 104, no. 3: 1341–428.

Schwartzman, Micah. 2012. 'What If Religion Is Not Special?' *University Chicago Law Review* 79, no. 4: 1351–428.

Tushnet, Mark. 2002. 'The Redundant Free Exercise Clause?' *Loyola University Chicago Law Journal* 33, no. 1: 71–94.

———. 2016. 'Abandoning Defensive Crouch Liberal Constitutionalism'. *Balkinization*, Friday, 6 May. https://balkin.blogspot.ca/2016/05/abandoning-defensive-crouch-liberal.html.

Part I

DIGNITY AS FOUNDATION OF LAW

Chapter One

'ACTS WHICH HAVE OUTRAGED THE CONSCIENCE OF HUMANKIND'

Clint Curle

When trying to comprehend an elusive concept, it is sometimes advantageous to seek out its opposite. Such is the case with human dignity. It can be difficult to define, but when we see or experience an affront to human dignity, we recognize it immediately. Such a method is especially appropriate when human experience provides such ample material on the opposite of human dignity. Unfortunately, we have no shortage of examples of the violation and degradation of human dignity across time and around the globe.

This chapter explores the interesting career of the legal phrase 'acts which have outraged the conscience of humankind'. The phrase emerged in nineteenth-century jurisprudence as part of an attempt to understand the boundaries of national sovereignty in international law, and more specifically, when it might be legally acceptable to violate national sovereignty for purposes of humanitarian intervention. The phrase was given prominence in the preambles to the Universal Declaration of Human Rights (UDHR, 1948) and continues to be an important reference today in the work of the International Criminal Court, the R2P doctrine and human rights generally. It is most frequently used as a legal threshold test to determine whether intervention to protect people's human rights is legitimate.

The central assumption of this chapter is that the concept of 'acts which shock the conscience of humankind' is a practical opposite to the idea of human dignity. By exploring the origins and use of the shocked conscience, we can gain clarity on the role that human dignity plays in international humanitarian and human rights law today.

As we will see, the oft-repeated appeal to an outraged conscience functions to moderate and, in a metaphorical sense, smooth the rough edges off legal positivist approaches to international humanitarian and human rights law and implicitly introduces some elements of the natural law tradition which are needed to sustain a conversation between legality and justice. Furthermore, this conversation about human dignity is conducted in a fashion that is dialogical in a pluralistic global environment, wherein the international humanitarian legal regime provides a forum in which nation states can negotiate the acts confronting the international community which truly shock the conscience, in conversation with past atrocities, and in this way implicitly affirm a core content of human dignity corresponding to the perceived demands of the present moment.

1. The Problem of National Sovereignty and International Humanitarian Intervention

To set the stage for the exploration of the concept of 'acts which shock the conscience', we need to understand the legal context in which it first arose. The bedrock principle of international law is national sovereignty (Parmar 2017). Nation states are the supreme powers within their territory. They have a right to exist, they are regarded as equals in a community of nation states and their boundaries are respected by other nation states which cannot legally interfere with matters within national boundaries.

Article 38(1) of the Statute of the International Court of Justice lists the sources of law that the court uses to resolve disputes as follows:

a) international conventions, whether general or particular, establishing rules expressly recognized by the contesting states;
b) international custom, as evidence of a general practice accepted as law;
c) the general principles of law recognized by civilized nations;
d) subject to the provisions of Article 59, judicial decisions and the teachings of the most highly qualified publicists of the various nations, as subsidiary means for the determination of rules of law.

Within the third category of 'general principles of law recognized by civilized nations' there resides a particular concept which permits a legal exception to the rule of national sovereignty: when a nation state engages in actions which are highly offensive to the public conscience, other nation states may intervene in a way that is recognized as legally legitimate.

The formulation of this concept in international law has evolved over time. A particularly provocative – and telling – variant is captured in the first part of the second recital of the Preamble to the UDHR: 'Whereas disregard and contempt for human rights have resulted in barbarous acts which have outraged the conscience of mankind'. The appeal to public conscience has been repeated several times since, notably in Protocol II of the Geneva Convention 1977, the Preamble of the 1997 Ottawa Treaty banning anti-personnel landmines and the 1998 Preamble of the Rome Statute of the International Criminal Court.

Michael Walzer (2004, 69) provides a commentary on this concept in *Arguing about War*:

> Non-intervention is not an absolute moral rule; sometimes, what is going on locally cannot be tolerated. Hence the practice of 'humanitarian intervention' – much abused, no doubt, but morally necessary whenever cruelty and suffering are extreme and no local forces seem capable of putting an end to them. Humanitarian interventions are not justified for the sake of democracy or free enterprise or economic justice or voluntary association or any other of the social practices and arrangements that we might hope for or even call for in other people's countries. Their aim is profoundly negative in character: to put a stop to actions that, to use an old-fashioned but accurate phrase, 'shock the conscience' of humankind.

We will look at the emergence of this concept in nineteenth-century negotiations around laws of war, chart its subsequent development through the twentieth century, with special attention to its use in the Preamble to the UDHR, interrogate how the phrase has been judicially considered and conclude with some reflections on what the enduring popularity of the phrase says about human dignity in international law.

2. Emergence of the Phrase 'Barbarous Acts Which Have Outraged the Conscience of Mankind'

The main focus of our discussion will be on the appeal to a shocked public conscience. We will initially address the 'acts of barbarism' section, which has largely been set aside today.

In the nineteenth century, it was common among international lawyers and diplomats to distinguish between two types of non-European peoples: 'barbarians' and 'savages' (Ringmar 2014). 'Savages' described peoples who lived in societies without a state. In the dominant European legal imagination, such peoples inhabited vast, untamed wilderness areas, with no means to defend their territories and no administration of these territories. 'Barbarians', on the other hand, were organized into states, but in the European imagination, they were arbitrary and despotic. Both 'savages' and 'barbarians' were contrasted with 'civilized' European states, with 'barbarians' occupying a mediating position between the two poles of civilization and savagery (Powell 1888). 'Barbarian' states had international standing but were not fully sovereign. This conceptual distinction, supported by European anthropological research, in large measure justified the era of colonial expansion by European states.

During the nineteenth century, characterizations of barbarism were sometimes used to describe egregious violations of the laws of war among European states. The codification of the laws of war represented by the Geneva Convention for the Amelioration of the Condition of the Wounded in Armies in the Field seems to have created the conditions for rhetorical appeals to 'barbarism' as the opposite of respect for the laws of war, which was equivalent to the opposite of civilized behaviour. For example, Polish descriptions of 'Russian barbarism' in relation to the Polish uprising of 1863–64 depicted the behaviour of Russian forces which targeted not only able combatants but also wounded combatants rendered defenceless, children, women and clergy. Marcin Wolniewicz (2013, 161) analyses the Polish framing of Russian behaviour thusly:

> The barbarism the Russians were accused of consisted, first of all, of violence: 'ferocious', 'brutal', 'bestial', 'cruel', as well as 'pagan', 'un-Christian', or even, 'satanic'. A violence that 'insults Christianity' whilst 'disproving the touted progress of civilization, which dishonours the age we live in'. [...] The dominant component of the descriptions of the Russian violence was its 'non-Europeanness'. Veiled at times with a 'mask of European polish', it usually appeared in a sheer 'nakedness of Asian barbarism'. This 'Asian barbarism' was, in turn, also a heterogeneous image. Its definitely excelling motif was an 'incursion of Asian hordes', which, according to 'the logic of Asian barbarism', strove for annihilation of the nation and destruction of the country. [...] The Mongols served as 'the model' for 'hordes': their devastating

invasions in the thirteenth century formed a vivid element of Polish historical awareness. Thus, Russia generally conducted in Poland 'a war worthy of the Mongols, finishing off the wounded, destroying everything with fire and sword'.

In sum, with the emergence of the codification of the laws of war in the first Geneva convention we also witness a contemporaneous emergence of a specific usage of 'barbarism' to describe extraordinary violence by European members of the international community who were ostensibly 'civilized'. In other words, acts of 'barbarism' were not used to describe the behaviour of so-called barbarian states but rather European states or colonies who disregarded the laws of war. So, for example, Canadian refusal to allow American fishing vessels emergency shelter in Canadian harbours during storms was described in 1890 as 'acts of barbarism fit only for savages' and 'as contemptible and odious as for a government conducting a naval war to fire on a hospital ship attested by her color and flag, and filled exclusively with the sick, wounded or dying, and their surgeons and nurses' (Nimmo 1890, 4).

As for the second part of the phrase, 'shock the conscience of humankind', it should be noted from the outset that at least from the English common law perspective, an appeal to conscience has been foundational to the jury trial system. Juries are regarded as the 'conscience of the community', and their findings of fact in a trial are respected. A verdict rendered according to conscience and reflecting the jury's conception of just deserts was divine in the sense that it was beyond judicial reproach (Green 1985, 20).

Applied to international humanitarian law, this appeal to conscience takes on special significance. Hersch Lauterpacht (1955, 752–53) noted,

> While no general rule of positive International Law can as yet be asserted which gives to States the right to punish foreign nationals for crimes against humanity in the same way as they are, for instance, entitled to punish acts of piracy, there are clear indications pointing to the gradual evolution of a significant principle of International Law to that effect. That principle consists both in the adoption of the rule of universality of jurisdiction and in the recognition of the supremacy of the law of humanity over the law of the sovereign State when enacted or applied in violation of elementary human rights in a manner which may justly be held to shock the conscience of mankind.

This opinion finds stronger expression in the subsequent edition of *International Law*:

> There is general agreement that, by virtue of its personal and territorial authority, a state can treat its own nationals according to discretion. But a substantial body of opinion and of practice has supported the view that there are limits to that discretion and that when a state commits cruelties against and persecution of its nationals in such a way as to deny their fundamental human rights and to shock the conscience of mankind, the matter ceases to be of sole concern to that state and even intervention in the interest of humanity might be legally permissible. (Jennins and Watts 1996, 442)

Such a bold appeal to an authority based in conscience which in certain circumstances trumps the foundational rule of respect for the sovereignty of nations is surprising to read in a tome which bears the name of Lassa Oppenheim, the famed international juror and avowed legal positivist who only recognized treaty and custom as sources of international law. In the first edition of *International Law*, Oppenheim was clear about his stance towards natural law: 'We know nowadays that a Law of Nature does not exist. Just as the so-called natural philosophy had to give way to real natural science, so that Law of Nature had to give way to jurisprudence, or the philosophy of the positive law. Only a positive Law of Nations can be a branch of the science of law' (Reisman 1994, 264).

3. The Martens Clause

The mainstream adoption of an appeal to transcendent principles of humanity and the conscience of humankind can be sourced in the Preamble to the 1899 Hague Convention with respect to laws and customs of war on land (Hague II). The clause, inserted by the Russian delegate to the conference (F. F. Martens), reads thus:

> Until a more complete code of the laws of war is issued, the High Contracting Parties think it right to declare that in cases not included in the Regulations adopted by them, populations and belligerents remain under the protection and empire of the principles of international law, as they result from the usages established between civilized nations, from the laws of humanity, and the requirements of the public conscience.

During the drafting of the Convention, a tension developed on the topic of the power of belligerents over occupied territories, and particularly the legal status of people engaged in armed resistance towards the occupying powers. In general, the great powers wished to establish strong international laws defining the powers of occupying armies. Belgium and other smaller states demurred, arguing that such an arrangement would simply give force the legitimization of law. To break the deadlock in the negotiation, Martens proposed his clause, which asserted that in areas where regulation of war was incomplete, international law was still present in the form of common usage between civilized nations, the laws of humanity and the requirements of public conscience.

There is a small body of scholarly writing devoted to the Martens clause. Some commentators see it as a signal advancement in international law, others as self-interest dressed up as humanitarian concern. See, for example, the positive assessment in Pustogarov (1999) and the more cynical analysis in Giladi (2014).

Cassese (2000) suggests that the innovation represented by the Martens clause – and it is debatable whether Martens intended this innovation – is that 'it approached the question of the laws of humanity for the first time not as a moral issue but from a positivist (or, to put it more accurately, from an apparently positivist) perspective'. Cassese explains:

> Previously, international treaties and Declarations had simply proclaimed the importance of such laws or humanitarian considerations. As a consequence, states had not been enjoined to abide by any strict legal standard upholding the laws of humanity; they had merely been called upon to not disregard the principles of humanity, qua moral principles, while acting in the course of a war. Absent international courts with compulsory jurisdiction or even

mandatory fact-finding bodies or commissions of enquiry, it was left to each belligerent to decide for itself whether or not it had behaved humanely while attacking the enemy or bombing its cities and villages. In short, these clauses had scant legal value. By contrast, the Martens Clause proclaimed for the first time that there may exist principles or rules of customary international law resulting not only from state practice, but also from the laws of humanity and the dictates of public conscience. (188–89)

In general, there are three broad camps reflected in the literature on the Martens clause. The first is that the clause merely serves to underscore the universal relevance of existing customary law in the absence of binding treaty provisions. The second camp holds that the clause establishes distinct sources of international law – namely the principles of humanity and the dictates of public conscience – which are distinct from treaty and existing customary law. The third camp contends that the clause has played an important role in motivating and inspiring the evolution of international humanitarian law in a humanizing direction. At the heart of this disagreement is a profound lack of consensus among scholars and jurists on the extent to which the criterion 'acts that shock the conscience' recognizes a natural law principle at the heart of positive international humanitarian law (Sutch 2012; Cassese 2000; and Meron 2000).

4. Migration and Development of the Phrase in International Law

The Martens clause in the 1899 Hague Convention marked an important point in the recognition of the role of conscience in international law. The clause, however, remained an insignificant insertion into the code of conflict until discovered by the diplomats who drafted the Nuremberg Charter's prohibition on crimes against humanity, after which the public conscience took on a more prominent role in the development of international humanitarian law (Lippman 1997).

The Martens clause was invoked at the Nuremberg trials to counter the argument that the Nuremberg Charter was being applied retroactively. Going beyond the context in which it was promulgated in 1899, the tribunal gave this interpretation of the Martens clause:

> The Preamble is much more than a pious declaration. It is a general clause, making the usages established among civilized nations, the laws of humanity and the dictates of public conscience into the legal yardstick to be applied if and when the specific provisions of the Convention and the Regulations annexed to it do not cover specific cases occurring in warfare, or concomitant to warfare. (Qtd in Meron 2000, 80)

One commentator suggests that the Martens clause was used to solve a central problem at Nuremberg. In order to define the criminality of the Nazi military command, the tribunal had to rely on the norms of natural law. But it had to do this in a way that apparently reflected the positivist orientation of international law. The Martens clause served as a connecting link between positive and natural law (Pustogarov 1999, 132). Other perspectives take issue with this interpretation of the Martens clause in subsequent usage to the present day, though if we restrict our focus to its use at Nuremberg, this function of the clause appears obvious.

The Nuremberg trials gave ample voice to the twin concepts of 'acts of barbarity' which 'shock the conscience'. For example, in the morning session of the trials on 17 January 1946, François de Menthon, the Chief Prosecutor for the French Republic, used the term 'barbarism' 24 times in reference to Nazi Germany's wartime activities in France. As one example:

> I propose today to prove to you that all this organized and vast criminality springs from what I may be allowed to call a crime against the spirit, I mean a doctrine which, denying all spiritual, rational, or moral values by which the nations have tried, for thousands of years, to improve human conditions, aims to plunge humanity back into barbarism, no longer the natural and spontaneous barbarism of primitive nations, but into a diabolical barbarism, conscious of itself and utilizing for its ends all material means put at the disposal of mankind by contemporary science. This sin against the spirit is the original sin of National Socialism from which all crimes spring. (Nuremberg Trial Proceeding 1946, 372)

Also in 1946, Lord Wright asserted the force of transcendent humanitarian principles:

> These are instances of what I have already adverted to, namely, a law or laws, not enacted by any sovereign lawmaking body, but depending for its creation on the voluntary assent of the civilized nations of the world, and on the humane feelings of civilized mankind enforceable, if need arise, by military Courts. The animating motive of these Conventions is admirably expressed in a sentence from Article 1 of the Preamble to the Hague Convention, No. IV, which recognized that these rules must be subject to development and revision as new necessities are realized or operate, as well as stating the governing principle of the rules in the following words, 'the inhabitants and the belligerents remain under the protection of the principles of the law of nations, derived from the usages established among civilized peoples, from the laws of humanity and from the dictates of the public conscience'. (Lord Wright 1946, 42)

How ought we to understand the meaning of conscience in this sense? Quincy Wright (1948, 14) (not to be confused with Lord Wright cited earlier) understood public conscience as synonymous with 'the opinion of the political organs of the world community as evidence of world public opinion'. Cherif Bassioni (1996, 69) noted that the idea of a shocked conscience is sometimes at odds with positive law. He provides the example of the Cambodian genocide, which does not easily fit the elements of the crime of genocide and yet due to its massive scale of killing, shocks the conscience. Bassioni acknowledges the aspect of subjectivity inherent in an appeal to conscience.

Veuthey takes a more specific view, proposing that the Golden Rule, with its variants present in virtually all major global religions, provides the core content for public conscience. He contends that in the Golden Rule's call to have concern for another, one's own human dignity is preserved (Veuthey 2003).

However, much of the global jurisprudence on the phrase has attempted to distance an appeal to conscience from public opinion. For example, Judge Frankfurter in *Rochin v. People of California* (1952) held that it was the proximity to torture which led to a characterization of a forced search as shocking to the conscience, the finding of which was a matter of judicial judgement rather than public opinion. Per Frankfurter:

> Applying these general considerations to the circumstances of the present case, we are compelled to conclude that the proceedings by which this conviction was obtained do more than offend some fastidious squeamishness or private sentimentalism about combatting crime too energetically. This is conduct that shocks the conscience. Illegally breaking into the privacy of the petitioner, the struggle to open his mouth and remove what was there, the forcible extraction of his stomach's contents – this course of proceeding by agents of government to obtain evidence is bound to offend even hardened sensibilities. They are methods too close to the rack and the screw to permit of constitutional differentiation. (172)

Likewise, the judicial reasoning of the Supreme Court of Canada disagrees with the appeal to broad public opinion to ascertain the content of public conscience. The 'shock the conscience' test was viewed not as a fluid temperature-taking of global public opinion, but rather as a way to talk about particular acts which violate the principles of fundamental justice which undergird international humanitarian and domestic human rights law. The test is not an appeal to subjectivity at all, but an appeal to principles of fundamental justice. Thus, in the Canadian legal context, extraditing individuals to a country where they are certain to undergo torture would shock the conscience, because such a decision would be contrary to the principles of fundamental justice (see *Schmidt v. The Queen* 1987; and *United States v. Burns* 2001).

Similar reasoning was employed at the International Criminal Court in *The Prosecutor v. Omar Hassan Ahmad Al Bashir* (2019) where the 'shock the conscience' test was not interpreted as a reference to subjectivity, pure emotionalism or public opinion but rather connected to violation of fundamental rules of international law along with a threat to international peace and security.

The International Law Commission (1963) commented that the international conscience is reflected in general multilateral treaties and rooted in the needs of international life, such as peace and order.

Judge Shahabuddeen's dissent in the International Court of Justice's Advisory Opinion on Nuclear Weapons (1996, 406) opined that

> the enormous developments in the field of human rights in the post-war years, commencing with the Universal Declaration of Human Rights in 1948, must necessarily make their impact on assessments of such concepts as 'considerations of humanity' and 'dictates of the public conscience'. […] The public conscience of the global community has thus been greatly strengthened and sensitized to 'considerations of humanity' and 'dictates of public conscience'.

The UN Human Rights Council (2018, para 1442) asserted that it is the scale and level of organization that elevates 'ordinary' criminal acts to those which 'shock the conscience of humanity' and become a concern for the international community as a whole.

The International Commission on Intervention and State Sovereignty which produced the Responsibility to Protect Report in 2001 described situations which 'shock the conscience' and create an exception to the non-intervention rule in the following fashion at paragraph 4.20:

- those actions defined by the framework of the 1948 Genocide Convention that involve large scale threatened or actual loss of life;
- the threat or occurrence of large scale loss of life, whether the product of genocidal intent or not, and whether or not involving state action;
- different manifestations of 'ethnic cleansing', including the systematic killing of members of a particular group in order to diminish or eliminate their presence in a particular area; the systematic physical removal of members of a particular group from a particular geographical area; acts of terror designed to force people to flee; and the systematic rape for political purposes of women of a particular group (either as another form of terrorism, or as a means of changing the ethnic composition of that group);
- those crimes against humanity and violations of the laws of war, as defined in the Geneva Conventions and Additional Protocols and elsewhere, which involve large scale killing or ethnic cleansing;
- situations of state collapse and the resultant exposure of the population to mass starvation and/or civil war; and
- overwhelming natural or environmental catastrophes, where the state concerned is either unwilling or unable to cope, or call for assistance, and significant loss of life is occurring or threatened.

One commentator, looking at the use of the phrase in the 1998 Rome Statute of the International Criminal Court, believes that the core idea of acts that shock the conscience is causing fear or anxiety in the international community as a whole (Burke 2018, 352).

To sum up, the appeal to public conscience – and to a shocked conscience – has been taken seriously by international lawyers. While its specific content is unsettled, one can discern an implicit appeal to a universal humanity animating all the discussions related to public conscience. Although the earliest commentators spoke to the subjectivity of the phrase, later jurisprudence has asserted a core of content around the idea of 'shocked conscience' that takes into consideration both the scale of human suffering involved and also principles of fundamental justice which are broadly recognized around the globe, such as the ban on torture. The general support of the international community is also a factor.

5. Application of the Phrase in the UDHR Preamble

As noted earlier, the second recitation of the Preamble to the UDHR states: 'Whereas disregard and contempt for human rights have resulted in barbarous acts which have outraged the conscience of mankind'. During the drafting process of the UDHR in 1947, the French delegate René Cassin remarked that 'in the period just passed there was wholesale denial of the right to life in a very light-hearted manner which outraged the conscience of all mankind' (Commission on Human Rights, Drafting Committee, First Session 1947, 11). Five days later, we see this appeal to an outraged conscience articulated in the proposed Preamble to the UDHR: 'Ignorance and contempt of human rights have been among the principal causes of the sufferings of humanity and of the massacres and barbarities which outraged the conscience of mankind before and especially during the last world war' (Commission on Human Rights, Drafting Committee, Initial Draft 1947). Johannes Morsink (2008) shows that the specific reference to World War II was subsequently removed in the lengthy drafting process. He continues:

> The drafters of the Declaration worked with the idea that (unless blocked) human beings have an operative moral conscience that tells them when they are about to engage in a gross violation of human dignity or when others have done so or are about to do so. This conscience puts us in touch with a realm of moral values and inherent rights the contours of which the drafters traced in their thirty Articles. This realm is an objective one in that ordinary people from all walks of life and from any of the world's cultural milieus can (unless blocked) enter it with their own unaided epistemic equipment. […] It was the outraged consciences of the peoples they represented that more than anything else gave the drafters a common drafting platform. They were so confident in their own reactions and so sure of how the persons and peoples they represented felt that they generalized these feelings of outrage over the rest of mankind, which is what they did when they used the phrase 'the conscience of mankind'. It is this moral confidence that makes the UDHR such a powerful moral beacon in our world. (17–18)

Hugh Starkey (2012, 10–11) voices a similar opinion about the UDHR:

> There is an assumption in the UDHR that there is a collective conscience that extends to the whole of humanity. This is highly speculative, since it was clearly the case that many well-educated citizens, who would have considered themselves to be civilised, participated in or supported war-time and pre-war atrocities. The UDHR is therefore asserting a new normative standard. Just as the main religious and humanist traditions aim to develop a conscience of good and evil, right and wrong in their followers, so the UDHR proposes the terms on which judgments of conscience can be made.

6. Implications for Our Understanding of Human Dignity in International Law

International lawyers do not talk much about human dignity. For the most part, we live in a positivist age which is allergic to metaphysics and ontology. And yet, we find an appeal to a shared conscience at the base of international humanitarian law. What explains the enduring attraction of the appeal to conscience?

There are at least two possible answers. First, international humanitarian law wants to progressively evolve while still maintaining a posture of legal positivism in a pluralistic environment. The negative appeal to conscience – specifically outraged conscience – within legal documents – mostly preambles – functions in a way that makes room for progressive jurisprudence while staying within the confines of legal positivism. Indeed, as a phrase capturing the negation of human dignity, 'acts of barbarism which shock the conscience' has fared better than the clearer and positive affirmations of the Four Freedoms statement which completes the second recitation of the UDHR Preamble, the source of which is Franklin Roosevelt's famous 1941 'four freedoms' speech. What the persistence of the phrase, despite its problems, indicates is the need for a transcendent appeal to something higher than law and politics – a stable universal. It reminds us of Antigone's response to King Creon in Sophocles' famed drama – the appeal to the unwritten law known by all, which places limits on what nation states and governments or their representatives can do to people (see Sophocles 2018, 17). The negative framing of the transcendent appeal in a shocked conscience does not go so far as to actually require a commitment to natural law. But from a functional point of view, the hint of natural law suffices. It avoids providing any sort of definition of human dignity whatsoever, except to indicate that we all know intuitively when human dignity has been deeply violated. Nevertheless, it asserts a moral core to the law identified through conscience. For an example of this interpretation of the role of conscience, consider the comments of the European Court of Human Rights in *Jalloh v. Germany* (2006), which involved police forcing a tube down the throat of a suspected drug dealer to induce vomiting in order to obtain evidence: 'It is a mistake, however, to forget that underneath – at the origin of the very legal standard to be subsequently applied – lies the moral resolution of those who not only have opinions or even convictions, but also the courage of those convictions' (per Judge Zupančič, concurring). This interpretation of the popularity of the Martens clause – that it introduces elements of natural law back into international humanitarian law which are required to bridge the gap between legality and justice – is one possible explanation for its endurance (see Ticehurst 1997).

The second interpretation of the popularity of the appeal to conscience is that its power is found precisely in its vagueness. It creates conditions for a broad pluralist dialogue about what does shock our conscience. This question – which acts are so outrageous as to shock the conscience of humankind? – is a negative way of inquiring into the existence and content of human dignity. In the manner in which it comes to us through preambles of international legal instruments, it is posed as an open-ended question which requires deliberation within and across boundaries and between states to answer, keeping in mind that ultimately conscience resides in individuals (Ignatieff 1996). As Veuthey (2003) avers, 'Public conscience is also the element which can burst open institutional shackles, and name the needs in their concrete, present reality, be they individual or collective'. He continues:

> Public conscience, or perhaps it would be more accurate to say 'public revulsion', has been the driving force behind every codification of international humanitarian law over the past 150 years. Rather than the proactive inscription of lofty ideals, the major humanitarian and human rights international instruments in use today are mainly the products of the painful lessons learned from the collective tragedies and humanitarian disasters of modern history. (202)

There is no assumption that the question can be answered once and for all. At the same time, the question does come with a historical framework intact. The Nuremberg and Tokyo trials and the UDHR provide an anchor for this dialogue in the atrocities of World War II, including the Holocaust of European Jews, the genocide of Roma and Sinti peoples, Nazi persecutions against Poles, Slavs, religious dissenters, persons with disabilities, socialists and communists, the so-called comfort women system of sexual exploitation set up by the Japanese Imperial Army, the list continues. Historically, we have agreed that these actions have outraged the conscience of humankind and represent a kind of photographic negative of human dignity. With these convictions – and images – from World War II in mind, what shocks the conscience of humankind today? In answering this question afresh, in a sustained conversation with the historical cases, international humanitarian law provides a global public forum in which affirmations of human dignity can be articulated and agreed upon.

John Humphrey (2000, 1:39), the Canadian diplomat who assisted in drafting the UDHR, wrote in his personal journal while he was at the UN: 'Moral bankruptcy is the reason for our failure to organize peace. I once thought that socialism could fill this moral gap; but now, although I still remain a socialist, I know better. For socialism is a technique and nothing more. What we need is something like the Christian morality without the tommyrot'. While the assessment of 'tommyrot' is a private comment taken from a diary and should be regarded in that light, Humphrey's broader point is germane. Human rights and international humanitarian efforts require a moral centre. Without such a centre, the tendency is to drift towards either a rigid legal positivism or an ever-expanding set of human rights claims that is incapable of distinguishing schoolyard bullying from Buchenwald. But in fact, the persistence of the concern around public conscience – and acts that shock the public conscience – is nothing less than an attempt to anchor humanitarian and human rights work in a moral centre, framed negatively. The negative framing leads to a dialogic process rather than a coherent statement of human dignity. And yet, it does serve to imperfectly anchor humanitarian and human rights work in a way that offers resistance to both rigid positivism and sentimentalized moral equivocation.

References

Bassioni, Cherif M. 1996. 'International Crimes: Jus Cogens and Obligatio erga Omnes'. *Law and Contemporary Problems* 59, no. 4: 63–74.

Burke, Róisín. 2018. 'United Nations Military Peacekeeper Complicity in Sexual Abuse: The International Criminal Court or a Tri-hybrid Court'. In *Thematic Prosecution of International Sex Crimes*, edited by Morten Bergsmo, 317–412. FICHL Publication Series No. 13, 2nd ed. Brussels: Torkel Opsahl Academic.

Canada v. Schmidt, [1987] 1 SCR 500.

Cassese, A. 2000. 'The Martens Clause in International Law: Half a Loaf or Simply Pie in the Sky?' *European Journal of International Law* 11: 187–216.

Commission on Human Rights, Drafting Committee, First Session. 1947. Summary Record of the Second Meeting Held at Lake Success, New York, on Wednesday, 11 June at 11:00 a.m. UN document E/CN.4/AC.1/SR.2.

Commission on Human Rights, Drafting Committee, Initial Draft. 1947. Preamble and articles 1–6, 16 June. UN document E/CN.4/AC.1/W.1.

Giladi, Rotem. 2014. 'The Enactment of Irony: Reflections on the Origins of the Martens Clause'. *European Journal of International Law* 25, no. 3: 847–70.

Green, Thomas A. 1985. *Verdict According to Conscience: Perspectives on the English Criminal Trial Jury 1200–1800*. Chicago, IL: University of Chicago Press.

Hague Convention with respect to laws and customs of war on land (Hague II). 1899. Accessed 31 December 2019. https://avalon.law.yale.edu/19th_century/hague02.asp.

Human Rights Council. 2018. Thirty-ninth session, 10–28 September, Agenda item 4, 'Human Rights Situations That Require the Council's Attention: Report of the Detailed Findings of the Independent International Fact-Finding Mission on Myanmar', 17 September 2018, para 1442. UN DOC A/HRC/39/CRP.2.

Humphrey, John. 2000. *On the Edge of Greatness: The Diaries of John Humphrey, First Director of the United Nations Division of Human Rights*, edited by Allan John Hobbins. Kingston: McGill-Queens University Press.

Ignatieff, Michael. 1996. 'Articles of Faith'. *Index on Censorship* 25, no. 5: 110–22.

The International Commission on Intervention and State Sovereignty. 2001. *The Responsibility to Protect*. Ottawa: International Development Research Centre.

The International Court of Justice's Advisory Opinion on Nuclear Weapons. 1996. *ICJ Rep. 226*, no. 403, 8 July.

International Criminal Court (ICC). 2019. Appeals Chamber, *The Prosecutor v. Omar Hassan Ahmad Al Bashir*, Joint Concurring Opinion of Judges Eboe-Osuji, Morrison, Hofmański and Bossa, 6. ICC-02/05-01/09-397-Anx1 06-05-2019 1/190 NM PT OA2.

Jalloh v. Germany (Application no. 54810/00) 11 July 2006. ECHR. https://hudoc.echr.coe.int/eng#{%22itemid%22:[%22001–76307%22]}.

Jennins, Sir Robert, and Sir Arthur Watts, eds. 1996. *Oppenheim's International Law*, 9th ed., vol. 1, Peace. London: Longmans.

Lauterpacht, Hersch. 1955. *Oppenheim's International Law*, 8th ed., vol. 1, Peace, edited by Hersch Lauterpacht. London: Longmans.

Lippman, Matthew. 1997. 'Crimes against Humanity'. *Boston College Third World Law Journal* 17 no. 2: 171–274.

Meron, T. 2000. 'The Martens Clause, Principles of Humanity and Dictates of Public Conscience'. *American Journal of International Law* 94: 78–89.

Morsink, Johannes. 2008. 'The Universal Declaration and the Conscience of Humanity'. For presentation at the conference: 'Rights That Make Us Human Beings. Human Rights as an Answer to Historical and Current Injustice', Nuremberg, 20 November.

Nimmo, Joseph Jr. 1890. 'The Chimera of Commercial Union with the Dominion of Canada'. *New York Tribune*, 23 June, 1–14.

Nuremberg Trial Proceedings Vol. 5. 1946. Accessed 31 December 2019. https://avalon.law.yale.edu/imt/01-17-46.asp.

Ottawa Treaty Banning Antipersonnel Landmines. Accessed 2 January 2020. http://www.icbl.org/media/604037/treatyenglish.pdf.

Parmar, Swati Singh. 2017. 'Understanding the Concept of "Sovereignty"'. *International Journal of Law* 3, no. 1 (January): 31–35.

Powell, J. W. 1888. 'From Barbarism to Civilization'. *American Anthropologist* 1, no. 2 (April): 97–124.

Protocol II of the Geneva Convention. 1977. Accessed 31 December 2019. https://www.icrc.org/en/doc/assets/files/other/icrc_002_0321.pdf.

Pustogarov, V. V. 1999. 'The Martens Clause in International Law'. *Journal of the History of International Law* 1: 125–35.

Reisman, W. Michael. 1994. 'Lassa Oppenheim's Nine Lives'. *Yale Journal of International Law* 19, no. 1: 255–84.

Ringmar, Erik. 2014. 'Recognition and the Origins of International Society'. *Global Discourse: An Interdisciplinary Journal of Current Affairs* 4, no. 4 (2 October): 446–58.

Rochin v. People of California, 342 U.S. 165 (1952).

The Rome Statute of the International Criminal Court. Accessed 31 December 2019. https://www.icc-cpi.int/resource-library/documents/rs-eng.pdf.

Sophocles. 2018. *Antigone*. Translated by R. C. Jebb. London: Global Grey. https://www.globalgreyebooks.com/antigone-ebook.html.

Starkey, Hugh. 2012. 'Human Rights, Cosmopolitanism and Utopias: Implications for Citizenship Education'. Institute of Education, University of London. Accessed 2 January 2020. https://discovery.ucl.ac.uk/id/eprint/1501657/1/Starkey2012Human21.pdf.

Statute of the International Court of Justice. Accessed 31 December 2019. https://www.icj-cij.org/en/statute.

Sutch, Peter. 2012. 'Normative IR Theory and the Legalization of International Politics: The Dictates of Humanity and of the Public Conscience as a Vehicle for Global Justice'. *Journal of International Political Theory* 8, nos 1–2: 1–24.

Ticehurst, Rupert. 1997. 'The Martens Clause and the Laws of Armed Conflict'. *International Review of the Red Cross* 37, no. 317 (April): 125–34.

United States v. Burns, [2001] 1 S.C.R. 283, 2001 SCC 7.

Universal Declaration of Human Rights. Accessed 31 December 2019. https://www.un.org/en/universal-declaration-human-rights/.

Veuthey, M. 2003. 'Public Conscience in International Humanitarian Action'. *Refugee Survey Quarterly* 22: 197–201.

Walzer, Michael. 2004. *Arguing about War*. New Haven, CT: Yale University Press.

Wolniewicz, Marcin. 2013. '"Russian Barbarism" in the Propaganda of the Polish January Uprising (1863–1864)'. *Acta Poloniae Historica* 107: 129–64.

Lord Wright. 1946. 'War Crimes under International Law'. *Law Quarterly Review* 62, no. 1 (January): 40–52.

Wright, Quincy. 1948. 'Legal Positivism and the Nuremberg Judgment'. *American Journal of International Law* 42, no. 2 (April): 405–14.

Yearbook of the International Law Commission. 1963. Vol. I, Summary records of the fifteenth session 6 May–12 July, 683rd Meeting, Monday, 20 May 1963, at 3 p.m. Chairman: Mr. Eduardo Jimenez de Arechaga, Law of Treaties (A/CN.4/156 and Addenda).

Chapter Two

ABSTRACT LANGUAGE AND INVISIBLE ASSOCIATIONS: THE NECESSITY FOR CLEAR LANGUAGE TO MAINTAIN GENUINE RIGHTS AND FREEDOMS

Iain T. Benson

Introduction: The Questions of Politics, Law and Religion in Relation to Lived Associations and Genuine Diversity

The Congress at which an early version of this chapter first appeared sought to address 'dignity, democracy and diversity' and hosted a workshop on the 'Inherence of Human Dignity' within which initial drafts of this and other chapters in this volume appeared.[1] I could not help but observe at the time that on the list of recent additions for other workshops at that conference was one entitled: 'The Advance of Conservative Tendencies in the Western World and the Risks for Democracy'. Clearly, what is meant by terms such as 'diversity' and 'conservative' and what might constitute 'risks to democracy' seemed very much to turn on how one envisions the state (law and democracy) and its functions and limits. For some people, terms such as 'dignity' and 'diversity' no longer describe the same sorts of things and so their nature and application are going to be widely disputed at a World Congress of this sort or, in fact, in the legal courtrooms or political chambers of nation states. All individuals are, in essence, part of a universal, shared humanity which is not defined by race, sex or religion as these are, strictly speaking, accidents not

[1] Part of this chapter is based on a presentation titled 'The Future of Religious Freedom', a conversation I participated in with Boris Van de Ham and Barry W. Bussey at the Faculty of Law, University of Leiden, Leiden, the Netherlands, 28 June 2019. I would like to thank Paul Cliteur for the invitation to attend Leiden as one of the 'opponents' to the examination of Bussey's PhD there in the Faculty of Law and for hospitality in relation to that. I also acknowledge the helpful insights from attendees at 'The Inherence of Human Dignity', World Congress of the International Association for the Philosophy of Law and Social Philosophy, Special Workshop on 'Dignity, Democracy and Diversity', University of Lucerne, Switzerland, 7–12 July 2019. For the invitation to Lucerne, I thank Angus J. L. Menuge and Barry W. Bussey. I would also like to thank my friends Kristof Vanhoutte and Vaile Roselli, who provided their home in Basel, Switzerland (a stone's throw from Nietzsche's house), as a place in which to prepare the bulk of this chapter. The 'Small Circle' Philosophical Discussion Group and its members in Europe and South Africa are also acknowledged for continued support and encouragement.

essences. So shared human dignity is defensible on the basis not of subordinate parts of group identity but, rather, in relation to the very essence of what constitutes humanness. Lest this be misunderstood, this is not to say that subordinate aspects, such as religious beliefs or national citizenships, are not important but, rather, to see them in relation to what is shared foundationally.

It is my argument that the essence of what constitutes humanness is the ability to believe differently and act on those beliefs despite the homogenous forces that use state power for conformity all the while employing the language of 'equality', 'diversity' and 'inclusivity'. Such forceful use of language can tend to weaken or even obliterate the different moral traditions that make us human. My argument here begins by pointing out that human dignity requires both a restricted self and a universal understanding. Our success depends upon our ability to work and live together while occupying the same or proximate social spaces. When self is unrestrained, there is a failure to appreciate and make allowances for the other, and when subordinate aspects dominate the sense of self, there is a risk that our universal humanity may be obscured.

My argument then proceeds to highlight the failure of law to recognize humanness in relation to diversity and universality held in tension. The sort of problem that is emerging from a failure to respect both sides of the tension is evidenced by a 2018 decision of the Supreme Court of Canada (SCC). In its refusal to permit the religious community at Trinity Western University (TWU) to have a law school functioning within belief systems that are legal but contested (relating to the nature of marriage), the SCC majority ignored diversity in its march to homogeneity, as I explain in greater detail later in this chapter. In the majority judgement in the TWU decision, the SCC framed a result in terms of what it believed we *should* be rather than what we *are*. I argue, instead, that we have to recognize that genuine diversity means lived disagreement.

Justice, as a virtue, has a long history of philosophical reflection centred on the essence of humanity that keeps alive, through respect for associations, the tension between the universal and the particular. When law loses sight of this tension, what is highlighted is not clear principle (such as respect for difference) but personal conceptions of feelings measured by the majority view – or simply the loudest and most strident voices. Such an approach to law leads, in parallel to abstract language in relation to rights, to abstract judicial creations, such as the SCC's invention of the concept of 'Charter values', despite the absence of any such language in the Canadian constitution. While such creations give courts flexibility to do what they want, these abstractions have little to do with justice, maintenance of the tension set out earlier or, ultimately, the necessary grounding for proper respect for human dignity itself.

This chapter concludes by observing that law does not have the capacity to deal with the areas of human essence covered by religion or provided by religious associations. Religions play an irreplaceable role in culture in that they address the problem of evil, the problem of virtue and the contemplation of the highest things. Law does not have the jurisdiction to deal with these important aspects of culture, nor should it step into the space rightly occupied by more traditional guardians of these sorts of moral questions. Religion provides solace and meaning despite the reality of evil; it strives for virtue in living a well-ordered existence and permits the contemplation of being. Law, on the other hand, is concerned with power and questions of legal and political ordering. When law and politics exceed their proper roles, they lose legitimacy and will destroy the aforementioned tension between universal humanity and associational differences.

We are now at a crossroads. We have a choice between affirming diversity on the shared basis of universal human nature as the very foundation of human dignity or making the law a subjugating force that denies diversity. If the latter course is followed, then religious communities and individuals will continue to experience law not as a protector of diversity and freedom but as an opponent threatening their very existence. Living in this situation is itself a practical denial of human dignity and human flourishing.

Restrictions on the Will versus the Unrestricted Self: Nature Is Restriction

Matters that are fixed by law, tradition, religion or nature itself pose restrictions on the individual will, and that is something that untrammelled wills do not like. As the mantra goes: 'you can be whatever you wish to be'.

As Eric Voegelin (1968, 99–100) reminds us in his most helpful book on Gnosticism and politics:

> Philosophy springs from the love of being; it is man's loving endeavor to perceive the order of being and attune himself to it. Gnosis desires dominion over being; in order to seize control of being the Gnostic constructs his system. The building of systems is a gnostic form of reasoning, not a philosophical one. […] All gnostic movements are involved in the project of abolishing the constitution of being, with its origin in divine, transcendent being, and replacing it with a world-immanent order of being, the perfection of which lies in the realm of human action.

What Voegelin traces so profoundly is the connection between the domination or denial of nature and the eventual movements that attempt to eradicate God. He notes, 'This gnostic movement of the spirit does not lead to the erotic opening of the soul, but rather to the deepest reach of persistence in the deception, where revolt against God is revealed to be its motive and purpose' (33).

Those familiar with the transgender movement may notice the relevance and applicability of Voegelin's comments on a related phenomenon when he writes:

> The nature of a thing cannot be changed; whoever tries to 'alter' its nature destroys the thing. Man cannot transform himself into a superman; the attempt to create a superman is to attempt to murder man. Historically the murder of God is not followed by the superman, but by the murder of man: the deicide of the gnostic theoreticians is followed by the homicide of the revolutionary practitioners. (64–65)[2]

---

2   Here, of course, the rejection of 'transgenderism' by those who believe nature determines and that sex is not 'assigned' at birth, but simply *observed*, is met with the astonishing claim that it is the rejection of this very move against nature that 'damages' the person claiming to be the other sex. That they cannot be the other sex is why recourse to the infinite plasticity of 'gender'

Nature, while it contains within it a certain kind of diversity, restricts what can be done against it, however much people may try and rationalize the departures. Diversity, as it is now in common usage today, does not mean being allowed to have diverse opinions based upon genuine differences that should be accommodated. It means something quite different. Law, in this new framework, is little more than a useful plausibility structure for cultural homogenization. My friend Cole Durham once put the modern position to me this way: 'We like pluralism as long as it is *our* pluralism'.

Law is no longer coherent. You may search for the application of coherent principles, but that is largely simply wishful thinking. What is going on, as any of us who have argued cases at the highest levels of the courts well know, is a jurisprudential shell-game. Permit me one quick example.

Trinity Western University and Judicial Avoidance by the Majority of the Canadian Supreme Court

In Western Canada, a private Christian university, TWU, sought to have a law school accredited. TWU had, a decade before, fought all the way to the SCC for approval of its final-year education program. The problem for the College of Teachers and then, in the recent round of public debates involving the Law Society of British Columbia, was that TWU had a 'Community Covenant' that had to be agreed to by all staff and students. This covenant indicated that certain things were not acceptable at the evangelical university. In particular, sexual relations were approved of only within traditional male-female marriage. Following a variety of regulatory approvals and then denials the matter of the law school ended up in the courts and what would have been precedential years ago was seen as no longer precedential given the fact that same-sex marriage had been legalized in Canada in the intervening years.

When the matter got to the highest court in the Province of British Columbia, the five-justice division of the British Columbia Court of Appeal (BCCA) in *Trinity Western University* 2016 held unanimously in favour of the university. By contrast, in *Trinity Western University* 2018[3] Canada's highest court chose to focus on the hypothetical hurt and exclusion of future students, without regard for those already there and any hurt or exclusion *they* may have felt. The religious association was rendered invisible by the SCC majority's approach.

---

is made. The parallels here to the pseudo-moral language of 'values' is clear. Gender is to sex what values are to virtues. The regnant will demands plasticity in all things it pushes against. It is, therefore, the claims of the subjective self that must trump culture and tradition. Voegelin would have little difficulty labelling this new transgender movement as both ideological and gnostic.

3   The SCC ruled in favour of the law societies in two companion decisions: *Law Society of British Columbia v Trinity Western University* [2018] 2 SCR 293, 2018 SCC 32 [hereinafter '*LSBC v. TWU* 2018'] and *Trinity Western University v. Law Society of Upper Canada* [2018] 2 SCR 453, 2018 SCC 33. I refer to them together as '*Trinity Western University* 2018'.

Even more astonishing, the Supreme Court majority simply avoided dealing with the central finding of the BCCA – the extremely strong language from the BCCA about the illiberal use of law by the LGBTTIQQ2SA[4] activists. Nowhere in the three SCC majority judgements do the seven judges (including the now-retired former Chief Justice Beverly McLachlin) deal with this passage from the BCCA:

> A society that does not admit of and accommodate differences cannot be a free and democratic society – one in which its citizens are free to think, to disagree, to debate and to challenge the accepted view without fear of reprisal. This case demonstrates that a well-intentioned majority acting in the name of tolerance and liberalism, can, if unchecked, impose its views on the minority in a manner that is in itself intolerant and illiberal. (*Trinity Western University* 2016, para 193)

How could this statement, from a unanimous bench of the decision under review, go completely uncommented upon by the majority judges of the SCC who overturned the British Columbia judges? What this oversight represents is a different worldview, not simply a different approach to judicial reasoning, and it is crucial to realize this. The abstract language of 'feelings', 'hurt' and exclusion was only applied to the activists and not the religious association.

Understanding the Nature and Importance of Moral Traditions to Coherent Politics and Law

What was needed and has not been provided by the SCC, perhaps because it has no workable theory to deal with the matter, is a robust conception of genuine diversity and co-existent disagreement. Language and tradition as discussed by writers such as Martin D'Arcy (*Christian Morals*), Michael Polanyi (*Personal Knowledge*), C. S. Lewis (*The Abolition of Man*), George Grant (*Philosophy in the Mass Age; English-Speaking Justice*) and Owen Barfield (*Speaker's Meaning*), when placed alongside the nature of ideology from Raymond Aron via Jacques Ellul (*Propaganda*), can show us how the shift from one set of moral conceptions to another leads to confusion and, in some cases, denial that the shift has occurred. Central to the moral traditions being overthrown in our time was the moral traditions' focus on the self not as 'constructing' reality but as 'conforming' to it. Contemporary law is often no longer mediating between these two fundamentally different conceptions, in part because it does not seem to realise they exist.[5]

---

[4]   This abbreviation, first used in the Province of Ontario and but one of many abbreviations for sexual identity groups, stands for lesbian, gay, bisexual, transsexual, transgendered, intersexed, queer, questioning, two-spirited (a First Nations term) and allies.

[5]   Two books would prove helpful to the aspiring jurist who wishes to comprehend the shift. The first, *The Abolition of Man* (1943) by C. S. Lewis; the second, *Philosophy in the Mass Age* (1966) by Canadian philosopher (himself influenced by Lewis while at Oxford) George Grant. Finally, Alasdair MacIntyre's highly influential *After Virtue: A Study in Moral Theory* (1984) should be essential reading across disciplines since it touches on the foundations of many of them.

Much of the language at times of transition from the world of objective goods perceived by natural reason to 'values' simply asserted by the subjective will, hides its 'faith' claims, since positivism (or objectivism as Polanyi terms it) forces faith claims to take on hidden meaning. What is not explicit, however, does not go away; it becomes unspoken or is deemed irrelevant. Thus both H. L. A. Hart (legal positivism) and John Rawls (contractualism) claimed that their theories could operate without metaphysics: this was, of course, inaccurate but has exercised a considerable and disabling influence on contemporary jurisprudence and jurists. The metaphysics of the person and culture itself are implicit if they are not explicit. Saying 'I am not taking a moral position' in relation to X does not mean one is not taking a moral position at all; what it means is that one does not wish to discuss the moral position one is, usually implicitly, taking.

It is time to argue that contemporary Western societies no longer have a coherent conception of law because they no longer share any of the convictions necessary to the place of reason in relation to nature or genuine diversity in relation to human freedom and universality. The only way out of this is to understand that genuine diversity (as opposed to using the rhetoric of diversity to bring about conditions of homogeneity) requires that we learn the nature of irreconcilable differences and the necessity of human freedom. These must be learned (relearned) in relation to the normative traditions that emerge from the life-worlds of associations that are threatened by the very nature of the systems represented by law and politics.[6]

In a recently much-noted (in Australia) case involving Instagram postings of biblical verses by a leading rugby player with fundamentalist Christian leanings, one Israel Folau, the issues of 'inclusion' and 'diversity' were raised in an interesting manner.

In his Instagram posts (this being a personal but widely public medium given his athletic fame), Mr Folau, quoting Gal. 5:19-21, suggested that various people were doomed to hellfire. The list included 'drunkards, homosexuals, adulterers, liars, fornicators, thieves, atheists, idolators' (by idolators he later made clear that he referred to Roman Catholics). It was the inclusion of homosexuals that was deemed to be an attack on 'inclusivity' by Rugby Australia, the sport's governing authority. Rugby Australia, in its various public pronouncements, stated that it was going to penalize Israel Folau because of its 'commitment to diversity'. This is, however, a curious reading of 'inclusion', as it led to the exclusion of the religious player in question from Australian rugby despite that association having an entire division of its organization devoted to 'Pride in Rugby' (to encourage advancement of LGBTQ+ players). As such, Rugby Australia's approach mirrored that of the SCC majority judges in *Trinity Western University* 2018. True inclusivity would demand that Folau's views in relation to public matters of concern be tolerated along with opposing perspectives, because everyone should not be forced

---

6   The regulation and restrictions of associations are not new. For restrictions on certain kinds of voluntary associations in ancient Rome, see Wendy Cotter, who notes that in Julius Caesar's edicts against guilds, the fear was of 'political sedition' and that 'only the most ancient were permitted to continue' (1996, 76). Even in ancient Rome, the argument from lineage carried weight and human associations were understood to be a place of resistance against the homogenization of the state.

to think the same way with respect to any of the listed activities – be it idols, alcohol or sexual conduct. At the end of this chapter I shall return to recent cases that raise similar issues and to the latest on the rugby player case in Australia.

The situation in Australia and elsewhere reveals that the language of 'diversity', 'equality', 'inclusivity', 'harm' and 'safety' itself is being hijacked to push particular agendas. This amounts to ideological bullying over differing beliefs regarding sexual morality where 'wrong beliefs' are deemed 'hateful' or 'exclusionary'. Moral evaluation and differing moral judgements are never mentioned – must not be mentioned – as those might lead to a *concrete* evaluation grounded in differing moral traditions. By following this asymmetrical approach, the majority of the SCC determined that TWU may not have a law school because of 'diversity' (see, e.g., *LSBC v. TWU* 2018, paras 39–43). Another example of the asymmetries that are developing is the recent Christian Medical and Dental Society decision from the Ontario Court of Appeal (2019 ONCA 393). In this decision, Ontario doctors opposed to abortion, euthanasia or gender reassignment surgery were informed, in essence, that they must choose another line of work if they do not want to make 'effective referrals', since their conscientious objection might make others feel 'stigma and shame' (para 141). In South Africa, in the same month as the ONCA decision, the *Gaum* decision of the Gauteng High Court (2019) ordered the Dutch Reformed Church to change both its doctrine and its rules on ordination in relation to same-sex marriage. This rare extension of judicial review power, again under the twin rubrics of 'equality' and 'diversity', used the 'harm' of exclusion to force changes to religious dogma, while in all three cases the exclusion of the religious individual or communities was ignored. Neo-orthodoxies replace former orthodoxies, the entire thing argued in new language that elides any analysis or respect for the religious believers or organizations whatsoever. The abstraction of languages parallels the invisibility of the communities being pressured by legal interpretations against genuine diversity.

In each case the idea of coexistent spheres of operation and belief, set out in such ringing tones by Justice Albi Sachs in the *Fourie* decision (2006) of the South African Constitutional Court, are ignored. An appropriate respect for different belief frameworks, perhaps operating on a presumption in favour of diversity, is being steamrollered in the direction of the homogenous and unitive state using the Orwellian language frames of equality, diversity and inclusivity. These have become, in their associational decontextualization, the very means of destroying different moral traditions. It would appear that in practical terms, the only sin is actual diversity and only progressive dogmas can continue to exist once the traditional dogmas have been exterminated as 'hurtful' or 'unsafe'.

Further Linguistic Abstraction as Merely Subjective 'Values' Replace the Cardinal Virtue of Justice

Aristotle in the *Nicomachean Ethics* (see Ross 1938) makes an observation that is rather startling for the modern mind (which is certainly *schooled*, but by the standards of any prior age, hardly *educated* – a distinction I learned from George Grant) because, in large part, the basic conceptions are no longer passed on and there has been a thinning of our language and concepts. Aristotle wrote that the student of politics must first study the *soul* and 'virtue above all things' (227). But what is the soul to contemporary politicians? And who knows what the virtues are anymore? Yet, justice is one of the cardinal virtues. Without virtues, you will only have personal conceptions of feelings driving law – and that is to be measured against something like the majority viewpoint or the loudest voices; hardly justice by any objective measure. In Canada it is common now to hear judges referring to 'Charter values' when the Canadian Charter of Rights and Freedoms says nothing whatsoever about any such category. It is a creation of the modern judicial mind craving plasticity. This is why judges have recourse to 'Charter values': they need not come from any settled jurisprudence or text and therefore create neither binding authority nor consistent application.

At the Catholic university in Australia where I teach, perhaps only one in a hundred of my students, the majority of whom went to Catholic schools, knows what is still in the Catholic Catechism: that the moral life is built around *virtues* – four cardinal (justice, wisdom, moderation and courage) and three theological (faith, hope and love). For Catholics now as for the general population, feelings replace virtues as 'values' of one's choosing. A willing and essentially unconstrained self is the key thing. How one 'feels' is the final judgement of what one should do according to one's own measure. We make the world valuable, we do not participate in a 'value' already given. This is, according to MacIntyre (1984, 26), the world of 'emotivism' where 'feelings are king', where 'causing hurt' is the *summum malum* and where 'being offended' is a breach of rights.

Barry W. Bussey (2017) and Justices Peter Lauwers and Brad Miller of the Ontario Court of Appeal (*Gehl v. Canada* 2017) have all written (the latter in a judgement) of the deeply troubling implications of so-called Charter values being used as the supposed basis of judicial reasoning. Yet this shibboleth, 'Charter values', appears with ever-increasing frequency in the new kind of interpretation that gives new length to the old criticism of the law of equity (given its uncertainty) as 'the length of the Chancellor's foot' (Selden 1984, 223–24). Charter values, being used by judges as a supposed base for their legal analysis, are worse than unpredictable: they provide a tabula rasa upon which the judicial mind can write whatever he or she wishes, unconstrained by text, debate, rigorous history or any particular philosophy at all. As George Grant (1986) said famously: 'values language is an obscuring language for morality used when the idea of purpose has been destroyed'.

Thus we have thinner notions: 'auto-nomos individuals' rather than 'moral persons', 'values' rather than 'virtues' and 'gender' rather than 'sex'; in all areas, the untrammelled will as the ground of supposed respect and dignity. Everywhere, we see abstraction and subjectivism in which the subjective will dominates what ought to be conformed to in nature, or what specific traditions set out as the appropriate stance of *response* (the root of which word, the Latin *spondere*, I learned from the late Kenneth Schmitz, is defined as 'to pledge' or 'to commit') to nature. The traditional accounts understand shared human nature, rationality and how these relate to an ordered cosmos as the ground and nature of what is around us and within which moral lives are worked out. The argument was that where this shared rationality and human nature was capable of understanding, we were able to see that *telos* or purpose framed necessarily the art or skill of *techné* within the order and purpose of the *cosmos* itself rather than a dis-ordered or dis-integrated *chaos*.

Matters have, however, changed – and changed radically and all around us. In the Canadian and South African decisions cited earlier we see evidence not only of different precedents but fundamentally different conceptions of meaning, history, culture and the scope and nature of the person and the state. Again, the different views are irreconcilable. So, the basic question for law is how it will approach irreconcilable disagreements and still respect freedom and difference, *not* how it will bring us to some gnostic reordering of society by the force of law.

Current 'pride' movements[7] are essentially civic totalism in the sense that they see law as the effective means of reordering rather than the free moral choices of persons through the *metanoia* of moral conviction and the exercise of free choices. This is why TWU, in the thinking of civic totalists, must not have its law school and Israel Folau must forfeit his million-dollar rugby contract. As a star he is a public figure and such views have no place in the public sphere any longer. The university and the athlete were the institutional and personal representatives of viewpoints no longer deemed *publicly* acceptable. There is a tension here because we know that the right to freedom of religion is also, as Article 18 of the International Covenant on Civil and Political Rights (1966) states, the right, 'individually or in community with others, in *public* or private to *manifest* his religion or *belief* in worship, *observance*, *practice* and *teaching*' (emphasis added). So, there would appear to be clear international recognition of this public dimension, yet restrictions are now being widely mounted using a panoply of ingenious arguments designed to suppress any negative assessments or appraisals of sexual conduct stemming from traditional religious viewpoints. This new dogmatic set of beliefs denying other dogmatic beliefs will not allow any religious or quasi-religious viewpoints other than its own.[8]

---

[7] It is interesting how these movements take, expressly, a religious formulation. Thus, 'pride', the form of the vices, is recrafted as something positive to march about in public opposition to Blessed Sacrament Processions. Formerly, Mardi Gras (Fat Tuesday), the night before Ash Wednesday and the beginning of Lent, was a period of abnegation, self-discipline and prayer. The rainbow symbol, it need scarcely be noted, was the promise of the covenant given by God to Noah after the flood. Here, in the contemporary frame, the religious symbols are parodied and inverted and the religious fervour and kenotic zealotry of the new movements are undeniable. The speedo and parodied vestments are viewed as merely amusing by people who have either lost sight of original meanings (if they ever knew them) or rejoice openly in public desecration – as suggested by the frequent portrayal of revellers dressed as nuns and priests on gay-pride floats. Rabbis and Muslim figures are not portrayed by the LGBT partygoers. As noted over the years by various commentators it is increasingly obvious that, as we might put it, 'Anti-Catholicism is the last publicly acceptable form of bigotry'.

[8] Various commentators have noted the tendency of a certain form of contemporary human rights to take on a religious or 'idolatrous' dimension: see, for example, Michael Ignatieff (2001). In this setting it ought not to be a surprise that some advocates of identity politics ironically come to exemplify the very zealotry and dogmatic, quasi-religious fundamentalism they often criticize in religious adherents.

Can Law Do What Religion Can in Relation to the Key Questions in Politics?

Let us consider some earlier approaches to identify certain key requirements of politics and law in order to show why and how religion can play an important and irreplaceable role in culture. Similarly, we should note law's lack of expertise or jurisdiction in comparison with each category here.

James Schall (1996) has stated that politics has three central 'problem' areas:

1. The problem of evil or coercion
2. The problem of virtue
3. The problem of contemplation of the highest things

He notes that 'the case for this unity is not often made within the discipline' (2–3). The incompleteness of political philosophy to completely explain the reality of evil or the possibility of good is, says Schall, 'a defect in the discipline but it does indicate its very limit, the nature of its own understanding of what it is, of what it can do [...] in reflecting on these very political things, political philosophy is open to metaphysics and revelation, themselves' (2–3). Politics, in a sense (and as William Galston noted some years ago), needs religion, and religious insights can inform it. Consider 'dignity' and its basis. If human dignity is to be a reality, taught and respected, it needs solid arguments in its favour. These are notably absent in liberalism. As we have moved into post-liberalism, the deficiencies in these key areas become more glaring with each rising issue involving life and ethics at the edges of life. The subjective will now dominates in each area. Abortion, euthanasia and now transgenderism show the incoherence that attaches to continued use of 'dignity' when this concept is no longer an objective reality but rather a socially contingent 'value' that may be inconsistently applied based on feeling rather than fact. If we are in a non-teleological flux, how can the choices for decision-making be anything but the 'power' that is the fixation of the neo-Marxists, the inevitable result of the loss of tradition according to MacIntyre or, generations earlier, Christopher Dawson, Michael Polanyi and C. S. Lewis? What principles beyond power could restrain the inflated subjective will? Only those created by consensus or coercion? If tradition has no heft, no moral weight, if it can be changed simply by majority viewpoint, then what is standing between such a system and the blunt force of 'might is right'?

Clearly, what Schall draws from the historical view of politics may also be said of the historical view of law; both are very different from the social imaginary of a 'public sphere' or 'secular world' in which ultimate questions about metaphysics and the nature of the human person, virtue and vice are considered 'irrelevant' or are left inchoate. George Jacob Holyoake's project of secularism (it was Holyoake who coined the term in 1851) set itself up expressly to reconstruct the public dimension of culture 'on a materialist basis' (see Benson 2004). Both H. L. A. Hart and John Rawls, as noted earlier, thought they could have theories free from metaphysics. Holyoake viewed metaphysical claims as inherently suspect and believed that they could be avoided (Benson 2004,

86–87), all the while ignoring his own metaphysical beliefs in just the manner referred to by Michael Polanyi (1958, 288), which I shall discuss further later.

Recall that Polanyi concluded that contemporary forms of knowledge *imagine* that it is possible to avoid metaphysical claims or the relevance of metaphysical commitments in human projects. This is, however, impossible, and what occurs is that the metaphysical assumptions are often hidden. Epistemological insecurity is papered over by avoidance or, worse, simplistic and superficial appeals to shared conceptions that exist only because they were developed in other traditions – and are no longer upheld by those 'teaching' those frameworks and concepts. Here the modern use of 'dignity' may serve as an example of a concept that is used frequently but whose origin and content is identified as arising from earlier religious conceptions. Hence, the meaning of 'dignity' is problematic if not impossible to derive without those religious underpinnings. Michael J. Perry (2010, fn. 50) observes, 'It is open to serious question whether a secular worldview can bear the weight of the claim that we should – that we have conclusive reason to – live our lives in accord with the fact that every human being has inherent dignity' (see also Rist 2002, 267; Grant 1985).

Another good example of this thinning of concepts alluded to earlier is the term 'values'. Philosopher Edward Andrew (1995, 170) has noted that 'there has been only partial awareness in the academy that the language of values entails that nothing is intrinsically good and no one is intrinsically worthy'. In my experience virtually everyone in my generation is unaware, initially, of the problem of 'values language' and many struggle against the implications of the realization that, perhaps, the language they have used in their professional work for many years is essentially baseless. Some ethicists argue that they wish to use 'values' because 'that is how people speak', but they have no real response to the critique but avoidance: and running away is not the best form of argument.[9] A more detailed work is needed to trace how 'values' and 'social values' with their deeply subjectivist framework came to trump the objective language of 'virtues'. Part of this work will be to trace how the subjective and monetary dimensions of both 'evaluation' and 'appreciation' came to dominate the recognition or knowledge of *intrinsic* worth.[10] The projections of the will on and over nature come slowly to replace the quest of the will to seek its place within the confines of nature.

---

[9]   In a phone conversation a year or two before he died (I was in Vancouver, Canada, and he was in his home in Halifax), George Grant told me how 'gratified' he was that I, in his words, '*got* the values point'. Grant pronounced himself 'baffled' by 'how difficult it is to get this point across'. Over 30 years later, I can completely understand his bafflement, though I see signs perhaps that we are at a tipping point since increasingly one comes across more popular writers and speakers suggesting that 'values' might not be the best term to use to convey moral meaning. If there is an increasing number of people unsatisfied with 'values', then we have, in significant measure, George Grant to thank for that since most other thinkers prior to him had, to a greater or lesser extent, failed to observe the subtle and corrosive effects of the widespread use of 'values language'.

[10]   Important here is John Macmurray (1936), who sets out with remarkable brevity and clarity how lived community and interpersonalism make religious empiricism richer than merely scientific empiricism but that both proceed from the same factual basis. The difference being that only religions can offer a strong argument for the essential basis for communion, community,

In his Gifford Lectures, published in 1958 as *Personal Knowledge*, Michael Polanyi noted something of great importance to why 'values' has come to dominate when he stated:

> Our objectivism, *which tolerates no open declaration of faith, has forced modern beliefs to take on implicit forms* [...] And no one will deny that those who have mastered the idioms in which these beliefs are entailed do also reason most ingeniously within these idioms, even while [...] they unhesitatingly ignore all that the idiom does not cover. (288, emphasis added)[11]

Further, in his less celebrated earlier book of published lectures, *Science, Faith and Society*, Michael Polanyi (1966 [1946]) noted the following three points that neatly undergird my observations on the inestimable importance of religion to the public interest in a free and democratic society. He writes first:

> If the citizens are dedicated to certain transcendent obligations and particularly to such general ideals as truth, justice, charity and these are embodied in the tradition of the community to which allegiance is maintained, a great many issues between citizens, and all to some extent, can be left – and are necessarily left – for the individual consciences to decide. The moment, however, a community ceases to be dedicated through its members to transcendent

---

interpersonal relationships and ultimately love. Materialism, according to Macmurray, is a diminished ground suffering from, as Hans Urs Von Balthasar (2004) would later term it, cosmological and anthropological reductions.

[11] See also, Owen Barfield (1984 [1967], 44–46):

> This is a crucial point [...] the most fundamental assumptions of any age are those that are implicit in the meanings of its common words. [...] One good reason for troubling to concentrate on the moment of change of meaning is that it directs our attention – awakens us – to fundamental assumptions so deeply held that no one even thinks of making them explicit.

Our time is paradigmatically (!) where we must rethink key terms, particularly under the conditions of so many hidden and implicit meanings within developing, or what should be developing, understandings of law in relation to 'pluralism' and religion. On 'paradigm shifts' in relation to law, drawing upon Thomas S. Kuhn (1970), see Iain T. Benson (2013, 43–44) where the historian, in relation to 'shared paradigms', is directed to

> compare the community's paradigms with each other and with its current research reports. In doing so, his object is to discover what isolable elements, explicit or implicit, the members of that community may have *abstracted* from their more global paradigms and deployed as rules in their research [...] if his experience has been at all like my own, he will have found the search for rules both more difficult and less satisfying than the search for paradigms [...] the search for a body of rules competent to constitute a given normal research tradition becomes a source of continual and deep frustration. (Emphasis in original)

What Kuhn says about scientific research applies equally to law. Though there are obvious differences, with respect to paradigms and rules, their changes and development and, in particular, the nature of 'hidden' or 'implicit' meanings, the two areas share common ground. See C. Niles (2003), 'Epistemological Nonsense', who also recognizes the relevance of Kuhn in relation to the analysis of key terms – in her case, 'secular'. See also Barry W. Bussey (2019).

ideals, it can continue to exist undisrupted only by submission to a single centre of unlimited secular power. (78–79)[12]

Polanyi also observes that:

> I do not assert that eternal truths are automatically upheld by men. We have learnt that they can be very effectively denied by modern man. *Belief in them can therefore be upheld now only in the form of an explicit profession of faith. In my view this would be quite impracticable but for the existence of traditions which embody such professions and can be embraced by men. Hence, tradition, which the rationalist age abhorred, I regard as the true and indispensable foundation for the ideals of that age.* (82–83, emphasis added)[13]

Another aspect of the relationship between law and religion is important to mention at this juncture. This is the danger to religion that occurs from placing too great a focus on law and politics which together constitute the regulatory part of the state (civil society, the other part, is often pressured by the regulatory part). This danger has been recognized by religious thinkers in all traditions throughout history (De Tocqueville being a notable example).

Conclusion: How Can Legal Language Become More Honest and Associations More Visible to Law?

Giorgio Agamben, a contemporary Italian philosopher, has referred recently to the religious significance of an overextension of legalism in our time. He highlights the polarity between the spiritual role of the law or state and that of religious associations. While state and law focus on the economy and time and governance of the world, the religious focuses on 'the economy of salvation' which points to eternity. Practical love, so important to life in community, cannot, without significant loss to its richness, be discussed only in terms of what is given in 'time' (and 'time' after all was key to our understanding of the *saeculorum* from which we derived 'the secular').

Agamben (2012, 35) makes the observation that 'the only way that a community can form and last is if these poles are present and the dialectical tension between them prevails. It is precisely this tension which seems today to have disappeared'.[14] He observes

---

[12] Polanyi does not address an implied dimension of his analysis, namely that the most important and primary locations for the maintenance of 'traditions' are associations, particularly religious associations. That is a point that is central to John Macmurray's (1936) work.

[13] Generally on the nature and importance of 'tradition', see Jaroslav Pelikan (1984, 56) citing Clifford Geertz: 'It is, in fact, precisely at the point at which a political system begins to free itself from the immediate governance of received traditions […] that formal ideologies tend first to emerge and take hold'.

[14] I acknowledge my debt here to my friend David Cayley of Toronto for this link to Agamben and to my friend Kristof Vanhoutte and the Small Circle Philosopher's group for discussions on this and related themes in recent years at meetings in Switzerland, Germany, France and South Africa.

that all that is left of the economy and governance when the community which points to an economy of grace has been eradicated is the economy's 'blind and derisive dominion to every aspect of social life' (35). Agamben – and we should recall that this was delivered as a sermon at Notre Dame in Paris – then delivers his chilling description of the times:

> With the eclipse of the messianic experience of the culmination of the law and of time comes an unprecedented *hypertrophy of law* – one that, under the guise of legislating every-thing, betrays its legitimacy through legalistic excess. I say the following with words carefully weighed. Nowhere on earth today is a legitimate power to be found; even the powerful are convinced of their own illegitimacy. The complete juridification and commodification of human relations – the confusions between what we might believe, hope and love and that which we are obliged to do or not do, say or not say – are signs not only of crises of law and state, but also, and above all, of crises of the Church […] the model of contemporary pol-itics – which pretends to an infinite economy of the world – is thus truly infernal. And if the Church curtails its original relation with the *paroikia*, it cannot but lose itself in time. For this reason, the question that I came here today to ask you, without any other authority than an obstinate habit of reading the signs of the time, is this: Will the Church finally grasp the his-torical occasion and recover its messianic vocation? If it does not, the risk is clear enough: It will be swept away by the disaster menacing every government and every institution on earth. (40–41, emphasis original)[15]

We are seeing law in the service of ideology today – ideology as defined by Raymond Aron and Jacques Ellul: 'a set of ideas accepted by individuals or peoples *without attention to their origin or value*' (Ellul 1965, 116, emphasis added).[16] Issue after issue shows us that law has the capacity to preserve genuine difference and disagreement as in the recent decisions involving a Northern Irish bakery (*Lee v. Ashers* 2018; see also Frau and Breda, Chapter 10 in this volume) or a university student (*The Queen (on the application of Ngole) v. The University of Sheffield*, 2019; hereinafter '*Ngole*'). In the *Lee v. Ashers* case involving a

---

[15] The word *paroikousa*, in Greek thought, refers to the sort of sojourning in which foreigners and those in exile dwelt. It was opposed to the Greek verb *katoikein* which designated how the citi-zens of a city, state, kingdom or empire dwelt. Thus, Agamben points to the stance the church should have towards the temporal world around it. While dwelling within time, the religious believers point to transcendent verities which they recognize must inform life together. Human communities cannot live without justice and love and both conceptions are larger than, but do not exclude, the law.

[16] Given what I have written about 'values', it is clear that Ellul did not see how this language is, itself, based on the ideology of the regnancy of the subjective self he does not accept. In this he shares erroneous expression with an illustrious group of thinkers that include, in the 'Homer nods' category, C. S. Lewis, Bernard Lonergan, Pope John Paul II, Joseph Pieper, Dietrich von Hildebrand, Jacques Maritain and a significant list of others. See Iain T. Benson (2018, 1–44). What one can say is that the movement now to see 'values language' as implicated deeply in the very 'poison of subjectivism' (Lewis) others may have missed or only partially understood is a notable feature of the current time. It is now no longer uncommon to see, for example, a scholar of the status of Remi Brague or Pierre Manent write that 'values' are in no way equiva-lent to what was understood by virtues in prior times – a point made over three decades ago by George Grant and others but that is only being more widely recognized today.

refusal to make a cake with a controversial message, the unanimous five justice United Kingdom Supreme Court held that people in the United Kingdom could not legally be forced to promote a message with which they fundamentally disagreed. In *Ngole*, university student Felix Ngole successfully appealed a trial judge's decision that would have upheld the University of Sheffield's decision effectively suppressing his religiously informed views on a public social media platform when he disapproved of homosexual acts. For these postings, the student had been removed from his sociology course by the university. Holding that the university had become entrenched and unreasonable in its position, the United Kingdom's second highest court maintained that the 'mere expression of views on theological grounds (e.g. that "homosexuality is a sin") does not necessarily connote that the person expressing such views will discriminate on such grounds' (*Ngole*, para 10).[17] In key ways, these two decisions in the United Kingdom parallel what has long been the law in Canada. The leading decision in that country (in which I served as a co-counsel on the partially successful appeal) involved Toronto printer Scott Brockie who refused to print materials for a Gay and Lesbian Advocacy Group (*Ont. Human Rights Comm'n v. Brockie (Brockie II)* 2003). Brockie had been ordered to print the materials by an Ontario Human Rights Inquiry Tribunal. In key respects, that decision was overturned, holding that the printer should not be forced to print materials that were irreconcilable with his religious beliefs (as opposed to 'ordinary business materials' which he was obligated to print).

In contrast to these decisions which preserve difference, we also have ample illustration of the law's failure to protect genuine diversity as in the decisions discussed earlier, the Canadian Supreme Court's lamentable TWU decision (2018) or the Ontario Court

---

[17] Interestingly, soon after the English decision in *Ngole*, the Australian Rugby Association settled its case out of court against Israel Folau for an undisclosed sum and issued an apology to him: 'While it was not Rugby Australia's intention, Rugby Australia acknowledges and apologises for any hurt or harm caused to the Folaus' (see https://www.abc.net.au/news/2019-12-04/rugby-australia-israel-folau-mediation-settlement/11765866). The settlement is rumoured to be in the millions of dollars. It is widely acknowledged that Rugby Australia was under pressure from one of its biggest sponsors, the airline Qantas, whose CEO, Alan Joyce, is a well-known LGBT rights supporter, to bring pressure to bear on Folau.

Australia is, at the time of writing, contemplating introducing a Commonwealth Religious Discrimination Act, part of which would provide protection on grounds of religion to employees wishing to express religious opinions in public. The rhetoric against such legislation suggests that any protection of a religious believer's rights of expression or belief constitutes a 'license to discriminate'. Obviously, such a view discloses an unstated premise that certain views should have no place in the public and that the mere articulation of public disagreement regarding sexual conduct is itself 'discrimination'. Civic totalism is in many ways becoming a default position though few recognize it for what it is: an illiberal attempt to foreclose public manifestation and debate about contested moral viewpoints. Proponents of judicial ordering (judicial supremacy) often speak of 'balancing' rather than 'accommodation' because they can 'balance' positions off the scale entirely (as in the TWU decision of the Supreme Court of Canada) rather than develop a modus vivendi of accommodation (as with the TWU decision of the British Columbia Court of Appeal). It is accommodation of diversity, not some supposed 'balancing', that supports genuine diversity.

of Appeal's equally troubling *CMDS* decision (2019). The former kind of decisions can achieve their results in a properly lasting manner only if courts and tribunals begin to recognize the other sorts as gnostic, illiberal, unrealistic and dangerous to freedom as they embody the homogenizing temptations of certain aspects of contemporary law, politics and culture. As set out at the beginning of this chapter, universal conceptions of respect and humanity can only continue to exist if genuine diversity allows differences to be manifest in society and homogeneity forced by law is rejected.

There is a fundamental tension between worldviews at issue here. One view respects or allows for dissent and difference, the other does not. We no longer inhabit the same jurisprudential worlds and our law and politics need to make this clear. Words such as inclusivity, 'values' and diversity, alongside de-contextualized uses of 'discrimination' and 'equality' unmoored from lived differences of moral traditions and meaning represented in associations, are solvents of human freedom, flourishing and moral/ethical languages, not means towards them. Traditions may be denied or derided but when 'things fall apart' they are what human communities have resort to. Even when, as now, we have succumbed to serious amnesia, what is written remains to be relearnt and reapplied in all ages past or yet to come – to the undying frustration and rage of the Conditioners or Innovators who strut and fret and march among us.[18]

References

Agamben, Giorgio. 2012. *The Church and the Kingdom*. Translated by Leland de la Durantaye. London: Seagull Books.

Andrew, Edward. 1995. *The Geneology of Values: The Aesthetic Economy of Nietzsche and Proust*. Lanham, MD: Rowman & Littlefield.

von Balthasar, Hans Urs. 2004. *Love Alone Is Credible*. Translated by D. C. Schindler. San Francisco, CA: Ignatius.

Barfield, Owen. 1984 [1967]. *Speaker's Meaning*. Middleton: Wesleyan University Press.

Benson, Iain T. 2004. 'Considering Secularism'. In *Recognizing Religion*, edited by Farrow, 83–98. Montreal: McGill-Queens.

———. 2013. 'An Associational Framework for the Reconciliation of Competing Rights Claims Involving the Freedom of Religion'. PhD diss., University of the Witwatersrand.

———. 2018. 'Values Language: A Useful Moral Framework or Cuckoo's Egg'. In *Creative Subversion: The Liberal Arts and Human Educational Fulfilment*, edited by David Daintree, 1–44. Redland Bay: Connor Court.

Bussey, Barry W. 2017. 'The Charter Is Not a Blueprint for Moral Conformity'. In *Religion, Liberty and the Jurisdictional Limits of Law*, edited by Iain T. Benson and Barry W. Bussey, 367–414. Toronto: LexisNexis.

.———. 2019. 'The Legal Revolution against the Accommodation of Religion: The Secular Age v. The Sexular Age'. PhD diss., University of Leiden.

Christian Medical and Dental Society of Canada v. College of Physicians and Surgeons of Ontario, 2019 ONCA 393.

---

[18] The terms 'Conditioners' and 'Innovators' along with 'Straighteners' are employed by C. S. Lewis (1943) to describe those haters of traditions whose machinations against nature and tradition lead inevitably, for reasons he spells out in detail, to what his book title suggests: *The Abolition of Man*.

Cotter, Wendy. 1996. 'The Collegia and Roman Law: State Restrictions on Voluntary Associations 64 BCE–200 CE'. In *Voluntary Associations in the Graeco-Roman World*, edited by John S. Kloppenborg and Stephen G. Wilson, 74–89. London: Routledge.

D'Arcy, Martin Cyril. 1949. *Christian Morals*. London: Longmans, Green.

Ellul, Jacques. 1965. *Propaganda: The Formation of Men's Attitudes*. New York: Vintage.

Gaum and Others v. Van Rensburg NO and Others (40819/17) [2019] ZAGPPHC 52; [2019] 2 All SA 722 (GP) (8 March 2019).

Gehl v. Canada (Attorney General), [2017] O.J. No. 1943, 2017 ONCA 319.

Grant, George. 1966. *Philosophy in the Mass Age*, 2nd ed. Toronto: Copp Clark.

———. 1985. *English-Speaking Justice*. Toronto: Anansi.

———. 1986. 'The Moving Image of Eternity'. Interview by David Cayley. Toronto: CBC.

Ignatieff, Michael. 2001. 'Human Rights as Politics and Idolatry'. In *Human Rights as Politics and Idolatry*, edited by Amy Gutman, 3–98. Princeton, NJ: Princeton University Press.

Kuhn, Thomas S. 1970. *The Structure of Scientific Revolutions*. Chicago, IL: Chicago University Press.

Law Society of British Columbia v Trinity Western University, [2018] 2 SCR 293, 2018 SCC 32.

Lewis, C. S. 1943. *The Abolition of Man*. New York: Macmillan.

MacIntyre, Alasdair. 1984. *After Virtue: A Study in Moral Theory*, 2nd ed. Notre Dame: Notre Dame University Press.

Macmurray, John. 1936. *The Structure of Religious Experience*. London: Faber & Faber.

Minister of Home Affairs and Another v. Fourie and (Doctors for Life International and Others, amici curiae) 2006 1 SA 524 (CC).

Niles, Christine. 2012. 'Epistemological Nonsense – The Secular/Religious Distinction'. *Notre Dame Journal of Law, Ethics, & Public Policy* 17, no. 2: 561–92.

Pelikan, Jaroslav. 1984. *The Vindication of Tradition*. New Haven: Yale.

Perry, Michael J. 2010. *The Political Morality of Liberal Democracy*. New York: Cambridge University Press.

Polanyi, Michael. 1966 [1946]. *Science, Faith and Society*. Chicago: University of Chicago Press.

———. 1958. *Personal Knowledge*. Chicago, IL: Chicago University Press.

Rist, John M. 2002. *Real Ethics*. Cambridge: Cambridge University Press.

Ross, W. D., ed. 1938. *Aristotle Selections*. New York: Charles Scribner's Sons.

Schall, James. 1996. *At the Limits of Political Philosophy*. Washington, DC: Catholic University of America.

Selden, J. 1984. 'Table Talk'. Quoted in *Sources of English Legal and Constitutional History*, edited by M. B. Evans and R. I. Jack. Sydney: Butterworths.

Trinity Western University v. The Law Society of British Columbia, 2016 BCCA 423.

Trinity Western University v. Law Society of Upper Canada, [2018] 2 SCR 453, 2018 SCC 33.

Voegelin, Eric. 1968. *Science, Politics and Gnosticism*. New York: Regnery Gateway.

Chapter Three

HUMAN DIGNITY AS AN EXPLICIT CONSTITUTIONAL NORM

Katya Kozicki and William Soares Pugliese

The theme of human dignity is essential for the comprehension of contemporary law. Human dignity is an indispensable principle for the interpretation of national and international law, awakening a series of discussions on topics ranging from its meaning to the most effective instruments for its protection. The present chapter aims to investigate a very particular topic, which is the effect of specifically provisioning human dignity as a fundamental principle in a constitution, such as Germany's Basic Law and Brazil's Constitution. The current analysis shall focus on the following subjects. Primarily, the chapter will examine the two most common concepts related to human dignity: principles and fundamental rights. These two definitions, although incompatible, are the most common theoretical concepts that allow interpretation of human dignity as a right. Second, the chapter examines the treatment human dignity has received in Germany, Brazil, the United States and Great Britain, with the first two countries having it as an explicit constitutional norm and the last two not. This section concludes that the explicit protection of human dignity in a constitution gives it a greater weight, or strength. Last, we argue human dignity also functions as an interpretative criterion for all the other provisions of a constitution, given its broad implications.

1. Introduction

Changes in the notion of human dignity have turned this notion into one of the central themes of contemporary law. Worldwide, appeals to human dignity emerged in response to violent episodes, such as World Wars I and II. Its focus, however, was not simply protecting people from shootings and explosions, but also from the degradation and humiliation caused by dictatorships and other authoritarian regimes. In short, human dignity is the term most countries' laws used to answer the call for a stronger protection of their own people. This means that human dignity is currently held as one of the most important rights in systems of law, with functions that surpass a guarantee, thus having a normative and interpretative role.

At the same time, human dignity was granted the status of a fundamental right in many constitutions. A fundamental right is, in short, a right with higher status that requires more attention from the state and also from private parties. Human dignity is not the first fundamental right. There were others which were considered as such before, such as liberty and property. This shows, however, how important human dignity is for countries that made this decision.

It is also important to realize human dignity is a notion that was developed in a different time than other fundamental rights, such as the already-mentioned liberty and property. During the seventeenth century, the discussion of the concept of fundamental rights was much more 'local', in the sense that framers of constitutions could be influenced by the ideas developed in different countries or continents, but the role of defining fundamental rights – and every other legal concept – was still an activity related almost exclusively to the circumstances concerning the nation in question. This has led to a few different interpretations regarding certain rights, including the idea of the 'Rule of Law', which is not the same in every constitution or country.[1]

In contrast, fundamental rights which developed in the second half of the twentieth century onward have had a different course. Information circulates faster, and legal solutions from one country are immediately published worldwide. Such is the case of human dignity. Cases concerning this subject, although related to specific countries, have quickly crossed borders. That is not to say solutions are the same, but interpretation of a fundamental right, at the present, is a broader and more complex task than it used to be. Also, it means human dignity may have a more universal meaning than other fundamental rights.

Most of the development of human dignity as a fundamental right has stemmed from countries with constitutions that have provisioned it explicitly. At the same time, constitutions that do not have human dignity in their framework, such as the Constitution of the United States, have also achieved protection for people on similar grounds and are currently part of the human dignity debate.

Considering this objective difference, the present chapter aims to investigate whether or not the specific provision of human dignity as a fundamental right in a constitution has, by itself, an effect. In order to do this, the first step of this chapter will be to define the main concepts related to the notion of human dignity in law. These are the dichotomy between rules and principles (mainly because human dignity is considered a principle in many countries) and the characteristics of fundamental rights (which is another common definition for human dignity).

Second, the chapter will discuss two effects of explicitly provisioning human dignity in a constitution. At first, we conclude that turning human dignity into a core value in a constitution gives it a strength, or weight, it may not have elsewhere. We also conclude that human dignity has achieved a normative or interpretative role for the system of law it is a part of. Because of this, human dignity has a very important role in the adjudication of cases.

The chapter applies a bibliographical approach, reviewing relevant research concerning the subject. The analyses of cases will be circumstantial, as a comparison between each interpretation of human dignity would be a much more complex task,

---

[1]   For this discussion, see Grote (2002).

not suited for the limits of a book chapter. It is also important to acknowledge that the authors' point of view arises from a country where human dignity plays a central role in the interpretation of law, where it is a fundamental right and where it is provisioned in the most important part of its constitution. Therefore, it has several different roles, an idea which may become clearer in the course of the text. Given that this text is a proposition from Brazilian authors, it is important for the reader to be aware that this analysis is primarily focused on the European constitutional theory and particularly on statutory interpretation – especially the lessons from the German academy.

2. Rules, Principles, Fundamental Rights: How Do These Concepts Work Together?

There are many concepts related to human dignity in comparative law. Sometimes, it is considered a principle, as opposed to a rule. In other definitions, it is called a fundamental right, meaning it is a right with specific characteristics that require the interpreter to consider it with more strength or caution. These concepts will be presented in this section.

The idea of a principle is not new. Actually, its development as a type of legal norm is directly related to constitutional law and to the inclusion of broader concepts into constitutions and other statutes. The proposition of reading human dignity as a principle is usually accompanied by lessons from Robert Alexy's *Theory of Constitutional Rights* (2002) or from Ronald Dworkin's *Taking Rights Seriously* (1977). This analysis will focus on Alexy's theory, simply because it is more related to the interpretation of a fundamental principle as it originates from a norm.

According to Alexy's (2002, 85) theory and to one of his main Brazilian commentators (Silva 2011, 20), the main difference between principles and rules is that the former should be viewed as optimization commands to be applied to the fullest extent possible, while the latter should be applied in order to realize exactly what they are meant to prescribe (Silva 2011, 45). There are several criteria to distinguish between rules and principles (69), the most used being generality. In broad terms, this criterion means that principles have a higher degree of generality than rules (Alexy 2002, 108); that is, they are applied to a wider range of cases. Thus, the difference between principles and rules is most evident in cases where the possible clash between two rules or between two principles is assessed. In Alexy's words, when one is facing a friction between two rules, one is facing a situation of conflict; when it is between two principles, there is a collision (91). These two solutions shall be explained in the next paragraphs.

The difference between rules and principles is logical, as the opposition between each of them shows. Both conflict and collision occur due to the existence of two norms which, if applied in isolation, lead to different and contradictory results. The conflict of rules only admits the application of one valid legal norm for a specific case. All others are invalid. It is inconceivable to have two concrete judgements that prove contradictory because there is only one standard, as Dantas (2004, 63) demonstrates.

On the other hand, when it comes to a collision of principles, there is a weighing of the two principles at issue to determine which will take precedence in the specific case in accordance with the 'collision law' doctrine (Alexy 2002, 93). The yielding of one does not invalidate the other.

'Collision law' maintains that there is no hierarchy of principles, because principles refer to situations and actions that cannot be mathematically quantified. In situations of conflict, the solution goes through the analysis of the case in the light of the principles with different weights and precedence according to the circumstances of the case. But this does not mean the absolute prevalence of one principle over another, since otherwise it would then be a conflict of rules (Dantas 2004, 96).

The procedure for finding a solution to a collision of principles is also in the plane of values. In this plane, the factual circumstances are evaluated in the dimension of the weight of the principle that should be the preponderant one, requiring, for such, the analysis of the constitutionally guaranteed values, the fundamental rights and other principles involved. In this sense, principles involved in the case will not be irrelevant, but one or more of them will yield to another that has more weight in the adjudication of the case.

The idea, here, is not to present a complete description of Alexy's theory. In reality, this short synthesis serves to demonstrate how, especially for European civil law, some constitutional provisions are defined as principles. In this sense, they have a very wide range of applications and strength, or weight, for the adjudication of cases. The notion that principles must be applied to the fullest extent possible is the best synthesis for the role principles have in these systems.

Another relevant aspect of including human dignity in a constitutional document is that, in general, it will be considered a fundamental right.[2] This is different than stating human dignity is a principle. To define human dignity as a fundamental right engraves it with some characteristics that turn it into a special type of norm. With reference to Rothenburg (2000), some of these characteristics must be introduced.

The first of these characteristics is the one that names the notion of a fundamental right: its *fundamentality*. What this means is that fundamental rights form the basis (axiological and logical) on which the legal order rests. As such, they work as a guide to the interpretation of law. A second feature of a fundamental right is its *universality*: the fact that every human being is entitled protection of such rights. Therefore, it is simple to argue the application of a fundamental right on a case, as one does not need to work with all the logical features of a rule. A third trait favoured by lawyers regarding fundamental rights is their *absoluteness*: fundamental rights have the highest hierarchy and would not tolerate unjustified restrictions. The absoluteness gives fundamental rights a power other norms do not have, as they rarely yield to other rules. On the contrary, fundamental rights are, seldom, the reason for defeasing the application of rules.

---

[2]   The expression 'fundamental right' must be understood as an expression from the *civil law* tradition. 'Right', in this sense, has a broader meaning, not only as an objective and specific claim, but as a general value of what is just.

A fourth and very important feature of fundamental rights is their *immediate applicability*. Therefore, at the moment a fundamental right is established, it does not need any other legal provision in order to be enforced. This is valid for cases concerning persons against the state and also in private law, as proposed by Canaris (1999). In other words, fundamental rights are strong, broad values that must be immediately applied by judges when deciding cases. It is, therefore, an indispensable argument for lawyers when a hard case is at court.

There may be a methodological issue at bay, here. Is it possible to define a principle as a fundamental right, at the same time? It appears the correct answer is negative, because these two classifications arise from different concepts of law. The notion of a principle is closely related to post-positivistic approaches, while the fundamental right elements are more connected to a soft positivism view. However, the scientific reply is not sufficient to prevent this conceptual confusion when lawyers present their reasons and when courts decide cases. So, there will be cases where a constitutional provision will be treated as a principle and others where it will be considered a fundamental right. In the worst scenarios, both views will be employed by some arguments that, while technically inaccurate, have a very strong presence before courts.

This section aimed to present two theoretical views for rights such as human dignity. First, they were presented as principles. Second, they were explained as fundamental rights. What these two have in common, although they are methodologically incompatible, is that they provide for very strong arguments arising from the rights that are explicitly provisioned in a constitution. This is exactly the case for human dignity. For this reason, Section 3 will focus on this specific right.

3. Human Dignity as an Explicit Norm

'Die Würde des Menschen' (The dignity of men) are the first words of the German Basic Law. That is to say, the first idea one will find when reading the German Constitution is that of 'human dignity'. Further reading will show that, for the German Republic, human dignity is inviolable and that state authority has the duty to respect and protect it. Although the German Constitution does not define human dignity, it shows how much this right is relevant to the German Republic and to its people (Enders 2010). The Basic Law was framed after World War II, and the choice of opening the Basic Law with this phrase was not a coincidence. Many other states had similar responses to war, such as other European countries, or to authoritarian periods, such as South American republics. The common trend, here, is that many of these countries' constitutions present human dignity as a central, or founding, idea in their texts. That is to say, human dignity can be considered a principle or a fundamental right, as explained earlier.

This is of absolute importance as human dignity, being a fundamental right or a principle, is considered by lawyers and by courts in an unlimited number of cases. As an example, Enders shows human dignity in Germany is, on the one hand, the 'supreme principle of the constitution', meaning it is a core value towards its general interpretation (2010, 3). On the other hand, the same human dignity principle is applied in specific cases such as the determination that torture is unconditionally prohibited and that there is a privilege against coercive self-incrimination (7).[3] Therefore, being the first norm of the German Basic Law, human dignity is in the center of the debates and one of the first principles to be considered in a legal argument.

Human dignity is also a part of the First Article of the Constitution of the Federative Republic of Brazil, from 1988. In this document, it is defined as the 'foundation' of the Brazilian republic. From its promulgation until today, human dignity has been a major argument for the country's Supreme Court to decide cases (Brazil 2017). For example, it was the central right at stake when the Supreme Court determined substantial change to the treatment of convicts in state prisons; it was also a core argument in order to forbid the use of handcuffs for respondents during court hearings, unless there is clear and present danger; human dignity was also an important right at play when the Court reviewed labour laws; last, the Brazilian Supreme Court also argued human dignity is related to the due process of law clause, stating a fast and adequate response from courts is essential for the enforcement of human dignity. This shows the wide range human dignity has reached in Brazilian law.

The examples from Germany and Brazil show that explicitly provisioning a principle in a constitution gives it a strength it would hardly achieve otherwise. It gains a gravitational strength, in the sense that it becomes relevant and allows for the development of a wide range of arguments, all deriving from the core idea of human dignity. That, in short, is a way to comprehend how the provision of human dignity in a constitution may affect its understanding.

We must consider, now, the situation of systems of law that do not contemplate human dignity as a right in their constitutions. This leads us to the United States and Great Britain. As American doctrine explains, the lack of a special, express provision on human dignity in the federal Constitution of the United States, for example, has demanded the development of theories expanding other fundamental rights in order to encompass the protection of human dignity (Barak 2015; see also Staffen and Arshakyan 2016).

The Fifth Amendment, for instance, determines no person shall be deprived of life, liberty or property, without due process of law. The Fourteenth Amendment furthers this notion, determining 'nor shall any state deprive any person of life, liberty, or property, without due process of law nor deny to any person within its jurisdiction the equal protection of the laws'. This has led to the Supreme Court constructing a theory where human dignity is a constitutional right, especially on the grounds of the substantial due process of law (Goodman 2005). Instead of simply affirming the right, the Supreme Court of the United States had to build this protection from other constitutional guarantees.

In Great Britain, the case is even more complex. General knowledge suggests that human dignity is not an important or pervasive feature of the law, although this notion is challenged by part of the academy (Bedford 2018). This does not mean Great Britain does not consider human dignity as an important feature of the law. This, most likely,

---

[3] There is no written norm concerning this subject. However, this ruling has been issued with grounds on the principle of human dignity. Therefore, it serves a general principle, but it is also relevant for very specific adjudications.

means British law has found other means to protect people without such a concept or without a cohesive term to encompass all of its effects.

In conclusion, the option to prescribe human dignity in constitutions does have theoretical effects. Combined with the civil law tradition, the definition of human dignity as a fundamental right turns this concept into a principle, giving it special strength, or weight, for lawyers to develop arguments from it. It also benefits from definition and the characteristics of fundamental rights, which launches human dignity in the centre of the debates, making it one of the first principles to be considered in a legal argument where it is explicitly provisioned.

4. Human Dignity as an Interpretative Criterion for Law

As already mentioned, rights such as human dignity play a pivotal role in the interpretation of law. This section will consider specific aspects regarding the relationship between constitutional rights and the interpretation and adjudication of cases. The basis for this process will be the theoretical work of Neil MacCormick. The reason for choosing this author is because his theory offers a definition of law that encompasses both civil and common law traditions while also accommodating the notion of principles, especially those arising from important constitutional provisions.

In his latest monograph, MacCormick (2007) has defined law as institutional normative order. This concept has been explained elsewhere (Kozicki and Pugliese 2018), and only its most important aspects will be presented here. In the same sense as Alexy's theory discussed previously, principles are considered generalized norms by MacCormick (2005), so that they have a broad impact on the system and carry values related to the normativity of the system. As such, the possibility of a solution by mere deduction is no longer defensible as it was in the previous century. This means that every case, as simple as it may seem, can be analysed and decided on in the light of the principles, even if there is a clearly incident rule.

Recognizing the relevance of Dworkin's work, MacCormick states that he altered his previous position (1978) and identifies the interpretative nature of law (2005, 39). Thus, the hypotheses in which justification by mere deduction is possible are smaller, being restricted to those in which a more complex problematization has not yet been developed, either in a concrete case or in theory. In any case, it is always possible to make an easy case difficult by means of interpretative resources and ultimately by focusing on the principles.

As they may change the understanding of any case, it is even more important to understand the techniques by which principles can be used in legal argumentation. More than that, principles assume an even more relevant role at the time of adjudication, which raises another problem for MacCormick: how to make his change of position compatible with the apparent expansion of powers that his new 'Theory of Law' confers on magistrates? In short, how is law, as an institutional normative order, capable of preserving the structure and guarantees of the rule of law, especially its promise of formal justice, based on equality and security, if it depends at all times on interpretations?

MacCormick's new argument starts from a premise: the legal context is not a blank sheet that allows us to reach any conclusion simply because it is reasonable. In offering a solution, the magistrate must base his conclusion on some proposition that has 'credibility as a legal proposition' (MacCormick 2005, 31), and the best way to do this is to 'show some coherence with other propositions that we may draw from state-established laws' (ibid.). Therefore, rules serve to guide and justify decisions in an institutional normative order. Laws, viewed for this purpose, are regarded as pre-interpretive material or as the raw material of a legal system.

What cannot be neglected, however, is that for the application of this raw material to take place 'it is necessary that some specific and contestable type of accusation or allegation of these facts be made against the individual threatened to suffer those consequences' (35). Such allegations must be proved in a case in which the counterparty can contest each element, whether probative or lawful.

The dialectical or argumentative character of judicial proceedings is an inescapable feature of the constitutional arrangement of the rule of law, as citizens are permitted to question and defend themselves against any charge. Thus, on the one hand, the legal system is clear and relatively determined; on the other hand, the possibility that law itself provides for a challenge to the rules makes it relatively undetermined. As good as the legislation is and as clear as the procedural rules are, the fact is that cases reach the courts as the subject of a discussion that includes factual and theoretical elements that need to be decided. In that decision, courts may apply earlier positions or establish new understandings that will resolve the case at hand without defining the legal issue conclusively – otherwise another party involved in a more recent process may challenge that understanding.

Therefore, applying the law involves its interpretation. Every standard must be understood before it can be applied. If this is how law works, decisions depend on good arguments to support interpretative conclusions (MacCormick 2005, 165). Among the interpretative arguments, there are three types of arguments that are considered persuasive to support the understanding of a legal text. The first type of argument is *linguistic*, that is, the one that uses the context of the rule itself as a source of reasons to justify it; the second is the interpretation that looks at the legal system as the context that gives meaning to the norm and is therefore called *systemic*. Finally, there are the *teleological-evaluative* arguments, which seek in the objectives or purposes of the legal text a way to give them better meaning. This brief synthesis of MacCormick's theory allows us to return to the role of principles and the concept of human dignity.

Principles will usually be related to the systemic and the teleological-evaluative arguments. So, unless a case is to be decided on the grounds of linguistic arguments alone, principles will play a part in the adjudication. Lawyers have clear knowledge of this and, as far as legal reasoning allows them, arguments based in principles are brought to advocate different decisions than literal interpretation of statutes would point to.

So, broader principles will be invoked in a wider range of cases. That is the distinctive feature of human dignity: its universal character allows it to be invoked in almost every case. This does not dilute the strength of human dignity. On the contrary, the need to enforce human dignity in the widest array of cases should result in a coherent system of protection of this right.

As a fundamental right, a principle and an interpretive criterion for law, human dignity is a key argument for positive change in law. At the moment human dignity is provisioned in constitutions, it induces different angles for cases to be examined and points judges to solutions that may even defeat rules in order to preserve the dignity of people – all of this inside what is considered an institutional, normative order.

Therefore, playing a role similar to the due process of law in the United States, human dignity is a substantive principle that justifies different views about Law and is the rationale for deciding cases by not applying specific rules.

5. Conclusion

The aim of the chapter was to investigate if the specific provision of human dignity as a fundamental right in a constitution has, by itself, any effect. The result of the research is affirmative. Three aspects must be highlighted.

First, defining human dignity as a fundamental right establishes the concept as a principle in European civil law. In this sense, human dignity has a very wide range of applications and strengths for the adjudication of cases.

Second, provisioning human dignity as a fundamental right in a constitution has the consequence of assigning it all of the characteristics of other fundamental rights. These traits, especially fundamentality, universality, absoluteness and immediate applicability, turn human dignity into a very broad value that must be immediately applied by judges when deciding cases. It is, therefore, an indispensable argument for lawyers when a problematic case is at court.

Last, provisioning human dignity in a constitution gives it a role as an interpretive criterion, inducing different angles for cases to be examined and pointing judges to solutions that may even defeat rules in order to preserve the dignity of people.

In conclusion, although the decision of provisioning human dignity in a constitution is still a political matter, it certainly has its effects in law. The most important one, it appears, is in the adjudication of complex cases.

References

Alexy, Robert. 2002. *A Theory of Constitutional Rights*. Oxford: Oxford University Press.

Barak, Aharon. 2015. 'Human Dignity in American Constitutional Law'. In *Human Dignity: The Constitutional Value and the Constitutional Right*, 185–208. Cambridge: Cambridge University Press. doi:10.1017/CBO9781316106327.016.

Bedford, Daniel. 2018. 'Human Dignity in Great Britain and Northern Ireland'. In *Handbook of Human Dignity in Europe*, edited by P. Becchi and K. Mathis, 1–45. Cham, Switzerland: Springer.

Brazil. 2017. *Coletânea Temática de Jurisprudência: Direitos Humanos*. Brasília: Supremo Tribunal Federal.

Canaris, Claus-Wilhelm. 1999. *Grundrechte und Privatrecht*. Berlin: de Gruyter.

Dantas, David Diniz. 2004. *Interpretação constitucional no pós-positivismo: teoria e casos práticos*. São Paulo: WVC.

Dworkin, Ronald. 1977. *Taking Rights Seriously*. Cambridge, MA: Harvard University Press.

Enders, Christoph. 2010. 'The Right to Have Rights: The Concept of Human Dignity in German Basic Law'. *Revista de Estudos Constitucionais, Hermenêutica e Teoria do Direito (RECHTD)* 2, no. 1: 1–8. São Leopoldo: Unisinos.

Goodman, Maxine D. 2005. 'Human Dignity in Supreme Court Constitutional Jurisprudence'. *Nebraska Law Review* 84, no. 3: 740–94.

Grote, Rainer. 2002. 'Rule of Law, Rechtsstaat, y Etat de Droit'. *Pensamiento Constitucional* 8, no. 8: 127–76. Lima: PUCP.

Kozicki, Katya, and William S. Pugliese. 2018. 'Direito, Estado e Razão Prática: a teoria do direito de Neil MacCormick'. In *O positivismo jurídico no Século XXI*, edited by Bruno Torrano and José Emílio Medauar Ommati, 145–81. Rio de Janeiro: Lumen Juris.

MacCormick, Neil. 1978. *Legal Reasoning and Legal Theory*. Oxford: Clarendon.

———. 2005. *Rhetoric and Rule of Law*. Oxford: Oxford University Press.

———. 2007. *Institutions of Law: An Essay in Legal Theory*. Oxford: Oxford University Press.

Rothenburg, Walter Claudius. 2000. 'Direitos fundamentais e suas características'. In *Revista de Direito Constitucional e Internacional*, vol. 30, 146–58. São Paulo: Revista dos Tribunais.

Silva, Virgílio Afonso. 2011. *Direitos Fundamentais: conteúdo essencial, restrições e eficácia*. São Paulo: Malheiros.

Staffen, Márcio Ricardo, and Mher Arshakyan. 2016. 'The Legal Definition of the Notion of Human Dignity in the Constitutional Jurisprudence'. In *12 Revista Brasileira de Direito*, 108–26. Passo Fundo: Faculdade Mreidional.

Chapter Four

DISCOVERING DIGNITY IN ADJUDICATION: THE JURISPRUDENCE OF THE COURT OF JUSTICE OF THE EUROPEAN UNION

Andrea Pin

Introduction

The post–World War II European legal order is an ideal place to explore the role of dignity in adjudication. As the great comparative law scholar Mauro Cappelletti put it, supranational jurisdictions seemed the perfect vehicle for the resurgence of 'natural law' after the totalitarian and war atrocities (1985, 31). Distrust of nationalism, fear of authoritarian executives and the necessity to put checks on tyrannical parliaments joined forces and gave birth to a particularly creative supranational judicial culture, which accorded a special place to dignity.

This chapter focuses on how the European Communities (EC) and the European Union's (EU) judiciary have understood human dignity. Although it changed its name at the replacement of the EC with the EU, the chapter will always refer to the Court of Justice of the European Union (CJEU) for the sake of brevity. The chapter's task requires some preliminary steps: outlining the status of EU law and the legal culture within which the CJEU has operated and a brief sketch of the growth of dignity within EU constitutionalism. An in-depth analysis of the CJEU's judgements that revolved around dignity will follow.

1. The CJEU: The EU's Legal Driver

The CJEU is widely considered the EU's main vehicle for the interpretation of EC and EU law (Stein 1981, 2). There is broad consensus that it has also been the main driver of the *development* of European legal integration since the EC's inception in the 1950s (Kelemen 2016, 120; Stein 1981, 1; Itzcovich 2017, 288–89). In many ways, its case law anticipated the legal ideas that were later enshrined in the EC and EU treaties and laws (Lenaerts 2007, 1030). Instead of merely clarifying the contents and the contours of EC and EU law, the CJEU has consistently shaped the law, extending it beyond the plain meaning of the words of the treaties and EU regulations (Weiler 2011, 688).

The CJEU's effectiveness is much indebted to the doctrine of 'direct effect', which it developed early in the 1960s. According to this doctrine, EC and later EU rules create rights that are directly enforceable by domestic courts without the need for states to execute them (*Van Gend En Loos*, C-26/62). It has thus enabled individuals and groups to claim EC and later EU rights, liberties and privileges in front of their domestic institutions, without waiting for them to implement EU regulations.

Thanks to the doctrine of EC and EU law 'supremacy', which the CJEU also developed, domestic judges have enforced EC and EU laws instead of domestic laws whenever the two intersect. When a domestic court perceives a conflict between EU law and domestic law, it must apply the former in place of the latter (*Costa v. Enel*, C-6/64).

Throughout the decades, the CJEU judiciary has intervened in several types of judicial proceedings. For the sake of this chapter, it will suffice to focus on three of them. First, through its various sections, the CJEU provides redress against EC or EU institutions' unlawful acts. Second, it addresses issues regarding EC or EU's employees. Third, and most importantly, the CJEU decides cases that reach it through the 'preliminary ruling procedure'. According to this procedure, domestic courts that need to apply a certain EU rule in a particular case may ask the CJEU to render a judgement that will clarify the correct interpretation of the EU rule itself. In order to do so, a domestic court must suspend the proceeding before it and send the CJEU a specific legal question that it must resolve in order to adjudicate the factual dispute at hand. The domestic proceeding will resume after the CJEU has delivered its judgement. The national court still retains discretion in deciding the ultimate outcome of the case before it, but it cannot depart from the CJEU's interpretation of the EU law at issue (Horspool et al. 2016, 86).

The CJEU has regularly employed an Advocate General (AG), who is a member of the EU judiciary but is not a judge. The AG routinely intervenes in the proceedings to advise the judges on how to rule in light of the EU's independent interest in the outcome (Baudenbacher 2003, 524). While the AG may summon litigants for informal hearings, her more important role is to deliver an opinion on impartial independent grounds from the parties to the underlying suit (Craig and De Burca 2011, 62), with the task of indicating to the CJEU the best course of action which furthers the EU's interests.

Also because of the writing style, a thorough understanding of the CJEU's case law normally requires reading both the AG's opinions and the CJEU's judgements. The CJEU's decisions derive predominantly from French judicial culture, a rather dry, formulaic prose. Since the CJEU has never permitted separate opinions, its judgements have normally reflected common grounds and avoided rationales that could generate controversy among its judges. Although its opinions have recently become lengthier and freer, they remain distinct from the more personal, detailed and colourful opinions of the AG (Itzcovich 2017, 286). The AG is more explicit and straightforward about the issues at stake and how the CJEU should handle them, as she can take more personal positions and make broader conceptual reflections, which are credited as providing inspiration for the CJEU's rulings.

The CJEU's style of legal interpretation devotes considerable attention to the purpose and not just to the plain reading of EU regulations. Moreover, it reads written rules in light of their probable effects, trying to identify which interpretive option is most likely to foster legal integration among the member states (Rasmussen 2008, 201). Although it has lately become more prudent in developing European integration through legal interpretation, it still prioritizes the development of EU law over case-law consistency over time (Itzcovich 2017, 289).

The CJEU has not merely pursued the goal of legal integration among the member states of the EU. The binding nature of its judgements has required it to anticipate their potential effects on the constitutional settings of the member states. Overall, its legal philosophy has sought the interpretation of EC and EU law that best pursues legal integration, while avoiding disruptive consequences.

Such aspects of the CJEU's jurisprudence and the very structure of the EU make an exploration of dignity particularly salient. Dignity has universal application, but the member states of the EU still differ in their legal toolkits and even in some of their legal values. Since the CJEU has tried to secure legal integration while avoiding legal and institutional conflicts, it has had to balance universalism with the need for state discretion. This has sometimes proven to be a rather difficult exercise in the field of human dignity, both from a conceptual and a practical viewpoint.

2. The Rise of Human Dignity within the EU

The zenith of the EU's consideration of human dignity is the Charter of Fundamental Rights of the European Union (2012/C 326/02) (hereinafter: Charter or EU Charter). The Charter cites the concept within its Preamble and opens with 'Dignity' its Title I. The same Title I grounds in dignity a variety of human rights: 'human dignity itself', the right to life, the right to the integrity of the person, the prohibition of torture and inhuman or degrading treatment or punishment and the prohibition of slavery. The Charter also emphasizes the connection between dignity and the protection of the elderly (Art. 25) and of the workers (Art. 31).

The Charter was drafted and adopted in the early 2000s, and later incorporated within the EU Treaty that entered into force in December 2009. By the early 2000s, however, the concept of human dignity was already present within its legal system, both directly and indirectly. As to explicit references to dignity, in the 1990s, the concept had already made its appearance within the recitals of some EC directives. Recitals do not enjoy strict normative effects, but provide norms with a context. In this respect, they show that the EC was sensitive to the issue of human dignity. As to implicit references to dignity, the CJEU constantly emphasized that it was building upon the edifice of the 'constitutional traditions' of the EC member states. Since many of them did protect human dignity in the early years after World War II, dignity was never absent from the constitutional framework that slowly developed into the EU.

The appearance of the European Charter, however, marked a turning point in the CJEU's jurisprudence of dignity. This happened mostly because of the symbolic role of the Charter and the philosophical shift that brought it to life. The achievements in the field of economic liberties, prosperity and peace that took place between the 1950s and the early 1990s made the original ideals of the European integration obsolete. Between the 1990s and the early 2000s, the EU had to reframe its overall purpose and took on the narrative of human rights to relegitimize itself (Pin 2019, 236). Human rights became common parlance within the EU and the unit by which the EU's performance would be measured. This emphasis on rights magnified the idea of human dignity as one of the EU's core components. As the AG once stated, the very existence of the EU was premised on 'the confidence […] that each Member State shares with all the other Member States, and recognizes that they share with it, a set of common values on which the Union is founded, such as respect for human dignity, freedom, democracy, equality, the rule of law and respect for human rights' (*Aranylosi and Caldararu*, C-404/15 and 659/15).

This new emphasis on fundamental rights did not dramatically change the EU's scope. The Charter, the rights it included and the policies that the EU implemented in the field of fundamental rights did not suddenly broaden the powers of the EU, which technically remained confined to a long, but not all-encompassing, list of areas, largely pertaining to business and economic activities. Most of the rights that the EU focused on still involved labour relations, competition and the economic freedoms that had prompted European integration. The EU certainly legislated in other extremely relevant areas – such as asylum seekers, refugees, reunification of the members of multinational families, within which dignity came to play a role (see, e.g., Recital 5 of the Directive 2994/38, and Directive 2003/86, both on family reunification within the EU); but, also in these fields, the classic EU's economic liberties retained their crucial role.

What follows tries to capture the development of the CJEU's case law that revolves around human dignity through the decades. It identifies some core aspects of human dignity, including its scope, conceptualizations, ramifications and status. Some of the cases discussed here do not focus specifically on dignity. Since the EU predominantly deals with economic issues, frontal clashes of fundamental rights hardly arise within CJEU judicial disputes. The CJEU, however, has found its way to tap the narrative of dignity within quintessentially economic disputes.

This analysis leaves in the penumbra the complex relationship between the CJEU and the European Court of Human Rights (hereinafter: ECtHR). Differently from the CJEU, the ECtHR and the other organs of the Council of Europe developed their reputation as protectors of human rights within the now-47 countries of the Council of Europe relatively soon after World War II. Although the European Convention of Human Rights' articles do not list dignity among the freedoms they protect, the ECtHR incorporated the concept of dignity early on, thus providing inspiration for the CJEU. Since the 2009 EU Treaty made reference to the Convention (Art. no. 6, para 3), it made the connection between the two courts official, thereby strengthening their link and reinforcing their habit of mutual citations (among many, see *N.S. v. Secretary of State for the Home Department*, C-411/19: AG opinion, para 148). Albeit influential, the ECtHR's jurisprudence on human dignity, however, hardly sheds light on how the CJEU has understood dignity. The ECtHR's reasoning has constantly been the target of criticism for being blurred and inconsistent, so it cannot be considered a reliable benchmark for understanding the CJEU's conceptualization of dignity (Brauch 2009, 278).

3. The Value of Dignity within the CJEU's Case Law

I. Dignity as Status

Since its early days, the CJEU had to deal with issues of dignity. At the beginning of its life, however, the CJEU did not deal with the idea of human dignity per se, but rather with dignity generally. It was confronted with the ancient understanding of dignity as status, ranking and reputation. In this respect, the CJEU's trajectory on dignity parallels the genealogy of dignity itself. As the idea of *human* dignity surfaced within the legal lexicon after being deployed for centuries to identify the multilayered ranks of societies, it also made its way into the CJEU's case law only after being utilized to express the values of reputation or of certain statuses (Waldron 2012, 14; but see Rosen 2012, 12).

At the beginning of European integration, most of the litigation was concerned with labour relations within EC institutions. Complaints that the reputation of an employee had been damaged and needed redress because of the public nature of the duty she discharged, or that a worker had failed to behave in the dignified manner required by her job, abounded (*Fonzi*, C-27 and 30/64; *Macevicius*, C-66/75; *Hirschberg*, C-219/75; *Mrs. V*, C-18/78; *Albertini*, C-338/82; *EESCEC*, C-150/98; *Katsoufros*, C-55/88). Such controversies gave birth to a sizeable stream of cases, which has never abated. Interestingly, however, the CJEU has never used a case to seize the opportunity to identify the significance and the contours of the concept of dignity as status. Probably, this usage of the word was so much in line with the long-standing understanding of dignity as 'reputation' that the CJEU never needed to clarify the meaning of the word.

On some occasions, however, the CJEU and its AG seemed to bridge the old understanding of dignity as status with the idea of humanity. This has happened when the CJEU has utilized the concept of dignity to save state limitations on advertisements for certain professions, in order to protect core legal values such as public trust or health (see, among many, *Société fiduciaire nationale d'expertise comptable v. Ministre du Budget, des Comptes publics et de la Fonction publique*, C-119/09). For example, when protecting the field of dentistry from advertisements (*Vanderborght*, C-339/15), the AG noted that

> the relationship of trust [between the dentist and the patient] would necessarily be undermined if dental care providers were permitted to advertise to the general public in order to promote their services. [...] the patient might legitimately fear that, when the practitioner advises or recommends that he follow a course of treatment, that advice or recommendation is motivated, at least in part, by the economic interests of the practitioner. (2016, para 107)

By emphasizing that EU law protects a profession's dignity *in order to* protect fundamental interests or goods such as health, or mutual trust within society, the AG has made explicit the connection between dignity as ranking and the protection of fundamental human values. In other words, it has connected the idea of dignity as ranking with the idea of human dignity, although it has never taken the opportunity to directly specify it.

II. Human Dignity

The CJEU has utilized the concept of human dignity more often than it has been able to reflect upon it. Of the variety of cases within which the idea was deployed, only a handful of them address the topic of human dignity squarely. Within this small number, many of the most interesting statements about dignity emanated from the personal, explicit and lengthy AG's opinions.

A. Dignity as humanity

The CJEU has had the chance to address the uniqueness of human nature. When confronted with a preliminary ruling on the applicability of the concept of 'victim' to legal persons, the CJEU and its AG identified a sphere of interests that belong only to human beings. More precisely, the CJEU stated that when EU rules refer to 'victims in criminal proceedings', they aim to protect 'the dignity of the individual', not legal persons (*Dell'Orto v. Saipem*, C-467/05, AG, para 57). Drawing such a bright line between natural and legal persons is permissible in the CJEU's view because only the former can suffer not just from material losses, but also from 'physical or mental injury and emotional suffering' (C-467/05, para 56). The special multidimensional vulnerability of humans thus becomes a marker of their unique dignity.

B. The beginning of dignity: The embryo

The EC Directive on the Legal Protection of Biotechnological Inventions (Directive 98/44/EC) generated controversy when technology made embryo manipulation a concrete possibility. *Brüstle v. Greenpeace eV* (C-34/10) focused on the utilization and patentability of embryo-related cells. More precisely, at stake was whether the qualification of embryo included a fertilized egg at the moment of conception or at a subsequent stage, since the Directive did not rule on this very aspect. The issue was relevant since the Directive excluded embryos from patentability. The CJEU thus had to adjudicate on the concept of embryo in order to identify the area of patentability.

The AG acknowledged the divisiveness of the controversy, as the definition of the embryo was one of the 'the main points of different philosophies and religions and the continual questioning of science' (C-34/10, para 39). The AG, however, wanted to make crystal clear that the CJEU had to decide exclusively on the legal plane and found that the 'principle of dignity', which the Directive included among its core values, was of paramount importance to adjudicate on the matter (C-34/10, para 96).

Although the variety of national disciplines made harmonization particularly challenging, the AG's opinion and the CJEU's judgements concurred that the concept of embryo had to be defined specifically for EU law. In the AG's words, 'If it were left to the Member States to define the concept of a human embryo, in view of the differences which exist in this regard, this would mean […] that an invention […] could be granted a patent in some Member States, while the patentability of such an invention would be excluded in others' (C-34/10, para 56). This would run against the Directive's purpose of harmonizing the legal protection of biotechnological inventions.

Since philosophical or religious considerations would have made any consensus impossible, the AG started with scientific evidence, as did the CJEU in its judgement. For the AG, science made plain that 'development from conception begins with a few cells [...] They hold within them the full capacity for subsequent division' (C-34/10, para 84). In the CJEU's view, because of such capacity, totipotent cells had to be considered 'the first stage of the human body which they will become' (C-34/10, para 85). This gave them a special value: cells that could develop into a full human being enjoyed the protection accorded by human dignity and could not be patentable. On the contrary, pluripotent cells did not enjoy the same protection as they did not have the same capacity. The CJEU thus used dignity to accord a special protection to a specific category of cells, without having to adjudicate strictly on the nature of the embryo.

C. The purpose of dignity and solidarity

In 2013, the CJEU clarified how the protection of human dignity is built into EU law. It stated that the 'right to human dignity and integrity' fleshes out the principles of 'social cohesion and solidarity'. It therefore requires the protection of vulnerable people, fostering a legal interpretation of EU rules in accordance with such a goal (*Fédération des maisons de repos privés de Belgique*, C-57/12). The statements that human dignity is a 'right' and that it substantiates 'social cohesion and solidarity' resonate with other CJEU's judgements that utilized the idea of human dignity. In fact, the preoccupations of solidarity and social cohesion are reflected in the case law that has grounded in dignity the requirement that individuals be provided with the basic means to live a decent life (*Jobcenter Berlin*, C-67/14). More broadly, the connection between human dignity and solidarity established by the CJEU echoes the central role that social justice has played in the process of European integration since its beginning.

Interestingly enough, however, this approach is not unilaterally protective of vulnerable people. Dignity can work as a double-edged sword, as happened in the famous *Dano* case (*Dano*, C-333/13; see also *Vertisce Arbeit Jobcenter v. Garcia-Nieto*, C-299/14). The case revolved around Romanian nationals who established themselves in Germany for a long period. They profited from the German welfare net protection as EU citizens, never sought a job and later requested the higher level of social protection that was accorded by domestic laws and that, according to EU citizenship laws, should have been extended to them as well. German institutions denied them such additional benefits, and a judicial dispute ensued. The CJEU justified the German denial of additional social protection for EU citizens. In the CJEU's eyes, the fact that the claimants did not participate in the economic life of the country justified distinguishing their treatment from other EU residents. Since they were already accorded some basic protection, their dignity was preserved. But forcing countries to do more for EU citizens not willing to enter the job market would have created 'a burden on the social assistance system of the host Member States' (*Dano*, C-333/13). In other words, the CJEU did not see the concept of dignity just as an equalizer, but rather as a bottom line beyond which diversification in welfare service was permissible.

D. Understanding human dignity

i. Absolute and Concrete Dignity

There are fields within which human dignity entails absolute protection. Prohibitions of inhuman or degrading treatment are 'absolute' precisely because they are grounded in dignity (*Petruhin*, C-182/15, para 56). This absoluteness has become a stable component of human dignity, mostly thanks to the case law that revolves around the processing of asylum seekers (*CK, HF, AS v. Slovenia*, C-578/16; *Cimade et a.*, C-179/11), repatriations (*MP v. Secretary of State*, C-353/16), extraditions (*Petruhin*, C-182/15) and the execution of the European Arrest Warrant that automatizes extradition among EU states (*ML v. Generalstaatsanwltschaft Bremen*, C-220/18). Dignity has thus become an important player in domestic disputes concerning non-nationals (*Zakaria*, C-23/12; *McCarthy v. Secretary of State*, C-202/13).

The absoluteness of human dignity's protection does not give birth to a formalist assessment of the potential threats to human dignity. The necessity of taking into consideration the concrete situation of individuals is a trademark of the CJEU's understanding of human dignity (among many, see *K. V. Staatsecretaris*, C-331/16, and *HK v. Belgische Staat*, C-366/16). The protection of human dignity requires, for instance, that minors enjoy special protection in the context of judicial proceedings. Their unique vulnerability requires that the parity of arms be adjusted to allow that their testimony is taken before the judicial proceedings take place, in order to preserve the freshness of their memory and prevent more damage to their lives (*X & Y, C*, C-507/10; *Pupino*, C-105/03). Or, to draw from another field, if domestic institutions fear that executing a European Arrest Warrant might pose a threat to an individual, they must investigate the concrete conditions that the extradition would entail for the individual (*Aranylosi and Caldararu*, C-404/15 and 659/15), without denying extradition simply because the subject to be extradited cites potential threats.

'Concreteness' is also a major component of the legal treatment of migrants and asylum seekers. The CJEU had to intervene several times on the practicability of returning asylum seekers to the EU country of first entry, as required by EU rules. In particular, the refugee crisis hit Greece while its national economy was on the verge of financial collapse. Asylum seekers who fled the Greek territories should have been deported back to Greece in order to process their asylum request. They complained that had they returned to Greece, they would have had to face inhuman conditions. The CJEU emphasized that, according to the EU Charter, the asylum seekers' dignity had to be not just respected, but also protected. In other words, countries that were supposed to return asylum seekers could not do so if they knew that systemic deficiencies of the state of destination would amount to degrading treatments for the asylum seekers (*N.S. v. Secretary of State for the Home Department*, C-411/19).

The CJEU reiterated a similarly concrete or contextual approach to immigration in a judgement about the standards for expelling undocumented third-country nationals. It evaluated the means through which domestic institutions could enact expulsions. Quick expulsions were deemed legitimate exclusively for those individuals who had lived only for a short period of time in a country. Those who had resided for longer periods were found to have developed bonds with the domestic society that could not be cut easily or without pain. Hence, the process of expulsion had to respect the stronger level of integration of the subject (*Z.Z. and O*, C-554/13).

By requiring that states consider an individual's actual concrete conditions before executing an European Arrest Warrant, or that they ensure non-nationals residing in an EU member state the means to live a decent life, the CJEU has put burdens on the shoulders of the states. The idea of solidarity that underpins dignity within the EU constitutional framework does not simply put shackles on the states; it also pushes them to engage in social welfare and human rights' transnational patrolling.

ii. Dignity and Time

Concreteness in protecting human dignity has also meant reading laws and regulations in a way that would acknowledge societal changes and protect vulnerabilities, once unknown or neglected. In *P. v. S. and Cornwall County Council* (C-13/94), the CJEU was called on to decide on the correct interpretation of a directive that aimed to secure equal treatment for men and women (Council Directive 76/207/EEC of 9 February 1976). P., the applicant, who was employed as a manager in an educational facility operated by the Cornwall County Council, underwent a gender reassignment process, about which she notified the Council. P. started with dressing and behaving as a woman and later underwent multistep surgeries. Before the surgery process was completed, P.'s contract was terminated. P. then claimed that she had been discriminated against on the basis of sex.

The Directive prohibited any discrimination 'whatsoever on grounds of sex, either directly or indirectly' (76/207/EEC). Since P. was technically still a male when dismissed, she could not claim that she was discriminated against for being a woman. The CJEU had to face the interpretative dilemma of deciding whether discrimination related to gender reassignment was protected under the Directive.

The AG Tesauro's opinion did not utilize the concept of dignity. It encouraged the CJEU, however, to remove social stigmas through an evolutionary interpretation of the Directive. He suggested that the 1976 Directive had to be interpreted in light of contemporary circumstances, not according to the meaning that attached to it when it was drafted. In mid-1970s, transsexualism was 'only just beginning to be "discovered"'; the Directive's meaning had to be accommodated now to include transsexuals (*P. v. S. and Cornwall County Council*, C-13/94, AG, para 23). 'In society as it is today, in which customs and morals are changing rapidly, [...] it would be unjustifiable to reject out of hand the problem of transsexuality [...] or simply to condemn it and consider it contrary to the law', he noted (C-13/94, AG, para 9). In Tesauro's view, the law had to engage with present-day challenges and read new social phenomena – such as transsexuality – into existing law. The legal interpretation of written laws therefore had to reflect social changes: 'outdated views' could not 'cut [the law] off from society as it actually is' (C-13/94, AG, para 9). It was necessary to 'keep up with social change' (C-13/94, AG, para 9).

In Tesauro's view, the CJEU was called to deliver a historical decision. It could not miss the 'opportunity of leaving a mark of undeniable civil substance' and 'taking a decision which [was] bold but fair and legally correct, inasmuch it [was] undeniably based on and consonant with the great value of equality' (C-13/94, AG, para 24).

The CJEU's judgement found that the Directive was 'simply the expression, in the relevant field, of the principle of equality, which [was] one of the fundamental principles of Community law' (C-13/94, judgement, para 18). In the CJEU's view, the scope of the Directive had to apply to 'discrimination arising […] from the gender reassignment' (C-13/94, judgement, para 20). P. had been dismissed 'on the ground that he […] intend[ed] to undergo, or [had] undergone, gender reassignment' and therefore had been 'treated unfavourably by comparison with persons of the sex to which he or she was deemed to belong before undergoing gender reassignment' (C-13/94, judgement, para 21).

The CJEU noted that 'to tolerate such discrimination would [have been] tantamount, as regards such a person, to a failure to respect the dignity and freedom to which he or she [was] entitled' (C-13/94, judgement, para 22). Albeit succinct, the CJEU's phrasing was quite important. It did not explain what dignity meant, but gave it key importance in deciding the case. By using this concept, the CJEU expressed the need to eradicate the social stigma attached to transsexualism. Interestingly, the CJEU emphasized the importance of respecting human dignity although the Directive did not mention the concept. Even more notably, this occurred long before this was enshrined in the European Charter. In other words, the CJEU gave dignity a pivotal role although this concept was not present within the Directive nor was it explicitly enlisted among the overarching principles of the EC legal system.

iii. Dignity and Personal Identity

The issue of sexual orientation later combined with that of asylum seekers. In two cases, the CJEU was confronted with the task of squaring a rather difficult circle. Some applicants for refugee status alleged that if they were deported to their home countries, they would face threats of persecution because of their sexual orientation (*A. B., C. v. The Kingdom of Netherlands*, Joint Cases C-148/13, C-149/13 and C-150/13). The CJEU had to assess whether and to what extent EU member states could verify the allegations without degrading the claimants' dignity.

AG Sharpston made powerful observations on the topic of sexuality, although she made reference to dignity very rarely. She noted that 'sexuality [was] a highly complex issue that [was] integral to [one's] personal identity and the sphere of human life' (C-148/13 to 150/13, para 36). On the one hand, it was immensely difficult to verify an 'averred sexual orientation' and it was 'unlikely that there [would] be documentary or other evidence to support an applicant's self-declared statement of […] sexual orientation' (C-148/13 to 150/13, para 43). On the other hand, human dignity forbade the usage of intrusive means to detect one's sexuality: the applicants could not 'be required to support requests for refugee status in a manner that undermine[d] their dignity or personal integrity' (C-148/13 to 150/13, para 52).

Sharpston quickly reviewed a set of approaches that, in her view, were not adequate to the task. Since 'within the [EU], homosexuality [was] no longer considered to be a medical or psychological condition', there was 'no recognized medical examination that [could] be applied in order to establish a person's sexual orientation' (C-148/13 to 150/ 13, para 60). Also 'explicit questions concerning an applicant's sexual activities and pro-clivities', utilization of stereotypes as proxies or requiring applicants to produce evidence such as films or photographs or to perform sexual acts in order to demonstrate their sexual orientation were obviously impermissible (C-148/13 to 150/13, paras 62–63). Sharpston thus circumscribed the possibilities of intruding into one's life, but still allowed for the possibility of assessing the credibility of an asylum seeker's claim.

The CJEU's judgement largely confirmed the AG's viewpoint, but used dignity as the main legal compass to navigate the issues at stake. It pointed out that, on the one hand, dignity ruled out tests that required the applicant to perform sexual acts. On the other hand, it called for an *in concreto* analysis of the situation of the applicant. Domestic institutions had to make concrete assessments of 'the individual situation and personal circumstances of the applicant' (C-148/13 to 150/13, para 57). In a nutshell, the CJEU made an extensive use of dignity, both by ruling out options and by pushing for an individualized assessment of the asylum seeker.

A few years later, another case gave the CJEU the opportunity to focus on psychologists' roles in assessing the asylum seeker's sexual orientation (*F. v. Bevandorlasi es Menekultugyi Hivatal*, C-473/16). The AG's opinion and the CJEU's judgement did not rule out as inconsistent with human dignity the option of employing psychologists. Psychologists could derive a claimant's sexual orientation by analyzing her personality: as scientific literature in the field did not distinguish homosexual and heterosexual personality, no serious diagnosis could have been reached. But they could be helpful in evaluating the general credibility of an applicant and make it easier for the asylum seeker to speak about persecution threats, fears or past experiences. The CJEU employed the concept of dignity to put limitations on what psychologists could do, as well as to encourage their involvement in the evaluation of asylum requests.

III. Theories of Dignity

The pivotal role of human dignity within the EU Charter boosted the AG's attempts to give this word a meaning. Some opinions dealt with the concept at length, taking pains to explain dignity's significance, edges, ramifications and even roots. The opinions that gave a strong contribution to the topic drew inspiration from two different intellectual sources: Kant and Dworkin.

A. Kant and the European roots of dignity

Shortly after the EU Charter with its emphasis on human dignity came into existence, the CJEU's AG Jacobs tried to make the Kantian ideal of dignity transparent. The *Kingdom of the Netherlands* case revolved around the limitations to genetic manipulations (C-377/98). The application was filed in 1998, before the Charter was drafted; but it was discussed in 2001, so the AG took the Charter into consideration while drafting his opinion. The Netherlands sought the annulment of a Directive that required member states to protect biotechnological inventions. Among the claims brought forward by the Kingdom was the breach of the fundamental right to respect for human dignity, in pursuance of which, however, the Directive prohibited the patentability of the human body at the various stages of its formation and development. Clearly inspired by the famous Kantian motto, the applicant submitted that the Directive did not make 'isolated parts of the human body' not patentable, thereby reducing 'living human matter to a means to an end, undermining human dignity' (C-377/98, AG, para 69). The AG subscribed to such a Kantian view of human dignity. He did not find any contradiction, however, between the Directive and the respect of human dignity, as the Directive itself ruled out the possibility of patenting the human body. The CJEU denied the claim, but did not challenge the claimant's Kantian reading of dignity.

A more eloquent Kantian inspiration may be found in respect of the *Omega* case, the CJEU's most famous dispute on dignity (C-36/02). A German undertaking imported and utilized British toys to run a recreational activity. Within it, players used guns that shot laser lights that were completely innocuous, aiming at other players who wore special vests. The local municipality, however, prohibited the game because it attempted to challenge public order. More precisely, such a game was seen as conflicting with the German Constitution's commitment to protect 'human dignity'. The case reached the CJEU because of the prohibition's impact on the common market: due to the prohibition, the foreign company could not offer its services and export its products in German territory.

The question that reached the CJEU was of particular significance. On one hand, it involved the EU's legacy, namely its economic freedoms. On the other hand, it was centred on the idea of 'human dignity'. This value was simultaneously the overarching principle of the German Constitutional order, a cornerstone of the EU Charter, and an important part of the new narrative that relegitimized the EU.

The way dignity was employed in the case was particularly delicate. Although Germany deployed it in order to carve out an exception to the EU freedom for its territory, the very concept of human dignity had undeniably a universal potential and appeal. Culturally speaking, the CJEU had to face a serious issue: the whole case could have been read as if the United Kingdom had tried to export an activity that Germans considered to be unacceptable on grounds of human dignity.

The domestic court that referred the case to the CJEU, however, tried to ease the problem by clarifying that the issue revolved around the clash between European economic freedom and the *German* national constitutional value of dignity. This interpretation viewed the case merely as a conflict between a local legal value and a general precept. But the same idea that the British were exporting something that was in open conflict with respect for human dignity hardly made this a uniquely German concern.

The CJEU was also confronted with a dilemma that was likely to re-emerge repeatedly in the near future: Were the economic freedoms – the old EC's pillars – giving way to fundamental domestic values? Or were powerful constitutional principles such as human dignity so weak that they had to give way to economic freedoms? What type of European integration was on its way, then? The whole argument had the potential to cause a cultural detonation.

But what was dignity, after all? The AG Stix-Hackl admitted that 'there [was] hardly any legal principle more difficult to fathom in law than that of human dignity' (C-36/02, para 74). The attempt that she made to provide an outline of the concept was, however, profound.

The AG drew from German legal doctrine on the topic. This is no surprise, given the paramount importance of the German contribution to the modern understanding of dignity, the fact that the case originated in Germany and that the AG herself was an Austrian lawyer. Enders, Brugger and Brieskorn were among the first authors that she cited. In a few words, the AG noted that human dignity was a concept that expressed 'the respect and value to be attributed to each human being on account of his or her humanity [...] Mankind itself [was] reflected in the concept of human dignity; it [was] what distinguishe[d] [the humans] from other creatures' (C-36/02, para 75). The AG, however, did not hide the problem beneath the concept: 'the question of what distinguishe[d] mankind inevitably prevail[ed] over the law; that it [was] to say, the substance of human dignity [was] ultimately determined by a particular "conception of man"' (ibid.).

The AG was required to draw some operational conclusions. In her view, dignity formed 'the underlying basis and starting point for all human rights distinguishable from it', and it was 'the point of convergence of individual human rights in the light of which they [were] to be understood and interpreted' (C-36/02, para 76).

Despite the variety of possible readings of dignity, the AG thought that it was possible to identify a common thread within dignity. Interestingly enough, she noted that 'human dignity [had] its roots deep in the origins of a conception of mankind in European culture that regard[ed] man as an entity capable of spontaneity and self-determination. Because of his ability to forge his own free will, he [was] a person (subject) and [could] not be downgraded to a thing or object' (C-36/02, para 78).

This reading of dignity is relevant at two different levels. First, it finds dignity's roots in Europe. Second, it is built as an historical development that reaches its peak with Kant. It is not by chance that the AG cites Kant in the footnote that explains the statement about the human capacity to spontaneity and self-determination. The AG specified that

> from a religious perspective, the dignity of man [was] based on his creation in the image of God and the universal promise of salvation for all mankind. It was political thinking during the 18th century that recognition that all mankind has its nature and reason in common was the cornerstone from which stemmed the demand that human dignity and human rights should be recognized. (C-36/02, fn. 50)

Kant thus stands out as the pinnacle of an intellectual development that led to the emancipation of individual freedom. The AG's reading is the average reading of human rights as a history of success of modern reason over the shackles of the past and the religious narratives (Gordon 2017, 290).

The AG quickly perused the success of dignity among contemporary international law declarations on human rights and post–World War II constitutions. This analysis, albeit cursory, allowed the AG to declare that human dignity normally functioned as a 'general article of faith or [...] as a fundamental evaluation or constitutional principle, rather than as an independent justiciable rule of law' (C-36/02, para 84). The conception of dignity as a right was therefore to be considered as a national exception.

The AG then tapped her reflections on the constitutional status of dignity into the clash between the German constitutional value and the EU protection of dignity, with the rather explicit goal of avoiding a conflict between the two. She acknowledged that dignity had slowly made its way into EU laws, through secondary legislation such as recitals of regulations and directives. In the AG's view, the CJEU had never identified dignity as a 'separate fundamental right' or 'an independent head of claim' (C-36/02, para 90). Therefore, the CJEU precedents, along with 'the inchoate nature of the concept of human dignity' itself, made it impossible to 'equate the substance of the guarantee of human dignity under the German Basic Law with that of the guarantee of human dignity as recognized in [EC] law' (C-36/02, para 92). Moreover, the AG was of the view that this mismatch allowed the CJEU to distinguish the principle of human dignity, which pervaded EU law, from the right to human dignity, which was a trademark of German constitutionalism.

The AG thus proposed to reconcile the clash by making room for the German reading of human dignity without superimposing it throughout the European territories. In her view, the court should not have allowed 'any interpretation of fundamental freedoms that compel[led] a Member State to permit acts or activities that [we]re an affront to human dignity' (C-36/02, para 93). The German measure could be seen as 'reasonably proportionate', as it did not overstep the boundaries of the discretion that the states had when they had to balance their public interests with European freedoms.

Each nation – the AG added – had the power to identify which interests were so fundamental to the extent that they overrode EC laws. 'The finding that a fundamental interest of society has been affected' to the extent that a freedom can be limited had to be 'determined in the light of national value judgments' (C-36/02, para 105). Within that case, the 'public displeasure' that the new undertaking received in Bonn testified to the conflict between the German understanding of human dignity and EC laws. The AG also substantiated her argument by citing the then-recent massacre of 26 April 2002, which took place in Erfurt, when a former student shot and killed 16 people.

The CJEU's judgement largely adhered to the AG's opinion and was able to square the circle by making three arguments. First, it emphasized that both the EU and Germany cherished human dignity. Second, it clarified that there was no requirement that the states had the same views on how to balance rights and interests. Third, it considered the German prohibition of the game as proportionate. By finding that, given the circumstances of the case, the prohibition was not disproportionate, it avoided a direct confrontation between the economic freedom involved and the protection of dignity.

B. Dignity, equality and Ronald Dworkin

S. Coleman v. Attridge Law and Steve Law is a perfect example of the capacity of dignity to trigger reflections that go beyond what the case at stake requires (C-303/06). The CJEU had to decide a dispute about the directive on equal treatment in employment and occupation (2000/78/EC of 27 November 2000). Sharon Coleman gave birth to a disabled son in 2002. In 2005, she accepted voluntary redundancy and stopped working for her employer. Shortly thereafter, she sued her former employer, alleging that she had been discriminated against. She specified that she had been treated less favourably, even in hostile terms, when she tried to accommodate her position's needs with the necessity of taking care of her son.

Coleman sought protection under the Directive that combated discrimination on grounds of sex, race, ethnicity, religion or belief, disability, age or sexual orientation. The interpretative issue focused on the fact that the Directive textually protected disabled people, but not those who were taking care of the disabled. The CJEU was very quick in bringing Coleman's situation within the umbrella of the Directive, thereby granting that type of protection against discrimination. It did so in rather plain terms, with very little attention given to the topic of dignity.

Although they concurred in the outcome, the CJEU's judgement and the AG's opinion differed widely in terms of rationales they offered for the decision and how they articulated their reasoning. AG Miguel Poiares Maduro took a very winding path. Instead of reflecting on the rationale for the Directive's prohibition of discrimination in order to extend it to cover Coleman, he embarked upon a lengthy journey regarding the meaning of dignity.

In order to do so, he first 'recall[ed] the values underlying equality': 'human dignity and personal autonomy' (C-303/06, para 8). Maduro then let Ronald Dworkin drive the argument:

> Human dignity entails the recognition of the equal worth of every individual [...] One's life is valuable by virtue of the mere fact that one is human, and no life is more or less valuable than another. As Ronald Dworkin has recently reminded [...], even when we disagree deeply about issues of political morality, the structure of political institutions and the functioning of our democratic states we nevertheless continue to share a commitment to this fundamental principle. Therefore, individuals and political institutions cannot act in a way that denies the intrinsic importance of every human life. (C-303/06, para 9)

Then Maduro introduced the topic of autonomy into the picture. Personal autonomy 'dictates that individuals should be able to design and conduct the course of their lives through a succession of choices among different valuable options' (C-303/06, para 9). In Maduro's view, 'recognising the equal worth of every human being means that we should be blind to considerations [based on religion, age, disability, or sexual orientation, among others] when we impose a burden on someone or deprive someone of a benefit' (C-303/06, para 10). Similarly, autonomy meant 'that people cannot be deprived of valuable options in areas of fundamental importance for their lives by reference to suspect classifications' (C-303/06, para 11).

Among the most subtle forms of discrimination was targeting people who are close to the subject of discrimination. According to Maduro, 'People belonging to certain groups are often more vulnerable than the average person, so they have come to rely on individuals with whom they are closely associated for help in their effort to lead a life according to the fundamental choices they have made' (C-303/06, para 14). This was exactly the case of Coleman. Although she had not been mistreated on account of '*her* disability', she certainly had been 'mistreated on account of "disability"'. And that was enough.

Maduro provided a very thorough explanation of why the Directive had to be interpreted as covering also the claimant's case. Much of his reasoning was centred on human dignity, but built up a rationale for the decision that was very loosely connected with the directive. Within the Directive, the idea of the autonomy of the individual was absent. The word 'dignity' appeared only once, when the Directive listed the various forms of harassment that constitute discrimination. On the contrary, Maduro construed a broad theory of dignity and autonomy based only on two titans of legal theory: Ronald Dworkin, whom he cited within the text and in a footnote, and Joseph Raz, who was cited in a footnote to substantiate his claim that human autonomy requires that a 'person is autonomous only if he has a variety of acceptable options available to him to choose from, and his life became as it is through his choice of some of these options' (1986, 204).

Moreover, Dworkin's only cited work is a book with which the author tried to overcome the deep ideological rifts that, in his view, contaminated American political and legal debate. In other words, AG Maduro's emphasis on the connection between dignity and democracy, or the morality of political institutions, was inspired by a book that primarily addressed the civic coexistence of widely differing worldviews in the United States (Dworkin 2006, 2).

The contrast between this AG's opinion and the one provided in *Omega* is striking. In *Omega*, the AG drew inspiration from a limited list of scholars, most of whom were German. However, *Omega* originated in Germany and the issue around which it revolved was the clash between the German and the EU conceptualizations of dignity. The German constitutional tradition itself had certainly played a major role in the success of dignity and could not be disregarded (Dupré 2015, 8). Maduro seems to have redirected intellectual sources to a topic that they did not address squarely; and he did so in order to decide a case that did not need them. He took a giant leap when he drew from Dworkin to decide a case that did not need Dworkin, autonomy, democracy or even dignity to be decided. It seems apparent that he did so in order to magnify and reconfigure the conceptualization of dignity, rather than to shed light on that particular dispute.

Conclusion

From a bird's eye view, within the CJEU's jurisprudence, human dignity has taken the form that fitted EU's patchwork constitutional framework, which balances national constitutional commands with the need for legal integration. It thus magnifies the importance of fundamental rights. It calls for administrative and judicial proceedings that respect humanity. It requires that individuals be treated in light of the circumstances they live within. It encompasses the point of view of individuals as well as of collectivities. It is a code word for social cohesion and solidarity. It precludes infringements upon rights beyond what is necessary and entails legal and social equality. It promotes an evolutionary interpretation of legal texts. It fights social stigmas. It protects the embryo from manipulation, in order to preserve the human being it is capable of becoming. It requires national and EU institutions to strike a balance among competing interests.

In this respect, the CJEU's case law on human dignity reflects the variety of meanings and functions that the concept itself has discharged in adjudication around the world (McCrudden 2008, 686, 693 and 713).

While the lack of separate opinions has probably limited the CJEU's judgements, the AGs have not shied away from making bold statements on human dignity. The AGs' opinions sometimes have thus become platforms for theorizations of dignity, with ambivalent results. The AG in *Omega* tried to capture the spirit of human dignity as understood in Europe, mostly by focusing on continental authoritative scholars that developed the understanding of the value of this concept within European constitutionalism. In *Coleman*, the AG gave human dignity a political and philosophical component drawing from legal philosophy in a way that seemed more reflective of contemporary intellectual reflections on dignity, rather than of the strands of thinking that actually gave the concept a shape and a place in constitutional and legal texts. The AGs have thus split between those who try to bring the original post–World War II understanding of dignity to the surface and those who aim to draw it into contemporary intellectual debates around dignity itself. The normative value of dignity has thus become the springboard for further intellectual explorations of dignity, making the concept a good vehicle for legal change.

What has probably changed, and dramatically so, is the reputation of human dignity in CJEU's adjudication. In *Omega*, the AG was persuaded that dignity within the EU did not operate as a self-sufficient legal claim, but was rather a principle that permeated EU legal culture. Later claims have not focused solely on human dignity, but they have certainly employed it as a powerful legal claim. Since *Omega*, human dignity has gained teeth.

References

A. B., C. v. The Kingdom of Netherlands, C-148, 149 and 150/13. CJEU.

Albertini, C-338/82. CJEU.

Aranylosi and Caldararu, C-404/15 and 659/15. CJEU.

Baudenbacher, Carl. 2003. 'Judicial Globalization: New Development or Old Wine in New Bottles?' *Texas International Law Review* 38, no. 3: 505–26.

Brauch, Jeffrey A. 2009. 'The Dangerous Search for an Elusive Consensus: What the Supreme Court Should Learn from the European Court of Human Rights'. *Howard Law Journal* 52: 277–318.

Brüstle v. Greenpeace eV, C-34/10. CJEU

Cappelletti, Mauro. 1985. 'Repudiating Montesquieu – the Expansion and Legitimacy of Constitutional Justice'. *Catholic University Law Review* 35: 1–32.

Charter of Fundamental Rights of the European Union (2012/C 326/02, 26 October 2012). https://eur-lex.europa.eu/legal-content/EN/TXT/?uri=CELEX:12012P/TXT.

Cimade et a, C-179/11. CJEU.

CK, HF, AS v. Slovenia, C-578/16. CJEU.

Costa v. Enel, C-6/64. CJEU.

Council Directive 76/207/EEC of 9 February 1976 on the implementation of the principle of equal treatment for men and women as regards access to employment, vocational training and promotion, and working conditions.

Council Directive 98/44/EC of 6 July 1998 on the Legal Protection of Biotechnological Inventions.

Council Directive 2000/78/EC of 27 November 2000 establishing a general framework for equal treatment in employment and occupation.

Council Directive 2003/86/EC of 22 September 2003 on the right to family reunification.

Craig, Paul, and Grainne De Burca. 2011. *EU Law*. Oxford: Oxford University Press.

Dano, C-333/13. CJEU.

Dell'Orto v. Saipem, C-467/05. CJEU.

Dupré, Catherine. 2015. *The Age of Dignity: Human Rights and Constitutionalism in Europe*. Oxford: Hart.

Dworkin, Ronald. 2006. *Is Democracy Possible Here?* Princeton, NJ: Princeton University Press.

Gordon, Robert W. 2017. *Taming the Past*. Cambridge: Cambridge University Press.

EESCEC, C-150/98. CJEU.

F. v. Bevandorlasi es Menekultugyi Hivatal, C-473/16. CJEU.

Fédération des maisons de repos privés de Belgique, C-57/12. CJEU.

Fonzi, C-27 and 30/64. CJEU.

Hirschberg, C-219/75. CJEU.

HK v. Belgische Staat, C-366/16. CJEU.

Horspool, Margot, Matthew Humphreys and Michael Wills-Greco. 2016. *European Union Law*, 9th ed. Oxford: Oxford University Press.

Itzcovich, Giulio. 2017. 'The European Court of Justice, Comparative Legal Reasoning'. In *Comparative Constitutional Reasoning*, edited by Andras Jakab, Arthur Dyevre and Giulio Itzcovich, 277–322. Cambridge: Cambridge University Press.

Jobcenter Berlin, C-67/14. CJEU.

K. V. Staatsecretaris, C-331/16. CJEU.

Katsoufros, C-55/88. CJEU.

Kelemen, Daniel R. 2016. 'The Court of Justice of the European Union in the Twenty-First Century'. *Law & Contemporary Problems* 29: 117–40.

Kingdom of the Netherlands v. European Parliament and Council of the European Union, C-377/98. CJEU.

Lenaerts, Koen. 2007. 'Interpretation and the Court of Justice: A Basis for Comparative Reflection'. *The Int'l. Lawyer* 41, no. 4: 1011–32.

Macevicius, C-66/75. CJEU.

McCarthy v. Secretary of State, C-202/13. CJEU.

McCrudden, Christopher. 2008. 'Human Dignity and Judicial Interpretation of Human Rights'. *European Journal of International Law* 19, no. 4: 655–724.

ML v. Generalstaatsanwltschaft Bremen, C-220/18. CJEU.

MP v. Secretary of State, C-353/16. CJEU.

Mrs. V., C-18/78. CJEU.

N.S. v. Secretary of State for the Home Department, C-411/19. CJEU.

Omega Spielhallen- und Automatenaufstellungs-GmbH v. Oberbürgermeisterin der Bundesstadt Bonn, C-36/02. CJEU.

P. v. S. and Cornwall County Council, C-13/94. CJEU.

Petruhin, C-182/15. CJEU.

Pin, Andrea. 2019. 'The Transnational Drivers of Populist Backlash in Europe: The Role of Courts'. *German Law Journal* 20, no. 2: 225–44.

Pupino, C-105/03. CJEU.

Rasmussen, Morten. 2008. 'The Origins of a Legal Revolution – the Early History of the European Court of Justice'. *Journal of European Integration* 14, no. 2: 77–98.

Raz, Joseph. 1986. *The Morality of Freedom*. Oxford: Clarendon.

Rosen, Michael. 2012. *Dignity: Its History and Meaning*. Cambridge, MA: Harvard University Press.

S. Coleman v. Attridge Law and Steve Law, C-303/06. CJEU.

Société fiduciaire nationale d'expertise comptable v. Ministre du Budget, des Comptes publics et de la Fonction publique, C-119/09. CJEU.

Stein, Eric. 1981. 'Lawyers, Judges, and the Making of a Transnational Constitution'. *American Journal of International Law* 75, no. 1: 1–27.

Van Gend En Loos, C-26/62. CJEU.

Vanderborght, C-339/15. CJEU.

Vertisce Arbeit Jobcenter v. Garcia-Nieto, C-299/14. CJEU.

Waldron, Jeremy. 2012. *Dignity, Rank, and Rights*. New York: Oxford University Press.

Weiler, J. H. H. 2011. 'The Political and Legal Culture of European Integration. An Exploratory Essay'. *International Journal of Constitutional Law* 9, no. 3–4: 678–94.

X & Y, C., C-507/10. CJEU.

Z.Z. and O, C-544/13. CJEU.

Zakaria, C-23/12. CJEU.

Chapter Five

THE NEW DIGNITY JURISPRUDENCE: A CRITIQUE

Angus J. L. Menuge

I. Introduction

The Preamble to the Universal Declaration of Human Rights (1948) demands 'recognition of the inherent dignity and of the equal and inalienable rights of all members of the human family'. Dignity is here understood as a fixed, universal and equal characteristic, intrinsic to being human. Since dignity precedes the state, the state cannot confer or remove it by legislation. Rather, the state must simply recognize and respect it. This idea – the *old dignity* – has precursors in the scriptural teaching that all human beings are made in the image of God; in the philosophy of Augustine, Aquinas, Locke and Kant; and in the US Declaration of Independence.

Over the past few decades, important rulings in the United States, culminating in *Obergefell v. Hodges* (Supreme Court of the United States 2015), reflect the emergence of quite a different concept of dignity – the *new dignity*. According to the new dignity, there is a deep connection between dignity and the autonomy of the inner self that seeks to realize its potential through a preferred lifestyle. Provided that a lifestyle does no harm, the state is required to respect it. If the state fails to do so, it *impairs* the dignity of those who choose that lifestyle. The remedy is legislation which grants the lifestyle legal protection and support, thereby *conferring* dignity on its practitioners. This move may create further pressure to legally require that citizens do not disrespect the dignity that has been granted. Dignity is no longer understood as fixed, universal and equal. The new dignity can vary between parties, depending on their different choices, so that a law may help or harm one party's dignity without helping or harming the dignity of others. And the new dignity does not precede the state, but can be removed or granted by acts of legislation. The state's job is to keep a close eye on (non-harmful) lifestyles as they emerge and ensure that dignity is dispensed as equitably as possible. This task is complicated by the fact that 'harm' is increasingly defined subjectively to include the perception of offense, making it hard to delimit lifestyles that are harmless.

In this chapter, I first present the key principles of the new dignity jurisprudence as they appear in several important US legal rulings (Section II). Next, I trace these principles back to their major philosophical precursors in the works of Rousseau, Kant (allegedly), Nietzsche, Sartre, Mill and our 'therapeutic' culture (Section III). I then argue that the resulting account is an unacceptable basis for jurisprudence (Section IV). This is because the new concept of dignity promotes legal decisions that are (1) unintelligible, (2) arbitrary, (3) inconsistent, (4) unstable and (5) untrustworthy. Rulings lose the appearance of legitimacy if it is not possible for a reasonable, well-informed person to understand why the decision was made (the decision is *unintelligible*), why that decision rather than another was made (the decision is *arbitrary*) or why the opposite decision could not be made on the same general grounds (*inconsistent* rulings). The account is also *unstable*, since the principles of new dignity allow one to argue that the process of redressing dignitary wounds sets up a cycle of compensatory discrimination, creating dignitary wounds in those whose rights have been abridged to aid the aggrieved party. As a result, the legal process is *untrustworthy*, because citizens can never be sure that what they consider a major advance for human dignity (analogous, they may think, to abolishing slavery or ending segregation) will not be reversed using the very same principles applied to make that advance. Indeed, this has already occurred, for example, where dignitary gains made by women have subsequently been abridged by demands to recognize the dignity of the transgender community (as discussed more fully in Section IV). The resulting, seemingly intractable conflict between competing dignity claims suggests that even the proponents of the new dignity need a more stable and rationally defensible concept to ground their jurisprudence. An adequate legal concept of dignity should allow one to respect the dignity of those formerly overlooked without requiring one to reverse uncontroversial gains that have already been made.

II. The New Dignity

A. Recent US Law

In the United States, perhaps the sharpest early statement of the new dignity concept is *Planned Parenthood v. Casey* (Supreme Court of the United States 1992), which, while disputing its basis, reaffirms the prior *Roe v. Wade* (Supreme Court of the United States 1973) decision legalizing abortion. *Casey* asserts a close connection between 'dignity' and 'autonomy' that warrants an allegedly constitutional 'right to privacy' on the decision whether or not to have an abortion: 'The woman's constitutional liberty interest […] involves her freedom to decide matters of the highest privacy and the most personal nature […]. The authority to make such traumatic and yet empowering decisions is an element of basic human dignity' (Supreme Court of the United States 1992, 915–16). On this view, dignity is dependent on the ability to exercise autonomy, and if the state interfered by prohibiting abortion, it would suppress autonomy and therefore abridge the dignity of the person considering abortion. Such dignity is not a fixed, invariant characteristic of all human beings but rather it can vary depending on the degree to which the state allows people to make their own choices. On this view, dignity is an *entitlement* of our liberty. According to the court, 'Part of the constitutional liberty to choose is the equal dignity to which each of us is entitled. A woman who decides to terminate her pregnancy is entitled to the same respect as a woman who decides to carry the fetus to term' (920).

While the old understanding saw respect as the appropriate response to an innate dignity, the new concept sees not only respect but dignity itself as something the state can grant.

The court held that the choice of whether or not to beget children is especially central to personal autonomy and could not be restricted without harming people's dignity. In a famous, but opaque passage we read:

> These matters, involving the most intimate and personal choices a person may make in a life-time, choices central to personal dignity and autonomy, are central to the liberty protected by the Fourteenth Amendment. At the heart of liberty is the right to define one's own concept of existence, of meaning, of the universe, and of the mystery of human life. Beliefs about these matters could not define the attributes of personhood were they formed under compulsion of the State. (851)

Interestingly, part of the cited reason for permitting abortion is not merely the liberty of ordinary action (like freedom of assembly) but the right to 'define one's own concept of existence, of meaning' and so on. There is a distinctly existentialist sound to the idea that individuals must be able to define what counts as a meaningful life for them. The underlying idea is that one has a right to choose one's identity by embracing a preferred lifestyle. Not to be allowed to do so harms one's dignity, and the state must then reform its laws so that dignity is dispensed more equitably.

There is a deep connection between the abortion cases and those permitting same-sex marriage. In *United States v. Windsor*, it was argued that New York's 'decision to give [same-sex couples] the right to marry conferred upon them a dignity and status of immense import' (Supreme Court of the United States 2013, 3) and that the DOMA (Defense of Marriage Act 1996) was unconstitutional because it 'humiliates tens of thousands of children now being raised by same-sex couples' (Supreme Court of the United States 2013, 23) and because 'the principal purpose and the necessary effect of this law are to demean those persons who are in a lawful same-sex marriage' (25). Here we see the beginnings of the idea, developed in *Obergefell v. Hodges* (Supreme Court of the United States 2015), that the state's constitutional obligation to uphold equal protection under the law means that it must strike down any laws that humiliate or demean people by denying them the recognition and benefits available to other citizens, because of their chosen lifestyle.

The *Obergefell* decision asserts that 'the fundamental liberties protected by the Fourteenth Amendment's Due Process Clause extend to certain personal choices central to individual dignity and autonomy, including intimate choices defining personal identity and beliefs' (Supreme Court of the United States 2015 syllabus, 2). In addition to the philosophically controversial idea that 'personal identity' is defined by our choices, the opinion makes it clear that dignity is something that can be harmed or conferred by legislation. A key part of the argument is an anti-humiliation principle, according to which equal protection implies that the law must not 'disparage' certain lifestyle choices: 'Under the Constitution, same-sex couples seek in marriage the same legal treatment as opposite-sex couples, and it would disparage their choices and diminish their personhood to deny them this right' (Opinion of the Court, 19). Further, DOMA laws are declared inconsistent with the Equal Protection Clause of the Fourteenth Amendment, because they harm and humiliate those (such as children) affected by those choices:

> Without the recognition, stability, and predictability marriage offers, [...] children suffer the stigma of knowing their families are somehow lesser. They also suffer the significant material costs of being raised by unmarried parents, relegated through no fault of their own to a more difficult and uncertain family life. The marriage laws at issue here thus harm and humiliate the children of same-sex couples. (Opinion of the Court, 15)

The remedy is legal reform that redresses 'dignitary wounds' (Opinion of the Court, 25) to same-sex couples and their families by extending to them 'the constellation of benefits the States have linked to marriage' (Opinion of the Court, 17).

As Clarence Thomas notes in his dissenting opinion, this is a significant departure from the understanding of liberty held by the framers of the US Declaration of Independence and of the US Constitution. The framers, like earlier lawmakers, saw liberty in primarily negative terms, as an absence of restraint or interference by the government in the lives of citizens: 'In the American legal tradition, liberty has long been understood as individual freedom *from* governmental action, not as a right *to* a particular governmental entitlement' (Thomas 2015, 7, emphasis original). Chief Justice John Roberts and Justices Antonin Scalia and Samuel Alito concurred with Clarence Thomas that the Constitution provides no basis for defining marriage, so this matter is something that should be entrusted to the states and the ordinary democratic process (Roberts 2015, 6). Justice Thomas also roundly rejected the idea that the new concept of dignity, as something harmed or conferred by the state, has any constitutional basis. In point of fact, the Constitution does not even mention 'dignity' and to the extent that the framers thought in those terms, they drew on a quite different understanding:

> The Constitution contains no 'dignity' Clause, and even if it did, the government would be incapable of bestowing dignity. Human dignity has long been understood in this country to be innate. When the Framers proclaimed in the Declaration of Independence that 'all men are created equal' and 'endowed by their Creator with certain unalienable Rights,' they referred to a vision of mankind in which all humans are created in the image of God and therefore of inherent worth [...] The corollary of that principle is that human dignity cannot be taken away by the government. (Thomas 2015, 16–17)

B. Principles of the New Dignity

From this brief review, we can see that the new dignity jurisprudence is committed to five key principles, which I will call (1) autonomy, (2) self-definition, (3) privacy, (4) anti-humiliation and (5) legal constructivism.

1. According to 'autonomy', all people have the right to choose a preferred lifestyle provided it does not infringe on the autonomy of others. It is up to each individual, and no one else, whether or not that individual has pets, is a vegetarian or engages in a variety of sexual relations with consenting others. On this view, dignity is rooted

in one's ability to make these choices without limitation or interference. In a recent video, a celebrity who affirmed a trans identity gave a paradigmatic expression of autonomy, insisting: 'You get to write your own story, live your life, live it *without any restrictions*, you can be you, you are in charge of how you want to live your life. [...] The time for you to love yourself, and express yourself the way you truly feel, is now' (NikkieTutorials 2020, 2:19–3:44, emphasis added).

2. According to 'self-definition', certain fundamental choices about how we live our lives are definitive of our identity. For example, *Obergefell* concurred with an earlier decision of the Supreme Judicial Court of Massachusetts that 'the decision whether and whom to marry is among life's momentous acts of self-definition' (Supreme Court of the United States 2015, Opinion of the Court, 13). On this view, part of one's dignity as a human being resides in one's ability to determine one's own identity.

3. 'Privacy' adds to this that even though one's actions and identity may be manifest in public, one's choices are private in the sense that society, including the law, has no right to interfere with one's personal choices about how to live and who one is.

4. According to 'anti-humiliation', any societal convention, practice or law that infringes on an individual's fundamental rights of autonomy and self-definition humiliates that individual by disrespecting the privacy of that individual's choices about how to live and what kind of person the individual is. When society does this, it inflicts 'dignitary wounds': it abridges or removes an individual's dignity because dignity is grounded in the ability to make one's own choices, and this ability has been impaired.

5. Finally, 'legal constructivism' maintains that appropriate legislation can not only *compensate* for dignitary wounds, but in an important sense, it can (and should) also *restore* or *confer* dignity. This is because the law can shield one's rights of autonomy and self-definition, ensuring that one's choices in these areas remain private. It can do this by striking down laws that infringe on the private sphere or by constructing new legal protections for preferred lifestyles and identities. In this sense, the law constructs human dignity by creating a private sphere in which autonomy and self-definition can operate without the humiliation of social intrusion.

III. Philosophical Roots of the New Dignity

In an insightful new book, Francis Fukuyama (2018) shows how (what I have called) the new dignity is a major assumption of contemporary identity politics. He traces the idea that dignity is rooted in autonomy to the works of Rousseau and Kant. The key doctrine he identifies in Rousseau is that 'the authentic inner self is intrinsically valuable, and the outer society [is] systematically wrong and unfair in its valuation of [it]' (10). As is well known, Rousseau believed that the noble savage in the state of nature was not sinful and that human vices are the result of a corrupted society, especially its distinctions of property and status. Resentment and conflict are inevitable because society reinforces the sense of inequality between individuals by bringing them together where comparisons are made: 'People became accustomed to [...] making comparisons; gradually they acquire the ideas of merit and beauty, which in turn produces feelings of preference [...] jealousy awakens with love, discord triumphs, and the gentlest of passions receives the sacrifice of blood' (Rousseau 1984 [1755], 114). But the mores, laws and conventions society uses to suppress this conflict also suppress the inner self and are an obstacle to self-realization. For Rousseau, society has developed to entrench inequality through 'a mass of rules, relationships, injunctions, and customs that is itself the chief obstacle to realization of human potential, and hence of human happiness' (Fukuyama 2018, 32). This account suggests that if the role of the state is to support human flourishing, legislation must promote and not obstruct the autonomous development of the inner self, so that individuals can live out their preferred lives without societal interference. When it comes to relationships with others, they must also not be externally defined, but autonomously chosen. Rather than the state defining appropriate relationships, each individual should be allowed to make, or dissolve, a contract with others as he or she sees fit.

Fukuyama claims that this emphasis on autonomy can also be traced to Kant, though I would argue that it is more accurate to say that the real source is a pervasive voluntarist misreading of Kant's ethics. Fukuyama correctly asserts that for Kant, the dignity of human beings is grounded in their nature as moral beings who have the freedom to make moral choices:

> Morality and humanity, in so far as it is capable of morality, is that which alone has dignity [...] For nothing has any worth other than that which the law determines for it. But precisely because of this, the legislation that determines all worth must itself have a dignity, i.e. unconditional, incomparable worth, for which the word *respect* alone makes a befitting expression of the estimation a rational being is to give it. *Autonomy* is thus the ground of the dignity of a human and of every rational nature. (Kant 2012 [1786], 4.435–4.436, 47–48, emphasis original)

A number of influential commentators on Kant, like Christine Korsgaard, have concluded that Kant is a voluntarist, who maintains that the autonomous self is the *source* of value, so that an action 'is good only because of the value conferred on it by the choice of a rational being' (Korsgaard 1996, 126).

Even this voluntarist reading of Kant differs from Rousseau, since it does not ratify just any desire of the inner self, but only those which conform to reason. While Rousseau's inner self might seek self-realization in any natural inclinations, Kant requires that one may only act in ways which one can universalize, and indeed prizes actions that are *against* inclination: he does not at all see 'autonomy as the capacity for individuals to choose the course of their own lives however they see fit' (Rosen 2012, 25). Further, Rosen persuasively argues that the voluntarist reading of Kant is mistaken: for Kant, moral value cannot be reduced to the dictates of rational autonomy because he believes that moral beings have a dignity and worth that is *prior* to autonomy:

> If value is really conferred by 'the choice of a rational being', as Korsgaard says, what about the value of that choosing being itself? Where does that come from? Either a rational being must have value because of its own choice (which looks like a vicious circle) or there must be at least one thing whose value does not come from the choice of a rational being. (Rosen 2012, 151)

As Rosen argues, this is clearly shown by Kant's opposition to suicide as a failure to respect the dignity of oneself as a moral being (147–50), and this is so even though a rational being might be able to universalize suicide under certain circumstances.

On Rosen's view of Kant, human beings have dignity because they are moral beings, *capable* of autonomously determining a moral option and of choosing that option. This is very different from the claim that (provided it meets appropriate standards of rationality) the choice itself is what *makes* the action good or right. On the first reading, autonomy is the *epistemic* power to discover what is morally right. On the second reading, autonomy is the *metaphysical* power to confer moral rightness. However, while I agree with Rosen that it is a misreading, it is this second reading of Kant that has influenced new dignity jurisprudence. The reasoning behind *Casey* and *Obergefell* requires much more than the modest claim that those seeking abortion or same-sex marriage are beings *capable* of making moral decisions. It requires the much stronger claims that: (1) there is no authority to determine the rightness or wrongness of those decisions higher than the individuals making them; and (2) their decisions are *self-validating*, that whatever they choose is right for them, at least in those circumstances. Abortion, same-sex marriage and their contraries are all presented as choices that are morally permissible because they belong to a private sphere of actions which are up to each individual and which must be free of external constraints like laws. The only thing that can be wrong here is the existence of laws that 'disparage' any of these choices.

This stronger reading of autonomy not only depends on Rousseau, but also betrays the influence of Nietzsche, Sartre and Mill. Enamoured of the Graeco-Roman aristocracy, in which only few had dignity, Nietzsche claims that the 'noble type of man regards *himself* as a determiner of values; he does not require to be approved of […] he knows that it is he himself only who confers honor on things; he is a *creator of values*' (2017 [1886], para 260, 165, emphases original). The new dignity jurisprudence both rejects and affirms Nietzsche's anti-egalitarianism. On the one hand, it sides with Rousseau and Kant in affirming the equal dignity of every individual's moral choices, something Nietzsche clearly denied. But on the other hand, where there is controversy about the correctness of these choices (as there is about abortion and same-sex marriage), final authority is given to a small number of experts. A majority of justices on the Supreme Court function in much the same way as Nietzsche's nobility, a point not lost on dissenting Chief Justice John Roberts: 'The majority's decision is an act of will, not legal judgment […] In our democracy, debate about the content of the law is not an exhaustion requirement to be checked off before courts can impose their will' (Roberts 2015, 3, 25). If Roberts and other dissenting justices are correct, where there is a conflict between the competing autonomies of citizens or of states, the new dignity jurisprudence maintains that one can resolve the conflict by appealing to the higher autonomy of the courts. In the process, Supreme Court justices move from interpreters of law to lawmakers. It is arguable that the new dignity jurisprudence depends on the Orwellian idea that all autonomous decisions have equal value, but some autonomous decisions are more equal than others.

Yet it would not be fair to say that the majority justices in the *Casey* and *Obergefell* rulings are simply disciples of Nietzsche. Those justices were driven in large part by *sympathy* for the plight of individuals whose autonomy was unduly burdened by intrusive laws. This sympathy traces to Rousseau's natural pity (and to the moral psychology of David Hume, Adam Smith and Charles Darwin). But it is antithetical to Nietzsche, who rejected the '*unmanliness* of that which is called "sympathy"'' (2017 [1886], para 293, 187, emphasis original) as life-denying. For Nietzsche, the fact that some people are oppressed creates no obligation for the nobility to do anything about it.

One reason for this departure from Nietzsche is that the new dignity jurisprudence values the authentic feelings of each individual and especially those whose self-expression is being repressed by society. This much traces to Rousseau's emphasis on permitting the development of the inner self. But the new dignity goes further than Rousseau's plea to allow the inner self to realize its potential (which does not change what that self essentially is), adding to autonomy the idea of *self-definition*. The thought is that rights of autonomy are not just about how we act, but also about the kind of person we can choose to become. This reflects the much more radical ideas of Jean-Paul Sartre and their influence on other existentialist philosophers and psychologists.

Sartre rejected the theistic idea that the 'essence' of a person existed as a concept in the mind of God before He created that person. Instead, he argued that man is 'a being whose existence comes before its essence, a being who exists before he can be defined by any concept of it […]. Man first exists: he materializes in the world, encounters himself, and only afterward defines himself […] he will be what he makes of himself' (Sartre 2007 [1945], 22). Of course, I am not suggesting that all advocates of the new dignity are atheists like Sartre. But they may hold that in a secular state, it would be inappropriate for courts to make the assumption that our identity is determined by God. So identity is understood in secular terms as a lifestyle with which a person chooses to identify. This could be a Catholic identity or a secular humanist identity, and it could be the identity of a single person or a married person. As a result, if a same-sex couple seeks marriage, they are not simply asking to be able to do something that opposite-sex couples are allowed to do: they are choosing to become a particular kind of person. Thus, if the law refuses to grant the legal status of marriage to same-sex couples, it does not merely restrict their freedom of action, it profoundly impedes their ability to *be* the person that they prefer.

There is some tension in the new dignity's account of privacy. On the one hand, the law is asked not to impede the development of the 'inner self' whose decisions are left to its own discretion. Yet, on the other hand, it is also obvious that individuals who prefer a non-traditional or controversial lifestyle typically do not merely ask to carry out that lifestyle without interference. They also seek public recognition and even approval. Indeed, John Roberts argued that this made the majority's privacy-based case for same-sex marriage incoherent: 'the privacy cases provide no support for the majority's position, because petitioners do not seek privacy. Quite the opposite, they seek public recognition of their relationships, along with corresponding government benefits' (2015, 18). Similarly, Fukuyama argues that most proponents of same-sex marriage 'wanted their political systems to explicitly *recognize* the equal dignity of gays and lesbians; the ability to marry was just a marker of that equal dignity' (2018, 19, emphasis original).

One explanation for this apparent inconsistency between appeals to privacy and a demand for public recognition is that the new dignity is concerned about dignity in more than one sense of the word. Rosen identifies no less than four distinct meanings of 'dignity' that are historically important: (1) 'dignity as a rank or status'; (2) dignity as 'intrinsic value'; (3) dignity as dignified behaviour; and (4) dignity as respect (Rosen 2012, 114). (See Chapter 12 in this volume for a similar, though not identical, analysis.) While the old dignity is particularly concerned with sense (2), and the new dignity partly retains this idea in the dignity of autonomous beings, it is also clearly concerned with dignity in senses (1) and (4). The concern that one is accorded the status of social recognition and that one's lifestyle is accepted seems profoundly rooted in the rise of a therapeutic culture. Fukuyama traces the need for our worth to be recognized to the Platonic idea of *thymos* or spirit: for Plato this is the faculty that makes judgements of worth, and an individual feels alienated when society sends the signal that his chosen identity is worthless. Fundamentally, this is a matter of self-esteem, which is diminished when others do not affirm a person's lifestyle choices. These ideas became prevalent in the existentialist psychology of the 1960s that encouraged the idea of self-realization through affirming one's deepest desires (Rieff 2006 [1966]; Taylor 1991; Vitz 1995). In turn, these psychological ideas permeated education through the self-esteem movement and led lawmakers to think in therapeutic terms, seeing law as a means to dispense recognition and affirmation to various self-actualization projects: 'A liberal society increasingly came to be understood not just as a political order that protected certain minimal individual rights, but rather as one that actively encouraged the full actualization of the inner self' (Fukuyama 2018, 92).

Fukuyama plausibly argues that it is the rise of the 'therapeutic society' which 'midwifed the birth of modern identity politics' which is 'everywhere a struggle for the recognition of dignity' (103–4). If dignity-as-status or dignity-as-respect is withheld from certain life-defining decisions, then dignitary wounds are being inflicted on those who make those decisions. Calling this a *humiliation* clearly reflects the therapeutic model according to which it harms people's self-esteem not to endorse their self-actualization projects. While legislation cannot change every citizen's opinion of those projects, it can give those projects the status and respect associated with legal recognition and protection. The law cannot construct the inner self, but it can remove obstacles to the development of that self, and it can construct and confer dignity-as-status and dignity-as-respect.

To be sure, on no sensible view can autonomy have unlimited scope. No one will support the autonomy of an individual whose inner self needs rape and murder to be fully actualized. So here the new dignity follows Mill in recognizing the minimal restraint that 'the only purpose for which power can be rightfully exercised over any member of a civilized community, against his will, is to prevent harm to others' (1978 [1859], 9). Otherwise, however, Mill believed each individual was entitled to see his life as an experiment in finding happiness. On this view, an individual will

> do well by himself and others if only he is left free of paternalistic and moral constraints to engage in experiments in living from which he, corporately and individually, will learn what conduces to happiness and what does not [...]. Freed from the old moralisms and religious and other superstitions – liberated to be the progressive being that, by nature, he is – he will flourish. (George 2013, 108–9)

But there is one more strand in the new dignity jurisprudence, noted by Justice Samuel Alito. Amongst the various limits to self-actualization – social expectations, conventions, laws and so on – there is one more: *language*. Alito argues that the majority opinion in *Obergefell* had a distinctly postmodern understanding of 'liberty' (2015, 2). As noted by Clarence Thomas, the standard meaning of 'liberty' in American law is 'freedom from physical restraint' (2015, 6), and the constitutional understanding is that government grants liberty by not interfering in our lives. But in a postmodern twist, the *Obergefell* decision redefines liberty in terms of the positive right to legal status and recognition. On this understanding, a person who engages in a controversial lifestyle is not necessarily at liberty simply because the state does *not* intervene to prevent it. If that person feels humiliated by a lack of social recognition and support for the lifestyle, true liberty is found only if the state *does* intervene, providing that lifestyle the appropriate measure of dignity-as-status and dignity-as-respect. In the process, the standard legal understanding of dignity as an intrinsic quality is shifted to meanings on which dignity is an entitlement. As the sick patient cannot be healthy unless he receives treatment, the humiliated victims of dignitary wounds cannot be truly free until the state dispenses the appropriate dose of dignity.

So, as Roberts, Scalia, Thomas and Alito all point out, new dignity jurisprudence is not rooted in the constitutional understanding of liberty and dignity, but rather in the demand to accept the new meanings of these terms that derive from the autonomous self-realization of the inner self. Autonomy has expanded not only to encompass defining oneself as a person, but also to redefining words so that they are subservient to one's will.

This is another place where Nietzsche and his postmodern heirs have clearly influenced new dignity jurisprudence. Based on his materialist worldview, Nietzsche argued that nature is devoid of moral worth – indeed, '*there are altogether no moral facts* [...] Morality is merely an interpretation of certain phenomena – more precisely, a misinterpretation*' (1976 [1888], 501, emphasis original). As I read him, Nietzsche meant that it is a misinterpretation if one supposes one is *discerning* a *pre-existing* moral fact; rather one is *giving* something value by an act of will. In a similar fashion, some justices apparently think that they can change the meaning of 'liberty' and 'dignity' to become entitlements the court can dispense. They can then *create* the legal fact of the liberty and dignity of a lifestyle by a legal act which confers status and respect.

IV. Critique of the New Dignity

Citizens of a democracy have a right to expect that the legal reasoning grounding major rulings that profoundly affect their common life together meets certain standards. Without professional expertise in the law, they expect any ruling, even where they disagree with it, to be *intelligible* in the sense that it is based on a clear rationale rooted in publicly accessible reason and fact. They also expect any ruling to be *non-arbitrary*, so it is clear why that ruling was made rather than another, and that the ruling is *consistent* in the sense that if A is ruled on ground G, G is not an equally strong justification for ruling not-A (or for not ruling that A).

Citizens are also rightly concerned that legal decisions have some reasonable prospect of *stability*; that they do not, in solving one problem, create more problems of the same kind, or problems that may naturally lead to conflicting appeals (e.g. if redressing discrimination against one party discriminates against other parties). And finally, to the extent that the law has the potential to serve as an engine of social progress, it is important that the law is *trustworthy* in the sense that major uncontroversial advances in the equile treatment of citizens cannot be easily reversed using the same principles employed to justify those advances.

Unfortunately, the new dignity jurisprudence fails to satisfy all five of these desiderata for legal reasoning: it supports rulings which are unintelligible, arbitrary, inconsistent, unstable and untrustworthy. And we will see that this is entirely predictable, given the philosophical sources of new dignity thinking identified in the previous section of this chapter.

A. *Unintelligibility*

The reasoning used to support the *Casey* and *Obergefell* rulings is unintelligible because it depends on a view of the autonomous inner self which is inconsistent with settled law and common sense.

In *Casey*, the view that liberty includes 'the right to define one's own concept of existence, of meaning, of the universe, and of the mystery of human life' (Supreme Court of the United States 1992, 851) licenses a subjectivist view of value, according to which the value of something, such as the unborn, depends on how an autonomous person values it. Yet even if a depressed man does not value himself, and is not valued by anyone else, his murder remains a crime. And if value is conferred by autonomous subjects, then, when some people want the unborn child and some do not, the child is both valuable and not valuable. If the child has intrinsic value, that value does not depend on whether or not the child is valued (extrinsic facts), and if it does not have intrinsic value, and all value is subjectively assigned, then by extension of the same logic, we have no account of why unvalued *adults* may not likewise be killed, nor of what to do if some value the child and some do not. Privileging the mother's valuation cannot resolve the issue if the expression of her 'inner self' is at odds with others whose concept of 'existence, of meaning, of the universe, and of the mystery of human life' leads them to value the child differently than she does. A reasonable person cannot understand why only one person's opinion of the value of the unborn matters or how wanting or not wanting a child can magically transform its value with no change in any of its intrinsic qualities.

Obergefell is also an unintelligible decision. Like previous abortion decisions, it heavily relies on a 'right to privacy', yet, paradoxically, it does not argue that same-sex couples be allowed to carry on their lives without governmental intrusion into the private sphere, which was already permitted, but instead demands 'public recognition for their relationships' (Roberts 2015, 18). The many references to 'dignity and autonomy' also do not constitute a credible rationale for the ruling. If 'autonomy' means simply the ability to make one's own lifestyle choices, then same-sex couples already had that ability. If it means the right to define oneself (in this case, as a married person), then the obvious problem is that the law cannot recognize every self-defined status. If my inner self tells me that I am king, it is a disappointing fact that the law does not have to recognize me as king. It is obviously not true that any time one's inner self leads one to self-define as an X, the law must recognize one as an X.

Further, a variety of tightly reasoned arguments had been made, prior to *Obergefell*, for retaining the traditional idea of marriage as the union of two opposite-sex people (Stanton and Maier 2004; Gergis et al. 2012). Since that had been the universal understanding of marriage in all societies until same-sex marriage was legalized in the Netherlands in 2001 (Roberts 2015, 4), the burden of proof was on those favouring a redefinition of marriage to show that the traditional understanding was irrational and unjust, yet no compelling, systematic refutation of the traditional view was provided. Finally, as John Roberts noted, the laws cited as precedents for *Obergefell* (e.g. laws prohibiting interracial marriage, or marriage to a prisoner or someone owing child support) were clearly irrelevant since they show only that 'particular restrictions to marriage *as traditionally defined* violate due process. These precedents say nothing at all about a right to make a State change its definition of marriage' (2015, 16, emphasis original). So, as with *Casey*, some people's preferences triumph over others without a coherent rationale.

B. Arbitrariness

Casey is arbitrary because its appeal to dignity and autonomy is insufficient to show that abortion is permissible if the mother wants to terminate a pregnancy. The reason is that there are other people whose 'dignity and autonomy' is compromised if they want the child to live so that they can fulfil the deep desire of their inner self to be a parent or grandparent. It may be that the mother of the child does not self-define as a mother, but her choice to terminate the pregnancy will frustrate the autonomy and dignity of anyone who chooses to self-define as father, grandmother or grandfather (or aunt, uncle, cousin etc.). Since inner selves may have conflicting means of self-realization, it is arbitrary for the law to side with one inner self at the expense of others, unless it appeals to additional factors, beyond dignity and autonomy, which differentially affect these selves, as in 'unequal burden' arguments.

The *Obergefell* decision is also arbitrary, as John Roberts points out. If the definition of marriage may be changed so that we do not humiliate the autonomous preferences of the inner self, then no reason has been given for extending marriage to same-sex couples but not extending it in other directions as well:

> Although the majority randomly inserts the adjective 'two' in various places, it offers no reason at all why the two-person element of the core definition of marriage may be preserved while the man-woman element may not [...] It is striking how much of the majority's reasoning would apply with equal force to the claim of a fundamental right to plural marriage. If 'there is dignity in the bond between two men or two women who seek to marry and in their autonomy to make such profound choices', [...] why would there be any less dignity in the bond between three people who, in exercising their autonomy, seek to make the profound choice to marry? (Roberts 2015, 20)

Indeed, the same reasoning used to justify the extension of marriage to same-sex couples would seem to support not only plural marriage, but self-marriage, and marriage to pets, inanimate objects, sports and ideologies, provided only that these are contracts to which all of the inner selves involved give their consent (see Bussey 2019, 48–49). When one raises this objection, a typical reply is, 'Well, I am not saying I support extending marriage to X'. But, on the assumptions of the new dignity, this response is irrelevant if there are people who claim that *their* self-realization depends on doing just that. To take an extreme case, suppose my deepest desire is to be married to whomever or whatever I feel close to at the moment – any number of people, any sex, any animal, plant or mineral I like. The law would rightly reject such a notion as impracticable, since it is impossible to keep track of all these marriages, and the executors of my will surely do not want to spend time determining what portion of my estate should be dispersed to my cat, my cactus or three people I met in the restaurant. But for all that, it might be the case that my inner self would find its greatest fulfilment only through this concept of marriage. So, when marriage is redefined only to favour the self-defining projects of *some* inner selves, it is clearly arbitrary.

C. Inconsistency

Arbitrariness is closely connected with inconsistency. If the chief ground for *permitting* abortion in *Casey* is to respect the autonomy and dignity of the inner self, then that same ground could also be used to *prohibit* abortion, since there are inner selves who cannot be fully actualized without the right to live as parents or grandparents, and so their self-defining projects are frustrated by abortion. (In Chapter 12 in this volume, Michael Quinlan makes a similar point about the way 'safe zones' around abortion clinics seek to preserve the dignity of those seeking abortion while denying such dignity to pro-life protestors.) And while the *Obergefell* decision permits marriage between *only two people* of the same or different sex, its ground of autonomy and dignity equally supports marriages between more (or less) than two people, and between a person and a non-person. Further, there may be opposite-sex couples who would find fulfilment in traditional marriage, but who are repelled by marriage as redefined by *Obergefell*. If so, then it seems that in order for the law to recognize the autonomy and dignity of these couples *and* that of same-sex couples, it must *both* retain the traditional understanding of marriage *and also* redefine marriage, which is inconsistent. Since the law cannot do both, it is clear that autonomy and self-actualization are not sufficient grounds to decide these cases.

D. Instability

The argument that women must have the right to choose whether or not to terminate a pregnancy is also unstable. If a woman wants an abortion, but her partner does not, and she argues that an abortion is required to achieve her personal goals, he can argue that her decision violates his right to be a parent and thus that her not having an abortion is required to achieve his personal goals. He can say that his choice to be a father has been disparaged and that his partner has inflicted 'dignitary wounds' on him by denying him the autonomy and dignity of defining himself as a parent. Likewise, those who seek trad-itional marriage may argue that this option has been taken away from them, since they do not seek an estate that is open to same-sex couples. The problem is that when the law changed the definition of marriage, it changed it for everyone, not just same-sex couples, and that means marriage of the previous traditional kind is no longer a legal option. Whatever one's conscience or church may say, the *law* no longer recognizes marriage as an exclusive union between one man and one woman. If legal recognition is necessary to confer dignity-as-status and dignity-as-respect on those seeking traditional marriage, then they can make the case that their choices have been disparaged and their dignity wounded by making it impossible for them to be legally married in that sense. They can even say that their children have been humiliated because they are not recognized as chil-dren of traditionally married parents.

E. Untrustworthiness

The instability of new dignity jurisprudence is closely connected to its untrustworthiness. Suppose one thinks that legalizing abortion and same-sex marriage are great advances for society. Still, since the legal reasoning used to make these advances is unintelligible, arbitrary, inconsistent and unstable, one can have no confidence that they will not be reversed by appeal to the very same principles used to make those advances. If one thinks these are advances on a par with abolishing slavery, ending segregation or giving women the right to vote – reforms which virtually no one would like to see reversed – one has good reason to argue that those advances should have a stronger rationale than that provided by the new dignity jurisprudence.

The right to abortion is held to be a matter of women's rights and also reproductive rights. But there are also parental rights which take seriously the rights of both male and female parents, and reproductive rights include the right to have (as well as not to have) a child, and can easily be extended to include the father's rights, as well as the mother's. Thus, if the central argument for the permissibility of abortion rests solely on the autonomy and dignity of the mother, it is liable to reversal by decisions promoting the rights of other relevant actors whose autonomy is compromised by abortion. Likewise, if same-sex marriage is held to be a matter of respecting the autonomy of same-sex couples, it can be argued that their autonomy could have been recognized in other ways (by civil unions and reform of discriminatory rules about insurance, visitation rights etc.) which do not require changing the definition of marriage. As noted earlier, changing the legal definition of marriage changes what marriage is, legally speaking, even for opposite-sex couples, and so they can make the case that their autonomy and dignity has been denied by the law and demand the right to have traditional marriage reinstated, at least as a discrete option.

But since the abortion and marriage issues are highly polarizing, it may help us appre-ciate this point by focusing on an example where many ordinary citizens think that some-thing has gone wrong with the law (though even this example has proven divisive enough, given the ostracism of leading feminists who have criticized the trans agenda). This is the emerging conflict between the great advances women have made in athletics and sport and the claims of the transgender community. On 23 June 1972, President Nixon signed into law various education amendments, including Title IX, which forbade any sex-based discrimination in institutions that receive federal funding. Over time, female students and their supporters were successful in arguing that Title IX requires schools and colleges to provide equal access to athletic and sporting activities (Rothman 2017). As a result of this reform, there has been a tremendous increase in the participation of women in athletic and sports teams and events (Lancaster, n.d.). However, in May 2016, under the Obama administration, the Department of Education sent a 'Dear Colleague Letter' which asserted that Title IX 'encompasses discrimination based on a student's gender identity, including discrimination based on a student's transgender status' (US Department of Education and Department of Justice 2016, 2). This led many public facilities to permit students to use the locker rooms and restrooms of the gender with which they identified, even if that differed from their biological sex at birth.

This interpretation of Title IX was contested, since the original wording refers only to sex, not gender, and assumes a biological rather than a psychological understanding of sex. In light of this controversy, a later 'Dear Colleague Letter' issued under the Trump administration in February 2017 withdrew and rescinded the earlier letter, but left the proper interpretation of Title IX to 'the States and local school districts' (US Department of Education and Department of Justice 2017, 2). While there is currently no one settled policy on transgender issues, a number of athletic and sporting organizations have allowed transgender athletes to compete, most often individuals born male who self-identify as female, and who maintain less than a maximum level of testosterone. Allowing such individuals to participate in women's teams and events has already led to a significant backlash at high schools in the 17 states that currently permit them to compete without restrictions (such as required sex-reassignment surgery or hormone therapy) against cisgender girls (those whose gender coincides with their biological sex at birth), on the grounds that the transgender individuals have unfair advantages in natural speed, size and strength (Associated Press 2019).

It appears undeniable that one of the drivers of the transgender movement in sport (and elsewhere) is the new understanding of the autonomy and dignity of the inner self. This is because the argument that a person born biologically male (female) who later self-identifies as a female (male) should be treated as a female (male) takes for granted the idea that identity is determined by subjective factors, such as the deepest desires of the inner self, not by objective markers, such as chromosomal differences, or obvious differences in the development of the body (biology). So, for example, it is thought that if a genetic man self-identifies as a woman, the individual can flourish only if the individual (1) functions as a woman (e.g. in sport) and (2) is recognized and affirmed as a woman by society. The law then sees its role as one of supporting the autonomy and dignity of the individual by ensuring that these two conditions are satisfied.

But this solution is clearly unstable. Even if identity claims have a subjective source, one can still choose to identify oneself on the basis of objective markers. A cisgender female can say that her identity *is* that of a cisgender female, and that for her to function and be recognized and affirmed as such, she needs (inter alia) to be able to participate in exclusively cisgender female events. And there is a close parallel with the marriage case: just as redefining 'marriage' to include same-sex couples changes the definition of marriage for everyone, including opposite-sex couples, so changing the definition of 'female', 'girl' and 'woman' to include transgender individuals changes the definition of these terms for everyone, including cisgender females. So, cisgender female athletes can argue that their distinctive cisgender identity is disparaged by conflating it with a transgender identity, and that allowing transgender individuals to dominate in their events (as they already have) inflicts dignitary wounds on cisgender females. As a result, cisgender females in athletics and sports can use new dignity principles to argue that they should be able to compete in exclusively cisgender events, allowing transgender individuals some alternative accommodation. Thus, the grounds of autonomy and dignity used to permit transgender individuals to participate in women's sports can just as well be used to carve out an exclusive category of cisgender female sports.

On reflection, the instability and untrustworthiness of the new dignity philosophy are not really surprising. Their common source is the underlying assumption that the law must recognize the lifestyle projects of inner selves and the failure to recognize that these projects can stand in irreconcilable conflict to one another. In practice, the method used to 'resolve' such conflicts makes appeal to passing opinions about the hierarchy of oppression, so that more humiliated groups receive more attention than others viewed as less humiliated – until, of course, the less humiliated become (or claim to have become) the more humiliated. Fukuyama argues that in the long run, organizing society around the dignity demands of competing identity groups is a recipe for incoherence and conflict:

> Identity politics […] engenders its own dynamic, by which societies divide themselves into smaller and smaller groups by virtue of their particular 'lived experience' of victimization […]. This has created demands for recognition on the part of groups who were previously invisible to the mainstream society. But this has entailed a perceived lowering of the status of the groups they have displaced, leading to a politics of resentment and backlash. (2018, 164–65)

And if the law is to retain and deserve the respect of its citizens, it must strive to maintain its hard-earned reputation for objectivity and impartiality, something clearly threatened by unstable and untrustworthy appeals to the ever-proliferating demands for dignity.

V. Conclusion

What we have seen is that important legal rulings in the past few decades reflect the emergence of a new concept of dignity, one that is centred on the demands of the autonomous inner self. We traced this concept to its precursors in earlier thinkers and saw how different it is from the older concept of dignity as an innate, intrinsic quality of all human beings. Finally, we argued that the new dignity philosophy is not a sound basis for jurisprudence because it leads to legal decisions that are unintelligible, arbitrary, inconsistent, unstable and untrustworthy. The new dignity philosophy is a recipe for profound personal, social and legal incoherence and conflict, and it does grievous harm to public trust in the objectivity, rationality and reliability of the law. It is therefore imperative for sharp legal and philosophical minds to articulate and defend compelling alternatives that will better support our common life together.

References

Alito, Samuel (Justice). 2015. Dissenting Opinion. *Obergefell v. Hodges*, 135 S. Ct. 1732, 576 U.S.

Associated Press. 2019. 'Transgender High School Athletes Spark Controversy, Debate in Connecticut'. 25 February. https://www.foxnews.com/sports/transgender-high-school-athletes-spark-controversy-debate-in-connecticut.

Bussey, Barry W. 2019. 'The Legal Revolution against the Accommodation of Religion: The Secular Age v. the Sexular Age'. PhD diss., University of Leiden.

Defense of Marriage Act (DOMA). 1996. Pub.L. 104–199, 110 Stat. 2419, enacted 21 September 1996, 1 U.S.C. § 7 and 28 U.S.C. § 1738C.

Fukuyama, Francis. 2018. *Identity: The Demand for Dignity and the Politics of Resentment*. New York: Farrar, Straus, and Giroux.

George, Robert P. 2013. *Conscience and Its Enemies: Confronting the Dogmas of Liberal Secularism*. Wilmington, DE: ISI Books.

Gergis, Sherif, Ryan T. Anderson and Robert P. George. 2012. *What Is Marriage? Man and Woman: A Defense*. New York: Encounter Books.

Kant, Immanuel. 2012 [1786]. *Groundwork of the Metaphysics of Morals*, rev. ed. Edited by Mary Gregor and Jens Timmermann. Cambridge: Cambridge University Press.

Korsgaard, Christine. 1996. *Creating the Kingdom of Ends*. Cambridge: Cambridge University Press.

Lancaster, Michael. n.d. 'Bridging the Gender Gap: The Positive Effects of Title IX'. https://www.athleticscholarships.net/title-ix-college-athletics-3.htm.

Mill, John Stuart Mill. 1978 [1859]. *On Liberty*. Edited by Elizabeth Rapaport. Indianapolis, IN: Hackett.

Nietzsche, Friedrich. 1976 [1888]. 'The "Improvers" of Mankind'. In *Twilight of the Idols* in *The Portable Nietzsche*, edited and translated by Walter Kaufmann, 501–5. New York: Penguin.

———. 2017 [1886]. 'Beyond Good and Evil'. In *The Essential Nietzsche*, translated by Helen Zimmern, 9–198. New York: Chartwell Books.

NikkieTutorials. 2020. 'I'm Coming Out'. YouTube video. https://www.youtube.com/watch?v=QOOw2E_qAsE.

Rieff, Philip. 2006 [1966]. *The Triumph of the Therapeutic: Uses of Faith after Freud*, 40th anniversary ed. Chicago, IL: University of Chicago Press.

Roberts, John (Chief Justice). 2015. Dissenting opinion. *Obergefell v. Hodges*, 135 S. Ct. 1732, 576 U.S.

Rosen, Michael. 2012. *Dignity: Its History and Meaning*. Cambridge, MA: Harvard University Press.

Rothman, Lily. 2017. 'How Title IX First Changed the World of Women's Sports'. *Time Magazine*, 23 June. http://time.com/4822600/title-ix-womens-sports/.

Rousseau, Jean-Jacques. 1984 [1755]. 'Discourse on the Origins and the Foundations of Inequality among Men'. In *A Discourse on Inequality*, translated by Maurice Cranston. London: Penguin Books.

Sartre, Jean-Paul. 2007 [1945]. *Existentialism Is a Humanism*. New Haven, CT: Yale University Press.

Scalia, Antonin (Justice). 2015. Dissenting opinion. *Obergefell v. Hodges*, 135 S. Ct. 1732, 576 U.S.

Stanton, Glenn, and Bill Maier. 2004. *Marriage on Trial: The Case against Same-Sex Marriage and Parenting*. Downers Grove, IL: IVP.

Supreme Court of the United States. 1973. *Roe v. Wade*, 410 U.S. 113.

———. 1992. *Planned Parenthood of Southeastern Pennsylvania v. Casey*, 505 U.S. 833.

———. 2013. *United States v. Windsor, Executor of the Estate of Spyer, et al.*, 570 U.S.

———. 2015. *Obergefell v. Hodges*, 135 S. Ct. 1732, 576 U.S.

Taylor, Charles. 1991. *The Ethics of Authenticity*. Cambridge, MA: Harvard University Press.

Thomas, Clarence (Justice). 2015. Dissenting opinion. *Obergefell v. Hodges*, 135 S. Ct. 1732, 576 U.S.

United Nations. 1948. Universal Declaration of Human Rights. http://www.un.org/en/universal-declaration-human-rights/index.html.

US Department of Education and Department of Justice. 2016. 'Dear Colleague Letter on Transgender Students'. 13 May. https://www2.ed.gov/about/offices/list/ocr/letters/colleague-201605-title-ix-transgender.pdf.

———. 2017. 'Dear Colleague Letter'. 22 February. https://assets.documentcloud.org/documents/3473560/Departments-of-Education-and-Justice-roll-back.pdf.

Vitz, Paul C. 1995. *Psychology as Religion: The Cult of Self-Worship*, 2nd ed. Grand Rapids, MI: Eerdmans.

Chapter Six

AGAINST GROUP DIGNITY: CONTEMPORARY HUMAN RIGHTS INSTRUMENTS AND THEIR ATTRIBUTIONS OF DIGNITY TO GROUPS

Dwight Newman, QC

I. Introduction

The starting point of this chapter is that recent international human rights instruments have begun to use the terminology of dignity in a fundamentally different way than in the rights instruments that first used it to refer to the inherent worth of the human person.[1] Specifically, recent human rights instruments have begun to refer to dignity that is attributed to groups or collective entities rather than simply to individual persons. It is important to try to understand why this change has occurred and, more significantly, what its consequences are. Understanding this shift in the context of international human rights instruments is important, because it is these instruments that have direct legal implications; at the same time, they effectively enshrine a philosophical concept, so the proper engagement with the concept within these instruments is philosophical but with attention to practical implications. Before considering consequences, though, it is necessary to set out in more detail the trajectory of the conceptual change by way of further background on the place of dignity within contemporary international human rights instruments.

The historic adoption of the Universal Declaration of Human Rights (UDHR) in 1948 included a normative recognition of the dignity of the human person. The Preamble emphasized the importance of recognizing 'the inherent dignity and of the equal and inalienable rights of all members of the human family' and of maintaining a faith in 'the dignity and worth of the human person', and Article 1 stated that 'all human beings are born free and equal in dignity and rights' (UDHR 1948). The preambles of the 1966 International Covenant on Civil and Political Rights (ICCPR) and International Covenant on Economic, Social, and Cultural Rights (ICESCR) reiterated

---

[1] Much of the work on this chapter was completed while the author was a Visiting Fellow at the Oxford University Programme for the Foundations of Law and Constitutional Government during the Trinity 2019 term.

that the 'recognition of the inherent dignity and of the equal and inalienable rights of all members of the human family is the foundation of freedom, justice and peace in the world' and that 'these rights derive from the inherent dignity of the human person' (ICCPR 1966; ICESCR 1966).

These instruments' use of a terminology of dignity was deeply grounded but involved some important innovative application in a human rights context. Prior to these invocations within a human rights discourse, the term has had many references over time, typically describing an elevated status or nobility of some rather than to a shared humanity of all (Debes 2017b; Rosen 2012). However, significant developments had occurred in the use of dignity terminology in the decades prior to the UDHR such that its usage of the term now worked to express a longer-standing, underlying idea of the inherent worth of each and every human person (Debes 2017b, 1–3; Moyn 2013). Notably, the term had come to be used in somewhat related ways in the Weimar constitution and, yet more significantly, in the 1937 Irish Constitution (Debes 2017b, 1–3; Moyn 2013, 96–99). Perhaps most influentially, Pope Pius XII's wartime lectures increasingly continued to use the terminology of dignity in a similar way as in the Irish constitutional context, employing the term to refer to the inherent worth of each person. It was this 'papal usage that proved of most direct relevance to post-War affairs' (Moyn 2013, 107).

On dignity, as on so many other matters, religious values and natural law played a key part in the initial enunciation of the UDHR and post-war human rights framework (Moyn 2013) – even if the human rights framework was ultimately to spiral away from original conceptions and to seek to become a theological usurper. Subsequently to the UDHR and the International Covenants, there has been a veritable explosion of dignity terminology in various normative and legal contexts, and there has been significant recent scholarly attention directed towards trying to understand this phenomenon and some of the significant shifts in the meaning of dignity in contexts like American constitutional law (Rosen 2012; McCrudden 2013; Düwell et al. 2014; Kateb 2014; Debes 2017a; Sangiovanni 2017). That shift in meaning is bracing. A current phrase like 'death with dignity' reflects a significant shift in a term used initially to express the inherent worth of the human person – not to be destroyed – towards an autonomy-focused and atomistic vision of the human self.

The origins of the concept have implications for the way it has been attacked. Some direct attacks on the concept of dignity object to its roots in religious values (Rosen 2014; Macklin 2003; Pinker 2008). It is possible to counter some of these attacks on their own terms, and some responses have valuably focused on showing how these criticisms have taken out of context and misinterpreted some of the religious language concerning dignity (Hanvey 2014, 213–14).

At the same time, other reformulations and reapplications of the concept – which might attempt to render it palatable to certain critics – amount in their effects to indirect attacks on the original idea of the inherent worth of the person. For example, the recent work by Sangiovanni (2017), which reformulates dignity into simply a principle against social cruelty, unwittingly limits its range of applications by indirectly undermining the traditional focus of dignity and essentially expositing just some limited strands of a larger concept. While well-meaning in addressing social ills, various efforts to reformulate a concept that did not need reformulation have tended to weaken it.

In discussions of shifts in the conceptual language of dignity, one relatively unexplored dimension has been the shift towards using the terminology of dignity in respect of groups or collective entities, so as to employ its rhetorical force against wrongs faced by these groups. This trend has received only limited attention (Waldron 2008; Werner 2014) and warrants more attention. Is this shift continuous with or a spiralling away from the original idea expressed by 'dignity' in the UDHR?

One such usage appeared in the preambular recitals to the 1981 African Charter on Human and Peoples' Rights, sometimes known as the Banjul Charter (ACHPR 1981). There, the preamble referred to the parties being *conscious* of their duty to achieve the total liberation of Africa, the peoples of which are still struggling for their dignity and genuine independence' (emphasis original). The operative sections of the Banjul Charter used the terminology of dignity only in an individual context, with Article 5's affirmation that

> every individual shall have the right to the respect of the dignity inherent in a human being and to the recognition of his legal status. All forms of exploitation and degradation of man particularly slavery, slave trade, torture, cruel, inhuman or degrading punishment and treatment shall be prohibited.

But the preambular reference opened the more collective possibility of peoples per se claiming 'their dignity', with the grammatically natural reading of the provision assuming a claim to that collective dignity.

A set of seemingly operative usages of group dignity appeared in 2007 in two provisions of the United Nations Declaration on the Rights of Indigenous Peoples (UNDRIP 2007). Article 15 of that instrument provides that 'Indigenous peoples have the right to the dignity and diversity of their cultures, traditions, histories and aspirations which shall be appropriately reflected in education and public information'. Article 43 provides that 'the rights recognized herein constitute the minimum standards for the survival, dignity and well-being of the indigenous peoples of the world'.

These references within the final text of UNDRIP represent a more limited set of uses of group dignity than had appeared in the course of developing the instrument. The 1994 Draft Declaration on the Rights of Indigenous Peoples had contained opening words in its preamble 'affirming that indigenous peoples are equal in dignity and rights to all other peoples' and a draft Article 2 stating that 'Indigenous individuals and peoples are free and equal to all other individuals and peoples in dignity and rights, and have the right to be free from any kind of adverse discrimination' (DDRIP 1994). Both provisions continue in the final text of UNDRIP but without reference to the term 'dignity', which was ultimately removed from these sections of UNDRIP in the complex course of international negotiations on the text of the instrument (Engle 2011; Inman et al. 2018; Anaya and Rodriguez-Pinero 2018). Nonetheless, Articles 15 and 43 of the final text do continue to envision that peoples could have a right to 'the dignity […] of their cultures, traditions, histories, and aspirations' and that one could speak of the dignity of peoples (UNDRIP 2007).

In some respects, though, the 1994 draft UNDRIP terms might have been a zenith, at least temporarily, for the concept of group dignity. The 2018 United Nations Declaration on the Rights of Peasants and Other People Working in Rural Areas – adopted through a relatively divided vote at the General Assembly partly due to concerns about its promulgation of further collective rights – has several standard references to individual dignity and only one reference to dignity associated with a collective context: 'Peasants and other people living in rural areas have the right to land, individually and/or collectively […] to achieve an adequate standard of living, to have a place to live in security, peace and dignity and to develop their cultures' (UNDROP, Art. 17(1)). Any collective reading of the latter dignity reference would be filled with ambiguity. In the context of these major instruments that have held back from stronger affirmations of group dignity, on one reading, group dignity might not seem to be on the march through human rights instruments at present.

That said, there are longer-term forces that may bring the concept back to the front. Various human rights scholars have referred directly to 'collective dignity' (e.g. Howard 1992; Neuhäuser 2011), scholarly projects like the Dignity Rights Project at Widener University Delaware Law School have included a focus on the 'dignity of peoples' as a project theme and numerous human rights bodies have continued to refer to such terms as 'dignity of peoples'. The intellectual and activist infrastructure continues to build towards including forms of group dignity in human rights instruments. For that matter, religious discussions of dignity, such as continuing Catholic discourse on the concept, also increasingly mention terms like 'dignity of peoples'. To take just one example, consider that para 2304 of the Catholic Catechism refers to 'dignity of peoples' when it states that 'peace cannot be attained on earth without safeguarding the goods of persons, free communication among men, respect for the dignity of persons and peoples, and the assiduous practice of fraternity'. Yet, there is very little explicit attention to what concepts of group dignity might mean or whether such usages of the concept are coherent or appropriate.

One notable defender of the coherence of group dignity has been the very prominent political theorist Jeremy Waldron, and it is worth turning next to his account. Thinking critically about his account will ultimately make it possible to see some of the difficulties in the concept of group dignity – indeed, ultimately, it will be possible to see three main arguments for resisting the idea, in what may be called the argument against concept-confounding, the argument against pure constructivism and the argument against anti-egalitarian construction. While there are valid collective rights – something I have defended in my own work on collective rights (Newman 2011) – the concept of inherent dignity most properly describes the inherent worth of the individual human person and references to group dignity largely represent confusion (or worse).

II. A Defence of Group Dignity: Waldron and Conceptual Openness

It would, of course, be possible for references to the dignity of groups to be using the word 'dignity' in some distinctive sense, whether an aesthetic sense, a metaphorical sense or some other sense more distinct from the UDHR claims concerning the dignity of human individuals. And, indeed, there have been legal and philosophical works that have used dignity in such ways, such as in referring to the 'dignity of legislation', the 'dignity of democratic debate', the 'dignity of law' or even 'the dignity of commerce' (Waldron 1999; Newman 2019; Newman and Thorburn 2015; Oman 2017). However, it is at least counterintuitive to read human rights instruments to be making a merely metaphorical use of the term when they apply it in the context of dignity having been part of other human rights instruments. Their usage must be taken more seriously than that, and it must be defended on its own terms.

One scholar who has sought to defend the concept of group dignity is the leading political theorist Jeremy Waldron, who has both published an article directly on 'The Dignity of Groups' and referenced the concept indirectly in his broader writing on dignity (Waldron 2008, 2012, 2017). In some ways, his defence of group dignity retains a tentative character, notably insofar as its conclusion is that the idea cannot be ruled out, rather than being a definitive defence of the claim. That said, he does argue that groups could be subjects of dignity for the three basic reasons that they can be irreplaceable, have self-determination rights and have claims to being of equal rank. At the same time, though, he also admits that the sense in which groups are subjects of dignity may not be the same foundational sense as that in which individual human persons have dignity, noting in particular that one would probably focus on the contribution that groups make to individuals and thus that their claim to dignity may not be to the same type of dignity as that claimed by individuals. Waldron's argument is sophisticated and thus subtle, and it is important not to dismiss it lightly given the serious thought he has put into it.

It is worth distinguishing two different strands of the argument. First, to the extent that it pertains to the claims of groups to self-determination or to the claims of groups to equal rank, it has a salience with some other briefly articulated arguments that groups could have claims to dignity which are borne out in the fact that they can hold rights and that they can have agency. Obviously, not everyone accepts these latter claims, but important strands of recent philosophical literature do offer accounts of collective agency and collective rights (see Newman 2007, 2012). Does a claim to agency, self-determination or group recognition and group rights also necessarily imply that groups have a claim to dignity?

Such an equation is by no means certain. It is entirely possible to defend collective rights on the basis that they contribute in irreducible ways to the interests of individuals – as in my account of collective rights – without being committed to a claim that groups possess *dignity*. Of course, if one broadens the concept of dignity so far as just to refer to any kind of worth or the holding of any kind of moral status, rights-holding groups would hold such a form of 'dignity'. But if there are reasons to consider dignity as focused on inherent worth, then arguments based on agency or rights-holding are misplaced. What is crucial is how the concept of dignity itself is to be understood, and the next section will argue for a narrower scope for dignity that happens to have the consequence of excluding an argument for group dignity grounded in agency or rights-holding.

An argument for group dignity grounded in the irreplaceability of groups is initially more difficult to challenge. However, such an argument depends on a more detailed, thick account of the irreplaceability of groups. My arguments here will not convince anyone who considers groups more real and more valuable than their individual members – and there are some such accounts held by theorists within certain African and Indigenous traditions that connect to some of the rights instruments at issue, though these accounts are by no means the sole strand of African or Indigenous philosophy and others do prioritize individuals in some respects (cf. Hull 2019; Maddison 2009; Newman 2011). But, without setting out to convince those with radically different starting viewpoints, it is possible to note that one can go very far in affirming the value of groups without going so far as to call them strictly irreplaceable.

This is because even if the ultimate value of groups remains their contribution to the lives of individuals, it may still be immensely difficult to envision a replacement group that contributes in the same ways as a given group, even while not technically impossible. Many liberal accounts of multiculturalism, notably those of Will Kymlicka and others following Kymlicka, do not go far enough in defending the distinctiveness of particular groups, but it is possible to go farther even while accepting the possibility of some limits (Newman 2011, challenging Kymlicka 1989 and 1995). Indeed, the very possibility of arguing for gradual reform of cultural traditions that limit the life opportunities of some (classes of) individuals – a possibility most would accept – presumes that it is appropriate to modify the character of groups so as to better serve individuals, thereby making clear that it is not groups themselves that must be preserved in fully inherent ways. Groups are valuable not as irreplaceable museum pieces but as living structures for the lives of individuals. But recognizing as much also undermines the possibility of a group dignity argument grounded in the irreplaceability of groups.

III. Arguments against Group Dignity

Matters become clearer yet when we consider that there are specific reasons not to purport to modify the scope of the concept of dignity in ways that make room for group dignity. There is value in conceptual clarity in human rights discourse (cf. Donnelly 2003, 87). We can consider three main arguments for resisting incorporating group dignity into the concept of dignity, in what may be called the argument against *concept-confounding*, the argument against *pure constructivism* and the argument against *anti-egalitarian construction*.

First, if the term 'dignity' presently refers to the concept of inherent worth – or, at least, did in the UDHR, subject to later confusions – let us call that the rigorous concept of dignity. The application of the concept to groups requires adjustment of that concept to move away from the rigorous concept of dignity. If one used an entirely different term, one could describe groups in terms of something with some connection to the concept. But if one uses the same term, even with a modifier as in 'group dignity', the original term is now subject to being read down away from the rigorous meaning with which it started. The concept is being confounded in a way that undermines the practical protection offered by the concept of dignity. Taken to the full implications, the attempt to protect valuable groups ends up having tendencies to undermine the protection of the inherent worth of the human person.

Analogous claims have sometimes been put without full explanations of the mechanism, such as in suggestions that overly extensive expansions of human rights may undermine existing rights (e.g. Hannum 2019, 57–79). The first branch of the problem, that of conceptual confounding, arises because the concept of 'dignity' as applied to groups must now be one such that groups can have dignity, which means that dignity must permit the replaceability of its subject. There is a departure from the rigorous concept of dignity, because 'dignity' can no longer refer to a concept of entirely inherent worth. There is a corrosive effect on the concept that arises from its extension beyond its original uplifting of the inherent worth of the human person. This effect arises because, for there to be 'group dignity', the concept of 'dignity' needs to extend in some way that applies to entities that do not have the same kind of inherent worth as the irreplaceable human person. There is ultimately a confounding of the concept that takes away from its original meaning and purposes.

Someone might wonder, of course, whether the use of a qualifier, as in 'group dignity', reduces this concern about confounding. One difficulty with such a proposition is that the international human rights instruments using the concept of dignity in relation to groups do not reference a separate concept of 'group dignity' but simply attribute dignity to groups. So, in some ways, the counterargument proposes a solution that is not actually being utilized and cannot easily be utilized. While it is of course possible to imagine an interpretation of the provisions referencing dignity for groups that attributes to them a different *group dignity*, there will nonetheless be ongoing confusion and confounding of the concept of *dignity* in the public mind. Even while there could theoretically be developed a different concept of *group dignity*, then, that is not what has been done, and even if it were, there would be collateral damage to the original concept of dignity that would not arise with the use of a different conceptual terminology.

Second, at a more fundamental level, if the term 'dignity' is taken to be subject to construction and modification to adjust it to different circumstances, that position tends to contradict any assumption that it expresses an objective moral truth. But a significant part of the rigorous concept of dignity and its reference to inherent worth is the idea that there is a worth beyond human construction. If one undermines that position by well-intended attempts to use dignity in other contexts, one undermines some of the central point of focusing on dignity in the first instance.

This issue may arise particularly for those who suggest that it is possible to construct variants upon the concept in order to suit the needs of justice for groups. While well-meaning in certain respects, such views nonetheless entail a view as to the malleability of concepts. And that malleability sits poorly with the very nature of dignity as a recognition of inherent worth – the nature of inherence is precisely that it involves a conceptual non-malleability or one is no longer speaking of something being inherent and above simple human construction.

Some of these claims may seem far-reaching in suggesting an actual contradiction as between constructability of the concept of dignity and an assumption that the concept expresses objective moral truths. But that they are far-reaching does not make them untrue. There is a genuine tension, and even contradiction, as between a claim that the concept of dignity can be altered to meet pragmatic needs of justice and a claim that the concept of dignity represents certain objective truths outside human alteration. The latter view may be unfashionable in certain circles, but, perhaps ironically, if the concept of dignity in the international human rights instruments is to have meaning and impact, then it must be above alteration for the sake of chosen new impacts.

Third, and in a certain more remote sense, if the term 'dignity' is constructed so as to include the dignity of groups, it has certain anti-egalitarian implications for individuals. The rigorous concept of dignity, in speaking of an inherent worth of irreplaceable individuated human persons, does not admit of trade-offs but affirms a basic equality, along the lines of that discussed in some of Waldron's writing (e.g. Waldron 2017; cf. also Waldron 2002). If that sort of basic equality also extends to groups of which some individuals are and are not parts, there is an overlay of a different set of egalitarian claims on top of the basic equality with which we started. And that will ultimately threaten the basic equality that can properly be associated with the rigorous concept of dignity.

The inherent worth of the human person can serve as a strong grounding for individual equality (Waldron 2017). While attention to the ways in which group membership impacts on different individuals differently can be a very appropriate part of engaging with individual equality, simplistic statements of group-based equality can actually undermine individual equality, for at least two reasons. First, while some groups promote individual equality, others may even directly undermine it. This would be true in full of certain hierarchical, gang-like structures that have no legitimate claims to group rights, or groups with caste-like systems that raise very troubling questions. Other sorts of groups might have equality-undermining aspects that raise complex questions but sit alongside real value in the group. In my past work on group rights, I have tried to devise a set of mediating principles to address these complex issues (Newman 2011). But the point for present purposes is that there should not be simple claims about the equality of groups if the value at issue is individual equality.

Second, there are tensions between treating groups equally in certain ways and treating equally the individuals within them. This is partly because there are appropriately more complex ways of engaging with the rights claims of groups that take account of their impact on the individual members within and on others outside the groups. I have attempted to engage with such complex systems at length in past work (Newman 2011). It matters whether it is possible to reform aspects of a group's practices so that it better serves its members without taking away from integral features of a group that does serve its members, and it matters whether a group engages with outsiders in a manner that would work reciprocally (Newman 2011, 2017). But the tension also arises from the internal diversity within groups. Simply engaging in equal treatment of groups may actually involve very unequal treatment of the individuals within those groups. For example, if one group is treated as being highly advantaged but has some very disadvantaged members within it, engaging in some sort of equality-oriented decision-making between the group and other groups will play out negatively for those individuals within the group that have a different status from the group as a whole. In certain circumstances, blanket assertions of group dignity may actually inappropriately endanger aspects of individual equality.

The extension of dignity to groups is a well-intended effort to express the deep value of groups. But it is damaging to the core concept of dignity in a way that recognition of other claims by groups are not. That there could be collective agency does not mean that there cannot be individual agency, for nothing in individual agency is threatened by the fact that there are other forms of agency. That there could be collective rights does not mean that there cannot be individual rights, because rights conflicts already arise between individuals, and so the mere possibility of rights conflicts or limits on rights does not threaten the core concept (Newman 2011). The core, rigorous concept of dignity is, by contrast, threatened by extensions of it that lessen its meaning, undermine its claims to objective moral truth and complicate the basic equality associated with it. There are thus powerful arguments against claims to group dignity precisely on account of the special nature and significance of the concept of dignity.

IV. Implications

There is real value in conceptual clarity in understanding international human rights (cf. Donnelly 2003, 87). That is not always a fashionable position, but it is an essential one for those who care about human rights and their fulfilment. The concept of human dignity, referring to the inherent worth of the human person, is a deeply important grounding for human rights to make sense at all (cf. Waldron 2002). Those who seek to alter the concept may be well-meaning in seeking to make it offer direct assistance against particular further injustices, especially when many groups have faced long-standing suffering, but they do unwitting harm to the concept that may undermine existing protections of human rights (cf. generally Hannum 2019).

An expanding body of literature has identified that a key difficulty with overly expansive readings of rights is that one ends up with a view of rights as subject to limitations in aid of all sorts of policy objectives, whether legislatively chosen or judicially chosen (cf., e.g., Hannum 2019; Webber 2010; Yowell 2018). Analogously, an overly expansive view of dignity undermines the significance of dignity in each instance. This is because dignity ceases to relate to inherent worth and ceases to be an absolute, instead becoming one defeasible consideration weighed alongside various other considerations. In 2006, the German Constitutional Court (*Bundesverfassungsgericht* 2006) issued a rare sort of judgement in deciding a case based directly on the right to dignity, and it struck down a law empowering the defence minister to make utilitarian choices about when to shoot down an aircraft that might have terrorists aboard amongst the passengers. While the case is not a simple one, one can see such a conclusion flowing from a concept of dignity stressing the inherent value of each human life. And one can also see that a view of dignity moved away from that focus, and treating dignity as just one (important) consideration, would lend itself more readily to permitting utilitarian calculations. Similar sorts of conclusions could follow for many other issues where an altered concept of dignity undermines the protection flowing from dignity, both in respect of dignity rights themselves and in respect of the full panoply of human rights grounded in dignity. There are very significant implications from a blurring of the concept.

Returning directly to group dignity, the idea of group dignity has appeared in some modern international human rights instruments in expanding ways. To the extent there may have been some slowing of its inclusion in actual human rights instruments, the idea has now taken hold in certain scholarly and activist circles. The most substantial scholarly defence of the idea has appeared in work by Jeremy Waldron, who has offered a sophisticated analysis of how it is that the idea might be justified and make sense. However, there are significant negative implications from altering the concept of dignity, with concept-confounding resulting in some undermining of the initial concept, with the constructivist approach involved tending to erode the objective moral claim inherent in the initial concept and the effects for individual equality also being potentially negative.

It would be meaningfully preferable not to include concepts of group dignity in international human rights instruments. The concept of dignity should remain clear and carefully delimited to the concept as adopted in the UDHR. That concept serves as an important grounding for human rights generally, and well-intended attempts to extend it actually do harm to it and to human rights.

That said, this chapter is by no means an argument against recognizing the important collective dimensions of rights and appropriate claims to group rights, which I have elsewhere defended (see especially Newman 2011). However, defences of collective rights or group rights need to be mounted on their own terms and not attached to a mistakenly altered account of human dignity. While groups are important and certain group rights are appropriately recognized, groups ultimately serve individual human rights; therefore, to speak of 'group dignity' is still to fall into an unfortunate conceptual confusion that has profoundly negative consequences for groups, for individuals and indeed for the human rights project. We should ultimately conclude against group dignity.

References

ACHPR (African Charter on Human and Peoples' Rights). 1981. Adopted 27 June 1981, Organisation for African Unity Doc. CAB/LEG/67/3 rev. 5, 21 I.L.M. 58 (1982); entered into force 21 October 1986.

Anaya, S. James, and Luis Rodriguez-Pinero. 2018. 'The Making of the United Nations Declaration on the Rights of Indigenous Peoples'. In *The UN Declaration on the Rights of Indigenous Peoples: A Commentary*, edited by Jessie Hohmann and Marc Weller, 38–62. Oxford: Oxford University Press.

Bundesverfassungsgericht [BVerfG] 15 February 2006, 1 BvR 357/05. http://www.bverfg.de/entscheidungen/rs20060215_1bvr035705.html.

Debes, Remy, ed. 2017a. *Dignity: A History*. Oxford: Oxford University Press.

———. 2017b. 'Introduction'. In *Dignity: A History*, edited by Remy Debes, 1–17. Oxford: Oxford University Press.

DDRIP (Draft Declaration on the Rights of Indigenous Peoples). 1994. U.N. Doc. E/CN.4/Sub.2/1994/2/Add.1.

Donnelly, Jack. 2003. *Universal Human Rights in Theory and Practice*. Ithaca, NY: Cornell University Press.

Düwell, Marcus, Jens Braarvig, Roger Brownsword and Dietmar Mieth, eds. 2014. *Cambridge Handbook of Human Dignity*. Cambridge: Cambridge University Press.

Engle, Karen. 2011. 'On Fragile Architecture: The UN Declaration on the Rights of Indigenous Peoples in the Context of Human Rights'. *European Journal of International Law* 22, no. 141: 141–63.

Hannum, Hurst. 2019. *Rescuing Human Rights: A Radically Moderate Approach*. Cambridge: Cambridge University Press.

Hanvey, James. 2014. 'Dignity, Persons, and *Imago Trinitatis*'. In *Understanding Human Dignity*, edited by Christopher McCrudden, 209–29. Oxford: Oxford University Press.

Howard, Rhonda E. 1992. 'Dignity, Community and Human Rights'. In *Human Rights in Cross-Cultural Perspectives: A Quest for Consensus*, edited by Abdullah A. An-Na'im, 81–102. Philadelphia: University of Pennsylvania Press.

Hull, George, ed. 2019. *Debating African Philosophy: Perspectives on Identity, Decolonial Ethics and Comparative Philosophy*. New York: Routledge.

ICCPR (International Covenant on Civil and Political Rights). 1966. United Nations General Assembly Resolution 2200A (XXI), 21 U.N. GAOR Supp. (No. 16) at 52, U.N. Doc. A/6316 (1966), 999 U.N.T.S. 171; entered into force 23 March 1976.

ICESCR (International Covenant on Economic, Social, and Cultural Rights). 1966. United Nations General Assembly Resolution 2200A (XXI), 21 U.N. GAOR Supp. (No. 16) at 49, U.N. Doc. A/6316 (1966), 993 U.N.T.S. 3; entered into force 3 January 1976.

Inman, Derek, Dorothée Cambou and Stefaan Smis. 2018. 'Evolving Legal Protections for Indigenous Peoples in Africa: Some Post-UNDRIP Reflections'. *African Journal of International and Comparative Law* 26, no. 3: 339–65.

Kateb, George. 2014. *Human Dignity*. Cambridge, MA: Harvard University Press.

Kymlicka, Will. 1989. *Liberalism, Community, and Culture*. Oxford: Clarendon.

———. 1995. *Multicultural Citizenship*. Oxford: Oxford University Press.

Macklin, Ruth. 2003. 'Dignity Is a Useless Concept'. *British Medical Journal* 327 (December): 1419–20.

Maddison, Sarah. 2009. *Black Politics: Inside the Complexity of Aboriginal Political Culture*. Sydney: Allen and Unwin.

McCrudden, Christopher, ed. 2013. *Understanding Human Dignity*. Oxford: Oxford University Press.

Moyn, Samuel. 2013. 'The Secret History of Constitutional Dignity'. In *Understanding Human Dignity*, edited by Christopher McCrudden, 95–111. Oxford: Oxford University Press.

Neuhäuser, Christian. 2011. 'Humiliation: The Collective Dimension'. In *Humiliation, Degradation, Dehumanization: Human Dignity Violated*, edited by P. Kaufmann, H. Kuch, C. Neuhäuser and E. Webster, 21–36. New York: Springer.

Newman, Dwight. 2007. 'Collective Rights'. *Philosophical Books* 48: 221–32.

———. 2011. *Community and Collective Rights: A Theoretical Framework for Rights Held by Groups*. Oxford: Hart.

———. 2012. 'Value Collectivism, Collective Rights, and Self-Threatening Theory'. *Oxford Journal of Legal Studies* 33, no. 1: 197–210.

———. 2017. 'The Challenging Parallelisms of Rights Claimed Based on Religious Identity and Sexual Identity'. In *Religious Liberty and the Law: Theistic and Non-Theistic Perspectives*, edited by Angus J. L. Menuge, 119–31. Milton Park: Routledge.

———. 2019. 'Allen Blakeney and the Dignity of Democratic Debate on Rights'. In *Back to Blakeney: The Revitalization of the Democratic State*, edited by David McGrane, John Whyte, Roy Romanow and Russell Isinger, 71–82. Regina: University of Regina Press.

Newman, Dwight, and Malcolm Thorburn, eds. 2015. *The Dignity of Law: The Legacy of Justice Louis LeBel*. Toronto: LexisNexis.

Oman, Nathan B. 2017. *The Dignity of Commerce: Markets and the Moral Foundations of Contract Law*. Chicago: University of Chicago Press.

Pinker, Steven. 2008. 'The Stupidity of Dignity'. *New Republic*, 27 May.

Rosen, Michael. 2012. *Dignity: Its History and Meaning*. Cambridge, MA: Harvard University Press.

———. 2014. 'Dignity: The Case Against'. In *Understanding Human Dignity*, edited by Christopher McCrudden, 143–54. Oxford: Oxford University Press.

Sangiovanni, Andrea. 2017. *Humanity without Dignity: Moral Equality, Respect, and Human Rights*. Cambridge, MA: Harvard University Press.

UDHR (Universal Declaration of Human Rights). 1948. United Nations General Assembly Resolution 217A (III), U.N. Doc. A/810 (1948) at 71.

UNDRIP (United Nations Declaration on the Rights of Indigenous Peoples). 2007. United Nations General Assembly, United Nations Declaration on the Rights of Indigenous Peoples, UNGA/RES/61/295, 13 September.

UNDROP (United Nations Declaration on the Rights of Peasants and Other People Working in Rural Areas). 2018. United Nations General Assembly, HRC/RES/39/12, 8 October.

Waldron, Jeremy. 1999. *The Dignity of Legislation*. Cambridge: Cambridge University Press.

———. 2002. *God, Locke, and Equality: Christian Foundation's in Locke's Political Thought*. Cambridge: Cambridge University Press.

———. 2008. 'The Dignity of Groups'. *Acta Juridica* 2008, no. 1: 66–90.

———. 2012. *Dignity, Rank, and Rights*. Oxford: Oxford University Press.

———. 2017. *One Another's Equals: The Basis of Human Equality*. Oxford: Oxford University Press.

Webber, Grégoire. 2010. *The Negotiable Constitution: On the Limitation of Rights*. Cambridge: Cambridge University Press.

Werner, Micha. 2014. 'Individual and Collective Dignity'. In *Cambridge Handbook of Human Dignity*, edited by Marcus Düwell, Jens Braarvig, Roger Brownsword and Dietmar Mieth, 343–54. Cambridge: Cambridge University Press.

Yowell, Paul. 2018. *Constitutional Rights and Constitutional Design*. Oxford: Hart.

Part II

RELIGIOUS LIBERTY AND HUMAN DIGNITY

Chapter Seven

RELIGIOUS LIBERTY AND THE HUMAN GOOD[1]

Robert P. George

The starting points of all ethical reflection are those fundamental and irreducible aspects of the well-being and fulfillment of human persons that some philosophers refer to as 'basic human goods' (see Finnis 2011, chs. 3–4). These goods – as more than merely instrumental ends or purposes – are the subjects of the very first principles of practical reason that control all rational thinking with a view to acting, whether the acts performed are, in the end, properly judged to be morally good or bad (Grisez 1965). The first principles of practical reason direct our choosing towards what is rationally desirable because humanly fulfilling (and therefore intelligibly available to choice), and away from their privations (Grisez 1965). It is, in the end, the integral directiveness of these principles that provides the criterion (or, when specified, the set of criteria – viz. the moral norms) by which it is possible rationally to distinguish right from wrong – what is morally good from what is morally bad – including what is just and unjust (Finnis 2011, 450–452). Morally good choices are choices that are in line with the various fundamental aspects of human well-being and fulfillment integrally conceived; morally bad choices are choices that are not.

To say the very abstract things I've just said is simply to spell out philosophically the point made by Martin Luther King in his *Letter from Birmingham Jail* about just and unjust laws – laws that honor people's rights and those that violate them. You will, perhaps, recall that the great civil rights champion anticipated a challenge to the moral goodness of the acts of civil disobedience that landed him behind bars in Birmingham. He anticipated his critics asking: How can you, Dr. King, engage in willful law breaking, when you yourself had stressed the importance of obedience to law in demanding that officials of the southern states conform to the Supreme Court's de-segregation ruling in the case of *Brown v. Board of Education*? Let's listen to King's response to the challenge:

> The answer [he says] lies in the fact that there are two types of laws: just and unjust. I would be the first to advocate obeying just laws. One has not only a legal but a moral responsibility

---

[1] An essay with this title first appeared in the *International Journal of Religious Freedom* 5:1 (2012), 35–44.

to obey just laws. Conversely, one has a moral responsibility to disobey unjust laws. I would agree with St. Augustine that 'an unjust law is no law at all'.

Now, what is the difference between the two? How does one determine whether a law is just or unjust?

A just law is a man-made code that squares with the moral law or the law of God. An unjust law is a code that is out of harmony with the moral law. To put it in the terms of St. Thomas Aquinas: An unjust law is a human law that is not rooted in eternal law and natural law.

Any law that uplifts human personality is just. Any law that degrades human personality is unjust. All segregation statutes are unjust because segregation distorts the soul and damages the personality. It gives the segregator a false sense of superiority and the segregated a false sense of inferiority. (King 1994 [1963])

So: just laws elevate and ennoble the human personality, or what King in other contexts referred to as the human spirit; unjust laws debase and degrade it. Now his point about the morality or immorality of laws is a good reminder that what is true of what is sometimes called 'personal morality' is also true of 'political morality'. The choices and actions of political institutions at every level, like the choices and actions of individuals, can be right or wrong, morally good or morally bad. They can be in line with human well-being and fulfillment in all of its manifold dimensions; or they can fail, in any of a range of ways, to respect the integral flourishing of human persons. In many cases of the failure of laws, policies, and institutions to fulfill the requirements of morality, we speak intelligibly and rightly of a violation of human rights. This is particularly true where the failure is properly characterized as an injustice – failing to honor people's equal worth and dignity, failing to give them, or even actively denying them, what they are due.

But, contrary to the teaching of the late John Rawls and the extraordinarily influential stream of contemporary liberal thought of which he was the leading exponent (Rawls 1988), I wish to suggest that good is prior to right and, indeed, to rights. Here is what I mean: To be sure, human rights, including the right to religious liberty, are among the moral principles that demand respect from all of us, including governments and international institutions (which are morally bound not only to respect human rights but also to protect them). To respect people, to respect their dignity, is to, among other things, honor their rights, including, to be sure, the right that we are gathered today to lift up to our fellow citizens and defend, the right to religious freedom. Like all moral principles, however, human rights (including the right to religious liberty) are shaped, and given content, by the human goods they protect. Rights, like other moral principles, are intelligible as rational, action-guiding principles because they are entailments and, at some level, specifications of the integral directiveness or prescriptivity of principles of practical reason that directs our choosing towards what is humanly fulfilling and enriching (or, as Dr. King would say, uplifting) and away from what is contrary to our well-being as the kind of creatures we are – namely, human persons.

And so, for example, it matters to the identification and defense of the right to life – a right violated not only when the death of another is sought as one's end or as a means to one's end, but also in cases in which someone's death is foreseen and accepted *unfairly* as a side effect of one's action in pursuit of an end – that human life is no mere instrumental good, but is an intrinsic aspect of the good of human persons – an integral dimension of our overall flourishing.[2] And it matters to the identification and defense of the right to religious liberty that religion is yet another irreducible aspect of human well-being and fulfillment – a basic human good.[3]

But what is religion?

In its fullest and most robust sense, religion is the human person's being in right relation to the divine – the more than merely human source or sources, if there be such, of meaning and value. Of course, even the greatest among us in the things of the spirit fall short of perfection in various ways; but in the ideal of perfect religion, the person would understand as comprehensively and deeply as possible the body of truths about spiritual things, and would fully order his or her life, and share in the life of a community of faith that is ordered, in line with those truths. In the perfect realization of the good of religion, one would achieve the relationship that the divine – say God himself, assuming for a moment the truth of monotheism – wishes us to have with Him.

Of course, different traditions of faith have different views of what constitutes religion in its fullest and most robust sense. There are different doctrines, different scriptures, different structures of authority, different ideas of what is true about spiritual things and what it means to be in proper relationship to the more than merely human sources of meaning and value that different traditions understand as divinity.[4]

For my part, I believe that reason has a very large role to play for each of us in deciding where spiritual truth most robustly is to be found. And by reason here, I mean not only our capacity for practical reasoning and moral judgment, but also our capacities for understanding and evaluating claims of all sorts: logical, historical, scientific, and so forth. But one need not agree with me about this in order to affirm with me that there is a distinct basic human good of religion – a good that is uniquely architectonic in shaping one's pursuit of and participation in all the basic human goods – and that one begins to realize and participate in this good from the moment one begins the quest to understand the more-than-merely-human sources of meaning and value and to live authentically by ordering one's life in line with one's best judgments of the truth in religious matters.

If I am right, then the existential raising of religious questions, the honest identification of answers, and the fulfilling of what one sincerely believes to be one's duties in the light of those answers are all parts of the human good of religion – a good whose pursuit is an indispensable feature of the comprehensive flourishing of a human being. If I am right, then man is, as Seamus Hasson puts it, intrinsically and by nature a religious being – *homo religiosus*, to borrow a concept, or at least a couple of words of Latin, from

---

[2]   There are, of course, many people today who contest my view that the life of a human being is intrinsically and not merely instrumentally valuable. So it needs to be defended. For a defense see Patrick Lee and Robert P. George (2008, 160–162). See also Germain Grisez, John Finnis, and Joseph M. Boyle, Jr. (1987, 304–309).

[3]   On religion as a basic human good, see Finnis (2011, 89–90).

[4]   For a deeply informed and sensitive treatment of similarities and differences in the world historical religions, see Augustine DiNoia (1992).

Eliade – and the flourishing of man's spiritual life is integral to his all-round well-being and fulfillment.

But if that is true, then respect for a person's well-being, or more simply respect for the person, demands respect for his or her flourishing as a seeker of religious truth and as a man or woman who lives in line with his best judgments of what is true in spiritual matters. And that, in turn, requires respect for his or her liberty in the religious quest – the quest to understand religious truth and order one's life in line with it. Because faith of any type, including religious faith, cannot be authentic – it cannot be *faith* – unless it is free, respect for the person – that is to say, respect for his or her dignity as a free and rational creature – requires respect for his or her religious liberty. That is why it makes sense, from the point of view of reason, and not merely from the point of view of the revealed teaching of a particular faith – though many faiths proclaim the right to religious freedom on theological and not merely philosophical grounds, to understand religious freedom as a fundamental human right.

Interestingly and tragically, in times past, and even in some places today, regard for persons' spiritual well-being has been the premise, and motivating factor, for *denying* religious liberty or conceiving of it in a cramped and restricted way. Before the Catholic Church embraced the robust conception of religious freedom that honors the civil right to give public witness and expression to sincere religious views (even when erroneous), in the document *Dignitatis Humanae* of the Second Vatican Council, some Catholics rejected the idea of a right to religious freedom on the theory that 'only the truth has rights'. The idea was that the state, under favoring conditions, should not only publicly identify itself with Catholicism as the true faith, but forbid religious advocacy or proselytizing that could lead people into religious error and apostasy.

The mistake here was not in the premise: religion is a great human good and the truer the religion the better for the fulfillment of the believer. That is true. The mistake, rather, was in the supposition made by some that the good of religion was not being advanced or participated in outside the context of the one true faith, and that it could be reliably protected and advanced by placing civil restrictions enforceable by agencies of the state on the advocacy of religious ideas. In rejecting this supposition, the Fathers of the Second Vatican Council did not embrace the idea that error has rights; they noticed, rather, that *people* have rights, and they have rights even when they are in error (see Hasson 2005). And among those rights, integral to authentic religion as a fundamental and irreducible aspect of the human good, is the right to express and even advocate in line with one's sense of one's conscientious obligations what one believes to be true about spiritual matters, even if one's beliefs are, in one way or another, less than fully sound, and, indeed, even if they are false (*Dignitatis Humanae* 1965, 2–3).

When I have assigned the document *Dignitatis Humanae* (1965) in courses addressing questions of religious liberty, I have always stressed to my students the importance of reading another document of the Second Vatican Council, *Nostra Aetate* (1965), together with it. Whether one is Catholic or not, I don't think it is possible to achieve a rich understanding of the Declaration on Religious Liberty, and the developed teaching of the Catholic Church on religious freedom, without considering what the Council Fathers proclaim in the Declaration on Non-Christian Religions. In *Nostra Aetate*, the

Fathers pay tribute to all that is true and holy, implying and then explicitly saying that there is much that is good and worthy in non-Christian faiths, including Hinduism and Buddhism, and especially Judaism and Islam. In so doing, they give recognition to the ways in which religion, even where it does not include the defining content of what the Fathers, as Catholics, believe to be religion in its fullest and most robust sense – namely, the Incarnation of Jesus Christ – enriches, ennobles, and fulfills the human person in the spiritual dimension of his being. This is to be honored and respected, in the view of the Council Fathers, because the dignity of the human being requires it. Naturally, the non-recognition of Christ as the Son of God must count for the Fathers as a falling short in the non-Christian faiths, even the Jewish faith in which Christianity is itself rooted and which stands according to Catholic teaching in an unbroken and unbreakable covenant with God – just as the proclamation of Christ as the Son of God must count as an error in Christianity from a Jewish or Muslim point of view. But, the Fathers teach, this does not mean that Judaism and Islam are simply false and without merit (just as neither Judaism nor Islam teaches that Christianity is simply false and without merit); on the contrary, these traditions enrich the lives of their faithful in their spiritual dimensions, thus contributing vitally to their fulfillment.

Now, the Catholic Church does not have a monopoly on the natural-law reasoning by which I am today explicating and defending the human right to religious liberty.[5] But the Church does have a deep commitment to such reasoning and a long experience with it. And in *Dignitatis Humanae*, the Fathers of the Second Vatican Council present a natural law argument for religious freedom – indeed they begin by presenting a natural-law argument before supplementing it with arguments appealing to the authority of God's revelation in sacred scripture. So let me ask you to linger with me a bit longer over the key Catholic texts so that I can illustrate by the teachings of an actual faith how religious leaders and believers, and not just statesmen concerned to craft national or international policy in circumstances of religious pluralism, can incorporate into their understanding of the basic human right to religious liberty principles and arguments available to all men and women of sincerity and goodwill by virtue of what Professor Rawls once referred to as 'our common human reason' (Rawls 1993, 137).

Let me quote at some length from *Nostra Aetate* to give you an appreciation of the rational basis of the Catholic Church's affirmation of the good of religion as manifested in various different faiths. I do this in order to show how one faith, in this case Catholicism, can root its defense of a robust conception of freedom of religion not in a mere *modus vivendi*, or mutual non-aggression pact, with other faiths, or in what the late Judith Shklar labeled a 'liberalism of fear', or, much less, in religious relativism or indifferentism, but rather in a rational affirmation of the value of religion as embodied and made available to people in and through many traditions of faith. So here is what *Nostra Aetate* says:

---

[5] On natural law and religious freedom in the Jewish tradition, see David Novak (2009). (Rabbi Novak kindly dedicated this fine work to me. Inasmuch as this is the first time I've had occasion to cite it in a public forum, I am happy to have the opportunity to express gratitude for what I consider to be a high honor.)

Throughout history even to the present day, there is found among different peoples a certain awareness of a hidden power, which lies behind the course of nature and the events of human life. At times there is present even a recognition of a supreme being or still more of a Father. This awareness and recognition results in a way of life that is imbued with a deep religious sense. The religions which are found in more advanced civilizations endeavor by way of well-defined concepts and exact language to answer these questions. Thus in Hinduism men explore the divine mystery and express it both in the limitless riches of myth and the accurately defined insights of philosophy. They seek release from the trials of the present life by ascetical practices, profound meditation and recourse to God in confidence and love. Buddhism in its various forms testifies to the essential inadequacy of this changing world. It proposes a way of life by which men can with confidence and trust, attain a state of perfect liberation and reach supreme illumination either through their own efforts or by the aid of divine help. So, too, other religions which are found throughout the world attempt in their own ways to calm the hearts of men by outlining a program of life covering doctrine, moral precepts and sacred rites.

The Catholic Church rejects nothing of what is true and holy in these religions. She has a high regard for the manner of life and conduct, the precepts and doctrines which, although differing in many ways from her own teaching, nevertheless often reflect truths which enlighten all men. Yet she proclaims and is in duty bound to proclaim without fail, Christ who is the way, the truth and the life (Jn. 1:6). In him, in whom God reconciled all things to himself (2 Cor. 5:1819), men find the fullness of their religious life.

The Church therefore, urges her sons to enter with prudence and charity into discussion and collaboration with members of other religious. Let Christians, while witnessing to their own faith and way of life, acknowledge, preserve and encourage the spiritual and moral truths found among non-Christians.

The Church has also a high regard for the Muslims. They worship God, who is one, living and subsistent, merciful and almighty, the Creator of heaven and earth, who has also spoken to men. They strive to submit themselves without reserve to the decrees of God, just as Abraham submitted himself to God's plan, to whose faith Muslims link their own. Although not acknowledging Jesus as God, they revere him as a prophet; his virgin Mother they also honor, and even at times devoutly invoke. Further, they await the Day of Judgment and the reward of God following the resurrection of the dead. For this reason they highly esteem an upright life and worship God, especially by way of prayer, almsgiving, and fasting.

Over the centuries many quarrels and dissensions have arisen between Christians and Muslims. The sacred Council now pleads with all to forget the past, and urges that a sincere effort be made to achieve mutual understanding; for the benefit of all men, let them together preserve and promote peace, liberty, social justice and moral values.

Sounding the depths of the mystery which is the Church, this sacred Council remembers the spiritual ties which link the people of the New Covenant to the stock of Abraham.

The Church of Christ acknowledges that in God's plan of salvation the beginning of her faith and election is to be found in the patriarchs and in Moses and the prophets. She professes that all Christ's faithful, who as men of faith are sons of Abraham (cf. Gal. 3:7), are included in the same patriarch's call and that the salvation of the Church is mystically prefigured in the exodus of God's chosen people from the land of bondage. On this account the Church cannot forget that she received the revelation of the Old Testament by way of that people with whom God in his inexpressible mercy established the ancient covenant. Nor can she forget that she draws nourishment from that good olive tree onto which the wild olive branches of the Gentiles have been grafted (cf. Rom. 11:1724). The Church believes that Christ who is our peace has through his cross reconciled Jews and Gentiles and made them one in himself (cf. Eph. 2:14–16). (*Nostra Aetate* 1965, 2–4)

Of course, from the point of view of any believer, the further away one gets from the truth of faith in all its dimensions – what the Council Fathers refer to in the passages I just quoted as 'the fullness of religious life' – the less fulfillment is available. But that does not mean that even a primitive and superstition-laden faith, much less the faiths of those advanced civilizations to which the Fathers refer, is utterly devoid of value, or that there is no right to religious liberty for people who practice such a faith. Nor does it mean that atheists have no right to religious freedom. The fundaments of respect for the good of religion require that civil authority respect (and, in appropriate ways, even nurture) conditions or circumstances in which people can engage in the sincere religious quest and live lives of authenticity reflecting their best judgments as to the truth of spiritual matters. To compel an atheist to perform acts that are premised on theistic beliefs that he cannot, in good conscience, share, is to deny him the fundamental bit of the good of religion that is his, namely, living with honesty and integrity in line with his best judgments about ultimate reality. Coercing him to perform religious acts does him no good, since faith really must be free, and dishonors his dignity as a free and rational person. The violation of liberty is worse than futile.

Of course, there are limits to the freedom that must be respected for the sake of the good of religion and the dignity of the human person as a being whose integral fulfillment includes the spiritual quest and the ordering of one's life in line with one's best judgment as to what spiritual truth requires. Gross evil – even grave injustice – can be committed by sincere people for the sake of religion. Unspeakable wrongs can be done by people seeking sincerely to get right with God or the gods or their conception of ultimate reality, whatever it is. The presumption in favor of respecting liberty must, for the sake of the human good and the dignity of human persons as free and rational creatures – creatures who, according to Judaism and Christianity, are made in the very image and likeness of God – be powerful and broad. But it is not unlimited. Even the great end of getting right with God cannot justify a morally bad means, even for the sincere believer. I don't doubt the sincerity of the Aztecs in practicing human sacrifice, or the sincerity of those in the history of various traditions of faith who used coercion and even torture in the cause of what they believed was religiously required. But these things are deeply wrong, and need not (and should not) be tolerated in the name of religious freedom. To suppose otherwise is to back oneself into the awkward position of supposing that violations of religious freedom (and other injustices of equal gravity) must be respected for the sake of religious freedom.

Still, to overcome the powerful and broad presumption in favor of religious liberty, to be justified in requiring the believer to do something contrary to his faith or forbidding the believer to do something his faith requires, political authority must meet a heavy burden. The legal test in the United States under the Religious Freedom Restoration Act is one way of capturing the presumption and burden: to justify a law that bears negatively on religious freedom, even a neutral law of general applicability must be supported by a compelling state interest and represent the least restrictive or intrusive means of protecting or serving that interest. We can debate, as a matter of American constitutional law or as a matter of policy, whether it is, or should be, up to courts or legislators to decide when exemptions to general, neutral laws should be granted for the sake of religious freedom, or to determine when the presumption in favor of religious freedom has been overcome; but the substantive matter of what religious freedom demands from those who exercise the levers of state power should be something on which reasonable people of goodwill across the religious and political spectrums should agree on – precisely because it is a matter capable of being settled by our common human reason.

Bibliography

Dignitatis Humanae. 1965. Accessed January 3, 2020. http://www.vatican.va/archive/hist_councils/ii_vatican_council/documents/vat-ii_decl_19651207_dignitatis-humanae_en.html.

DiNoia, Augustine. 1992. *The Diversity of Religions: A Christian Perspective*. Washington DC: Catholic University Press.

Finnis, John. 2011. *Natural Law and Natural Rights*. 2nd edition. Oxford: Oxford University Press.

Grisez, Germain. 1965. 'The First Principle of Practical Reason: A Commentary on the *Summa Theologiae*, 1–2, Question 94, Article 2'. *Natural Law Forum* 10: 168–196.

Grisez, Germain, John Finnis, and Joseph M. Boyle, Jr. 1987. *Nuclear Deterrence, Morality and Realism*. Oxford: Clarendon Press.

Hasson, Kevin J. 2005. *The Right to Be Wrong: Ending the Culture War over Religion in America*. New York: Encounter Books.

King, Martin Luther. 1994 [1963]. *Letter from Birmingham Jail*. New York: Harper Collins.

Lee, Patrick and Robert P. George. 2008. *Body-Self Dualism in Contemporary Ethics and Politics*. New York: Cambridge University Press.

Nostra Aetate. 1965. Accessed January 3, 2020. http://www.vatican.va/archive/hist_councils/ii_vatican_council/documents/vat-ii_decl_19651028_nostra-aetate_en.html.

Novak, David. 2009. *In Defense of Religious Liberty*. Wilmington, DE: ISI Books.

Rawls, John. 1988. 'On the Priority of Right and Ideas of the Good'. *Philosophy and Public Affairs* 17, no. 4: 251–276.

Rawls, John. 1993. *Political Liberalism*. New York: Columbia University Press.

Chapter Eight

HUMAN DIGNITY FOUND IN RELIGIOUS COMMUNITY

Barry W. Bussey

I. Introduction

Jonathan Haidt, a social psychologist and professor of ethical leadership at New York University's Stern School of Business, notes that 'you've got to look at the ways that religious beliefs work with religious practices to create a religious community' (2012, 250).[1] Since 'religions are social facts', says Haidt, religion 'cannot be studied in lone individuals' any more than a bee can be isolated from the hive (287). Rather, one must view religion as a collective phenomenon that has individual dimensions. As Emile Durkheim (1964 [1915]) observed, humans are *homo duplex*. We exist at two levels: 'as an individual and as part of the larger society' (225). We have a 'profane' realm (Haidt calls it the 'chimp' domain), where we are concerned with our day-to-day living, worrying about our wealth, health and reputation, but with a nagging sense of something more, of greater importance (Durkheim 1964 [1915], 226). Most of our time (90 per cent, according to Haidt) is spent in the profane. The other realm (10 per cent) is 'higher' – it is the 'sacred' – where the collective (Haidt calls it the 'bee' domain) emotions temporarily pull us away from the profane to the spiritual. Haidt suggests that religion has a 'hive switch' that causes us to switch back and forth (2012, 189–220).

We are, then, 90 per cent 'chimp' and 10 per cent 'bee'. It is that 10 per cent I want to focus on in this chapter. The bee domain of human experience is often sidelined by the modern era's hypersensitivity to individual desire and disproportionate focus on satisfying individual expectations with little regard for communal obligations. Sometimes that focus is at the expense of the greater public good. This chapter argues that the communal religious experience of individuals forms a vital part of who they are: their

[1] I want to acknowledge the tremendous assistance of Angus Menuge and Amy Ross in providing helpful suggestions that I have incorporated in this chapter.

The opening paragraph of this chapter is taken from an article I previously published: 'The Right of Religious Hospitals to Refuse Physician-Assisted Suicide', *Supreme Court Law Review* (2018) 85 S.C.L.R. (2d), 189 at 199–200. This chapter unpacks that paragraph to provide further thought and reflection on the concept of religious community and human dignity.

being. My point is not that we are literally created by communal religious experience, but that it is only through such experience that we actualize our full potential as relational beings. So, by analogy, the person who wants to be a hockey player and has the potential to be one can exist even if the state bans hockey; but, in another sense, he cannot be a hockey player (actualize his potential) unless playing hockey is permitted. Likewise, as an inherently relational and religious being (*homo religiosus*), one cannot realize one's potential outside of a community of shared religious experience. In that sense, one cannot be a Catholic without a Catholic Church. Therefore, denying communal religious experience to a person is like denying vital food for that person's body, leading to stunted development and sickness. As such, it deserves our respect as a crucial part of their human dignity.

This is in no way meant to belittle the importance of individual freedom. Rather, my point is that a communal aspect of freedom exists in much the same way that Haidt identifies a duality in human nature. Recognizing the 'hive' aspect of the individual does not discount or invalidate freedom based on the liberation of the individual from state oppression. However, in maintaining individual freedom, we must not lose the reality of human existence in community and community in human existence. As will be explored, the individual/communal paradox of human dignity is part of what makes us so beautifully complex and contributes to a meaningful life.

The argument will proceed as follows: Section II explores the sociality of human beings and the imperative to be engaged in an entity greater than ourselves; Section III examines the nature of religious community and its role in fulfilling the human desire to be part of something beyond oneself. I use Dietrich Bonhoeffer's theology on the community of believers in the Lutheran Christian tradition as an example. Section IV considers the law's struggle with granting religious freedom protection to religious communities. Here I use several cases of the Supreme Court of Canada (SCC) that illustrate the difficulty the courts are having in recognizing the human dignity of (or through) religious communities; Section V considers the concept of human dignity and the relationship to religious communities; finally, I conclude by stitching together the different strands of the argument that, in addition to religious communities fulfilling a basic human desire to belong, there are sound reasons why human dignity considerations would support the proposition that religious communities, in their own right, be recognized as having constitutional protection of their respective religious beliefs and practices.

II. Religious Community and Aristotle's Political Animal

'Man is by nature a political animal', Aristotle (1944) opined. In his view, this was because humans have the unique ability to speak and perceive the 'good and bad and right and wrong and the other moral qualities' (Book 1, section 1253a). And 'it is [the] partnership in these things that makes a household and a city-state' (ibid.). Humans are social beings. They are concerned with what makes life meaningful, and thus partner together in community to debate and live out the essence of being. In other words, to live out what nature intended for human life to flourish. Not only do humans require time for solitude and contemplation; they need the relational aspects of the household, the village, the city and, today we would add, the nation state. There is life beyond the self – the I. There is the You. The other. The family. The neighbour. The country. These interrelationships depend on one's definition of self vis-à-vis the other and the understanding of one's responsibility towards the other to ensure that there is mutual peace to pursue happiness. It is in this sense, then, that human beings are political. That fact has consequences for individual meaning and for the collective success of society. Aristotle's world was hierarchical,[2] a far cry from the liberal democratic egalitarian approach we now embrace. But what is significant for our purposes is the continuity of ancient times with our present: the recognition that human beings must maintain communal relationships in order to thrive.

Our modern context is complicated. Many academics have moved away from traditional notions of community[3] to forms of community that are only recently recognized as such. One example is the depiction of sexual identities as a community, expressed in various acronyms, with seemingly no limit.[4] These postmodern concepts of communal identity have little relation to what Aristotle understood as community. However, this appeal to the collective still furthers the evidence of science that we are social beings with an innate desire for community, even if the claim for community is non-traditional.

By contrast, the globalist view of humanity argued that human beings should not be grouped ethnically, nationally or religiously. Instead, we are all one – human. And, as such, we ought to put away those 'social constructs' that create barriers.[5] Until recently

---

[2] For example, he recognized and accepted master-slave relationships as being part of nature.

[3] The Online Etymology Dictionary entry for 'community' notes the historical roots of the word as meaning '"a number of people associated together by the fact of residence in the same locality", also "the common people" (not the rulers or the clergy), from Old French comunité "community, commonness, everybody" (Modern French communauté), from Latin communitatem (nominative communitas) "community, society, fellowship, friendly intercourse; courtesy, condescension, affability", from communis "common, public, general, shared by all or many"'.

[4] Barb Perry of the University of Ontario Institute of Technology held an 'LGGBDTTTIQQAAPP Inclusive Training' seminar for the Elementary Teachers' Federation of Toronto. According to the poster advertising the event, as described in a *Daily Mail* article (2017), the acronym stands for lesbian, gay, genderqueer, bisexual, demisexual, transgender, transsexual, twospirit, intersex, queer, questioning, asexual, allies, pansexual, polyamorous. According to Dan Evon (2017) of snopes.com, Perry used the acronym 'to draw workshop participants [...] by acknowledging that keeping track of diverse LGBTQ identities can be overwhelming'. For a somewhat tongue-in-cheek discussion of the 'proliferation of sexual identities' listed in the acronym, see also Litwin (2016).

[5] Comedian Trevor Noah (2017) expresses this sentiment in his comedy routine:

> There's one thing you will never waste your money on. It's travelling the world. Be in another place and discover a different point of view. Traveling is the antidote to ignorance. That's so true. It changes your mind, your perspective, how you believe, what you believe. You know one of the greatest things you can do [...] is traveling to a country where they don't speak your language. That's probably my favorite thing – going through a place where they don't speak English just to make you realize how insignificant you really are, you're not the center of the universe, there's another world that exists beyond you. I try and do that all the time.

it was common to hear the argument that it was time to take down national borders and allow for the free flow of people and goods. The European Union was touted as a model to emulate in the movement towards 'our increasingly non-exclusive and fluctuating relationship to collective belonging and practice' (Walker 2016, 31). Then there was BREXIT (Looney 2017). Currently we are witnessing a marked increase of populist movements that are changing the political landscape away from the globalist, non-border approach. Such movements may well be the result of a cultural backlash against progressive ideologies (ten Napel 2020; see also Inglehart and Norris 2016). The COVID-19 crisis appears to be accelerating the anti-globalist trend as countries shut their borders to foreigners for fear of spreading disease. Additionally, the pandemic is taken as proof positive by the nationalists of their argument that their respective countries cannot rely on other countries especially in times of emergency (Farrell and Newman 2020; Irwin 2020).

Despite these winds of change we are left with the same conclusion: humans are political animals. They require community. We have a cohesive nature that binds and, as we shall see, also blinds us in our communities (as Jonathan Haidt observes). Haidt explores interesting leads from moral psychological research as to why people do not get along with their partisan and ideological opposites. His review of the scientific literature confirms that we are 'deeply intuitive creatures whose gut feelings drive our strategic reasoning' (Haidt 2012, 40). Our reasoning involves the passions. Based on personal bias, people make moral judgements quickly and emotionally. Moral reasoning is, therefore, a search for reasons to justify our already-made judgements (ibid.).[6] Where do those gut instincts come from? They have a long gestation period from our communal upbringing.

Haidt, as noted earlier, argues we are 90 per cent chimp and 10 per cent bee. The dominance of the chimp nature is due to the historic necessities of competition with other individuals to survive. In addition, Haidt asserts that we are Glauconian, meaning we are generally more concerned with the appearance of virtue than the reality (223).[7] The concept of 'virtue signalling' has a rather long history.

However, Haidt observes that we are '*conditional hive creatures*' meaning that under special conditions we can 'transcend self-interest and lose ourselves (temporarily and ecstatically) in something larger than ourselves' (223, emphasis original). This he calls a 'hive switch' that allows groups to be more cohesive and therefore more successful vis-à-vis other groups (ibid.). What binds the individual to the collective has not gotten as much attention in scientific studies as the individual has been emphasized. Haidt reminds us

---

[6]   Haidt's view seems rather cynical. It appears to undermine freedom of conscience, since any moral argument is merely emotion, not truth. I do not have time to explore this in depth here and plan to spend some time on this issue in further writing.

[7]   Haidt's reference to Glaucon is instructive. Glaucon was Plato's brother, who argued that people free 'from all reputational consequences tend to behave abominably' (Haidt 2012, n. 3, 223). Glaucon in Plato's *Republic* spoke to Socrates about what would happen if a man had the mythical ring Gyges, which makes the wearer invisible at will. Such a man would become totally corrupted, Glaucon maintained. Socrates argued in response for the rule of philosophers who would govern with reason not passion, to ensure that they pursued only what was truly good for all and not for themselves (Haidt 2012, 72–74).

that the work of Emile Durkheim, the 'father' of sociology, is still relevant and helpful in understanding the individual and group dynamics.

Durkheim wrote in the late nineteenth and early twentieth centuries. 'For that which makes a man', Durkheim said, 'is the totality of the intellectual property which constitutes civilization, and civilization is the work of society. Thus is explained the prepondering role of the cult in all religions, whichever they may be' (1964 [1915], 418). By 'cult', Durkheim means the actions motivated by religion – the religious rites and the religiously inspired virtues:

> This is because society cannot make its influence felt unless it is in action, and it is not in action unless the individuals who compose it are assembled together and act in common. It is by common action that it takes consciousness of itself and realizes its position; it is before all else an active co-operation. The collective ideas and sentiments are even possible only owing to these exterior movements which symbolize them, as we have established. Then it is action which dominates the religious life, because of the mere fact that it is society which is its source. (418)

To make the point clear, Durkheim takes it a step further. He observes that to understand the world we must understand religion. 'In summing up, then', he says:

> Nearly all the great social institutions have been born in religion. Now in order that these principal aspects of the collective life may have commenced by being only varied aspects of the religious life, it is obviously necessary that the religious life be the eminent form and, as it were, the concentrated expression of the whole collective life. If religion has given birth to all that is essential in society, it is because the idea of society is the soul of religion. (418–19)

Durkheim notes that people are *homo duplex*, that is, we exist at two levels: as an individual and as part of the larger society (Haidt 2012, 225). On one level, we relate one to one in our day-to-day relationships – family members, co-workers – where we keep our autonomy and personality intact. On the second level, we bond to the social entity as a whole and lose our individuality in favour of the actions and influence of that entity.

Religion is the basis upon which we connect with those of like mind. There is a mutually reinforcing element that flows between the individual and her religious association. The individual consciousness is given direction and discipline from that association:

> All religions, even the crudest, are in a sense spiritualistic: for the powers they put in play are before all spiritual, and also their principal object is to act upon the moral life. Thus it is seen that whatever has been done in the name of religion cannot have been done in vain: for it is necessarily the society that did it, and it is humanity that has reaped the fruits. (Durkheim 1964 [1915], 420)

Durkheim keenly observed that the value of religion is found in its ability to transfer to the individual a cause that is beyond reach of the one person – in fact, it is beyond reach of society as a whole – but all are united in seeking to obtain it. All religions point to a better day, the Promised Land or heaven, where evil no longer exists in society. Such a society is not an empirical fact:

> It is a fancy, a dream with which men have lightened their sufferings, but in which they have never really lived. It is merely an idea which comes to express our more or less obscure aspirations towards the good, the beautiful and the ideal. Now these aspirations have their roots in us; they come from the very depths of our being; then there is nothing outside of us which can account for them. Moreover, they are already religious in themselves; thus it would seem that the ideal society presupposes religion, far from being able to explain it. (Ibid.)

The concept of the ideal society, which religion strives to achieve, is essential. According to Durkheim, the ideal does not exist outside of our real society as forming two separate polar opposites. Instead, the ideal and the 'real' society are part of the one society. The religious ideal allows our current society to strive for all things better. After all, a 'society can neither create itself nor recreate itself without at the same time creating an ideal' (422).

As Durkheim so eloquently puts it:

> It is in assimilating the ideals elaborated by society that [the individual] has become capable of conceiving the ideal. It is society which, by leading him within its sphere of action, has made him acquire the need of raising himself above the world of experience and has at the same time furnished him with the means of conceiving another. For society has constructed this new world in constructing itself, since it is society which this expresses. Thus both with the individual and in the group, the faculty of idealizing has nothing mysterious about it. It is not a sort of luxury which a man could get along without, but a condition of his very existence. (423)

Durkheim's one-hundred-year-old observations continue to be discussed by current scholars. His view of *homo duplex* remains persuasive (Haidt 2012, 257). While 'we live most of our lives in the ordinary (profane) world', 'we achieve our greatest joys in those brief moments of transit to the sacred world, in which we become "simply part of a whole"' (244). Religious beliefs and practices create a community, giving hope for a better future in a way that is much more effective than the secular attempts at community building. Although academics like Richard Dawkins and the late Christopher Hitchens have vilified 'sacred' beliefs and practices as being irrational, inefficient and costly, these are now seen as the very glue that binds people together. 'There is now a great deal of evidence', says Haidt, 'that religions do in fact help groups to cohere, solve free rider problems, and win the competition for group-level survival' (2012, 256). As D. S. Wilson says, 'Religions exist primarily for people to achieve together what they cannot achieve on their own' (2002, 159).

III. Religious Community and the Individual

It is important for policymakers to appreciate the depth of thought that occurs within a religious community as it wrestles with the tension between individual and communal responsibilities. This is not necessarily unique to the Christian faith; however, given the insights and applicability of his analysis, not to mention the profound influence his writing has had on ethics and theology in the latter part of the twentieth century, I will use the work of Lutheran theologian Dietrich Bonhoeffer to provide some evidence of the themes and dynamics which Haidt and Durkheim observed as influencing religious followers.

In *Sanctorum Communio*, Bonhoeffer (1998)[8] argues that a Christian is a free-willed individual who has responsibilities towards human communities as well as to God. According to Bonhoeffer, 'The whole nature of human spirit [Geistigkeit], which necessarily is presupposed by the Christian concept of person and has its unifying point in self-consciousness [...] is such that it is only conceivable in sociality' (66). 'There is', Bonhoeffer maintains, 'no distinctly human empirical social relation *unless there exist a community appropriate to its essence*' (ibid., emphasis original). In other words, the community – particularly the religious community – is of fundamental significance to the individual's identity, self-awareness and purpose. Affirming the full human dignity of the individual therefore rests upon, and results from, the recognition of an individual's sense of belonging in community.

Rather than prioritizing or subordinating the individual to the whole, Bonhoeffer's formulation provides a balance in which the '*personal and social being have equal weight*' (76, emphasis original). Thus, community as a metaphysical unit '*can be interpreted as a collective person with the same structure as the individual person*' (77, emphasis original). In this sense, the whole represents the part. Thus, when there is harm to the community, there is harm to its members because those members find their full expression and identity only in community. Through reciprocity of wills, the 'collective person' may acquire its own dignity, which is necessarily predicated on the worth and purpose of the individual. Both the person and the 'concrete community with specific goals' (78) achieve greater fulfilment through their mutual relationship. For Bonhoeffer, 'the person comes into being only when embedded in sociality, and the collective person comes into being together with the individual person. It is neither prior to, nor a consequence of, the individual. That is, the collective person exists only where there are individual persons' (ibid.). Moreover, much like an individual person, the community 'has its own center of activity that experiences love, compassion, shared joy [...] and its own way of acting, alongside other individual persons, in the sense of equal weight and monadic image' (103).

These insights on community have a theological application. Bonhoeffer maintains that 'God does not think of people as isolated individual beings, but in a natural state of communication with other human beings' (79–80). It is here one discovers his or her reality of being. As 'God created man and woman directed to one another', so He does not 'desire a history of individual human beings, but the history of the human *community*' (80, emphasis original). Nor does God 'want a community that absorbs the individual into itself, but a community of human beings' (ibid.). This autonomy of the individual is important for maintaining freedom of conscience, as noted later in this chapter, while

---

8   I want to acknowledge Amy Ross's assistance in refining my summary of Bonhoeffer's work.

also allowing courts to recognize that the community itself has a uniquely transcendent worth and function. Bonhoeffer holds that both the collective unit and the individual unit have the same structure in God's eyes, where 'community and individual exist in the same moment and rest in one another' (ibid.).

From this perspective, then, the divinely formed religious community may derive a God-given dignity in a similar way that the human being, made in God's image, possesses inherent dignity or worth.

Distinguishing the religious collective in theological terms – as opposed to a more superficial commonality, which in Bonhoeffer's formulation distinguishes the lecture hall from a true 'community of will' (83) – may offer a productive way to ascribe dignity to religious groups without undermining or eroding the notion of dignity, since it maintains the 'objective moral claim inherent in the initial concept' (see Newman, Chapter 6, 102).

Bonhoeffer observes that 'communal acts of will do not run parallel to each other toward a purpose beyond the persons themselves; rather, in communities, the direction of the personal wills is the same – that is, they are reciprocal' (1998, 83). In other words, the individual is neither subsumed by nor fused with the community, since 'community of will and unity of will only build upon the inner separateness of I and You […] The person who is united with me in common intention is structurally just as separate from me as the one who is not so united. Between us lies the boundary of being created as individual persons' (84). Likewise, individuals are free to 'say adieu' and depart from the community (103, quoting Freyer, *Theorie des objektiven Geistes*, 81).

In recognizing the individual this way, Bonhoeffer acknowledges that there is bound to be strife. Within the community, individuals are bound to experience a conflict of wills with other individuals and with the community itself. However, 'strength unfolds only in strife' (Bonhoeffer 1998, 85). Ultimately, tension is resolved by the 'cooperation of wills' which comes as a result of the 'social synthesis' of the community. The community is 'built upon the separateness and difference of persons, constituted by reciprocal acts of will, finding its unity in what is willed, and counting among its basic laws the inner conflict of individual wills' (86). While Bonhoeffer himself does not extend this definition to encompass the dignity of the community, his analysis seems to be consistent with Newman's observations regarding the 'internal diversity within groups' (100). By emphasizing both the separateness and synthesis of the individuals, it may be possible to contemplate collective dignity in such a way that does not, as Newman cautions, 'inappropriately endanger aspects of individual equality' (101). Bonhoeffer stresses that in community, 'all are led to carry their individual viewpoints to the limit, to be really serious about it, in keeping with the basic sociological laws of social vitality. But – to put it paradoxically – the more powerfully the dissimilarity manifests itself in the struggle, the stronger the objective unity' (1998, 192). A shared spirit unites the 'plurality of persons into a single collective person without obliterating either their singularity or the community of persons' (ibid.). He appears to suggest that a healthy society attains unity by tolerating dissent and disagreement and that totalitarian societies are not really unified (as they claim) but are profoundly divided because they cannot accommodate dissent.

Importantly, the resolution of conflict occurs within the framework of an 'objective spirit' which 'leads an individual life "beyond" the individual persons, and yet it is real only through them. The more alive the individual persons, the more powerful the objective spirit. [...] To withdraw from it is to withdraw from the community. It wills historical continuity as well as the social realization of its will' (100).

Thus, the concept of the objective spirit depends on – and flows from – an understanding of the collective person as having a divine destiny. A community has an eschatological character that it shares with history. Indeed, 'the deepest significance of community is 'from God to God' (ibid.). Unlike society which is time bound – once its purpose is completed, it ends – the religious community does not end. It is eternal as God is eternal. This, then, is the basis of a human community's 'holiness', whether physical, as in blood and clan; historical, as with a nation; or life-shaping, as in marriage and friendship. 'This holiness reveals the fundamental indissolubility of all these life structures' (101).

In particular, the Christian community is that coming together of human beings who are renewed by the Holy Spirit away from the severance of basic relations that lead to a demanding confrontation between 'I and You', to 'a giving way' (191). As Bonhoeffer explains:

> A Christian comes into being and exists only in Christ's church-community and is dependent on it, which means on the other human being. One person bears the other in active love, intercession, and forgiveness of sins, acting completely vicariously. This is possible only in the church-community of Christ, and that itself rests, as a whole, on the principle of vicarious representation, i.e., on the love of God. But all are born by the church community, which consists precisely in this being-for-each-other of its members. (Ibid.)

In addition to articulating the structure and function of a religious community, the principles established in Bonhoeffer's work provide a strong justification for the legal accommodation of religious freedom and freedom of conscience. He characterizes religion as a source of authority. The church derives its authority from the divine word, which provides an uncompromising standard that supersedes all other authority. It follows that the law, therefore, does not have the jurisdiction to demand allegiance in matters of religious conviction, since the individual and collective person are compelled by conscience to obey the sovereign word.

Bonhoeffer argues that the 'absolute authority of the word[9] demands absolute obedience, that is, absolute freedom; the relative authority of the church calls for relative obedience, which means relative freedom' (250). Bonhoeffer thinks that the freedom of the Christian is found in 'costly grace', by taking up our cross and following Christ. That sets us free not to be slaves of our own ego but adopted sons of God.

The church has a responsibility not only to preach but to speak authoritatively. Once the church has spoken, its membership has only 'a relative freedom' to the matter upon which the church has taken a stand (251).[10] The church is owed a 'relative

---

[9] 'Word' seems to be a reference to Scripture, Christ and the word of the church.

[10] Bonhoeffer says that 'as a theologian – and every Protestant Christian is a theologian – [I] have only a relative freedom'. On that basis, I say 'membership'.

obedience' even to the point of demanding sacrifices. However, this does not threaten freedom of conscience, since Bonhoeffer immediately qualifies this by reiterating that it is a 'relative' obedience, a 'relative' freedom. The relative bond to the church can be broken only 'if it stands in the way of my absolute commitment to the word' (ibid.). Therefore, the church's authority is derivative and representative. Bonhoeffer notes that it 'remains for God alone to know when the moment has come when an individual within the church is forced to oppose its authority' (252). Somewhat paradoxically, 'this turning point against the church's authority can at any rate only be an act of supreme obedience that is most deeply committed to the church and the word within it, but never a merely capricious act' (ibid.). This explains Bonhoeffer's decision later when he disobeyed the 'German Christian' Church, which violated the First Commandment by requiring absolute obedience to the Nazi Party. It was out of love for the German Church and its true identity that he and others formed the Confessing Church.

Within Bonhoeffer's theological framework, the individual is free to speak his mind on the interpretation and meaning of church pronouncements, religious lifestyle commitments and the like. Indeed, the individual is recognized as having human worth and dignity which is Kantian in approach. Bonhoeffer 'must be read against the background of the categorical claim that the personal dignity of a human being can be preserved only if that person never merely serves as a means to an end' (von Soosten 1998, 299). Yet, the individual is part of the religious community even to the point of having to sacrifice his or her individuality for the sake of the whole. There is a recognition that the community transcends oneself. There is, then, not only a psychological 'hive' switch, but also, within the religious community, a theological basis for such a switch. At the same time, Bonhoeffer admits that the individual is ultimately responsible to God. Community and individual are thus both subject to the divine. Herein lies the tension that the law must struggle to understand. Acknowledging this dialectic is key to providing justice – to recognizing the dignity not only of the individual, but of the religious community as well. In the section that follows we will consider how the Canadian courts have fared recently in recognizing these distinctions.

IV. Religious Communities and the Lack of Constitutional Protection

The SCC once lauded itself as 'jealously guarding' freedom of religion.[11] However, its recent jurisprudence involving religious communities has belied such an assertion. Three cases highlight the SCC's disregard of the communal aspects of religion: the *Hutterian Brethren of Wilson Colony* case (2009), the *Loyola High School* case (2015) and the *Trinity Western University* law school cases (2018).

---

[11] 'The protection of freedom of religion afforded by s. 2(a) of the Charter is broad and jealously guarded in our Charter jurisprudence' (*Reference re Same-Sex Marriage* 2004, para 53).

Hutterian Brethren of Wilson Colony

The Hutterian Brethren, a Christian communal colony in Alberta, refuse to have their pictures taken because they believe photography violates the Second Commandment of God not to make as idols 'any likeness of what is in heaven above or on the earth beneath' (Exod. 20:4, NASB). From 1974 to 2003, the Alberta government allowed this group an exemption from the general requirement for photographs on a driver's licence. However, that policy changed to require all provincial drivers to be photographed and images stored in a facial recognition database. Only 453 Albertans held non-photo licences at the time of the change – a mere 0.02 per cent of the total number of licences issued. Of the 453, 250 belonged to the Hutterian Brethren community.

On judicial review, both lower Alberta courts supported the Hutterian Brethren's constitutional freedom, holding the government's limit on that freedom was unjustified. The courts rejected the Alberta government's accommodation proposals as they still required a photograph. The Hutterites proposed that they carry a licence without a photograph but that it be marked stating that it could not be used for identification purposes. The Alberta government refused.

At the SCC, the court was sharply divided, but the majority accepted the government's limit on religious freedom as being justified. Former Chief Justice McLachlin, writing for the four-member majority, held that there was an infringement of religious freedom. However, McLachlin was concerned that freedom of religion 'presents a particular challenge' because 'much of the regulation of a modern state could be claimed by *various individuals* to have a more than trivial impact on a sincerely held religious belief' and that 'giving effect to each of their religious claims could seriously undermine the universality of many regulatory programs' (para 36, emphasis added). Such reasoning could allow any dump truck to run through a picket fence. It appears to have been the first time the court favoured government policy in complex regulatory regimes at the expense of religious freedom. At first blush, one might understand the reluctance of the court to allow a significant damper on the government's ability to carry out the work of governing in the modern context, that is, an increasingly multicultural and diverse society. However, in this case the Alberta government gave the exemption for 29 years with no evidence of any harm or 'overall detriment of the community' (para 36) whatsoever. McLachlin's reasoning is hardly convincing.

McLachlin's impoverished view of religious communities is evidenced by her acceptance of the Alberta government's argument that the photograph was required to combat identity theft – with no mention of the 700,000-plus Albertans without any driver's licence, who would therefore not be in the facial recognition database. Instead, the concern centred on the 250 Hutterian Brethren who had strong, deeply held beliefs against their photographs being taken. The reasoning was particularly odd given that the primary purpose for the photograph on a driver's licence has nothing to do with identity theft but rather with driver identification. McLachlin held the government's concern was of 'pressing and substantial importance' to justify the limit on their religious freedom. The harmful effects of the limit were proportional in her view because Alberta's system needed to be in line with that of other provinces. Moreover, the Hutterian Brethren matters were simply the result of 'a multicultural, multireligious society where the duty of state authorities to legislate for the general good inevitably produces conflicts with *individual beliefs*' (para 90, emphasis added). The fact that McLachlin repeatedly characterized the communal convictions of the Hutterites as a matter of 'individual beliefs' is particularly telling, especially since the Hutterites themselves argued for a much more complex notion of religious faith in community. They explained that 'each Colony member has a specific set of responsibilities assigned to him or her, some of which require the member to drive. If a Colony member cannot carry out these responsibilities, it "causes our religious commune to function improperly, thereby eroding the fabric of our *social, cultural and religious way of life*"' (para 8, emphasis added).

Unfortunately, the SCC failed to properly understand and ascertain the role of religious community and the individual's commitment to community faith. It shirked its responsibility in understanding *what* the community believes and the *extent of commitment* the members have to maintaining that belief and practice. Without that knowledge, the law is bound to minimize the effect of its decision on the claimant.

For example, the SCC was ready to accept the Alberta government's attempt at accommodation which would have involved keeping the photo requirement but 'eliminating or alleviating the need for [the Hutterites] to carry photos' (para 57). In other words, let the picture be taken but don't carry it. The SCC majority thought that was a reasonable compromise to reduce the impact on the members' s. 2(a) Charter rights. The court neither understood nor appreciated the Hutterites' religiously motivated aversion to photographs. Carrying photos was troubling, but having one's picture taken in the first place was the real problem, since it created an idol. The SCC's lack of appreciation was part of a systemic failure to consider the *substance* and *extent of the commitment* of the Hutterites to their religious belief and practice. The entire legal analysis is grossly impaired when there is a failure to understand the religious community.[12] Unless this lack of interest is corrected there is little chance for meaningful dialogue between the normative commitments of law and religion. It cannot happen because the law has a blind spot. The law does not recognize its own weakness in favouring the state over religious communities in such situations.

McLachlin stated, 'This Court has recognized that a measure of leeway must be accorded to governments in determining whether limits on rights in public programs that regulate social and commercial interactions are justified under s. 1 of the *Charter*' (para 35). In the determination of minimal impairment she reiterated, 'In making this assessment,

---

12 For more on the incongruous, reductionist decisions that may result when courts fail to understand the complexities of religion, see Chiu (2020). Implicit in Chiu's argument is the harm done to human dignity if the law disregards the complexities of religious belief and behaviour. He notes that 'any important life experience must engage with what is real and true, and the religious aspect of life is receptive to such questions. Moreover, since the quest to find such truth is impossible to do alone, by its nature the search for the sacred requires observance in a communal context'. He concludes that without a full, complete vision of religion, 'we run the risk of doing an injustice to the very essence of what it means for humanity to thrive in community' (35).

the courts accord the legislature a measure of deference, particularly on complex social issues where the legislature may be better positioned than the courts to choose among a range of alternatives' (para 51). Yet, the 29 years of experience in accommodating this religious community was evidence enough that the government needed no deference.

McLachlin's admission of deference is remarkable because it reveals a willingness to understand the government but not so the religious claimant. The court took pains to determine the *what* of the government's position and even the *extent of commitment* the government must have to regulate, in this case, photographs for the driver's licence. Unfortunately, the same regard was not given to the Hutterites. The failure of the law to properly understand the religious beliefs and commitment of the Hutterian Brethren led to an inability to find a resolution that would have met the purpose of the state objective *and* shown respect for the religious practice.

At least one alternative readily comes to mind that would have solved the problem. The Hutterites suggested their non-photo bearing licence be clearly marked as ineligible for identification. The court refused that suggestion because of identity theft. However, an appropriate resolution would be fingerprinting the licensee so that both name and identifying characteristic (fingerprint) would be linked without the possibility of replication.

The court's review of the balance between the salutary and deleterious effects of the government position was 'whether the limit leaves the adherent with a meaningful choice to follow his or her religious beliefs and practices' (para 88). To answer this enquiry the court must know the seriousness of the limit upon the claimant. Though the court had no knowledge of the *extent of commitment* to that belief, it ruled that the community members had a choice to follow their religious beliefs.

The court admitted that 'in judging the seriousness of the limit in a particular case, the perspective of the religious or conscientious claimant is important' (para 90). Yet it was quick to point out that the 'bare assertion' of the claimant that the limit curtails his practise 'does not, without more, establish the seriousness of the limit […] We must go further to evaluate the degree to which the limit actually impacts on the adherent' (para 90).

The fundamental flaw in this approach is that the court made its determination based on what *it* perceived as the actual impact on the community, rather than having a clear, unequivocal understanding of the Hutterite position. For the court it was a matter of ensuring that the Hutterites had a 'meaningful choice' to practise their faith – that choice was to pay extra for transportation to and from their communal compound. The court said that it was 'a cost on those who *choose* not to have their photos taken' (para 96, emphasis added).

However, for the Hutterites, the issue is not a *choice*; it is an obligation of the conscience that goes to the core of who they are, not simply as individuals, but as a community with a deep sense of historical continuity and social unity. The failure of the law to take into account the *what* of the claimant's belief and practices, and the *extent of commitment* to that belief and practice, could not be more evident.

For the foreseeable future, the young children of the Hutterite community will be left to wonder why their parents cannot drive them upon the free-flowing highways of the country. The answer that the Supreme Court would like them to give is that as parents they *chose* not to have their photographs taken. Of course, those parents will say nothing of the sort. Rather, their consciences as informed by their reading and understanding of the Second Commandment dictate that they must not – for fear of eternal consequences – allow their likeness to be produced in any form. They will share to the coming generation that they are unwelcome to participate in one of Canadian society's most ubiquitous privileges – to drive. All because the law's sympathy does not extend to their religious obligation to refuse photographs. But the concern goes much deeper than driving. For the Hutterites, the dilemma involves their very ability to function as an agrarian community with deeply ingrained customs and shared responsibilities; if one member cannot fulfil his or her role (like selling eggs and fresh produce at the local farmer's market), this does not just interfere with that member's rights, it affects the entire commune's ability to operate, teach, worship and sustain themselves both physically and spiritually. There is also an element of unity with the past as well as the present community, which calls to mind Bonhoeffer's description – 'It wills historical continuity as well as the social realization of its will'. Thus, to abandon a particular belief is also to sever this deep and powerfully maintained bond with traditions that have defined the Hutterites for generations.[13]

McLachlin rejected the Hutterites' claim that to deny them their licence 'because they refuse to abandon their religious belief in the Second Commandment but issuing licences to the comparator group simply because they do not share such religious belief' was demeaning and infringed their human dignity (para 107). She saw it differently. Governments issue a licence to those who meet the statutory requirements (in this case a photograph) and not based on religious belief.

She went further and said that even if there was a distinction on religion, the government's decision 'arises not from any demeaning stereotype but from a neutral and rationally defensible policy choice' (para 108). What is missing here is McLachlin's appreciation that even neutral and rational government policies may be discriminatory. She rejected the comparison to the *Andrews v. Law Society of British Columbia* case (1989) where the SCC held that the Canadian citizenship requirement for membership in the Law Society of British Columbia violated the Charter and was unreasonable. Interestingly, it was Justice McLachlin's BC Court of Appeal (BCCA) decision (1986) that was before the SCC in *Andrews*. She stated then that the first question under a s. 15 challenge is

> whether the impugned distinction is reasonable or fair, having regard to the purposes and aims and its effect on persons adversely affected. I include the word 'fair' as well as 'reasonable' to emphasize that the test is not one of pure rationality but one connoting the treatment of persons in ways which are not unduly prejudicial to them. (609–10, qtd in *Andrews* 1989, 162–63)

She found none of the Law Society's arguments convincing and felt the citizenship requirement was 'clearly prejudicial', concluding that 'the requirement of citizenship for admission to the practice of law is unreasonable or unfair' (616, qtd in *Andrews* 1989, 163).

---

[13] I want to acknowledge Amy Ross for this insight.

If we weigh these two cases on the scales of justice, it seems rather counterintuitive to conclude that discrimination on the basis of citizenship is an unacceptable limit; but a photograph that offends religious conscience is an acceptable limit. More than that, in the *Hutterian Brethren* case, Chief Justice McLachlin went so far as to say the 'Colony members' claim is to the unfettered practice of their religion, not to be free from religious discrimination' (2009, para 108). From my reading of the case, there was nothing to suggest that the Hutterite colony was saying any such thing. They simply wanted the government to continue recognizing what it had permitted for 29 years. Moreover, in *Andrews*, there was no revoking of a previous accommodation as there was in the Hutterite case.

While it is true, in the very strict sense, that the Hutterites will be able to go on in their religious practice, but with the increased cost of hiring transportation, the fact remains that they have to face a terrible burden because of the law's inability to understand their plight. Their vulnerability will be seen in the increased personal danger or delays in getting transportation to medical facilities for those in need; the increased burden to maintain a livelihood in getting goods to market; and the reliance upon outside sources for the delivery of supplies; in all likelihood, it will be reasonable to assume they will face further ridicule because of their plight in the community at large.

Justice Abella, in dissent, emphasized the communal aspect of religious freedom (para 130–33). She quoted from former Justice Bertha Wilson in *Edwards Books* (1986), who stated:

> It seems to me that when the Charter protects group rights such as freedom of religion, it protects the rights of all members of the group. It does not make fish of some and fowl of the others. For, quite apart from considerations of equality, to do so is to introduce an invidious distinction into the group and sever the religious and cultural tie that binds them together. It is, in my opinion, an interpretation of the Charter expressly precluded by s. 27 which requires the Charter to be interpreted 'in a manner consistent with the preservation and enhancement of the multicultural heritage of Canadians'. (808–9, qtd in *Hutterian Brethren* 2009, para 130)

Abella also highlighted the understanding of the European Court of Human Rights[14] in this regard:

> The right of believers to freedom of religion, which includes the right to manifest one's religion in community with others, encompasses the expectation that believers will be allowed to associate freely, without arbitrary State intervention. Indeed, the autonomous existence of religious communities is indispensable for pluralism in a democratic society and is thus an issue at the very heart of the protection [of religious freedom]. …
>
> In addition, one of the means of exercising the right to manifest one's religion, especially for a religious community, in its collective dimension, is the possibility of ensuring judicial protection of the community, its members and its assets. (Para 118, qtd in *Hutterian Brethren* 2009, para 131)

---

[14] In the case *Metropolitan Church of Bessarabia and Others v. Moldova* No. 45701/99, ECHR 2001-XII.

Justice LeBel also took up the communal aspect in his reasons:

> Religion is about religious beliefs, but also about religious relationships. […] [This appeal] raises issues about belief, but also about the maintenance of communities of faith. We are discussing the fate […] of a community that shares a common faith and a way of life that is viewed by its members as a way of living that faith and of passing it on to future generations. (Para 182)

Justices Abella and LeBel's reasons, though in dissent, were the first indication in a long while that the SCC had turned its mind, in a serious way, to the communal nature of religious freedom. However, to date, the SCC has yet to clearly articulate the law in this respect.

The underlying assumption throughout the *Hutterian Brethren* case is that the deference given to the government is reasonable because the matter deals with 'a complex regulatory response to a social problem' (para 37) where the limit is the inability to access conditional benefits or privileges of the state. If the limit were penal, 'threatening the liberty of the accused' (ibid.), then the law would not provide the same deference. Thus, it becomes a question of degree as to the nature of the limit. If the limit has to do with public privilege, as the issuing of a driver's licence, then the government is given deference; if, however, it has to do with personal liberty, then there is little deference.

This position denies the basic equality of rights protection under the Charter. To give deference to the state is to favour the state up front. The decision gave an unfair advantage to the state. The claimant is by definition the weaker party in the litigation – lack of resource capacity to commit to a long-term fight and lack of public support or influence has already put the claimant in a subservient position to counter the designs of the state. On the face of it the Charter promises that any limits to guaranteed rights will have to be demonstrably justified in a free and democratic society. A tipping of the scales in favour of the state results in a situation where the justification will be less than robust.

Further, why in principle should there be a different standard for a regulatory limit involving a public benefit, service or privilege, as opposed to a limit involving personal liberty? Both are actions of the state, which has virtually unlimited power and ability to enforce its will upon the individual. Both limit a guaranteed right. What exempts the state from having to put forward an energetic justification of its limit in the one but not the other? 'Nothing' is the appropriate response.

It would be more just if the deference towards the state came not from the regulatory versus penal axis of the limit but rather from the optional versus obligatory axis of the religious belief and practice. Thus, if a religious belief were optional, then it would be reasonable for the state to be given deference in its limit. If, however, the religious belief were obligatory, then it should not matter whether the limit were regulatory or penal – as both, in the eyes of the claimant, would amount to the same.

This approach may prove useful because (1) the state is without parallel in its capacity to put forth its position in whatever situation it finds itself; (2) the onus on the state to justify its limit would not have to be so robust for matters that have lower religious significance to the claimant.[15]

The *Hutterian Brethren* decision highlights the fact that Canadian jurisprudence has not yet articulated the collective aspect of religious freedom. It is not because the law has not recognized that right, but because, until recently, there has been no sustained attack on that communal right to warrant such analysis. It was among those rights 'taken for granted to be the unchallengeable rights of Canadians' (*Boucher v. R.* 1951 at 285 per Rand J). However, that has changed. This case highlighted government actors' willingness to challenge communal religious rights for political purposes. The pre-supposition appears to be that the secular state interest is supreme and must prevail. Therefore, mediating institutions such as religious communities are a nuisance when they refuse to comply. This decision prepared the way for further erosion in religious freedom rights in subsequent cases, ultimately leading to the disastrous decisions in the Trinity Western University (TWU) law school case, which marked a new low in Canadian jurisprudence on religious freedom.

Loyola High School

In 2008 the province of Quebec implemented a mandatory core curriculum that included the course Ethics and Religious Culture (ERC) which sought to teach beliefs and ethics of different world religions from a neutral and objective perspective.[16] That is a tall order for any government to attempt as governments can never be totally neutral in

---

[15] One has to recognize that given the nature of litigation, there may be few instances where a claimant pursues the protection of a religious practice that is considered optional. But there are some – consider that for many religious groups it may not be obligatory to have a house of worship, yet if a government regulation somehow had the effect of preventing a congregation from having a building in which to worship, they would fight to maintain that right. It is suggested that in that case, where having a building is not obligatory for the claimant, the onus on the government to justify its limit would not be as high. It is perhaps intuitive that the majority of claimants would go through the tribulation of Charter litigation only if the religious practice were mandatory.

[16] Note Michael J. Perry's (1989) observation regarding Bruce Ackerman's (1980) position on government neutrality:

> The justification of government's choice to be neutral between two competing positions – or the justification of its choice not to be neutral, or, indeed, the justification of any contested choice government makes with respect to any matter at all – cannot possibly be neutral among all competing conceptions of human good, if, as will invariably be the case with respect to real-world political controversies: according to some conceptions of human good (at least one) it is good for us, qua political community, to do one thing (e.g., be neutral between the contending positions) while according to other conceptions (at least one) it is good for us to do something else (e.g., forsake neutrality for partiality). In contending for one or another contested choice, the justification must side with – it must ratify or affirm – one or another competing conception of the good. There is simply no way for political justification to avoid such partiality and achieve the neutrality Ackerman seeks. (480–81)

religious ethics,[17] even if the law requires neutrality to prevent favouring one religion over another.[18] The ERC had three components: world religions and religious culture, ethics, and dialogue. It was meant to be secular and cultural, and the teachers were required to be objective and impartial.

Loyola High School, being a Roman Catholic school, objected to the ERC's requirement that its teaching of the Catholic faith must be secular and that its teachers were to be objective and impartial. Loyola was willing to teach other religions objectively and respectfully but on ethical matters it would emphasize Catholic teaching. Further, it could not agree to their teachers being strictly neutral as the ERC required. Therefore, it sought an exemption from the Quebec government. The government refused. Loyola went to court for judicial review of Quebec's decision.

Justice Rosalie Abella wrote the majority decision and applied an analysis of 'Charter values' in determining whether the Quebec government's refusal was unreasonable. The court's 'Charter values' process, known as the *Doré* analysis (2012), is a recent evolution of its approach in reviewing government Charter rights infringement in regulatory matters. It gives the government greater deference when it makes discretionary administrative decisions. In other words, it is easier for the government to justify violations of the Charter in the guise of public interest. It has, in my view, greatly solidified the court's *Hutterian Brethren* sentiment but with a different legal analysis.

Abella held that Quebec's refusal to allow Loyola an exemption to teach the Catholic faith from a Roman Catholic perspective was 'a disproportionate, and therefore unreasonable interference with the values underlying freedom of religion of those individuals who seek to offer and who wish to receive a Catholic education at Loyola' (para 6). However, she went on to hold that there was no impairment of Loyola's freedom of religion to require Loyola 'to offer a course that explains the beliefs, ethics and practices of other religions in as objective and neutral a way as possible, rather than from the Catholic perspective' (para 6). It seems, at least on the face of the matter, improbable that a private religious school could be expected to teach a course about another religious community's beliefs, ethics and practices in a way that would be entirely neutral. Is it not the case that we would expect a sectarian school, by its very nature, to be unable to

---

[17] Franklin I. Gamwell points out that 'every political decision takes sides among religions, because it implies some judgment about the character of religious truth. As long as the body politic decides not to proscribe abortion, for instance, it decides implicitly against the religious convictions of the Moral Majority and (at least some of) the Roman Catholic Church' (1982, 281).

[18] Justice Gascon (*Mouvement laïque québécois v. Saguenay (City)*, 2015) held that the state has 'a duty of religious neutrality', in that the 'state may not act in such a way as to create a preferential public space that favours certain religious groups and is hostile to others. It follows that the state may not, by expressing its own religious preference, promote the participation of believers to the exclusion of non-believers or vice versa' (para 75). Further, the 'state's duty to protect every person's freedom of conscience and religion means that it may not use its powers in such a way as to promote the participation of certain believers or non-believers in public life to the detriment of others. It is prohibited from adhering to one religion to the exclusion of all others' (para 76).

present beliefs, including those that go contrary to its very identity, in a neutral manner? However, it is possible to speak respectfully of differing beliefs while still not endorsing them as being equally acceptable or valid: that is, the school could most certainly teach other religions in a way that affirms the dignity and worth of all humans (regardless of what they believe).

In arriving at her decision Justice Abella did not think it necessary to address the issue of 'whether Loyola itself, as a corporation, enjoys the benefit of s. 2(a) rights, since the Minister is bound […] to exercise her discretion in a way that respects the values underlying the grant of her decision-making authority, including the *Charter*-protected religious freedom of the members of the Loyola community' (34). The court's failure to address the communal rights of Loyola was a missed opportunity to clarify the religious freedom rights of religious communities distinct from those of the community's individual members.

As noted earlier, there is confusion about the extent of religious communal rights in Canadian law. It is surprising that Abella, who expressed such strong support for communal rights in the *Hutterian Brethren* decision, would not capitalize on this opportunity. Instead, her reasoning is less enthusiastic towards religious communities. Now she expects them to set aside their religious views for 'national values'. A preview of her thinking on 'national values' came during oral argument when she asked Loyola's counsel, 'Is any religion's view of its own ethical framework to be held to be secure from the obligation to teach this course? Does it matter for instance if the particular religion teaches an ethical framework which contradicts what we have said about the *Charter*, if it has views that are fundamentally opposed to what we consider national values?' (*Loyola* Transcript 2014, 7, ll. 16–22).

While state neutrality permits religious pluralism, she says, that 'does not mean that religious differences trump core national values' (para 46). In her words, 'These shared values – equality, human rights and democracy – are values the state always has a legitimate interest in promoting and protecting. They enhance the conditions for integration and points of civic solidarity by helping connect us despite our differences' (para 47). Meanwhile, 'religious freedom must therefore be understood in the context of a secular, multicultural and democratic society with a strong interest in protecting dignity and diversity, promoting equality, and ensuring the vitality of a common belief in human rights' (ibid.). Abella then noted that the state 'has a legitimate interest in ensuring that students in *all* schools are capable, as adults, of conducting themselves with openness and respect as they confront cultural and religious differences' (para 48, emphasis original).

One does not have to think too hard to find scenarios where 'national values' may be at odds with long-held and long-understood religious norms. This is especially true when we consider the struggle that religious communities face when hiring or firing individuals who do not share their religious norms; or, as seen in the TWU law school case, when religious communities wish to maintain certain standards of behaviour for members of a church or students at a religious school. 'National values' of 'equality' and 'human rights' can be used by the courts to force such communities to hire those who do not subscribe to the beliefs of the religious employer; or to accept those who want to attend religious schools or universities yet oppose religious teachings. While there are exemptions for religious communities in human rights legislation, we now know, as in the TWU law school case, the courts are prepared to ignore such protections. Ironically, in the name of diversity, everyone must accept the court's ideology of what 'diversity' means.

For Justice Abella, these 'values' enhance 'integration' and 'civic solidarity' by ensuring that we connect despite our differences. There can be no doubting that a multicultural society needs to have means of creating a civic understanding of mutual responsibilities. Religious communities, by their nature, tend to be absolutist in their truth claims – as Loyola demonstrated. However, that is increasingly coming under scrutiny by a secular society that is intolerant of difference. Unfortunately, Abella's 'national values' do not seem to include respect for each other's differences, even though we may subscribe to mutually exclusive religious understandings. Rather, these national values appear to advocate for a syncretization of views with the state. The irony is that Abella appears to be saying that respecting diversity means we must all agree with the state's 'national values'. Hardly diverse. That is not liberal democracy – at least not what we once understood as such.

In a very strange twist, it was Chief Justice McLachlin (along with Justice Moldaver) who came out supporting communal rights to religious freedom. Given McLachlin's appalling lack of support for the Hutterian Brethren community's religious freedom, her apparent change of heart was notable. Unfortunately, her later decision in the TWU cases showed that such a change of heart was short-lived indeed.

McLachlin and Moldaver JJ held that Loyola could rely on the right of religious freedom. They asserted, 'The communal character of religion means that protecting the religious freedom of individuals requires protecting the religious freedom of religious organizations, including religious educational bodies such as Loyola. Canadian and international jurisprudence supports this conclusion' (para 91). They referenced Abella and LeBel in *Hutterian Brethren* and noted that 'the individual and collective aspects of freedom of religion are indissolubly intertwined. The freedom of religion of individuals cannot flourish without freedom of religion for the organizations through which those individuals express their religious practices and through which they transmit their faith' (para 94). In their view it resembles freedom of expression, freedom from unreasonable search and seizure and trial within a reasonable time which applies to corporations (ibid.).

The dissenting judges further emphasized the fact that international human rights instruments recognize the communal character of religion, such as Article 18 of the Universal Declaration of Human Rights (1948), Article 9 of the European Convention on Human Rights and Article 18 of the International Covenant on Civil and Political Rights. They point out, since the Charter should be presumed to have the same level of protection as found in the international human rights documents that Canada has ratified, 'it follows that the collective aspect of freedom of religion should find protection under the *Charter*' (para 97).

McLachlin and Moldaver 'conclude that an organization meets the requirements for s. 2(a) protection if (1) it is constituted primarily for religious purposes, and (2) its operation accords with these religious purposes' (para 100). After finding that Loyola met these requirements, they held that Loyola's right was infringed by Quebec and that it was not reasonable. They would not require, as did the majority, that the matter go back to the government ministry for re-evaluation but would grant Loyola the remedy of overturning the government's decision and the exemption it requested.

Given the favourable *Loyola* decision, there was, within the religious communities, a sense of optimism that finally the SCC was open to recognizing and articulating the boundaries of the communal right of religious freedom. While the majority did not address the issue, as they deemed it unnecessary, they nevertheless recognized the communal aspects of the right. Further, McLachlin and Moldaver set forth a road map for a future court to establish the right on a more secure footing. The TWU law school case seemed to be the ideal case to deal with this issue. But, alas, it was not to be due to the political nature of the issue at hand.

Trinity Western University Law School Cases

I have written much on the TWU law school case (e.g. Bussey 2020, 2019, 2016–17, 2017a, 2017b, 2015, 2018a), which to my mind represents the lowest bar yet reached by the Canadian courts in their (mis)treatment of a religious community with politically unpopular beliefs. The legal profession, the Ontario judiciary and the SCC all proved unwilling to uphold the religious community's enumerated, constitutional right to religious freedom when that freedom came into perceived conflict with equality rights.[19]

The point of this review, then, is not to repeat what has already been said, but to focus specifically on the court's failure to address the collective rights of TWU as a religious institution. The court's inability to appreciate the complex nature of the religious community resulted in two decisions (*Law Society of British Columbia v. Trinity Western University*, 2018 SCC 32, [2018] 2 SCR 293, hereinafter *LSBC v. TWU*; and *Trinity Western University v. Law Society of Upper Canada*, 2018 SCC 33, [2018] 2 SCR 453) which trivialized the religious freedom rights of the university while upholding only a partial concept of human dignity.

TWU is an evangelical Christian university in Langley, British Columbia. In 2012 it put forth a proposal to the Federation of Law Societies of Canada for the first and only faith-based law school in Canada. Once the proposal arrived at the Federation, academics and professionals across the country raised opposition because of TWU's mandatory Community Covenant Agreement (CCA), which defined marriage as the union of one man and one woman. The CCA was deemed discriminatory against LGBTQ+ individuals who might want to apply to the law school. As a result, the Law Society of British Columbia, the Nova Scotia Barristers' Society and the Law Society of Upper Canada (now the Law Society of Ontario) all voted against accreditation, resulting in litigation. While courts in British Columbia and Nova Scotia ruled in favour of TWU, the courts in Ontario upheld the law society. Both the BC and ON cases were appealed to the SCC.

---

[19] It is worth noting that, in fact, religion is also an equality right under section 15 of the Charter; it is, therefore, misleading to characterize equality and religious freedom as somehow mutually exclusive.

With apparent disregard for enumerated Charter rights, provincial and federal human rights legislation and its own precedent, a divided SCC ruled in favour of the respective law societies. As in the *Loyola* case, the majority applied the *Doré* framework, using conveniently malleable 'Charter values' (over and against Charter rights) as a reference point in deferring to the law societies. Significantly, the court made an explicit connection from the *Hutterian Brethren* decision through *Loyola* to TWU, as the majority cited both cases as justification for its values-based analysis in *LSBC v. TWU* (para 57 and again in para 100).

Even worse, the SCC denied the obvious when it claimed: 'Far from controversial, these values are accepted principles of constitutional interpretation' (*LSBC v. TWU*, para 41). Such an assertion seems particularly baffling given the robust rejection of Charter values by the concurring and dissenting opinions in the decision (McLachlin CJC, para 115; Rowe J, paras 166–75; dissent of Côté and Brown JJ, paras 307–11), not to mention a swath of legal literature that exposes the discord over the doctrine (Macklin 2014; Harding and Knopff 2013; Benson 2008; Horner 2014). Indeed, some clear-sighted members of the bench at the Ontario Court of Appeal have observed that '*Charter* values lend themselves to subjective application because there is no doctrinal structure to guide their identification or application' (*Gehl v. Canada* 2017, para 79). This 'is particularly acute when *Charter* values are understood as competing with *Charter* rights' (ibid.; see also *E.T. v. Hamilton-Wentworth District School Board* 2017 at paras 103–4). It remains a pity that the Supreme Court has, to date, failed to acknowledge the disaster that its Charter values jurisprudence has become.

That disaster resulted in the court's rejection of the communal right of religious freedom. Remarkably, the court was willing to view the law society as 'the collective face of a profession' (per McLachlin CJ, concurring, para 140), but seemed unable to comprehend TWU as a 'collective person' or 'community of wills' in the sense portrayed by Bonhoeffer. Despite passing references to 'communal practice' (para 99; see also para 64), the SCC largely characterized religion as a matter of individual (rather than shared) belief. In fact, in his concurring reasons, Justice Rowe explicitly rejected the argument that TWU, as a community, possessed any religious freedom rights at all. Instead, he insisted:

> While acknowledging this communal aspect, I underscore that religious freedom is premised on the personal volition of individual believers. Although religious communities may adopt their own rules and membership requirements, the foundation of the community remains the voluntary choice of individual believers to join together on the basis of their common faith. Therefore, in the context of this appeal, I would decline to find that TWU, as an institution, possesses rights under s. 2 (*a*). I note that, even if TWU did possess such rights, these would not extend beyond those held by the individual members of the faith community. (*LSBC v. TWU*, per Justice Rowe, concurring, para 219)

By characterizing the case as a 'conflict between the pursuit of statutory objectives and *individual* freedoms' (100, emphasis added), the SCC was able to conclude that denying approval of the law school was not 'a serious limitation on the religious rights of members of the TWU community' since 'no evangelical Christian is denied the right to practise his or her religion as and where they choose' (para 102). The fact that the institution would be unable to operate according to its religious principles was of 'minor significance' (paras 87 and 104). In essence, Justice Rowe was saying that there can be no such thing as a Christian university, only Christians at a university that conforms to 'national values' or 'Charter values', with whatever relics of the Christian heritage the state permits to be retained.

Importantly, dissenting Justices Brown and Côté came to the opposite conclusion after acknowledging a much richer view of religion. While they, too, avoided the question of institutional religious freedom rights, they argued astutely that 'ensuring full protection for the "constitutionally protected communal aspects of … religious beliefs and practice" requires more than simply aggregating individual rights claims under the amorphous umbrella of an institution's "community"' (para 316). Brown and Côté cited Dwight Newman's observation that religion is 'not just about individuals praying alone but about *communities* of faith living out their traditions and religious lives' (Newman 2016, 9, emphasis added). In their view, then, the law societies' decision to withhold accreditation 'represents a profound interference with religious freedom: it is a measure that undermines the core character of a lawful religious institution and disrupts the *vitality of the TWU community*' (para 324, emphasis added).

The majority's struggle to accept the communal nature of religion also hampered its ability to perceive and protect the dignity of religious adherents. Hence, the SCC was emphatic about possible dignitary harm to members of the LGBTQ community while remaining silent on the prospect of any such harm to members of the religious community. The court should *at least* recognize a parallel between sexual identity claims and religious identity claims (see Newman 2018). The SCC took pains to explain that 'substantive equality […] prevents "the violation of essential human dignity and freedom" and "eliminate[s] any possibility of a person being treated in substance as 'less worthy' than others"' (para 95). The majority rejected TWU's commitment to 'treat all persons with dignity, respect, and equality, regardless of personal differences' (para 97, quoting the university's Community Covenant), insisting instead that 'LGBTQ students enrolled at TWU's law school may suffer harm to their dignity and self-worth, confidence and self-esteem, and may experience stigmatization and isolation' (para 98). Former Chief Justice McLachlin, in concurring reasons, further argued that 'the Covenant singles out LGBTQ people as less worthy of respect and dignity' (para 138).

Once again, only Justices Brown and Côté recognized that any appeal to dignity must consider both the dignity of LGBTQ students *and* that of the religious community. To maintain true secularism and pluralism, 'it is necessary to ensure that the dignity of *all members* of society is protected. "Tolerance", then, means forbearing, and allowing for difference. […] The "public interest", broadly understood, is therefore served by accommodating TWU's religious practices, including the Covenant' (*LSBC v. TWU*, para 334–35, emphasis added). Moreover, in their incisive refusal to rely on 'Charter values', Côté and Brown pointed out '*Charter* values like "equality", "justice", and "dignity" become mere rhetorical devices by which courts can give priority to particular moral judgments, under the guise of undefined "values", over other values and over

Charter rights themselves' (para 309). Their observation underscores the problematic use of 'dignity' by the majority, which resulted in a skewed application of the concept. Thus, as Greg Walsh astutely notes in Chapter 11 of this volume:

> Without the Court providing a definition of how it understands dignity, it was left simply to affirm [its] proposition as correct without being able to provide any further justification for its position. This meant it was unable to engage with the claim made by TWU that it could both require adherence to the Covenant and respect the dignity of LGBT students and the wider community especially considering the caring environment that TWU was dedicated to creating. (195)

In short, TWU simply wanted to expand its course offerings within a private, religious communal setting. As a religious community with enumerated constitutional rights to practice its faith without fear of reprisal, the university was also exempted from human rights legislation that respected its religious difference in a secular society. Moreover, TWU had already fought and won a similar case concerning its education degree at the SCC. Yet, it was ultimately denied its communal religious freedom due to the unpopularity of its moral teachings. In reality, Justice Abella's 'national values' in *Loyola* bore fruit in the TWU case. 'National values' (yet another confusing and pliable term along with 'Charter values') evidently do not respect or allow religious communities to hold divergent beliefs without facing real consequences in government licencing and accreditation – whether that be driver's licences or university accreditation. Such treatment, I suggest, denies individual dignity and the dignity of the religious community to fulfil its religious mission.

V. Human Dignity and the Relationship to Religious Communities

Dwight Newman (Chapter 6 in this volume) observes astutely that academic parlance on dignity in human rights discourse is evolving from the inherent dignity of the human person towards a more ubiquitous use of the term for other legal contexts. Dignity, as a human rights concept, was highly influenced by natural law and theological reflections arising from religion. However, as Newman reports, there has been a spiralling away from these 'original conceptions' resulting in the modern human rights framework becoming 'a theological usurper' of sorts (94).

Newman's concern is the application of dignity to communities of people rather than individuals. He rightly points out that 'there is very little explicit attention to what concepts of group dignity might mean or whether such usages of the concept are coherent or appropriate' (96). Newman is not convinced that group claims to agency, self-determination or group recognition imply that groups have a claim to dignity. He argues that dignity must be narrowly defined to the inherent worth of the individual. He accepts that groups have value for their contribution to individual lives and that such groups would be difficult to replace for those individuals (98). But the fact that groups may be modified to better serve individuals is an admission, says Newman, that groups have no inherent dignity (100).

First, Newman is a purist in his definition of 'dignity'. He prefers a 'rigorous concept of dignity' reserved for the inherent worth of individuals, not groups. To apply it to groups is to read down the rigorous meaning for the individual and undermine 'protection of the inherent worth of the human person' (99). It is a confounding of two different conceptualizations creating confusion.

Second, to allow the term 'dignity' to be malleable to different circumstances contradicts 'any assumption that it expresses an objective moral truth' (ibid.). International instruments with the term 'dignity' will lose their objective authority when the term is subjectively applied to different constructs such as 'group dignity'.

Third, he maintains that the 'rigorous concept of dignity'[20] maintains an egalitarian emphasis on the individual. But if dignity is applied to groups, then 'there is an overlay of a different set of egalitarian claims on top of the basic equality with which we started. And that will ultimately threaten the basic equality that can properly be associated with the rigorous concept of dignity' (100).

Newman's concern about legal terms losing their articulate and robust original meaning is valid, especially in light of activist elements in the human rights context that advocate for changes in the meaning of terms to suit their public policy goals. Perhaps the most obvious example is the term 'marriage'.[21] Another, more recent example of this is the controversial use of 'Charter values' as noted earlier. Lawyers, forever creative in rhetoric and reason, push and shove a term into a space where it would not normally fit. 'Dignity' appears, according to Newman, to be facing a similar fate.

If Newman is correct in his assessment that applying 'dignity' to groups means the inherent worth of the irreplaceable human being is compromised, then we have cause to worry. To support the need for conceptual clarity in human rights, it is important to recognize that the argument I make is not to say that a group has inherent dignity in the sense of the inherent dignity of the individual, which would read down or take away from the individual's dignity. Rather, what I am proposing arises *out of* the inherent dignity of the individual.

My proposal is, therefore, part and parcel of recognizing and affirming the individual's inherent worth and dignity. It is also supported by the work of Haidt and Durkheim showing that religious community forms a vital part of an individual's identity. And it is on that basis that respect is due to the religious community. This includes legal recognition of communal rights, including the right of a religious community to establish and maintain its beliefs and to expel those who no longer wish to abide by the religious group's moral teachings. The religious community, as noted in Bonhoeffer's work discussed earlier, has formulated its own sense of identity and membership expectations.

---

[20] Meaning, in this case, the 'inherent worth of irreplaceable individuated human persons'.

[21] See *Reference re Same-Sex Marriage* (2004): 'Canada is a pluralistic society. Marriage, from the perspective of the state, is a civil institution. The "frozen concepts" reasoning runs contrary to one of the most fundamental principles of Canadian constitutional interpretation: that our Constitution is a living tree which, by way of progressive interpretation, accommodates and addresses the realities of modern life' (para 22).

The law, it seems to me, must recognize the unique status of religious communities as part of, not in addition to, the inherent worth and dignity of the individual. Only rarely do we see this expressed in the jurisprudence of the world's courts. One of those rare occasions was when Justice Albie Sachs, writing for the Constitutional Court of South Africa, stated:

> Freedom of religion goes beyond protecting the inviolability of the individual conscience. For many believers, their relationship with God or creation is central to all their activities. It concerns their capacity to relate in an intensely meaningful fashion to their sense of themselves, their community and their universe. For millions in all walks of life, religion provides support and nurture and a framework for individual and social stability and growth. *Religious belief has the capacity to awake concepts of self-worth and human dignity which form the cornerstone of human rights. It affects the believer's view of society and founds the distinction between right and wrong. It expresses itself in the affirmation and continuity of powerful traditions that frequently have an ancient character transcending historical epochs and national boundaries.* (*Christian Education South Africa v. Minister of Education* 2000, para 36, emphasis added)

In this passage it is important to note the communal aspects of religious freedom. The principled reason for this is that the accommodation accorded to persons makes little sense if it is not also accorded to groups. Failing to protect the group, in addition to depriving groups of any recognition when it is clear that their associational dimension is important to society, also robs the person of the collective and associational dimension of the right. With respect to religion, this collective dimension of 'communion' (the root concept within our term 'community') is a core aspect of the religion chosen by the individual. It goes to the centre of their individuality.[22]

I suggest the communal right is not the aggregate of individual members' rights but a right of the religious community as such. If the religious freedom of groups was simply an aggregate of members' rights, then it would mean that a greater latitude would be given to 'state intervention into the internal affairs of such groups since the focus would be vindicating individuals and their interests, not the group and its interests' (Ahdar and Leigh 2013, 375–76). But keep in mind that this group right is an element of the inherent worth and dignity of the individual to choose to be part of the religious community. It is a religious freedom right of a religious group, as Julian Rivers notes: 'Collective religious liberty in this sense is the liberty of a community of people sharing a common religious faith to organize themselves and structure their corporate life according to their own ethical and religious precepts' (2001, 231).[23]

It is true that the group is made up of individuals, but we are talking about a group of individuals of one mind. Of course, not everyone will agree, as in Bonhoeffer's discussion on the church. However, the church, the religious organization, the religious community

---

[22] Note that an earlier form of this paragraph was originally published in Bussey (2018b, 211).
[23] See also Iuliano, who suggests that when aggregations of people display mutual awareness and rational unity, being the performative core of personhood, then such aggregations 'should be conceived of as persons in their own right' (2015, 87).

as a group of individuals, has the right to decide the group's fate. It is not up to any one individual or subgroup of the organization to decide, with the assistance of the state, to force its view and/or practices on the group. The group has integrity in and of itself, and the law ought to respect its self-determination.

Therefore, the religious community is to determine and administer its own internal religious affairs without state interference. And, indeed, Canadian courts are reluctant to interfere with decisions made by religious groups unless they violate legal and proprietary right (for Ogilvie's seven principles by which courts have been guided in deciding to intervene in church matters, see Ogilvie 2010, 219–20; see also *Wall* 2018).

Religious organizations may also exercise moral authority over their members. That is to say, who can and cannot be a member; and what rules of conduct members are expected to comply with to maintain their membership. Section 27 of the Canadian Charter preserves the multicultural heritage of Canada defined as 'various ways of life […] rooted in the authentic life of a people seen as a community bound together by pervasive traditions and moral ties' (Brotz 1980, 41–42).

David Novak aptly describes this concept of moral authority being part of collective religious freedom:

> Freedom of religion is my right to be a member or not to be a member of a religious community, and thus freely submit myself to its moral authority. However, freedom of religion becomes what could be called an 'empty right' if the religious community I freely choose to join does not have the liberty to morally govern me and my fellow community members. Therefore, my right of religious freedom presupposes the communal right of a religious community to exercise its moral authority. That moral authority is its liberty. (2009, 88)

Notice how Novak aptly frames the communal right to the individual's choice: 'My right of religious freedom presupposes the communal right of a religious community to exercise its moral authority'. The inherent worth and dignity of the individual human being means I have the right to limit my personal freedom and make that subject to the will of the religious community. However, I also reserve the right to withdraw from that religious community on my own volition.

VI. Conclusion

In this chapter I argued that religious freedom is more inclusive than solely an individual liberty. It has a communal component. The communal aspect of religious freedom is not due to the fact that the community has an inherent dignity claim similar to the inherent worth of the individual referenced in the international human rights instruments. I accept the warning of Dwight Newman not to conflate 'group dignity' with 'dignity' of the individual. What I suggest is that there is within the concept of the dignity of the individual a component that finds expression in community. In other words, recognizing communal rights is indeed a recognition of human dignity in a fuller sense.

Part of my reasoning for this position flows from the work of Jonathan Haidt, who has argued that within human nature there is a prominent individual domain and communal domain. He has suggested that we are, as a species, 90 per cent 'chimp' and 10 per cent 'hive'. We live our lives more for ourselves, or, as I suggest, *sola singula*, than we do communally. Haidt observes, building on the work of Emile Durkheim, that we also desire something beyond ourselves, seeking a communal experience in the same way that a bee belongs in a hive. This is significant, in my view, because it helps explain our 'groupishness'.

Durkheim saw religion as a civilizing force. Indeed, recent scholarship has also concluded that humankind's evolutionary destiny involves a spiritual element. Scott Atran states, 'No other mode of thought and behavior deals routinely and comprehensively with the moral and existential dilemmas that panhuman emotions and cognitions force on human awareness and social life, such as death and deception. As long as people share hope beyond reason, religion will persevere' (2002, 280).

Unfortunately, the Canadian law has not seen fit to fully recognize or address the communal aspect of human dignity in the religious context. There yet remains a myopic focus on the 'chimp' nature of humanness rather than the 'hive' nature. Religious community forms part of the individual desire to go beyond oneself. It has always been with us and will remain so. Religious community, therefore, must be recognized for what it is: part of the inherent worth and dignity of the irreplaceable human being. It is through that dignity lens that religious community can finally receive the focus in the law that it is due.

References

Ackerman, Bruce. 1980. *Justice in the Liberal State*. New Haven, CT: Yale University Press.

Ahdar, Rex, and Ian Leigh, eds. 2013. *Religious Freedom in the Liberal State*, 2nd ed. Oxford: Oxford University Press.

Alberta v. Hutterian Brethren of Wilson Colony, 2009 SCC 37 (CanLII), [2009] 2 SCR 567. Retrieved 20 April 2020. http://canlii.ca/t/24rr4.

Andrews v. Law Society of British Columbia, 1986 2 B.C.L.R. 305, 27 D.L.R. (4th) 600, [1986] 4 W.W.R. 474.

Andrews v. Law Society of British Columbia, 1989 CanLII 2 (SCC), [1989] 1 SCR 143.

Aristotle. 1944. *Aristotle in 23 Volumes*, vol. 21, *Politics*. Translated by H. Rackham. Cambridge, MA: Harvard University Press. *Perseus Digital Library*. Book 1, section 1253a. Retrieved 25 April 2020. http://www.perseus.tufts.edu/hopper/text?doc=Perseus:text:1999.01.0058:book=1:section=1253a.

Atran, Scott. 2002. *In Gods We Trust: The Evolutionary Landscape of Religion*. Oxford: Oxford University Press.

Benson, Iain T. 2008. 'Do "Values" Mean Anything at All? Implications for Law, Education and Society'. *Journal for Juridical Science* 33, no. 1: 1–22.

Bonhoeffer, Dietrich. 1998. *Dietrich Bonhoeffer Works*. Vol. 1, *Sanctorum Communio*. Minneapolis, MN: Fortress.

Boucher v. R., 1950 CanLII 2 (SCC), [1951] SCR 265.

Brotz, Howard. 1980. 'Multiculturalism in Canada: A Muddle'. *Canadian Public Policy* 6, no. 1: 41–46.

Bussey, Barry W. 2015. 'Space Enough for a Christian Law School'. *Oxford Journal of Law and Religion* 4, no. 2: 303–7. https://www.academia.edu/12531774/Space_Enough_for_a_Christian_Law_School.

———. 2016–17. 'Rights Inflation: Attempts to Redefine Marriage and the Freedom of Religion: The Case of Trinity Western University School of Law'. *Regent University Law Review* 29, no. 2: 197–257. https://papers.ssrn.com/abstract=2969788.

———. 2017a. 'The Charter Is Not a Blueprint for Moral Conformity'. *Supreme Court Law Review* 79: 367–414. https://papers.ssrn.com/abstract=3032525.

———. 2017b. 'The Legal Revolution against the Place of Religion: The Case of Trinity Western University Law School'. *Brigham Young University Law Review* 2016, no. 4: 1127–213. https://ssrn.com/abstract=2951912.

———. 2018a. 'Law Matters but Politics Matter More: The Supreme Court of Canada and Trinity Western University'. *Oxford Journal of Law and Religion* 7, no. 3: 559–68. https://doi.org/10.1093/ojlr/rwy046.

———. 2018b. 'The Right of Religious Hospitals to Refuse Physician-Assisted Suicide'. *Supreme Court Law Review* 85: 189–223.

———. 2019. 'The Law of Intervention after the TWU Law School Case: Is Justice Seen to Be Done?' *Supreme Court Law Review* 90: 265–96. https://ssrn.com/abstract=3381257.

———. 2020. 'Making Registered Charitable Status of Religious Organizations Subject to 'Charter Values'. In *The Status of Religion and the Public Benefit in Charity Law*, edited by Barry W. Bussey, 159–203. London: Anthem.

Christian Education South Africa v. Minister of Education, 2000 (4) SA 757 (CC).

Chiu, Raymond. 2020. 'Religion and Public Benefit'. In *The Status of Religion and the Public Benefit in Charity Law*, edited by Barry W. Bussey, 23–36. London: Anthem.

DailyMail.com Reporter. 2017. 'Canadian Elementary School Teachers Attend "LGGBDTTTIQQAAPP" Inclusiveness Training Session: Would You Understand the Title?' Accessed 17 April 2020. https://archive.is/kZBXu.

Doré v. Barreau du Québec, 2012 SCC 12 (CanLII), [2012] 1 SCR 395. Retrieved 22 April 2020. http://canlii.ca/t/fqn88.

Durkheim, Emile. 1964 [1915]. *The Elementary Forms of the Religious Life*, 5th ed. Translated by Joseph Ward Swain. London: George Allen & Unwin Ltd. https://ia802700.us.archive.org/4/items/elementaryformso00durkrich/elementaryformso00durkrich.pdf.

E.T. v. Hamilton-Wentworth District School Board, 2017 ONCA 893.

European Convention on Human Rights. 213 U.N.T.S. 221.

Evon, Dan. 2017. 'Is This "LGGBDTTTIQQAAPP" Inclusiveness Training Session Flyer Real?' Accessed 17 April 2020. https://www.snopes.com/fact-check/lggbdtttiqqaapp-lgbt-inclusiveness-training-flyer/.

Farrell, Henry, and Abraham Newman. 2020. 'Will the Coronavirus End Globalization as We Know It? The Pandemic Is Exposing Market Vulnerabilities No One Knew Existed'. *Foreign Affairs*, 16 March 2020. https://www.foreignaffairs.com/articles/2020-03-16/will-coronavirus-end-globalization-we-know-it.

Freyer, Hans. 1923. *Theorie des objektiven Geistes*. Berlin: Verleg und Druck Von B. G. Teubner. https://archive.org/details/theoriedesobjekt00frey/mode/2up.

Gamwell, Franklin I. 1982. 'Religion and the Public Purpose'. *Journal of Religion* 62, no. 3: 272–88.

Gehl v. Canada (Attorney General), [2017] O.J. No. 1943, 2017 ONCA 319.

Haidt, Jonathan. 2012. *The Righteous Mind: Why Good People Are Divided by Politics and Religion*. New York: Pantheon Books.

Harding, Mark S., and Rainer Knopff. 2013. 'Constitutionalizing Everything: The Role of "Charter Values"'. *Review of Constitutional Studies* 18, no. 2: 141–60.

Highwood Congregation of Jehovah's Witnesses (Judicial Committee) v. Wall, 2018 SCC 26 (CanLII), [2018] 1 SCR 750. Retrieved 21 April 2020 [*Wall*]. http://canlii.ca/t/hs9lr.

Horner, Matthew. 2014. 'Charter Values: The Uncanny Valley of Canadian Constitutionalism'. *Supreme Court Law Review: Osgoode's Annual Constitutional Cases Conference* 67.

Inglehart, Ronald F., and Pippa Norris. 2016. 'Trump, Brexit, and the Rise of Populism: Economic Have-Nots and Cultural Backlash'. HKS Working Paper no. RWP16-026. https://ssrn.com/abstract=2818659 or http://dx.doi.org/10.2139/ssrn.2818659.

International Covenant on Civil and Political Rights, 999 U.N.T.S. 171. GA Res 2200A (XXI), UN GAOR, 21st Sess, Supp no. 16, UN Doc A/6316, 16 December 1966.

Irwin, Neil. 2020. 'It's the End of the World Economy as We Know It – Experts Suggest There Will be "a Rethink of How Much Any Country Wants to be Reliant on Any Other Country"'. *New York Times*, 16 April 2020. https://www.nytimes.com/2020/04/16/upshot/world-economy-restructuring-coronavirus.html.

Iuliano, Jason. 2015. 'Do Corporations Have Religious Beliefs'. *Indiana Law Journal* 90, no. 1: 47–99.

Law Society of British Columbia v. Trinity Western University, 2018 SCC 32 (CanLII), [2018] 2 SCR 293. Retrieved 20 April 2020. http://canlii.ca/t/hsjpr.

Litwin, Fred. 2016. 'Not My Rights Movement'. *Convivium*. Accessed 21 April 2020. https://www.convivium.ca/articles/not-my-rights-movement.

Looney, Sarah. 2017. 'Breaking Point? An Examination of the Politics of Othering in Brexit Britain'. TLI Think! Paper 69/2017. Available at SSRN: https://ssrn.com/abstract=3014638 or http://dx.doi.org/10.2139/ssrn.3014638.

Loyola High School v. Quebec (Attorney General), 2014 Transcript of oral hearing at the Supreme Court of Canada, 24 March. Transcript by www.stenotran.com.

Loyola High School v. Quebec (Attorney General), 2015 SCC 12 (CanLII), [2015] 1 SCR 613. Retrieved 21 April 2020. http://canlii.ca/t/ggrhf.

Macklin, Audrey. 2014. 'Charter Right or Charter-Lite? Administrative Discretion and the Charter'. In *Supreme Court Law Review: Osgoode's Annual Constitutional Cases Conference* 67, edited by J. Cameron, B. Berger and S. Lawrence, 561–88. Toronto: York University.

Metropolitan Church of Bessarabia and Others v. Moldova, no. 45701/99, ECHR 2001-XII.

Mouvement laïque québécois v. Saguenay (City), 2015 SCC 16 (CanLII), [2015] 2 SCR 3. Retrieved 21 April 2020. http://canlii.ca/t/gh67c.

Newman, Dwight. 2016. 'Ties That Bind: Religious Freedom and Communities'. S.C.L.R. (2d) 75: 3–20.

———. 2018. 'The Challenging Parallelism of Rights Claims Based on Religious Identity and on Sexual Identity'. In *Religious Liberty and the Law: Theistic and Non-Theistic Perspectives*, edited by Angus J. L. Menuge, 119–31. Milton Park: Routledge.

Noah, Trevor. 2017. 'Afraid of the Dark'. Netflix. Retrieved 17 April 2020. https://www.netflix.com/ca/title/80134969.

Novak, David. 2009. *In Defense of Religious Liberty*. Wilmington, DE: ISI Books.

Ogilvie, M. H. 2010. *Religious Institutions and the Law in Canada*. Toronto: Irwin Law.

Online Etymology Dictionary. 'Community'. Accessed 25 April 2020. https://www.etymonline.com/word/community.

Perry, Michael J. 1989. 'Neutral Politics'. *The Review of Politics* 51, no. 4 (Autumn): 479–509.

R. v. Edwards Books and Art Ltd., 1986 CanLII 12 (SCC), [1986] 2 SCR 713. Retrieved 22 April 2020. http://canlii.ca/t/1ftpt.

Reference re Same-Sex Marriage, 2004 SCC 79 (CanLII), [2004] 3 SCR 698. Retrieved 29 April 2020. http://canlii.ca/t/1jdhv.

Rivers, Julian. 2001. 'Religious Liberty as a Collective Right'. In *Law and Religion: Current Legal Issues*, vol. 4, edited by Richard O'Dair and Andrew Lewis, 227–46. Oxford: Oxford University Press.

von Soosten, Joachim. 1998. 'Editor's Afterword to the German Edition'. In *Sanctorum Communio*, by Dietrich Bonhoeffer. Minneapolis, MN: Fortress.

ten Napel, Hans-Martien. 2020. 'Wat was er eerder, de democratische recessie of de wederopleving van het populisme?' *Hans-Martien ten Napel* (website). https://hansmartientennapel.com/2020/04/20/wat-was-er-eerder-de-democratische-recessie-of-de-wederopleving-van-het-populisme/.

Trinity Western University v. Law Society of Upper Canada, 2018 SCC 33 (CanLII), [2018] 2 SCR 453. Retrieved 20 April 2020. http://canlii.ca/t/hsjpt.

Universal Declaration of Human Rights. 1948. G.A. Res. 217 A (III), U.N. Doc. A/810, at 71.

Walker, Neil. 2016. 'The Place of Territory in Citizenship'. Edinburgh School of Law Research Paper no. 2016/20. Forthcoming in Baubock, R., I. Bloemraad and A. Shachar, eds. *The Oxford Handbook of Citizenship*. Available at SSRN: https://ssrn.com/abstract=2849018 or http://dx.doi.org/10.2139/ssrn.2849018.

Wilson, David Sloan. 2002. *Darwin's Cathedral: Evolution, Religion, and the Nature of Society*. Chicago, IL: University of Chicago Press.

Chapter Nine

WHAT 'RULE OF LAW' PROGRAMS NEED IN THE TWENTY-FIRST CENTURY

Dallas K. Miller

I. Introduction and Rule of Law Background

With the collapse of communism and the end of the Cold War, the rule of law became a prominent plank in foreign aid platforms originating in the West. Rule of law training over the past 30 years has exploded, with the European Union, the United Kingdom and the United States leading the way. Major Western nations have included, as part of their foreign aid budgets, a rule of law component promising 'to move countries past the first, relatively easy phase of political and economic liberalization to a deeper level of reform' (Carothers 1998, 95).

The emphasis on rule of law training in the recent past coincides with the focus on 'dignity' in the legal academy and with foundational international documents. The Charter of the United Nations (1945) sought to avoid the 'scourge of war' by reaffirming faith in fundamental human rights and 'in the dignity and worth of the human person'. This was followed by the Universal Declaration of Human Rights (UDHR 1948) which begins with the 'recognition of the inherent dignity [...] of all members of the human family' being foundational to freedom, justice and the rule of law. The UDHR emphasis on dignity makes it a foundational term and concept for any international rule of law analysis.

Other foundational international legal documents include Article 3 of the Geneva Conventions, Article 7 of the International Covenant on Civil and Political Rights (ICCPR 1966) and certain provisions of the European Convention on Human Rights, all of which emphasize dignity in the context of human rights and rule of law. Yet, scholars have struggled with the meaning of dignity in the international legal context, particularly since the Cold War seemed to take the focus off a robust articulation of the term. The repeated and early assertion of the word was not sufficient. Indeed, repeated use of a term without proper development can cause it to become a platitude without significant content or meaning. Fortunately, legal scholars have shown how international law can use the concept of human dignity to better recognize, promote and protect both the rule of law and human rights. An example of this is Jeremy Waldron, who gave the 2011 Sir David Williams Lecture at the University of Cambridge. In giving meaning to the term 'dignity', he presented this fulsome description:

> Dignity is the status of a person predicated on the fact that she is recognized as having the ability to control and regulate her actions in accordance with her own apprehension of norms and reasons that apply to her: it assumes she is capable of giving and entitled to give an account of herself (and of the way in which she is regulating her actions and organizing her life), an account that others are to pay attention to; and it means finally that she has the wherewithal to demand that her agency and her presence among us as a human being be taken seriously and accommodated in the lives of others, in others' attitudes and actions towards her, and in social life generally. (Waldron 2012, 202)

After two decades of the rule of law being the focus of foreign aid and attempts at building justice systems in the former Soviet bloc, leaders in the legal community began concentrating their efforts in a more tangible way. The World Justice Project, founded in 2006, applies a multidisciplinary approach to reducing corruption, eliminating human rights abuses and providing a more natural governance model based on the rule of law. The instrument developed by the World Justice Project is the rule of law index, using eight categories to measure how the rule of law is actually experienced in practical, everyday situations: constraints on government powers, absence of corruption, open government, fundamental rights, order and security, regulatory enforcement, civil justice and criminal justice. All categories are essential, but two are absolutely key to the advancement of rule of law and human rights protection: governmental constraints and fundamental rights. Prominent on this list and foundational for any advancement of human rights generally are freedom of opinion and expression, freedom of belief and religion, and freedom of assembly and association (World Justice Project 2017–18).

For nations emerging from communist control or colonial rule, these two categories – constraints on government power and protection of fundamental rights – are particularly vital when it comes to correcting dysfunctional or failed justice systems (see, e.g., Haugen 2014, 172). Efforts to assist these countries are, in fact, supported by a rule of law approach that is backed by a dignity focus. Dignity-infused rights protections, along with substantive and procedural due process and allowance for legal argument and professional legal representation, could not exist if dignity did not play a key role in rule of law advancement. Indeed, a holistic approach to rule of law could not occur without dignity playing a key part:

> Once we accept that human dignity requires litigants to be heard, the justification of the advocate becomes clear. People may be poor public speakers. They may be inarticulate, unlettered, mentally disorganized, or just plain stupid. They may know nothing of the law, and so be unable to argue its interpretation. Knowing no law, they may omit the very facts that make their case, or focus on pieces of the story that are irrelevant or prejudicial. They may be unable to utilize basic procedural rights such as objecting to their adversary's leading questions. Their voices may be nails on a chalkboard or too mumbled to understand. They may speak a dialect, or for that matter know no English. None of this should matter. Human dignity does not depend on whether one is stupid or smooth. Hence the need for the advocate. (Luban 2005, 819)

Rule of law advancement and attempts to bring structural change to failed legal systems coincide with the recent legal approach to human dignity. Giving someone the 'right to be heard' or to have appropriate legal representation and be able to answer the case against one is part of giving that person dignity or treating her with dignity in the legal process. It is also part of building a rule-based justice system. Law protects dignity by protecting human rights, providing a forum for legal advocacy and treating individuals as dignified human agents. This is what rule of law programs do (Waldron 2012, 204–16).

One of the most insightful works in this area is the 2010 bestseller by Tom Bingham entitled *The Rule of Law*. In this work, Bingham seeks to provide a comprehensive analysis and guide for the application of international rule of law. Within the text he interacts with historic British constitutional principles, plus international law principles as well as the constitutional experience of the United States. The work is seen as a template for a rule of law paradigm that can be used in emerging states as they seek to develop a system of justice that makes a nation secure, but respects and protects rights and holds government to account.

The purpose of this chapter is to provide a mild critique of Bingham's work due to a significant omission. My criticism could be categorized as obtuse or minor, but it does appear that in at least one area – that of international religious freedom – Bingham's work is not as comprehensive as it could be. As well, he seems to understate the value of this fundamental human right. Since he also neglects to focus on dignity, there may very well be a connection between the two omissions.

II. Tom Bingham – Biographical Sketch

Thomas Henry Bingham, or Baron Bingham of Cornhill, was the second child born in 1933 to a dentist and her physician husband. At age 7, Tom was enrolled at Hawthorns, an all-boys preparatory school outside of London, and from there went to Sedbergh School, set in a beautiful part of Cumbria. A gifted student, he shone at his studies. He loved the countryside and excelled in fell running (cross-country) and received prizes for his poetry. He also had an appreciation for religious studies and at one time considered ordination.

Bingham spent two years in the national service, an entirely positive experience as he joined the Royal Ulster Rifles and served in Hong Kong. On scholarship to Oxford in 1954, he began a PPE (politics, philosophy and economics) program, later changing to a history concentration. During his studies he spent one summer on a Coolidge Fellowship and toured the United States, spending time at Civil War sites and observing court proceedings. His interest in the US system resulted in a major paper, 'Slavery and Secession (1850–1862)'.

Bingham's strong interest and academic background in history (especially constitutional documents) had him considering law before he finished his degree at Oxford. He was admitted to Gray's Inn as a student and began his dining in Hall (pupilage) over several terms. Without a formal law degree but based on keeping term at Gray's Inn, Bingham was called as a barrister and easily managed the bar admission course and exam. Between his Oxford studies and his work as a barrister, Bingham benefitted richly under the wise tutelage of Justice Finnemore, following him as a marshal (unpaid assistant) in the northern circuit, which gave him helpful exposure to the business of the court, both civil and criminal.

In 1959 Bingham passed the bar exams and went to a prestigious law firm, Gibson and Weldon. He served his 12-month pupilage and became a tenant in the barristers' chambers known as Fountain Court while the Head of Chambers was Leslie Scarman QC, who himself went on to be a distinguished member of the judiciary. As a barrister, Bingham quickly became known for his skill, appearing in a reported case early in his career. He took silk in 1972,[1] gained a domestic and international reputation as a premiere commercial litigator and acted as counsel for public inquiries covering important issues of his day.

In 1980 Tom Bingham was appointed by Lord Chancellor Hailsham as a Judge of the Queen's Bench, Commercial Division, at the age of 46 – young for a judicial appointment in the United Kingdom, but certainly he was at the top of his profession. After six years on the Queen's Bench division, he was elevated to the Court of Appeal. He enjoyed the collegiality and exchange of views on the appellate court. Towards the end of his term in the Court of Appeal, he was asked to conduct a public inquiry into the Bank of England's failed supervision of the Bank of Credit and Commerce International. Upon completing the public inquiry, he was made Master of the Rolls and then became Lord Chief Justice in 1996 and Senior Law Lord in the House of Lords in the year 2000.

Tom Bingham was likely the greatest English judge since World War II. He truly was in a category of his own, and cleverness is only part of the story. Early on in his life he developed talents for hard work, determination and self-discipline, which stood him in good stead throughout his career. He retained a Victorian attitude towards the number of hours required for him to achieve success. He possessed the capacity to persevere in disappointment. He did a commendable job in each important position that came his way, serving with integrity, judgement, courtesy and kindness. His work as a jurist both on and off the bench strengthened the rule of law in the United Kingdom. His focus on protecting the rule of law both domestically and internationally is well displayed in his final work, *The Rule of Law* (2010), published the year he died.

III. *The Rule of Law*

Tom Bingham's book had its genesis in the 2006 Sir David Williams Lecture at the University of Cambridge. Bingham chose as his subject the rule of law, as he felt the term needed explanation in light of its increased use in common parlance:

> I was not quite sure what it meant, and I was not sure that all those who used the expression knew what they meant either, or meant the same thing. In any event, I thought it would be

---

[1]   That is, he was awarded the honorary designation of Queen's Counsel (QC).

valuable to be made to think about the subject, the more so since the expression had recently, for the first time, been used in an Act of the British Parliament, described rather portentously as 'an existing constitutional principle'. (2010, vii)

Bingham accomplished a rare feat in writing a legal text that became a bestseller to a non-legal audience. It was chosen as 'book of the year' by three major newspapers in 2010 and was awarded the Orwell Prize for best political book in 2011. Part of the reason for its popularity and lucidity is that it was not written from an ivory tower academic perspective. Tom Bingham practiced and implemented the rule of law in his many experiences and opinions as a judge.

Reviewer Irving Stevens (2011) notes that Bingham did not set forth any grand statement of intent for the purpose of the book; rather, its strength lies in Bingham's simply embarking on publicly thinking about the rule of law. Through his clear writing style, he has forced the reader to do the same. The book was particularly timely in light of the language in certain acts of the British Parliament that referenced the rule of law, in the Lord Chancellor's new Oath of Office and in the Constitutional Reform Act of 2005. Stevens praises Bingham for articulating the rule of law as 'one of the greatest unifying factors, perhaps the greatest, the nearest we are likely to approach to a universal [secular] religion' (242). No doubt Bingham saw the headquarters or 'Vatican' of that religion to be the United Kingdom, as evidenced by his mining of British history going back to the 1215 Magna Carta.

Stephen Sedley (2010), a Lord Justice of the appeal court, in a review of Bingham's book in the *Guardian*, applauds him for wrestling with the definition of the rule of law, which is more than simply public administration and adjudication governed by duly enacted laws. In order to avoid the positivist dilemma that would prevent apartheid South Africa and Nazi Germany from coming under that definition, Sedley welcomes Bingham's grafting of a second key element – an irreducible list of basic human rights administered and adjudicated upon by impartial and independent courts.

In a solid philosophical critique of Bingham's argument, John Gardner (2010) in the *London Review of Books* commends Bingham for his erudition, patience and accessible style – rare qualities in legal writing. He applauds his 'thick' account of the rule of law, which requires respect and protection for human rights – not formally protected in the United Kingdom until legislation passed just before Bingham's published work. Although Gardner endorses Bingham's definition of rule of law, he is critical of Bingham's justification for it or the mode of reasoning used to achieve it. For example, he touches on the one clear, uncomfortable position of Bingham's – parliamentary sovereignty. Gardner posits that the rule of law and parliamentary sovereignty together require judges to disregard and thereby invalidate certain parliamentary provisions that prevent acts from entering law, but also that all acts of Parliament must enter the law. According to Gardner, the 'doctrine of parliamentary sovereignty' does not allow courts to invalidate statutes 'on human rights grounds' but it does on 'rule of law grounds' (15–16).

It may be that Bingham was guided more strongly by history than by critical analysis or logic. Bingham argues clearly for deferring to parliamentary sovereignty, asserting that 'the British people have not repelled the extraneous power of the papacy in spiritual matters and the pretensions of royal power in temporal in order to subject themselves to the unchallengeable rulings of unelected judges' (2010, 268).

Bingham uses a comparative and international law approach in his book. He also posits his work as a comprehensive theory. Reviewers and commentators of *The Rule of Law* are virtually unanimous in their praise for its clarity in style and content as well as its accessibility to the larger public outside of lawyers and legal academia. In his 2006 Cambridge lecture, Bingham starts off with the principle encapsulating the rule of law; that is, 'that all persons and authorities within the state, whether public or private, should be bound by and entitled to the benefit of laws publicly and prospectively promulgated and publicly administered in the courts'.

Part I of the book is a historical study of the rule of law. The strength in Bingham's book is in his laying out eight rules necessary in understanding the implications of the rule of law, each of which comprises a chapter in Part II:

(1) The law must be accessible and so far as possible intelligible, clear and predictable.
(2) Questions of legal right and liability should ordinarily be resolved by application of the law and not the exercise of discretion.
(3) The laws of the land should apply equally to all, save to the extent that objective differences justify differentiation.
(4) The law must afford adequate protection of fundamental human rights.
(5) Means must be provided for resolving, without prohibitive cost or an inordinate delay, bona fide civil disputes which the parties themselves are unable to resolve.
(6) Ministers and public officers at all levels must exercise the powers conferred on them reasonably, in good faith, for the purpose for which the powers were conferred and without exceeding the limits of such powers.
(7) Adjudicative procedures provided by the state should be fair.
(8) The rule of law requires compliance by the state with its obligations in international law, the law which, whether deriving from treaty or international custom and practice, governs the conduct of nations. (2010, 37–129)

The principles in Part II are the focus of this chapter's critique. These suggestions are made in terms of historic completeness. My criticisms are due to the unfolding of the international human rights problems in the twenty-first century. These problems have shown that Bingham's work is lacking an appropriate description of the fulsome human rights protection that includes the protection of international religious freedom.

IV. Critiques

A. Failure to Utilize Natural Law in Articulating the Rule of Law and the Need for Human Rights Protection

For a true rule of law program to operate, Bingham claims it must afford adequate protection for fundamental human rights. His assertion is correct, but he lacks clarity on his reason for this claim. He seems to avoid the issue of any foundational principles that will ground human rights in an absolute sense.

One can do no better than quote Mahatma Gandhi on the superiority of the British system to advance the rule of law:

> I discovered that the British Empire had certain ideals with which I have fallen in love, and one of those ideals is that every subject of the British Empire has the freest scope possible for his energies and honour and whatever he thinks is due his conscience. I think that this is true of the British Empire, as it is not true of any other Government [...] And I have found that it is possible for me to be governed least under the British Empire. Hence my loyalty to the British Empire. (1922, 22)

Unlike Gandhi, Bingham seems unusually timid to proclaim the advantages of the British historic strength on this issue. In fact, he allows Valery Zorkin, the Chairman of the Constitutional Court of the Russian Federation, to do the heavy lifting for him in a comparative analysis of various legal systems. Zorkin denies that law is simply what is dictated by political authority or state issue, and he considers the parallel development of Soviet Communism and German Nazism as substantiation. About the USSR under the influence of Stalinism, he says that, because 'the law was identified with statutory law, and law was identified with the will (or rather dictatorship) of the proletariat [...] whatever was prescribed by the state in the form of statutory law was lawful'. Hitler's approach, though antagonistic to communist ideology, still ended in the same result, for German law 'existed only as a body of statutory law' because it was 'an expression of the will of the German nation, and the will of the German nation was incorporated in the Führer'. Both systems killed millions because 'for both the law was given and contained in the statutes' (Bingham 2010, 67–68).

Bingham acknowledges that it is up to individual states to decide what rights to protect. However, couldn't this question-begging approach be used to support Nazi regimes and Soviet Gulags? The trials at Nuremberg would not have proceeded had we left it to 'states to decide what rights they would protect' (68), nor could we call Stalin's genocidal regime against the Ukraine what it actually was: genocide. If one has a solid, dignitarian view of the human person, one cannot leave to individual states the right to pick and choose what protections to afford. The stakes are far too high.

Bingham's approach seems to give too much latitude to the legal positivist. It also does not clearly assert that basic human rights standards are a form of natural law that must be defended on an epistemic basis. Bingham fails to acknowledge how, in the nineteenth century, legal positivists replaced natural law theory, which held that there was a higher standard outside of positive law and a basis on which positive law needed to be judged.

Bingham, in seeking to develop a rule of law theory, begins with an early positivist, A. V. Dicey, who popularized the notion that law is the command of the sovereign, giving wind to the sails of legal positivism that led to the gross human rights abuses of the twentieth century. Legal positivism was argued as the defence theory at the Nuremburg trials to resist the prosecutor's claim that there was a law above laws. Justice Robert Jackson, summing up at the Nuremburg tribunal, illustrates the problems with a positivist defence, insisting that the 'International Military Tribunal […] rises above the provincial and transient and seeks guidance not only from International Law but also from the basic principles of jurisprudence which are assumptions of civilization' (1948, 398).

Without a natural law approach, criticism of an apartheid South Africa or Amin's Uganda cannot be made by British jurists. Legal positivism by its very nature limits one's right to the confines of its own legal system. If no legal philosophy supersedes the nation state and overrides relativistic approaches to rights protection, we end up in a system where rights abuses occur without a philosophical basis on which to criticize or condemn them. Belgian legal philosopher Perelman describes this principle:

> This conception of juridical positivism collapses before the abuses of Hitlerism […] The universal reaction to the Nazi crimes forced the Allied chiefs of state to institute the Nuremberg trials and to interpret the adage *nullum crimen sine lege* in a nonpositivistic sense because the law violated in the case did not derive from a system of positive law but from the conscience of all civilized men. The conviction that it was impossible to leave these horrible crimes unpunished, although they fell outside a system of positive law, has prevailed over the positivistic conception of the grounding of the law. (1980, 47)

In seeking to justify the inclusion of fundamental human rights as an essential sub-rule, Bingham would have benefitted from an analysis by a contemporary, Jean Porter, who – through detailed analysis of political and legal scholars such as Mary Ellen O'Connell, Neil MacCormick and Ronald Dworkin – considered the authority of a state to both govern itself and assert international claims. Porter concludes her lengthy section, 'Authority Within and Beyond the State', with the work of Mary Ellen O'Connell, who references a 'higher law' or a 'natural law' that provides ultimate grounding for formal enactments in a legal system and basic human rights protections. The norms against genocide, apartheid, extrajudicial killing, slavery and torture have been held in the general principle of law articulated by the great jurists of classical Roman times and are generally understood to issue from reason inspired by the natural order. Such values as necessity, proportionality and good faith regulate enforcement measures. 'While most of international law is based on positive acts of consent', Porter asserts, 'ultimately the ontology and legitimacy of international law is based on more than consent, just as it is more than sanctions' (2010, 343).

Bingham ponders the dilemma of what rights should be included because there 'is no universal consensus on the rights and freedoms which are fundamental even among civilized nations' (2010, 68). Bingham equivocates too much on this topic, given the consensus on basic rights and freedoms. The UDHR spells out the essential rights included in many established democracies' bills of rights. Even if Bingham is correct in his belief that it is difficult to determine which rights are fundamental, legal theorists should not necessarily shy away from the task. Who else should address these difficult issues?

B. *Religious Freedom – a Modern Principle?*

Protecting human rights against government encroachment or abuse necessarily leads one to a natural rights theory. Human dignity also leads one to a justice system that closely relates to natural rights theory and, indeed, is dependent on it. One scholar has succinctly expressed the point:

> The theory that law must uphold human dignity is logically tied to the conception of political justice that rests upon natural rights. Natural rights theory, so formulates principles of law that regard each person as a moral agent whose life, liberty, and property may not be controlled by others. Government control, even of a democratic sort, is justified only if it protects and preserves the rights of life, liberty, and property. Although people sometimes try to vote them away, as if they were granted and revocable by society, government, or the state, these rights are inalienable, even when positive law disregards them. Thus, although slavery was sanctioned by positive law, it was immoral because persons are by nature free agents not slaves. (Machan 1977, 830)

The European Convention of Human Rights, as the basis of the Human Rights Act of 1998, states:

> Article 9 – Freedom of thought, conscience and religion
>
> (1) Everyone has the right to freedom of thought, conscience and religion; this right includes freedom to change his religion or belief and freedom, either alone or in community with others and in public or private, to manifest his religion or belief, in worship, teaching, practice and observance.
>
> (2) Freedom to manifest one's religion or beliefs shall be subject only to such limitations as are prescribed by law and are necessary in a democratic society in the interests of public safety, for the protection of public order, health or morals, or for the protection of the rights and freedoms of others.

Bingham seems to be gratified that religious freedom is now a modern, unquestioned value that has gotten past its 'chequered history' (2010, 77). He implies this is unique among the rights claims listed under this sub-rule. However, his assessment may be too simplistic a description of the history of freedom of thought, conscience and religion.

The rule of law requires the protection of fundamental rights such as freedom of belief and practice, but these rights cannot be absolute – a point Bingham takes great pains to emphasize. Individual religious rights claims must, according to Bingham, be balanced against the rights of others, necessitating the drawing of lines. He does not put these strict limitations on any of the other rights enumerated in this chapter. For instance, the right to a fair trial of an accused person is not balanced against the rights of victims or witnesses.

Bingham is noticeably uncomfortable with the religious liberty claims that may challenge the status quo in Britain. All extreme cases of unacceptable religious practices cited by Bingham are religious practices that are not historically British: human sacrifice; self-immolation of widows; female genital mutilation; polygamy; and other practices by Sikhs, Rastafarians and Muslims (77).

Bingham fails to elucidate the historic basis for religious freedom in the United Kingdom that gave rise to the First Amendment in the US Bill of Rights and the clear statement of religious liberty in Article 18 of the UDHR. He goes into great detail in historically showing how the judiciary evolved into an independent institution using seventeenth- and eighteenth-century controversies in England and the founding of the United States. But he fails to do any similar historic analysis regarding religious freedom. Examples of toleration and the granting of religious freedom in the seventeenth and eighteenth centuries are not mentioned by Bingham. Indeed, he fails to reference the seventeenth-century classical liberal thinker who was instrumental in developing this right: John Locke. Given Bingham's expertise in the history of jurisprudence, instead of a passing reference to the struggle of religious liberty as having a chequered history, one would have expected a more rigorous historic review of some of its foundational texts.

John Locke's writings, *Two Treatises of Government* (1689) and *A Letter Concerning Toleration* (1689), were published after the Glorious Revolution in England. Locke lived at a time when political absolutism and the wars of religion prevailed. Both these political realities helped make religious liberty what we now take for granted and what Bingham refers to as a chequered past.

Contrary to Hobbes, John Locke reasoned that society in a 'state of nature' has a basic moral law operating: human life must be protected so that people can fulfil their divine calling and serve their God. Both monarchical divine right and the all-powerful Leviathan state as postulated by Hobbes rob people of their consent. Locke was one of the first political theorists to offer a rational, moral and theological basis for consensual government. His theory worked out into a view of religious identity based on reason and not inheritance. One's religious faith is arrived at by reason, it is voluntary and meeting in a religious community is also voluntary. His firm belief in the need for humanity to have a relationship with God drove him to see that government had one central obligation: to protect the freedom of every individual to discover the truth about God and his moral demands. To Locke, preservation of a person's conscience from governmental coercion was so important that a government which fails to uphold and protect the natural right of religious freedom fails to do its job.

Locke wanted reform so that every person, regardless of religious identity, would receive the same civic freedom to pursue the dictates of conscience. Locke claimed that 'no issue was more consequential than the question of salvation, no political right was more important than the freedom to worship God without the threat of sanctions or violence'; hindering this freedom was 'a violation of an individual's natural rights' (Loconte 2014, 234).

Locke's work contributed to the Act of Toleration of 1689, which was foundational in protecting religious freedom in its modern context. The liberalism of Locke never really took hold to its fullest extent at the time but, almost one hundred years after his writings, the American founders richly benefitted when they established a nation completely rebuilt on the concept of religious freedom.

Bingham would have gained so much more had he focused on the key figures of the seventeenth and eighteenth centuries crucial to working out the principles underlying Article 9(1), as he did in his summary of judicial independence. His approach to religious liberty fails due to a lack of historic analysis.

C. Who Offends Religious Freedom?

Who offends a person's religious freedom? It is primarily the state. Bingham misses this point entirely. Most of his effort is spent on what could go wrong with too much religious freedom, such as the dangers of legislation and regulation and their application on terrorism suspects. He dedicates one chapter to terrorism and the rule of law and how courts can and should deal with terrorist suspects. The focus is not surprising given that he wrote many decisions relating to cases in the United Kingdom arising out of the war in Iraq.

His approach to religious freedom would have been enriched had he dealt with religious freedom as he did terrorism. What follows is an attempt to make Bingham's analysis of Article 9(1) stronger. It is clear in his analysis on terrorism that, in order for suspects' rights to be protected, the actions of the legislature and executive must be closely monitored by the courts. As well, courts must be courageous in upholding the rule of law and in protecting basic individual rights.

While expressing concern about religions and religious practices outside of Britain, his British-centric approach appears obvious and is a weakness. By citing some of the most egregious religious practices Bingham finds them completely unacceptable:

> A society such as ours could not countenance human sacrifice, or the self-immolation of widows on their husbands' funeral pyres, or female genital mutilation, however strongly those practices might be valued by those who follow other religions and traditions. In many countries of the world man may lawfully have several wives, but not here: one, at a time, is enough. (2010, 77)

It may have been helpful to examine fully the foundational statement on religious freedom in the UDHR and cite examples of where individuals require protection from infringement on rights articulated in Article 18:

> Everyone has the right to freedom of thought, conscience and religion; this right includes freedom to change his religion or belief, and freedom, either alone or in community with others and in public or private, to manifest his religion or belief in teaching, practice, worship and observance.

When one examines the wording in this article it is clear that it is drafted with the view that human beings have the right to be respected in this very important and intimate portion of their lives. Individuals are given a choice to believe and follow their religious community and, indeed, they are treated with such dignity that they are granted personal agency and autonomy such that they are free to change their religious community.

It seems that Bingham fails to grasp that government, or the state, is the main perpetrator in abusing religious freedom, just as it abuses the rights of suspected terrorists. He fails to take the same type of analysis in dealing with religious freedom abuses internationally.

D. *Religious Freedom – an International Crisis*

Bingham spends much time on the international rule of law in the context of terrorism, but he focuses only on religious freedom in a domestic context. As well, he neglects to connect the importance of religious liberty with rights of freedom of expression, assembly and association (Bingham 2010, 76–80). As I have argued elsewhere (Miller 2017, 70), widespread deprivation of rights makes it abundantly clear that serious human rights infringement by state authorities has, at its core, a complete denial of the right of freedom of thought, conscience and religion.

Studies examining religious freedom from the perspectives of government restrictions and social hostilities conclude that religious persecution is increasing internationally. The most recent study reveals that countries with 'high' or 'very high' levels of government restriction have risen to 28 per cent of the nations of the world; similarly, 27 per cent of nations have 'high' or 'very high' levels of social hostility towards religion. A contributing factor to this increase may be the rise of nationalism (Pew Research Center 2019, 4).

Statistics and graphs showing the increase of religious restrictions are noteworthy, but the enormity of the problem is best illustrated by examining one country: China. The *2017 Report on International Religious Freedom* estimates that hundreds of thousands of Uighur Muslims have been forcibly sent to re-education centres, and others have been repatriated, detained or killed, or have disappeared in China. This has prompted many Chinese Uighur Muslims to seek asylum on the grounds of religious persecution. The report records that China regularly imprisons people for their religious beliefs and fails even modestly to adhere to internationally recognized rights of religious freedom (US Department of State 2018, 2).

The rule of law message that Western nations seek to send to the Middle East and Asia is that they must adopt the liberal international order. A description of the liberal international order is the entire theme of Bingham's book. However, messages such as Bingham's are simply not getting through to nations like China, according to one specialist in foreign policy:

> American religious freedom policy has played only a small part in the grand strategy of liberating China. Chinese Communist religion policy has always constituted an assault on fundamental human rights. It has caused vast human suffering. It has consistently violated the rights of conscience; the right to be free of torture, unjust imprisonment, and other assaults on human dignity; and the right of religious freedom as laid out in international law, including Article 18 of the International Covenant on Civil and Political Rights (which China has signed but not ratified).

[…] The impoverished view of religious freedom as mere 'freedom to believe and worship' has taken hold among some in our foreign policy establishment, and [has] played a role in the highly rhetorical and largely ineffective international religious freedom diplomacy adopted by the State Department over the past two decades. It is difficult to mount an effective strategy to advance religious freedom in China, or anywhere else, if you believe that religious freedom entails primarily a private right of belief and worship, with no legitimate role for religion in public affairs. (Farr 2019, 5–7)

The neutral view articulated by Bingham makes it difficult to be overly critical of an international problem like religious freedom in China. This failure to have a robust and forceful position on international religious freedom is aided and abetted by the United Nations system, which one religious freedom expert describes as having become so capacious that countries with the most inhumane practices, such as North Korea's burning alive of political prisoners, brag about their human rights protections: 'The effort to secure basic freedoms in the form of civil and political rights has been diluted by the proliferation of human rights in the form of new treaties and expansive judicial interpretations' (Rhodes 2019, 10).

A clear, rights-based system focusing on primary fundamental freedoms, including religious freedom, is necessary for rule of law advancement internationally. The need in much of the world is great. The ability of the United Nations is limited and oftentimes a failure. Texts such as Bingham's *Rule of Law* would do much better if written with a more forceful religious freedom component covering international issues.

V. A Dignitarian Conclusion

Dignity is not something that Bingham explicitly deals with in his book, nor does he refer to it in other writings. In the area of religious freedom his work would have benefited by looking at this through the lens of dignity. Perhaps this omission is due to the cases he dealt with later in his career being the interaction between the courts and other branches of government and not specifically related to human rights. However, in other writings Bingham goes to great lengths in emphasizing that the law favours liberty and, by implication, the dignity of all human beings.

The learned jurist Aharon Barak wrote about the importance of judges giving content to vague constitutional concepts. Throughout his life, both on the bench and in his academic writing, Bingham has given content to the concept of *liberty*. His work would have been much stronger had he at least begun to give constitutional content to the emerging concept of dignity as a constitutional principle. Dignity has become a term that cries out for content as many constitutional courts throughout the world have struggled with it (Barak 2013, 363).

Simultaneous with Bingham's writings was the emergence of a strong academic interest in human dignity and its relationship to human rights in general. The jurisprudence of the European Court referenced by Bingham does not have human dignity in its foundational document, the European Convention on Human Rights. However, the jurisprudence of the court is replete with references to human dignity coming from the UDHR and the two UN international conventions (Costa 2013, 401).

According to *Kokkinakis v. Greece* ((1994) 17 EHRR 397, at para 31), one of the earliest decisions by the Strasbourg Court on Article 9 finds:

> As enshrined in Article 9 (art. 9), freedom of thought, conscience and religion is one of the foundations of a 'democratic society' within the meaning of the Convention. It is, in its religious dimension, one of the most vital elements that go to make up the identity of believers and their conception of life, but it is also a precious asset for atheists, agnostics, sceptics and the unconcerned. The pluralism indissociable from a democratic society, which has been dearly won over the centuries, depends on it.

> While religious freedom is primarily a matter of individual conscience, it also implies, inter alia, freedom to 'manifest [one's] religion'. Bearing witness in words and deeds is bound up with the existence of religious convictions.

> According to Article 9 (art. 9), freedom to manifest one's religion is not only exercisable in community with others, 'in public' and within the circle of those whose faith one shares, but can also be asserted 'alone' and 'in private'; furthermore, it includes in principle the right to try to convince one's neighbour, for example through 'teaching', failing which, moreover, 'freedom to change [one's] religion or belief', enshrined in Article 9 (art. 9), would be likely to remain a dead letter.

This broad-based, foundational approach to religious freedom implies dignitarian justification. It is not a theme that Bingham uses or alludes to in his reference to Article 9.

In seeking to justify religious freedom by way of dignity, Julian Rivers perhaps best describes why judges generally have problems in dealing with religious freedom cases:

> Legal and political theorists find freedom of religion intensely problematic. It is therefore not surprising that when judges find themselves interpreting and applying broad constitutional or human rights provisions protecting freedom of religion, then answers they give to fundamental questions of scope and justification are sketchy or non-existent. In its first case under article 9 ECHR, the European Court of Human Rights (ECtHR) describes freedom of religion as 'one of the foundations of a "democratic society"'. It is 'one of the most vital elements that go to make up the identity of believers' and also a 'precious asset for atheists, agnostics, sceptics and the unconcerned'. Although the case-law under the European Convention has developed extensively since that first decision in *Kokkinakis*, the ECtHR has hardly added to these preliminary foundational considerations. There is no doubt that in the minds of the Strasbourg judges that freedom of religion is important, but exactly what it is and why it matters is elusive. (2013, 405)

The proper use of dignity in an historic context may very well be helpful in further editions of *The Rule of Law*.

One of the most comprehensive analyses of human dignity is the work by Christopher McCrudden (2013), *Understanding Human Dignity*, best described as the conflict between human rights and a theologically based vocabulary influencing justice, starting in classical times and working its way through centuries of Christian thought, culminating in the 1891 encyclical *Rerum Novarum*. Through this process the foundational concept of dignity is established historically and theologically, and its terminology of dignity-infused twentieth-century discourse so important to our language today. However, the conflict with the terminology of dignity arises in using twenty-first century terminology devoid of theological foundation. This is hinted at by The Right Honourable Baroness Hale of the Supreme Court of the United Kingdom, providing a preface to McCrudden's work:

> The law may eventually have reached this point, but the lawyers did not invent such a major shift in political thinking. The people did that. Freedom fighters, levellers, feminists even, who knew that they were not being accorded their proper respect as human beings and sometimes called this dignity. Philosophers and theologians supplied the thinking behind it. But how did they get from the hierarchical to the universal view of human worth? From the idea that God ordained the rich man in his castle and the poor man at his gate to the idea that such differences are made by man and not by God? And have they all got there? Surely there are some differences that are ordained by God, if only in the hierarchy of an apostolic church which does not yet admit that women may have that dignity. So what does it mean to say that man is made in the image of God? Or is it, as some would say, the other way round? (2013, xv)

Justice Hale asks, 'Or is it, as some would say, the other way round?' In other words, she suggests that we are making God in humankind's image.

Much work needs to be done in this area, and my rather modest criticism and proposal for Bingham's work made with much trepidation can be summarized by suggesting that a thoroughgoing analysis of dignity be implemented in his analysis of foundations for human rights and basic human rights protection, especially that of religious freedom. However, such twenty-first century use of dignity analysis cannot be done without properly using Bingham's own, partially historic analysis and a theological corrective that will keep judges from making the mistakes that Julian Rivers has identified.

References

Barak, Aharon. 2013. 'Human Dignity: The Constitutional Value and the Constitutional Right'. In *Understanding Human Dignity*, edited by Christopher McCrudden, 361–80. Oxford: Oxford University Press.

Bingham, Tom. 2006. 'The Rule of Law'. Presentation, sixth in the Centre for Public Law series of lectures honouring Sir David Williams, Cambridge, 16 November. Accessed 9 August 2019. https://www.cpl.law.cam.ac.uk/sir-david-williams-lectures/rt-hon-lord-bingham-cornhill-kg-rule-law.

———. 2010. *The Rule of Law*. London: Allen Lane.

Carothers, Thomas. 1998. 'The Rule of Law Revival'. *Foreign Affairs* 77, no. 2: 95–106.

Charter of the United Nations and Statute of the International Court of Justice. 1945. 1 UNTS XVI. https://www.un.org/en/charter-united-nations/#:~:text=The%20UN%20Charter,integral%20part%20of%20the%20Charter.

Costa, John-Paul. 2013. 'Human Dignity in the Jurisprudence of the European Court of Human Rights'. In *Understanding Human Dignity*, edited by Christopher McCrudden, 393–402. Oxford: Oxford University Press.

European Convention on Human Rights. 1950. European Council of Human Rights. Entered into force 1953. https://www.echr.coe.int/Documents/Convention_ENG.pdf.

Farr, Thomas F. 2019. 'Diplomacy and Persecution in China'. *First Things*, May. Accessed 7 November 2019. https://www.firstthings.com/article/2019/05/diplomacy-and-persecution-in-china.

Gandhi, Mahatma. 1922. *Speeches and Writings of M.K. Gandhi*, 3rd ed. Madras, India: G.A. Natesan.

Gardner, John. 2010. '"How to Be a Good Judge". Review of *The Rule of Law*, by Tom Bingham'. *London Review of Books* 32, no. 13: 15–16. Accessed 7 November 2019. https://www.lrb.co.uk/v32/n13/john-gardner/how-to-be-a-good-judge.

Geneva Convention Relative to the Protection of Civilian Persons in Time of War (Fourth Geneva Convention). 1949. 75 UNTS 287. Art. 3. International Committee of the Red Cross. Entered into force October 1950. https://ihl-databases.icrc.org/applic/ihl/ihl.nsf/WebART/365-570006.

Hale, Brenda. 2013. 'Preface'. In *Understanding Human Dignity*, edited by Christopher McCrudden, xv–xvii. Oxford: Oxford University Press.

Haugen, Gary. 2014. *The Locust Effect*. Oxford: Oxford University Press.

Human Rights Act. 1998. UK Public General Acts 1998, c. 42. http://www.legislation.gov.uk/ukpga/1998/42/contents.

International Covenant on Civil and Political Rights. 1966. United Nations General Assembly Resolution 2200A (XXI), 21 U.N. GAOR Supp. (no. 16) at 52, U.N. Doc. A/6316 (1966), 999 UNTS 171. Entered into force 23 March 1976.

Jackson, Robert. 1948. 'Closing Address in the Nuremberg Trial' (under 'One Hundred and Eighty-Seventh Day, Friday, 26 July 1946, Morning Session', 397–432). In *Proceedings in the Trial of the Major War Criminals before the International Military Tribunal*, vol. 19, Nuremberg, Germany. Accessed 7 November 2019. https://www.loc.gov/rr/frd/Military_Law/pdf/NT_Vol-XIX.pdf.

Locke, John. 1689. *A Letter Concerning Toleration*. Accessed 7 November 2019. https://socialsciences.mcmaster.ca/econ/ugcm/3ll3/locke/toleration.pdf.

———. 1823 [1689]. *Two Treatises of Government*. Vol. 5 of *The Works of John Locke*. Rpt, London: Thomas Tegg. Accessed 7 November 2019. http://www.yorku.ca/comninel/courses/3025pdf/Locke.pdf.

Loconte, Joseph. 2014. *God, Locke, and Liberty: The Struggle for Religious Freedom in the West*. Plymouth: Lexington Books.

Luban, David. 2005. 'Lawyers as Upholders of Human Dignity'. *University of Illinois Law Review*, no. 3: 815–45.

Machan, Tibor R. 1977. 'Human Dignity and the Law'. *DePaul Law Review* 26, no. 4: 807–32.

McCrudden, Christopher, ed. 2013. *Understanding Human Dignity*. Oxford: Oxford University Press.

Miller, Dallas. 2017. 'The Right to Religious Freedom: A Judicial Approach'. In *Religious Liberty and the Law: Theistic and Non-Theistic Perspectives*, edited by Angus Menuge, 69–86. Abingdon: Routledge.

Perelman, Chaïm. 1980. 'Can the Rights of Man Be Founded?' In *The Philosophy of Human Rights*, edited by Allen Rosenbaum, 46–54. Westport, CT: Greenwood.

Pew Research Center. 2019. 'A Closer Look at How Religious Restrictions Have Risen around the World'. Washington, DC. Accessed 7 November 2019. https://www.pewforum.org/2019/07/15/a-closer-look-at-how-religious-restrictions-have-risen-around-the-world/.

Porter, Jean. 2010. *Ministers of the Law: A Natural Law Theory of Legal Authority*. Grand Rapids, MI: Eerdmans.

Rhodes, Aaron. 2019. 'Toward a Reformation of International Human Rights'. *Providence* (Institute on Religion and Democracy) 13 (Winter): 9–11.

Rivers, Julian. 2013. 'Justifying Freedom of Religion: Does "Dignity" Help?' In *Understanding Human Dignity*, edited by Christopher McCrudden, 405–19. Oxford: Oxford University Press.

Sedley, Stephen. 2010. '"*The Rule of Law* by Tom Bingham": Review of *The Rule of Law*, by Tom Bingham'. *Guardian*, 20 February. Accessed 7 November 2019. https://www.theguardian.com/books/2010/feb/20/rule-law-tom-bingham-sedley.

Stevens, Irving. 2011. '"The Rule of Law". Review of *The Rule of Law*, by Tom Bingham'. *Denning Law Journal* 23: 242–48.

Universal Declaration of Human Rights. 1948. United Nations General Assembly Resolution 217A (III), U.N. Doc. A/810 (1948) at 71.

US Department of State. 2018. *2017 Report on International Religious Freedom*. Accessed 7 November 2019. https://www.state.gov/reports/2017-report-on-international-religious-freedom/china-includes-tibet-hong-kong-and-macau/.

Waldron, Jeremy. 2012. 'How Law Protects Dignity'. *Cambridge Law Journal* 72, no. 1: 200–22.

World Justice Project. 2017–18. *Fundamental Rights (Factor 4)*. Accessed 7 November 2019. https://worldjusticeproject.org/our-work/wjp-rule-law-index/wjp-rule-law-index-2017%E2%80%932018/factors-rule-law/fundamental-rights-factor.

Chapter Ten

BALANCING COMPETING DIGNITY CLAIMS: INSIGHTS FROM THE UNITED KINGDOM AND ITALY

Matteo Frau and Vito Breda

This chapter discusses balancing the prerogative to manifest identity-based beliefs such as the support for same-sex marriage and the prerogative to refuse the transmission of such a message by a service provider.[1] We argue that both prerogatives are manifestations of human dignity that have normative and pragmatic implications that should be assessed within a deliberative arena such a parliament and regional assemblies. The argument is supported by a comparative analysis of recent UK jurisprudence and the evaluations of the statutory measures that inform Italian and European law.

The first manifestation of human dignity in the case is a prerogative granted to a historically discriminated-against identity to access publicly offered services. The second manifestation of human dignity is the prerogative of individuals who are managing a business to refuse to provide a service on the basis that what is asked of them is perceived as contravening their religious beliefs. In this chapter we provide a review of the Northern Irish, British and Italian systems of rules that inform the accommodation of this dilemma. These three systems are, albeit differently, committed to protecting human dignity and they comply, again distinctively, with the set of international obligations that are derived from membership in the Council of Europe and the European Union.

The analysis shows that while there are strong indications that international jurisdictions are dynamically changing the balance between the prerogative to manifest and the prerogative to refuse identity-based claims, the process of accommodating competing manifestations is still better left to the national and regional deliberative arenas. This chapter is divided into three sections. The first part discusses the process of balancing competing dignity claims. The second analyses the *Lee v. Ashers Baking Company* case. The third section discusses the statutory measures that inform Italian law on cases in which there might be an allegation of discrimination. The comparison shows that even in a legal system such as the Italian one where there is generally entrenched constitutional

---

[1] The authors gratefully acknowledge the valuable assistance of Barry W. Bussey and Amy Ross in the preparation of this chapter. We are also grateful to Angus J. L. Menuge for so generously giving the opportunity to join this project.

protection against discrimination, it is not guaranteed that the courts will consider the refusal to reproduce identity-based beliefs as discriminatory without a specific statutory intervention by the Italian Parliament.

Balancing Competing Dignity Claims

In this comparative chapter it will be argued that balancing the prerogative to manifest identity claims that promote same-sex marriage, like the one discussed in *Lee v. Ashers Baking Company Ltd (Northern Ireland)* (2018; Foster 2016; *Lee v. McArthur* 2016), and the prerogative to refuse to transmit certain messages should be decided within a legislative arena that represents that distinctive community. Mr Lee was a gay rights activist who ordered a cake with a printed slogan, 'Support Gay Marriage', from Ashers Baking Company, a bakery in Northern Ireland. The McArthurs, evangelical owners of the bakery, declined his order and refunded his money.[2] The argument will be developed through a comparative analysis of the Italian law and British common law.

This chapter argues that UK Supreme Court intervention in the implementation of the Equality Act (Sexual Orientation) Regulations 2006 (hereafter, the SOR 2006) is out of tune with choices made by regional institutions that operate in a divided society. There are two self-standing reasons for such a stance. First, the debate over the protection of minorities in a modern democracy cannot be separated from the manifestation of beliefs that contribute to a shared sense of identity for group members (Bauman 2001, 101; Breda 2007; 2018, 850). In instances such as the one discussed in *Lee v. Ashers*, there are two conflicting prerogatives involved (*Lee v. McArthur* 2016, 22:707). Mr Lee has the prerogative to manifest a claim (e.g. the support for gay marriage) that he perceives as an integral part of his identity as a homosexual individual (Bauman 1998; *Lee v. Ashers* 2018, 848; Gerstmann 2017). The McArthurs, on the other hand, have the prerogative to refuse to have their company be the medium for Mr Lee's message because it is perceived as incompatible with their religious beliefs (*Lee v. Ashers* 2018, 848). Both these prerogatives are derived from a liberal commitment to protect and foster human dignity (Coughlin 2013; Hasson 2003; Muftugil 2017; Oppenheimer 1996).

These manifestations of belief contribute to the deliberative process that allows modern democracy to seek a reasonable representation of social reality, and to pass laws and regulations that try to change (or preserve) human conduct. For instance, the obligation expressed in the First Amendment of the US Constitution is one of the first recognitions of the role of religious identity in modern liberal democracy (Baum 2002; Macedo 1995). However, the protection that religious identities hold in the United States is based on their historical contributions to democracy and is not an assertion that the sets of beliefs carried by these groups have a special status in the political arena that might trump other competing ideas or beliefs (Baum 2002; Bellah 1967; Breda 2017; Doe 2011; Thiemann 1996).

---

[2]   This case will be discussed in greater detail in the next section.

The recognition of the role of communities has expanded to include national identities (Breda 2004; 2018; Casanas Adam 2017; Government of Wales Act 1998, ch 38; The Northern Ireland Act 1998, ch 47, 199; UK Parliament n.d.), linguistic communities (Turgeon and Gagnon 2013) and, more recently, groups of individuals who have a distinctive type of sexual orientation (First Minister and the Deputy First Minister (NI) 2006; Oppenheimer 1996). Again, the recognition of these groups is part of a process that appreciates the full scope of cultural diversity in modern democracy (Bauman 1999; Breda 2013). This is the case even if these beliefs might be perceived as antithetical to the enlightened projects which ultimately protect human dignity and ensure that modern deliberative democracy is functioning as an – albeit imperfect – truth-finding political device (Habermas 2006). This point is often contested because it is perceived that the system of values that ensures free speech is a Trojan horse for religious extremism and anti-democratic political activities (Laclau and Mouffe 2001; Mouffe 1992).

There is a rich and articulated literature that focuses on open deliberative democracies and the space allocated to ideologies (e.g. nationalism and religious extremism) which might undermine them (Canovan 2000; Enns 2010; Gagnon and Sauca 2014; Habermas 1975; 1991; 1995; Orgad 2009; Rosenfeld and Sajo 2012). It is, however, outside the scope of this chapter to provide a general overview of the interaction between the prerogative to manifest beliefs and their role in a multicultural society. The issues discussed in this chapter instead engage the balance between either expressing or refusing to express certain beliefs. According to the religious convictions in question, marriage is axiomatically connected to procreation and homosexual conduct is viewed as sinful (*Lee v. Ashers* 2018, 857; *Lee v. McArthur* 2016, 22:723). In most European legal systems, both beliefs (regarding marriage and homosexual conduct) might be connected to a distinctive manifestation of a set of privately held ideas which might or might not be associated with a comprehensive ideology (Hasson 2003; Oppenheimer 1996). The manifestation of these ideas is connected to a web of international and national legal obligations that seek to balance the right not to be discriminated against and the right not to be forced, as a service provider, to reproduce utterances (Charter of Fundamental Rights of the European Union 2012/C 326/02, Articles 9–11, 16; European Convention on Human Rights (ECHR) 1950, Articles 9, 10). Northern Ireland, for historical reasons, has established in the Government of Ireland Act 1920 an articulated statutory system that is unique to the region and is aimed at ensuring that private businesses do not discriminate on the basis of religious group (Brennan 1997; Hughes 2016; Rafter 2012; UK Parliament 1920, sec 5). The SOR 2006 extended such a protection to gay people. The Government of Ireland Act 1920 was, and still is, considered the result of eminently political activity.

The McArthurs' refusal to have their company involved in the preparation of a cake for Mr Lee was perceived as illegitimate by the Northern Irish District Court, the Northern Ireland Appeal Court and, obviously, the Equality Commission for Northern Ireland (*Lee v. McArthur* 2016). The UK Supreme Court differed in its findings (*Lee v. Ashers* 2018). In *Lee v. Ashers*, Baroness Hale explained that a reasonable connection could not be made between the promotion of gay marriage, the identity group associated with

Mr Lee's sexual orientation and a specific group of individuals to whom the message was directed, that is, family and friends.

In the next part of this chapter, we will argue that such a conclusion is internally dissonant but that there are indications both from an analysis of the epistemic activities carried out by the UK courts and the law applicable in Italy that confirm the contextual nature of the dilemma. That is, the balancing exercise between differing prerogatives is part of a pragmatic activity that should be decided by parliament in which those views are represented. These prerogatives are not a part of what Zucca calls the *sphere of inviolability* of human dignity (2007, 38) nor, within the limit of reasonableness, endangering the functioning of modern democracy. For instance, in modern multicultural societies parliaments, regional assemblies and city councils constantly curtail, for pragmatic reasons, identity-based demands over the use of minority languages by service providers. It is unavoidable that individual dignities might be negatively affected. A Kanak-speaking resident of New Caledonia, for instance, might be forced to ask for a service (e.g. the printing of a good wishes card) in French – a language that was colonially imposed on her and kept her ancestors in a form of serfdom. A service provider might also, based on his nationalist view, refuse to provide the transmission of a message in Kanak by his greeting card company because it is perceived as hindering his French identity (Marrani 2013). It is a prerogative of the New Caledonia Territorial Congress and the French National Assembly to set the boundaries of the use of the Kanak language by business owners (Breda and Mihailovic 2019; Noumea Accord 2002). These types of debates occur day in and day out in all multinational societies and deliver a large spectrum of laws and local deliberations (Keating and McGarry 2001). Unavoidably the result of the deliberative process is a temporary winner and loser. However, it is the possibility of questioning previous political decisions and the dynamic nature of the issue that make a deliberative arena the most suitable place for setting the balance between expressions of human dignity in the service market.

An individual (or a group of individuals) might ask, in whatever medium, whether her identity establishes a contractual relation with a service provider which should act, it is reasonable to expect, as a commercial entity within a distinctive regulatory system composed by multiple overlays of European, national and, in the case of Northern Ireland, regional norms. The requirement of openness was also a prerequisite – at the time in which the case was decided – of the United Kingdom's membership in the European Union. The key aim of the regulatory framework is, among other goals, to increase the economic efficiency of transactions and reduce unfair practices across the European market (Charter of Fundamental Rights of the European Union 2012/C 326/02, Articles 9–11, 16, 21; Council Directive 2000/78/EC, secs 10–11; ECHR 1950, Articles 9, 10; European Union, Consolidated Version of the Treaty on the Functioning of the European Union, 26 October 2012, OJ L., Articles 2, 6). It is also worth mentioning that in Europe, several borders were inherited from the Westphalia treaties which divided European kingdoms along religious borders (MacCulloch 2010, ch 21).

In this process that is dominated by pragmatic decisions, a legal system also has a deontological duty to protect the rights of individuals (Brittain 2015; Charter of Fundamental Rights of the European Union 2012/C 326/02; ECHR 1950). The normative obligation includes a commitment to protect the human dignity of its citizens by ensuring that they have the freedom to pursue and manifest their individual conceptions of the common good (Zucca 2007). Balancing competing visions of the common good requires a pragmatic assessment of socially perceived values alongside the financial or social costs for the commonwealth. For instance, and as mentioned earlier, the Northern Irish legal system has, for historical reasons, civil penalties associated with discriminatory business practices based on sectarianism. Only relatively recently has an EU directive extended the protection against discrimination towards sexual orientations to all member states, yet, such a protection is limited to the area of labour law (Council Directive 2000/78/EC, s. 12, 29, 31).

The argument here is not that such prerogatives do not have a normative value; some of them, in a case of an eventual lacunae, can be accommodated by the courts. The narrative that is defended is instead that a comparative analysis of the cluster of precedents and legislative/administrative activities that seek a balance between these types of rights shows an indication that such measures aimed at protecting coinciding but conflicting prerogatives are part of an ongoing deliberative activity over normative and pragmatic issues that are not settled. Again, deliberative arenas and not courts are the best institutions to determine the balance between concurrent manifestations of identity-based beliefs.

First, the debate over the accommodation of two prerogatives will not be discussed from a contractual perspective. In the case of *Lee v. Ashers*, a baker agreed to provide a service and collected a fee without properly assessing the implications of the identity-based message requested by a patron (2018, 849). This type of mistake could be due, within the margin of error that is part of all comparative analyses, to a mistake in the *determining motive* (ibid.). The subsequent refusal to comply with the terms of the contract on the basis of a misinterpretation of the requested task is likely to be constructed as a unilateral mistake by a commercial entity which does not normally have pernicious effects on the contract (Gordley 2004, 435). In particular, the *error made regarding the basic assumptions* is not considered relevant to the formation of a valid contract in most legal systems (Eisenbergt 2003, 1581; Gordley 2004, 440). It could be argued that *Lee v. Ashers* was intended to have general implications for the market. That is, consumers would have to spend time evaluating the set of beliefs that is intrinsic to the person from whom they are asking a service. This is not, it could be argued, necessarily a bad development in a multicultural society; yet it objectively reduces the speed of commercial transactions and might blur the line between the doctrine of the mistake relating to the object of a contract (e.g. the service of writing on a cake) with the error relating to the subjects of the contract. The doctrine of a mistake in the formation of the contract tends to be distinctive of a legal system, yet James Gordley points out that the relevance of the basic assumptions that a person holds as self-evident truth should not, normally, be part of the evaluation of pre-contract assessments: 'the propensity to question one's assumptions varies from one person to the next. It would be odd to deny relief to the timorous and grant relief to the sanguine' (2004, 440). Again, this contract law aspect of *Lee v. Ashers* will not be discussed in detail; it is, however, important to note that judicial decisions that balance prerogatives have general and direct implications for commercial transactions, and again this is an area of policy that is eminently political and not jurisdictional (Eisenbergt 2003; Gordley 2004).

Second, the argument defended here is not that judges should refrain from discussing disputes over rights. Neil Foster has recently explained that courts do have a role in adjudicating private interactions which involve a shared or mutual manifestation of religious beliefs (2020, 179). This chapter also does not suggest that judges should not work out the answers to disputes regarding the implementation of statutory material. The argument is rather this: it is unreasonable for court to grant, as might be the case in Italy, a prerogative to a group of individuals, such as the LGBTQ community, when a deliberative assembly, like the Italian Parliament, had the opportunity to create those prerogatives, but remained silent. Similarly, in cases in which the deliberative arena, as has been the case in Northern Ireland, extended those prerogatives – which were originally allocated to Northern Irish religious communities – to gay people, the courts cannot restrict them without their decision being perceived as an illegitimate intervention by an external entity.

This is particularly so in Northern Ireland, where all group interactions are heavily regulated. Northern Ireland is a modern consociative democracy within a large democratic state (Breda 2018, 5, 73; Wolff 2004). Consociative regional democracies such as Quebec in Canada (Keating 2001), New Caledonia in France (Chappell 2013) and South Tyrol in Italy are *low-trust* multi-ethnic societies (Wolff 2004). The negative aspects are well known. For instance, in the past four years, the Northern Ireland Assembly has been only sporadically active. In addition, and due to distinctive historical circumstances (e.g. in the past either or both communities were victims of an attempted physical or cultural genocide), they adopt a system of governance that seeks to increase the level of transparency in legal systems to reduce the level of animosity between identity groups (Keating and Wilson 2014; Wolff 2004). The Northern Ireland Act 1998, for instance, provides that regional government is composed of representatives of all major political parties and not, as is expected in a deliberative democracy, exclusively by the party that collected the majority of the casted votes at the last election (Hadden and Boyle n.d.; The UK Government and the Government of Ireland 1998). The sharing of cabinet roles among members of opposing political parties, which might also claim to represent different identity groups, is intended to enhance the level of accountability of the executive and all its institutions. It is often the case that political groups that have taken the role of representing identities have a vested interest in undermining deliberative institutions which might make them politically accountable at the regional level. In the case of Northern Ireland, the undefined relation between regional and national parties might contribute, for instance, to a faltering deliberative democracy.

The level of transparency within the activity of public institutions is also coupled with the enhanced protection against discriminatory practices by service providers that have been a part of Northern Irish statutory regime since 1920. This chapter will discuss, in detail, the regional statutory measures that prevent businesses from implementing discriminatory practices, yet it is important to note that in consociative democracies, institutional and legal developments are imbued by the overarching requirement of preserving a peaceful coexistence between communities (Brennan 1997; Boyle and Hadden 1995; Coakley 2017; Hughes 2016; UK Parliament 1920). In other words, it is reasonable to suggest that balancing the prerogative to ask for the manifestation of an identity belief (e.g. the support for same-sex marriage) with the prerogative to refuse the transmission by a service provider of such a manifestation (because it is antithetical to a religious belief) is part of an attempt to reduce the increasing sectarian tension that is, within the United Kingdom, unique to Northern Ireland.

Third, and perhaps as a corollary to the previous point, the issue discussed in cases such as *Lee v. Ashers* will not be considered from the perspective of a conflict between fundamental rights. Debates over the nature of fundamental rights have been part of the staple diet of the debate between natural law lawyers and positivists for over two centuries, and it is outside of the remit of this chapter to discuss the implications of such a rich literature (Alexy 2003; Dworkin 1978; Fuller 1958; Hart 1997; Zucca 2007). It is also reasonable to suggest that cases such as *Lee v. Ashers* might be perceived as one of the latest manifestations of the pragmatic effect of such a debate. However, the attempt to analyse the case from this perspective would be possible only if one or both claims purported by both parties were fundamental to modern democracy (Alexy 2003; Dworkin 1978). Zucca adopts the term *sphere of inviolability* (2007, 44) to categorise rights that are fundamental to the protection of human dignity. These rights are protected in the constitution, and they tend, within the limit of reasonableness, to be constructed in absolute negative terms (Alexy 2003; Dworkin 1978; Zucca 2007, 44).

It is, it might be argued, possible to construct the claims that are related to this prerogative as a universal claim. For instance, a claim analogous to the one put forward by Mr Lee in *Lee v. Ashers* can be constructed with these words: individuals should not be treated differently on the basis of a distinctive manifestation of who they are without questioning the level of protection that the legal system allocates to the concept of human dignity. The counterargument, which is a product of another rather complex narrative, might be summarised in these terms: a business should not be forced to transmit words that it perceives as incompatible with the identity of its owner without questioning the level of protection that a legal system allocates to the concept of human dignity. Both claims are constructed as a negative, absolute right that excludes any other interfering claims, and they assume a related unlimited state's obligation to allocate resources to protect the individuals who exercise them (Alexy 2003; Zucca 2007). However, neither of the claims (e.g. the universal demand not to be discriminated against on the basis that one individual belongs to a protected group, and the right not to write someone else's utterances) is unlimited. Protected categories are indeed set by parliaments and the right not to transmit communication is consistently and systematically trimmed by the state's intervention in defamation cases where public broadcasters and academic publishers are forced to publish retractions and apologies. This is independent from the beliefs of the owners of the service provider (Graham 2009; Kenyon 2010, 698; Milo 2008; Tan 2016). So, the debate over the protection of the manifestation of identity claims in consociative democracies such as Northern Ireland, South Tyrol and Quebec tends to be more articulated because the political stability or indeed civil coexistence is dependent on a continued and dynamic process of mediation between similarly supported yet conflicting prerogatives. In Northern Ireland, for instance, the debate over the admissibility of discriminatory practices by service providers commenced in 1920, and it originally focused exclusively on reducing the economic cost of sectarian discrimination (Boyle and Hadden 1995; Brennan 1997; Goodall et al. 2015; UK Parliament 1920, sec 5). The result of that historical development was a unique, as far as we know, system of civil liabilities that aimed to reduce the effect of sectarianism on the open market.

Fourth, both the United Kingdom and Italy were, at the time in which the case was decided, members of the European Union and of the Council of Europe that implies a large overlap of international obligations (Brittain 2015; Charter of Fundamental Rights of the European Union 2012/C 326/02; ECHR 1950; European Union, Consolidated Version of the Treaty on the Functioning of the European Union, 26 October 2012, OJ L). Distinctive of the United Kingdom is the limited effect of the ECHR and of the Charter of Fundamental Rights (Joint Committee on Human Rights 2006; Kavanagh 2009; O'Cinneide 2008). In addition, a British court cannot void acts of the British Parliament (Breda 2015b). There is an undergoing appeal of the *Lee v. Ashers* case in the European Court of Human Rights which is likely to focus on the freedom to express political opinion. This element of the case will not be discussed in this chapter.

Fifth, *Lee v. Ashers* discussed the support for same-sex marriage as a case of discrimination to provide a service on the basis of the sexual preferences of a patron and on the grounds of his/her political opinion, but in this chapter we will focus exclusively on the balance between the prerogatives. Sixth, the District Court judge erroneously perceived the *Lee v. McArthur* case as a direct discrimination case, whereas the facts actually related to a case of indirect discrimination. The McArthurs did not have a policy that directly discriminated against homosexuals. They held, instead, a belief that had the effect of discriminating, by association, against gay and lesbian individuals who promoted same-sex marriage. This element of the case will not be discussed in this chapter.

The Ashers Case: The Text and Co-Text of Factual Narratives

Lee v. Ashers sits at the intersection of multiple debates, but in this chapter we will focus on the balancing exercise between the prerogative to manifest (or refuse to manifest) identity-based beliefs that are an expression of human dignity. In this section we will analyse the case and its historical development from Mr Lee's complaint, to the Equality Commission in Northern Ireland, to the decision by the UK Supreme Court (*Lee v. Ashers* 2018).

Mr Lee ordered (either on 8 or 9 May 2014) a bespoke cake in one of the shops that belong to the Ashers Baking Company. The order was taken by one of the owners who was told the cake was for a private function (*Lee v. Ashers* 2018, 847; *Lee v. McArthur* 2016, 22:702). It was to celebrate the end of 'Northern Ireland Anti-Homophobic Week' (*Lee v. McArthur* 2016, 22:702). Among the decorations requested to be put on the cake was the message: 'Support Gay Marriage' (22:702). The order was accepted on Friday, but, the following Monday, after Mr McArthur consulted his wife Amy, who co-owns the Ashers Baking Company, they decided to cancel the order and reimburse Mr Lee (*Lee v. Ashers* 2018, 848). The reason given to Mr Lee was that the bakery was a 'Christian business', and it should not have accepted the order (ibid.). The McArthurs confirmed that they perceived support for same-sex marriage as inherently sinful since it is intrinsically connected to the support of sexual relationships between same-sex individuals (*Lee v. McArthur* 2016, 22:704). Mr Lee complained to the Equality Commission for Northern Ireland, which, after an exchange of communication with the McArthurs, ordered a payment of damages to Mr Lee for a breach of the statutory duty not to discriminate on the grounds of the sexual orientation of the person (e.g. sec 3 SOR 2006) who is seeking to obtain a service or a good (e.g. sec 5.1 SOR 2006). The McArthurs refused to comply, and the case went to the Northern Irish district judge who considered the claim that they theoretically would have refused the order if it had been made by a heterosexual individual, and so in theory they did not have a motive to discriminate against a protected category, but she noted that the Equality Act (Sexual Orientation) did not require an assessment of the intention of the service provider. It was sufficient to engage section 5.1 of SOR 2006 that the message was intrinsically associated with a group of individuals of same-sex orientation (*Lee v. McArthur* 2016, 22:707). The Northern Irish Court of Appeal qualified the decision of the district judge but confirmed the violation of section 5.1 of SOR 2006. However, the UK Supreme Court assessed the case and disagreed with the finding of the Court of Appeal. The Supreme Court deemed the conduct of Mr Lee and the message he requested to be written on the cake as insufficient to engage section 5.1 of the SOR 2006. The case is currently under review by the European Court of Human Rights.

From a contextual analysis of the events mentioned in the case, however, there are reasonable indications that such an evaluation was made too quickly. The role of religion in the region is plainly stated in the Court of Appeal's decision: 'The Context [...] Northern Ireland has a large and strong faith community. The commitment to religion is fulfilled not just by regular worship but informs every aspect of the way those of faith conduct their lives. Many of those are people who have played an active part in commerce and taken on leadership roles within the commercial world' (*Lee v. McArthur* 2016, 22:712). That statement, which suggests an effect from a divided society in commerce, is coupled with an analysis of the lingering effect of homophobia: 'The LGBT community has endured a history of considerable discrimination in this jurisdiction [...] Those who were gay were reluctant to expose their sexuality and some were subjected to blackmail and other intimidation' (ibid.). In this context, an order for a cake designed to celebrate same-sex marriage is a clear expression of an identity belief associated with a specific, historically marginalized group. The Court of Appeal again delivers the point in a concise narrative: 'The benefit from the message or slogan on the cake could only accrue to gay or bisexual people' (22:699). The UK Supreme Court perceived it otherwise and supported an improbable scenario based on the likelihood that a heterosexual individual, in the same place and under the same circumstances, would have made a similar order and would have obtained a similar refusal.

This is a hypothetical interpretation that falls short of what is expected from a contextual analysis of the text (Azuelos-Atias 2010). For instance, Levinson notes that a series of activities are required to extract the significance from a text. It is expected that the interpreter does consider contextual elements that imbue the text with its actual significance. The activity of finding meaning includes searching for:

(i) knowledge of role and status (where role covers both role in the speech event, as speaker or addressee, and social role, and status covers notions of relative social standing); (ii) knowledge of spatial and temporal location; (iii) knowledge of formality level; (iv) knowledge of the medium; (v) knowledge of appropriate subject matter; [and] (vi) knowledge of appropriate province. (Levinson 1983, 23; Skoczeń 2016, 4)

These are the elements that might give an indication of the meaning of the message in a distinctive context. There are, as mentioned earlier, indications that such an evaluation was carried out by the Court of Appeal.

Indeed, the factual narrative in this case includes an evaluation of an utterance (and not the process of interpreting legal text which is cognitively distinctive of a legal community). In other words, the text 'Support Gay Marriage' here is a fact, not a legal narrative. The court ought to search for a representation of the past based on scientific evidence and a plausible reconstruction of the events in narrative form (Azuelos-Atias 2010; Coleman and Leiter 1993). This analysis is discussed by the Court of Appeal in the review of the facts. It is also evaluated, logically we might add, in an obiter:

> It would be ironic if the constitutional protections against legislative or executive discrimination based on religious belief or political opinion, as introduced by the Northern Ireland Constitution Act 1973 and the Northern Ireland Act 1998, were to become the instruments for the support of differential treatment of fellow citizens based on religious belief and political opinion. (*Lee v. McArthur* 2016, 22:723)

It was, for the Court of Appeal, impossible to dissociate the prerogative to refuse a service (based on religious belief) to Mr Lee as unrelated to a group of citizens that is protected against these types of discrimination. It is, again within the margin of error of a cognitive process, reasonable to suggest that the Northern Irish District Court and the Northern Irish Court of Appeal did heed a connection between the conduct of Mr Lee, the Ashers Baking Company and the effect of a protected category, but found it so obvious that it was not worth mentioning.

The Supreme Court assumed that a lack of reference in the court of appeal decision to the context overlooked the relevant aspect of the case: 'Not only did the district judge not make such a finding in this case, the association would not have been close enough for her to do so' (*Lee v. Ashers* 2018, 852). Again, there are indications that the Court of Appeal decision did find the connection but assumed it to be so obvious that it did not mention it. This diverging interpretation on which cognitive process should be adopted to evaluate the facts in *Lee v. MacArthur* and the subsequent *Lee v. Ashers* case had a domino effect on the decision of the case.

Similar conclusions, albeit for different reasons, might be derived from the idea that the text 'Support Gay Marriage' could be interpreted as inclusive of third parties. Baroness Hale stated that the result of the utterance might be for the 'benefit of the children, the parents, the families and friends of gay people' (*Lee v. Ashers* 2018, 852) (and not exclusively gay people). The argument here is that Mr Lee's requested utterance has such a general valence that it might include individuals who were intended to be covered by the SOR 2006, whereas the order is intended to protect only a limited group of individuals. However, this narrowing of the aim of SOR 2006 sits at odds with the legal status of same-sex civil partnerships in the Northern Ireland Civil Partnership Act 2004 c. 33. Same-sex civil partnerships are already recognised in Northern Ireland by the Civil Partnership Act, and all the categories mentioned by the court such as children (e.g. secs: 72–75, 196, 199–203) and relatives (e.g. ch 5) do not receive, outside of the benefit of a change in the labelling of the ceremony they might be attending, an advantage from supporting marriage for homosexual individuals ('Registering a Civil Partnership' 2015).

The last item on the farrago of assumed potential beneficiaries is the category of 'friends of gay people' but again this is a germane narrative that will reduce the valence of the SOR 2006 order to an illogical extent (*Lee v. Ashers* 2018, 852). Based on analogous reasoning, it could be argued that a publican in Northern Ireland should not be forced to add a ramp for disabled individuals at the entrance to her pub because it might benefit the friends of disabled people. Again, this is not a very persuasive argument. The court's subtlety on reducing the protection of a discriminated category, as well as its dislocation of Mr Lee's utterance from its context, indicates that the Supreme Court might not have dedicated enough time to the pragmatic implications of the decision.[3] Again, the aim of this chapter is not to provide the right answer to the dilemma engaged by the *Lee v. Ashers* case. Quite the opposite. The argument defended here is that balancing prerogatives to manifest and refuse identity-based beliefs in the marketplace requires a pragmatic evaluation that is the domain of deliberative arenas in which those statutes are enacted. Cases such as *Lee v. Ashers* show the intrinsic limitation of an external jurisdictional accommodation of these dilemmas.

The Italian Job: Balancing a Pragmatic Prerogative to Assert and Deny the Manifestation of Identity-Based Beliefs

In the previous sections, we discussed the case history of *Lee v. Ashers* as one instance in which the courts tried to balance two concurring manifestations of human dignity. Both religious identity claims and sexual identity claims ought to be respected in a modern, pluralist society. Hence, balancing the rights of either identity is a pragmatic issue that ought to be settled in a deliberative context rather than a legal arena. There is, as shown in our analysis of *Lee v. Ashers*, a perceptible difference in the managing of these claims in consociative democracies such as Northern Ireland. In this section, we will show that the Italian legal system currently protects the manifestation of religious beliefs, and it is silent in relation to the protection of sexual orientation. It is silence that prevents judges giving support to the manifestation of sexual orientation beliefs. This is a delicate point.

---

[3]   The bizarre aspect of the decision is that a Catholic can pop into a bakery in Belfast and ask an Anglican baker to write 'No Marriage for Priests' on a cake. An Anglican can ask a Jewish baker to write 'Porkchops Are Divine Food'. These customers and their requested slogans belong to protected categories and the messages are legal. The refusal will trigger civil penalties. Again, this illustrates why these issues require a pragmatic balancing of prerogatives.

The chapter shows the distinctive contextual nature of the process that balances the prerogative to manifest identity-based beliefs and the prerogative to refuse the transmission of such beliefs by a commercial firm. It is not to say that religious or sexual orientation prerogatives are not a manifestation of human dignity.

The Italian legal system does not establish a specific set of rules regulating the expected behaviours of service providers. However, that does not mean that the judges are tasked to cover the lacunae. Italian judges have an explicit constitutional commitment to recognise human dignity and implement international law (Senato della Repubblica 1948, Articles 2, 3(1)). As part of internally and internationally recognised principles, human dignity has, according to Ruggeri and Spadaro, a 'super-constitutional value' (1991, 343). There is, it is plausible to suggest, a tendency to transform this super-constitutional value into extensive protection against discrimination. As was the case for Northern Ireland, there are historical reasons for having enhanced protection against discrimination (Bonaventura 2016; Breda 2013; 2015a; Ward 1997). Following the collapse of the fascist regime, the 1948 Constitution recognised, for instance, the importance of forming an association with other individuals (Dworkin 1978; Zucca 2007) such as with religious groups (Flick 2015; Senato della Repubblica 1948, Article 2). Italy, as compared to the United Kingdom, does not include a region in which a community is divided along sectarian lines (Breda 2018, ch 3).

However, over the years, Italian institutions have developed a distinctive sensibility for the process of the accommodation of religious beliefs based on three pragmatic experiences. First, the accommodation of religious beliefs is part of diplomatic relations with the Vatican State (Holy See 1929; Long 1990, 251–60; Spano 2009). Second, a large part of the population is baptised as Catholic and there are multiple areas of overlap between the perception of acceptable civic coexistence and religious rules (Breda 2013). Third, the area of protection of religious freedom inserted in the 1948 Constitution was developed as a response to the hard lessons learned during fascism in which institutional discrimination focused on all non-Catholic organizations and was a proxy for an attempt to commit genocide against the Italian Jews (Spano 2009).

These elements combined with a lack of statutory measures that protect sexual preferences suggest that service providers have a prerogative to refuse a service because of a religious belief. Again, the argument here is not that such a prerogative is to be considered a normative aspect of a modern legal system, because the UK Supreme Court and the Italian Constitutional Court might reach a convergence of ideas.

What is distinctive of the Italian jurisprudence is, perhaps, the recognition of a direct connection between religious freedom as an individual prerogative and as a social activity (Italian Constitutional Court 1975, 188). Decision n. 188 of the Constitutional Court, for instance, asserted that 'the religious sentiment, which lives in the depths of the individual conscience and extends to more or less numerous groups of people linked together by the bond of the practising of a common religion, must be considered among the most important constitutional assets' (Point 4). There is, in other words, a general obligation of not interfering in the activity of individuals who are engaged in the manifestation of a religious belief, because the religious freedom is the aspect of personality in which the value of human dignity is most intensely manifested (Modugno 1995, 22). From this perspective, Italian jurisprudence appears to be in tune, so to speak, with the jurisprudence of the European Court of Human Rights (ECHR) and of the Court of Justice of the European Union (CJEU 2017; *Kokkinakis v. Greece* 1993, 17 EHRR 397).

However, the constitutional commitment not to interfere in the practice of religious freedom is limited by the commitment to foster the individual's social and economic development as a manifestation of private autonomy (e.g. Article 2(2)) or as a manifestation of partaking in a communal activity (e.g. Article 41). This obligation to protect individual manifestations of an identity-based belief is trammelled, in cases such as *Lee v. Ashers*, by an international obligation to not interfere in the expression of religious beliefs (Italian Constitutional Court 1996, Point 3.1).

What is distinctive of the Italian constitutional law system is a constitutional commitment to foster private economic initiatives (e.g. Article 41). Is that to say businesses are always right? Again, this commitment is constitutionally limited: 'It may not be carried out against the common good or in such a manner that could damage safety, liberty and human dignity' (Senato della Republica 1948, Article 41). So, it is a prerogative of the parliament to direct economic enterprises in a way that is perceived as enhancing a free market economy, but in such a steering activity, statutory measures should consider the implications for the dignity of members of the community (ibid.). Crucially, there is no specific protection, as is the case in Northern Ireland, against direct or indirect discrimination by service providers based on sexual orientation.

The next question would be whether courts might consider the case by referring to an analogous case. There are indeed a series of statutory measures that might inform a judge who is assessing cases that are analogous to *Lee v. Ashers*.

This is a speculation, but we suggest that an Italian judge would not consider the conduct of the Ashers Baking Company as triggering a civil liability. To begin with, in relation to the obligation to have an open market of goods and services, Italy has a series of specific statutory measures that seek to prevent discriminatory practices (Italian Parliament 1998, Article 43(2)b). This statutory asset is coupled with highly articulate European legislation that seeks similar aims. There is, for instance, a qualification of the freedom of enterprise that is regulated by Council Directive 2000/43/EC (implemented in Italy by Law n. 215 2003) which ensures protection against ethnic discrimination. Council Directive 2004/113/EC (implemented in Italy by legislative decree Law n. 196 2006) prevents gender discriminatory practices (Italian Parliament 2006). The issue here might be whether these categories amount to a closed list. If the answer were negative, Italian judges could expand the boundaries to include protection for gays and lesbians. This category is already protected in labour law. Since the enactment of Council Directive 2000/78/CE, sexual preferences are illegitimate grounds for discrimination.

Again we are moving in the realm of wild speculations, but it seems improbable that an Italian judge might perceive the lack of protection for a minority group that has been historically discriminated against as justifying an extension, *á la* Northern Ireland, in the Italian legal system.

Such an eventuality appears highly unprovable for a series of deductive reasons. In 2004, when the parliament implemented Directive 2004/113/EC, it had the opportunity to include sexual orientation as a newly protected group but crucially decided not to do so. Second, there remains a possibility that Italian judges might derive a commitment to cover a gap in the legislative activity of the Italian parliament by referring to the general principles of European law. The Court of Justice of the European Union has already arrived at the definition of non-discrimination as a *general principle of community law* deduced from the constitutional traditions of member states, and currently enhanced by the connection between the Charter of Fundamental Rights of the European Union and the ECHR (Brittain 2015; *Mangold v. Helm* 2005, C-144/04). The *Mangold* case was the first to affirm the existence of a general principle of non-discrimination (based on age) independent of Directive 2000/78/EC and capable of producing horizontal direct effects (*Mangold v. Helm* 2005, C-144/04). In addition, the 2014 ruling on the Association de Médiation Social case by the CJEU incidentally clarifies that the principle of non-discrimination enshrined in Article 21(1) of the charter is sufficiently clear to be considered as a subjective individual right that might be protected by a court (*Association de médiation sociale v. Union locale des syndicats CGT* 2014, C-176/12, 144).

However, it is unlikely that such reasoning will find traction in a court. Both religious identity claims and sexual identity claims ought to be respected in a modern, pluralist society. Hence, balancing the rights of either identity is a pragmatic issue that ought to be settled in a legislative context rather than a legal arena. In addition, the imposition of damages on businesses that are caught discriminating on the basis of the sexual preferences of their patrons might be outside of the judicial competence allocated to an Italian court. Article 23 of the Italian Constitution prevents institutions such as courts and tribunals from imposing personal or financial obligations on individuals without a specific statutory competence to carry out such an activity. So the recognition of an international obligation does not generate an automatic remedy that has a horizontal effect on private businesses (Neuvonen 2015). In short it is a wild speculation to expect that an Italian judge would consider a business activity (or the refusal to provide a service) as so deeply offensive of human dignity (e.g. Article 41) that he or she would insert a new category of protection in the Italian legal system.

This point is delicate and so we must be precise. The argument defended in this chapter is not that a historically discriminated against community such as gay people should not be protected. Rather the argument is this: the balance of the prerogative to manifest ideas that are associated with a minority group and the protection of service providers to refuse a service requires a specific intervention by parliaments because the two prerogatives are part of pragmatic assessments that are normally left to legislatures.

Conclusion

In this chapter we discussed the process of the accommodation of the prerogative to assert and refuse the printing of claims. Both prerogatives are, we argued, a manifestation of human dignity that could be associated with the protection of elements of human flourishing. The recent case of *Lee v. Ashers* is one of the latest attempts by the judicial system to accommodate the two conflicting prerogatives. We asserted, however, that the process of balancing the two prerogatives is better left to regional and national parliaments.

This is the case for multiple reasons. First, we explained that the two claims (i.e. the right to manifest identity-based beliefs and the refusal to reproduce such claims) cannot be constructed in absolute terms. It is, in most European legal systems, up to the parliament to decide the limit to the freedom of speech. Similarly, public institutions do have the prerogative to force the publication of information that is perceived as beneficial for a community.

Second, balancing the two prerogatives has the effect of limiting private initiatives and, as a result, distorting the functioning of an open market of goods and services. Both the United Kingdom and Italy, at the time of writing this chapter, are part of the European Union and both legal systems have implemented international obligations to reduce the level of discrimination against minorities. It is important to mention the lingering presence of sectarianism in all Northern Irish economic activities. In a small village, there will be two butchers. It is known that one is Catholic and the other is Protestant. The same goes for pubs. So, in this way, a semblance of peace is present, but it is always tinged with sectarian rivalry or division.

Third, the level of protection against the discrimination of minorities is contextually dependent. The analysis of the *Lee v. Ashers* case shows, for instance, that in Northern Ireland, homosexual people's access to the market of goods and services is protected in a way that, for historical reasons, is distinctive from the rest of the United Kingdom and Europe. In contrast with Italy and England, LGBTQ citizens in Northern Ireland receive the same level of protection against discrimination that is granted to religious communities.

We explained that religious communities and also religious minorities have a history of sectarian discrimination in both Britain and Italy. In the United Kingdom, religious communities were not a protected category until the enactment of the Human Rights Act 1998. A similar level of protection was established in Italy in 1948. Northern Ireland, in comparison to the rest of the United Kingdom and Italy, adopted statutory measures aimed at reducing the divisive effect of sectarianism. Again, it is reasonable to suggest that such a policy was driven by the desire to ensure an open market rather than an attempt to protect rights *à la* Dworkin. Regardless, the result was the comparatively extensive protection of the prerogative to access the market by an identity group and a related obligation to keep it open. The SOR 2006 includes homosexual people in the list of protected categories.

The Supreme Court in *Lee v. Ashers*, it is reasonable to suggest, misunderstood the direct link between identity and claims in a consociative democracy like the one in Northern Ireland. The connection between identity (of gay people) and claims is axiomatic in consociative democracies and, in the appeal case, it was subsumed. The Supreme Court instead perceived the connection as unengaged. The decision focused only on 'the message' and on the beneficiaries of such a message.

The analysis of dissonant elements in the *Lee v. Ashers* case shows the contextual nature of the process that each legal system might adopt in balancing the prerogative to manifest beliefs. It is not the aim of the chapter to suggest that either of the two prerogatives should trump the other. The analysis of the Italian legal system shows, for instance, that an automatic compliance with international obligations to reduce all forms of discrimination and an articulated constitutional protection of human dignity might not be the proxy for a definitive normative stance in relation to the protection of the prerogative to manifest identity-based beliefs. Again, the argument here is not that Italian law and international law might never provide the protection to the prerogative given to homosexual people to have their identity-based claim reproduced by a service provider. This balance is likely to change in the near future. It might change because the balance between the prerogative to manifest identity-based claims and the prerogative to refuse the reproduction of such claims by a company (for religious reasons) is eminently a pragmatic activity. Parliament, not judges, should assess the effects of coinciding but conflicting manifestations of identity-based beliefs and the effects that such a balance might have in an open society.

References

Alexy, Robert. 2003. 'Constitutional Rights, Balancing, and Rationality'. *Ratio Juris* 16, no. 2: 131–40.

Association de médiation sociale v. Union locale des syndicats CGT (2014) C-176/12. ECJ Grand Chamber. Accessed 12 August 2019. https://eur-lex.europa.eu/legal-content/EN/TXT/PDF/?uri=C ELEX:62012CJ0176&from=EN.

Azuelos-Atias, Sol. 2010. 'Semantically Cued Contextual Implicatures in Legal Texts'. *Journal of Pragmatics* 42, no. 3: 728–43. https://doi.org/10.1016/j.pragma.2009.07.009.

Baum, Gregory. 2002. *Nationalism, Religion and Ethics*. Montréal: McGill-Queen's University Press.

Bauman, Zygmunt. 1998. 'On Postmodern Uses of Sex'. *Theory Culture and Society* 15, no. 3/4: 19–34.

———. 1999. *In Search of Politics*. Cambridge, UK: Polity.

———. 2001. 'Identity in the Globalising World'. *Social Anthropology* 9, no. 2: 121–30.

Bellah, Robert. N. 1967. 'Civil Religion in America'. *DAEDALUS* 134, no. 4: 40–55.

Bonaventura, Florence Di. 2016. 'Italy and Lega Nord: Stories of Communities, National (Dis)Integration and Spaces of (Restricted) Citizenship'. *Società Mutamento Politica: Rivista Italiana Di Sociologia* 7, no. 13: 289–307. https://doi.org/10.13128/SMP-18288.

Boyle, Kevin, and Tom Hadden. 1995. 'The Peace Process in Northern Ireland'. *International Affairs* 71, no. 2: 269.

Breda, Vito. 2004. 'Democracy and Constitutional Recognition: The Political Role of Nationalism in Modern Democracy'. PhD diss., University of Edinburgh.

———. 2007. 'Constitutional Identities in a Liquid Society'. In *Liquid Society and Its Law*, edited by Jiri Priban, 153–70. Aldershot: Ashgate.

———. 2013. 'Balancing Secularism with Religious Freedom: In Lautsi v Italy the European Court of Human Rights Evolved'. In *Legitimizing Human Rights*, edited by Angus J. L. Menuge, 127–42. Farnham, UK: Ashgate.

———. 2015a. 'Shari'a Law in Catholic Italy: A Non-agnostic Model of Accommodation'. In *The Sociology of Shari'a: Case Studies from around the World*, edited by Adam Possamai, James T. Richardson, and Bryan S. Turner, 119–37. Boundaries of Religious Freedom: Regulating Religion in Diverse Societies. Cham, Switzerland: Springer International.

———. 2015b. 'Lingering with Intent: The UK Constitutional Review'. In *Constitutional Review and Democracy*, edited by Miodrag A. Jovanovic, 165–84. The Hague: Eleven International.

———. 2017. 'Constitutional Patriotism'. In *Handbook of Patriotism*, edited by Mitja Sardoč, 1–13. Cham, Switzerland: Springer International.

———. 2018. *Constitutional Law and Regionalism: A Comparative Analysis of Regionalist Negotiations*. Northampton: Edward Elgar.

Breda, Vito, and Andreja Mihailovic. 2019. 'New Caledonia: The Archipelago That Does Not Want to Be Freed'. *Comparative Law Journal of the Pacific* 24 (Small Countries): 69–95.

Brennan, Niamh. 1997. 'A Political Minefield: Southern Loyalists, the Irish Grants Committee and the British Government, 1922–31'. *Irish Historical Studies* 30, no. 119: 406–19.

Brittain, Stephen. 2015. 'The Relationship between the EU Charter of Fundamental Rights and the European Convention on Human Rights: An Originalist Analysis'. *European Constitutional Law Review* 11, no. 3: 482–511.

Canovan, Margaret. 2000. 'Patriotism Is Not Enough'. *British Journal of Political Science* 30, no. 3: 413–32.

Casanas Adam, Elisenda. 2017. 'The Referendum on Catalonian Independence: The Position of the Catalan Authorities'. *UK Constitutional Law Association Blog*. https://ukconstitutionallaw.org/2017/10/03/elisenda-casanas-adam-the-referendum-on-catalonian-independence-the-position-of-the-catalan-authorities/.

Chappell, David A. 2013. *The Kanak Awakening: The Rise of Nationalism in New Caledonia.* Honolulu: University of Hawaii Press.

Charter of Fundamental Rights of the European Union 2012/C 326/02. OJ L. Accessed 17 March 2017. https://eur-lex.europa.eu/legal-content/EN/TXT/PDF/?uri=CELEX:12012P/TXT&from=EN.

CJEU. 2017. *Achbita and Another v. G4S Secure Solutions* NV All ER 108.

Coakley, John. 2017. 'Adjusting to Partition: From Irredentism to "Consent" in Twentieth-Century Ireland'. *Irish Studies Review* 25, no. 2: 193–214.

Coleman, Jules L., and Brian Leiter. 1993. 'Determinacy, Objectivity, and Authority'. *University of Pennsylvania Law Review* 142, no 2 (December): 549–638.

Coughlin, John J. 2013. 'Separation, Cooperation, and Human Dignity in Church-State Relations'. *Jurist* 73: 539.

Council Directive 2000/78/EC, OJ L 303, 2.12.2000, 16–22.

Council Directive 2004/113/EC, OJ L 373, 21.12.2004, 37–43.

Doe, Norman. 2011. *Law and Religion in Europe: A Comparative Introduction.* Oxford: Oxford University Press.

Dworkin, Ronald. 1978. *Taking Rights Seriously.* Cambridge, MA: Harvard University Press.

Eisenbergt, Melvin A. 2003. 'Mistake in Contract Law'. *California Law Review* 91, no. 6: 1573–643.

Enns, Phil. 2010. 'Habermas, Democracy and Religious Reasons'. *Heythrop Journal* 51, no. 4: 582–93.

The European Convention on Human Rights. 1950. ECHR. https://www.echr.coe.int/documents/convention_eng.pdf.

European Union. Consolidated Version of the Treaty on the Functioning of the European Union, 26 October 2012, OJ L, 2012/C 326/01. https://eur-lex.europa.eu/LexUriServ/LexUriServ.do?uri=OJ:C:2012:326:FULL:EN:PDF.

First Minister and the Deputy First Minister (NI). 2006. The Equality Act (Sexual Orientation) Regulations (Northern Ireland). Vol. 439.

Flick, Giovanni Maria. 2015. *Elogio Della Dignità.* Città del Vaticano: Libreria editrice vaticana.

Foster, Neil. 2016. 'The Ashers "Gay Cake" Appeal – One of These Things Is Not Like the Others'. *Law and Religion Australia* (blog), 25 October. https://lawandreligionaustralia.blog/2016/10/25/the-ashers-gay-cake-appeal-one-of-these-things-is-not-like-the-others/.

———. 2020. 'Respecting the Dignity of Religious Organisations: When Is It Appropriate for Courts to Decide Religious Doctrine?' *University of Western Australia Law Review* 47, no. 1: 175–219.

Fuller, Lon L. 1958. 'Positivism and Fidelity to Law: A Reply to Professor Hart'. *Harvard Law Review* 71, no. 4: 630–72.

Gagnon, Alain-G., and José María Sauca. 2014. *Negotiating Diversity Identity, Pluralism and Democracy.* Brussels: P.I.E. Peter Lang.

Gerstmann, Evan. 2017. *Same-Sex Marriage and the Constitution.* Cambridge: Cambridge University Press.

Goodall, Kay, Peter Hopkins, Simon McKerrell, John Markey, Stephen Millar, John Richardson and Michael Richardson. 2015. 'Community Experiences of Sectarianism'. Edinburgh: Scottish Government Social Research. https://www.gov.scot/publications/community-experiences-sectarianism/.

Gordley, James. 2004. 'Mistake in Contract Formation'. *American Journal of Comparative Law* 52, no. 2: 433–68. https://doi.org/10.2307/4144457.

Government of Wales Act 1998 Ch 38.

Graham, L. Bennett. 2009. 'Defamation of Religions: The End of Pluralism'. *Emory International Law Review* 23: 69.

Habermas, Jürgen. 1975. *Legitimation Crisis*. Translated by Thomas McCarthy. Boston, MA: Beacon.

———. 1991. *The Structural Transformation of the Public Sphere: An Inquiry into a Category of Bourgeois Society*. Cambridge, MA: MIT Press.

———. 1995. 'Address: Multiculturalism and the Liberal State'. *Stanford Law Review* 47, no. 5: 849–53.

———. 2006. *The Divided West*. Cambridge: Polity.

Hadden, Tom, and Kevin Boyle. N.d. 'Northern Ireland: Conflict and Conflict Resolution'. In *Ethic Conflict and Human Right*, edited by Kumar Rupesinghe, 53–64. Tokyo: United Nations University Press.

Hart, H. L. A. 1997. *The Concept of Law*, 2nd ed. Edited by Penelope Bulloch and Joseph Raz. Oxford: Oxford University Press.

Hasson, Kevin. 2003. 'Religious Liberty and Human Dignity: A Tale of Two Declarations'. *Harvard of Law & Public Policy* 27: 81–92.

Holy See, Kingdom of Italy. 1929. *Lateran Pacts*.

Hughes, Brian. 2016. 'Loyalists and Loyalism in a Southern Irish Community, 1921–1922*'. *Historical Journal* 59, no. 4: 1075–105. https://doi.org/10.1017/S0018246X15000576.

Italian Constitutional Court. 1975. Decision n. 188. Accessed 11 August 2019.

———.1996. Decision n. 334. Accessed 11 August 2019.

Italian Parliament. 1998. *Law n. 286 1998*.

———. 2006. *Law n. 196 2006*.

———. 2011. *Law n. 150 2011*.

Joint Committee on Human Rights. 2006. 'Joint Committee on Human Rights – Twenty-Third Report'. UK Parliament. https://publications.parliament.uk/pa/jt200506/jtselect/jtrights/239/23902.htm.

Kavanagh, Aileen. 2009. *Constitutional Review under the UK Human Rights Act*. Cambridge: Cambridge University Press.

Keating, Michael. 2001. *Nations against the State: The New Politics of Nationalism in Quebec, Catalonia and Scotland*, 2nd ed. Basingstoke: Palgrave Macmillan.

Keating, Michael, and John McGarry. 2001. *Minority Nationalism and the Changing International Order*. Oxford: Oxford University Press.

Keating, Michael, and Alex Wilson. 2014. 'Regions with Regionalism? The Rescaling of Interest Groups in Six European States'. *European Journal of Political Research* 53, no. 4: 840–57.

Kenyon, Andrew T. 2010. 'What Conversation? Free Speech and Defamation Law'. *Modern Law Review* 73, no. 5: 697–720.

Kokkinakis v. Greece [1993] ECHR 20, (1994) 17 EHRR 397. Accessed 11 August 2019.

Laclau, Ernesto, and Chantal Mouffe. 2001. *Hegemony and Socialist Strategy: Towards a Radical Democratic Politics*, 2nd ed. London: Verso.

Lee v. Ashers Baking Company Ltd (Northern Ireland). 2018 H.R.L.R. 22 843. UKSC.

Lee v. Mcarthur. 2016, 22 H.R.L.R 700. Court of Appeal (Northern Ireland).

Levinson, Stephen C. 1983. *Pragmatics*. Cambridge: Cambridge University Press.

Long, Gianni. 1990. *Alle Origini Del Pluralismo Confessionale: Il Dibattito Sulla Liberta Religiosa Nell'eta Della Costituente*. Bologna: Il Mulino.

MacCulloch, Diarmaid. 2010. *A History of Christianity: The First Three Thousand Years*. London: Penguin.

Macedo, Stephen. 1995. 'Liberal Civic Education and Religious Fundamentalism: The Case of God v. John Rawls?' *Ethics* 105, no. 3 (April): 468–96.

Mangold v. Helm (2005) C-144/04. n.d. ECJ. Accessed 12 August 2019.

Marrani, David. 2013. *Dynamics in the French Constitution: Decoding French Republican Ideas*. Abingdon: Routledge.

Milo, Dario. 2008. *Defamation and Freedom of Speech*. Oxford: Oxford University Press.

Modugno, Franco. 1995. *I "nuovi diritti" nella giurisprudenza costituzionale*. Torino: Giappichelli.

Mouffe, Chantal. 1992. *Dimensions of Radical Democracy: Pluralism, Citizenship, Community*. London: Verso.

Muftugil, Onur. 2017. 'Human Dignity in Muslim Perspective: Building Bridges'. *Journal of Global Ethics* 13, no. 2: 157–67.

Neuvonen, Päivi Johanna. 2015. '"Inequality in Equality" in the European Union Equality Directives: A Friend or a Foe of More Systematized Relationships between the Protected Grounds?' *International Journal of Discrimination and the Law* 15, no. 4: 222–40.

'Noumea Accord: Agreements, Treaties and Settlements – New Caledonia'. 2002. *Australian Indigenous Law Reporter* 7 no. 1: 88 – 96.

The Northern Ireland Act 1998 Ch 47.

O'Cinneide, Colm. 2008. 'The New Human Rights Culture'. In *Constitutional Futures Revisited: Britain's Constitution to 2020*, edited by Robert Hazell, 159–78. Basingstoke: Palgrave Macmillan.

Oppenheimer, Mark. 1996. '"The Inherent Worth and Dignity": Gay Unitarians and the Birth of Sexual Tolerance in Liberal Religion'. *Journal of the History of Sexuality* 7, no. 1: 73–101.

Orgad, Liav. 2009. '"Cultural Defence" of Nations: Cultural Citizenship in France, Germany and the Netherlands'. *European Law Journal* 15, no. 6: 719–37.

Rafter, Kevin. 2012. 'Redefining the Irish Presidency: The Politics of a "Non-Political" Office, 1973–1990'. *Irish Political Studies* 27, no. 4: 576–95. https://doi.org/10.1080/07907184.2012.734450.

'Registering a Civil Partnership'. 2015. Nidirect. 19 October.

Rosenfeld, Michel, and Andras Sajo. 2012. 'Constitutional Identity'. In *The Oxford Handbook of Comparative Constitutional Law*, edited by Michel Rosenfeld and Andras Sajo, 756–76. New York: Oxford University Press.

Ruggeri, Antonio, and A. Spadaro. 1991. 'Dignità dell'uomo e giurisprudenza costituzionale (prime notazioni)'. *Politica del diritto*, no. 3: 343–77.

Senato della Republica. 1948. Constitution of the Italian Republic.

Skoczeń, Izabela. 2016. 'Minimal Semantics and Legal Interpretation'. *International Journal for the Semiotics of Law – Revue Internationale de Sémiotique Juridique* 29, no. 3: 615–33.

Spano, Francesco. 2009. 'La "rivoluzione discreta": A centosessan'anni dalle Lettere Patenti'. *Quaderni Di Diritto e Politica Eclesiastica* 1: 219–32.

Tan, Kevin. 2016. 'Defaming Politicians, Scandalising the Courts: A Look at Recent Developments in Singapore'. In *Democracy, Media and Law in Malaysia and Singapore: A Space for Speech*, edited by Andrew T. Kenyon, Tim Marjoribanks and Amanda Whiting, 1st ed, 105–28. Abingdon: Routledge.

Thiemann, Ronald F. 1996. *Religion in Public Life : A Dilemma for Democracy*. Washington, DC: Georgetown University Press.

Turgeon, Luc, and Alain-G. Gagnon. 2013. 'The Representation of Ethnic and Linguistic Groups in the Federal Civil Service of Belgium and Canada'. *Canadian Public Administration* 56, no. 4: 565–83. https://doi.org/10.1111/capa.12040.

The UK Government and the Government of Ireland. 1998. 'The Belfast Agreement: An Agreement Reached at the Multi-Party Talks on Northern Ireland 1998. Cm 3883 (the Belfast Agreement)'.

UK Parliament. 1920. Government of Ireland Act 1920 c.67.

———. 1998. Human Rights Act 1998 c.42.

————. 1998. Scotland Act 1998 Ch 46 Schedule 7.

Ward, David. 1997. ' "Italy" in Italy: Old Metaphors and New Racisms in the 1990'. In *Revisioning Italy: National Identity and Global Culture*, edited by Beverly Allen and Mary Russo, 81–99. Minneapolis: University of Minnesota Press.

Wolff, Stefan. 2004. 'The Institutional Structure of Regional Consociations in Brussels, Northern Ireland, and South Tyrol'. *Nationalism and Ethnic Politics* 10, no. 3: 387–414.

Zucca, Lorenzo. 2007. *Constitutional Dilemmas: Conflicts of Fundamental Legal Rights in Europe and the USA*. Oxford: Oxford University Press.

Chapter Eleven

TRINITY WESTERN UNIVERSITY AND THE FUTURE OF CONSERVATIVE RELIGIOUS EDUCATION

Greg Walsh

I Introduction

The extent to which minority religious communities should be protected when their convictions differ from mainstream society is one of the more challenging aspects faced by our lawmakers.[1] A central area where this challenge arises is education where religious schools, universities and other educational organizations are established and operated according to religious convictions that violate deeply rooted beliefs about justice held by others in society.

The extent to which such religious organizations should be allowed to operate was addressed by the Supreme Court of Canada in *Law Society of British Columbia v. Trinity Western University and Brayden Volkenant* [2018] 2 SCR 293 (hereinafter: *Law Society of B.C.*) and *Trinity Western University and Brayden Volkenant v. Law Society of Upper Canada* [2018] 2 SCR 453 (hereinafter: *Trinity Western*).

Trinity Western University is a private Christian university based in the Canadian province of British Columbia. It required all staff members and students to agree to a code of conduct known as the Community Covenant Agreement (hereinafter: the Covenant) as a condition of attendance or employment. The Covenant expressed traditional Christian beliefs and required a person to live according to a set of moral principles that included abstaining from 'sexual intimacy that violates the sacredness of marriage between a man and a woman' (3). The Covenant applied to the conduct of employees and students on and off campus, and members were expected to hold each other accountable for complying with the Covenant, which could include making a complaint to the university administration that a person was violating the Covenant.

In 2012, the university decided to establish a law school for approximately 170 students. It received approval from the Federation of Law Societies of Canada, but was

---

[1] I would like to thank Barry W. Bussey and Amy Ross for their helpful comments on an earlier draft of the chapter. Commentary on the chapter is welcome and can be sent to greg.walsh@nd.edu.au.

ultimately rejected by the law societies of Ontario, Nova Scotia and British Columbia (Bussey 2019, 141–52). The law societies refused to accredit the proposed law school on the basis that requiring students to abstain from sexual activity outside a heterosexual marriage would adversely impact LGBT students and the wider community.

Trinity Western University and one of its graduates (who hoped to attend the law school) (hereinafter: both referred to as 'TWU') asked the courts to review the decisions of the law societies. The Supreme Court and Court of Appeal of both British Columbia and Nova Scotia ruled in favour of TWU. In Ontario, the Divisional Court and the Court of Appeal ruled for the law society. The Supreme Court of Canada (hereinafter: the Court) ruled in favour of the law societies of British Columbia and Ontario (it did not consider the ruling in Nova Scotia as there was no appeal from the decision in that jurisdiction). The Court held that the denial of accreditation was within the statutory power of the law societies, that the procedures adopted in reaching a decision were valid and the denial of accreditation did not violate the Canadian Charter of Rights and Freedoms (hereinafter: the Charter). It was a split decision with seven justices ruling for the law societies (the majority judgement by Abella, Moldaver, Karakatsanis, Wagner and Gascon JJ and two concurring judgements by McLachlin CJC and Rowe J) and a dissenting judgement by Côté and Brown JJ. In response to the Court's decision, TWU amended its policies so that the Covenant is now optional for students while still being compulsory for staff members (Trinity Western University n.d.).

TWU argued that the law societies violated their freedoms of conscience, religion, expression and association protected by Section 2 of the Charter and their right to equality protected by Section 15 of the Charter. The Court rejected TWU's assertion that the Charter was violated, relying on a range of grounds, including an extensive use of the terms 'equality', 'dignity' and 'diversity'. The Court also based its conclusion on other grounds, including that accreditation would have an adverse impact on the quality of legal professionals, that there was no violation of some of the rights relied upon by TWU (Rowe J, for example, argued there was no violation of religious liberty) and that public confidence in the competency of the law societies would be undermined. In particular, the Court relied on the harm that accrediting the law school might have caused especially to members of the LGBT community such as the difficulties LGBT law students would encounter as law students at TWU and the emotional harm that might be experienced by LGBT individuals by a decision to approve the law school.

The aim of this chapter is not to consider the merits of the Court's final decision but instead to assess the legitimacy of how it approached justifying its decision by relying on equality, dignity and diversity. These concepts are typically central to human rights analyses so a critical assessment of their role in the Court's reasoning is useful to determine whether they were applied in a manner that was fair to the interests of all parties.

The Court's approach in *Law Society of B.C.* is the central focus of the chapter as it was in this case that the justices provided detailed reasons for their conclusions, while in the accompanying *Trinity Western* decision, the Court often simply repeated or referred to its reasoning in *Law Society of B.C.* Considering the similarity between the cases, the comments about the merits of the reasoning in *Law Society of B.C.* are also relevant to the reasoning in *Trinity Western*.

II Equality

Central to the Court's decision on the reasonableness of denying TWU accreditation was the claim that the Covenant violated the equality rights of LGBT students and subjected them to unjust discrimination. The Covenant would have forced LGBT students to affirm that same-sex sexual activity was unethical (at least for TWU students) and to refrain while students from expressing their sexuality even if they were legally married. On the adverse impact of the Covenant, then Chief Justice McLachlin wrote:

> TWU's insistence on the mandatory Covenant is a discriminatory practice. It imposes burdens on LGBTQ people on the sole basis of their sexual orientation. Married heterosexual law students can have sexual relations, while married LGBTQ students cannot. The Covenant singles out LGBTQ people as less worthy of respect and dignity than heterosexual people, and reinforces negative stereotypes against them. It puts them to a choice – attend TWU or enjoy equal treatment. Those LGBTQ students who insist on equal treatment will have less access to law school and hence the practice of law than heterosexual students – heterosexual students can choose from all law schools without discrimination, while one law school, the TWU law school, would only be available to LGBTQ students willing to endure discrimination. (*Law Society of B.C.*, para 138)

This adverse impact on LGBT students that 'effectively impose[d] inequitable barriers on entry to the school and ultimately, inequitable barriers on entry to the profession' led the majority to hold that the Law Society of British Columbia (LSBC) was justified in denying accreditation as they had 'an overarching interest in protecting the values of equality and human rights' (para 41). Similarly, Rowe J declared that the denial of accreditation was reasonable 'given the Covenant's imposition of discriminatory barriers to admission' and the importance of 'promoting equal access to the legal profession' (para 258). McLachlin CJC agreed, holding that the LSBC could not 'condone a practice that discriminates by imposing burdens on LGBTQ people on the basis of sexual orientation, with negative consequences for the LGBTQ community, diversity and the enhancement of equality in the profession' (para 146).

A The Meaning of Equality

The central problem with the Court's reliance on equality was its failure to engage fairly with the concept of equality. The dissenting justices, Côté and Brown JJ, for example, argued that 'the majority's preferred value of "equality" [...] without further definition [is] too vague a notion on which to ground a claim to equal treatment in any and all concrete situations, such as admission to a law school' (*Law Society of B.C.*, para 310). The majority, the justices declared, had 'advance[d] "equality" in a purely abstract sense, such that it could mean almost anything' (ibid.).

There is nothing in the Court's judgement that indicates that it engaged with the philosophical complexities concerning the concept of equality and its applicability in resolving moral disputes. Peter Westen, for example, famously argued that although appeals to equality have produced many desirable social changes, it is an 'empty' concept that can be used to support conflicting moral positions:

> Equality will cease to mystify – and cease to skew moral and political discourse – when people come to realize that it is an empty form having no substantive content of its own. That will occur as soon as people realize that every moral and legal argument can be framed in the form of an argument for equality. People then will answer arguments for equality by making counterarguments for equality. Or simpler still, they will see that they can do without equality altogether. (1982, 596)

Sherif Girgis similarly contests a range of commonly held views about equality – including that it is inherently valuable, the basis of other moral principles and that we are equal in dignity – while still recognizing that it can play a useful role in emphasizing important norms of moral reasoning (2014, 144–45). Further concerns exist about whether the widely accepted view that there is no hierarchy of human rights is being undermined by lawmakers affirming the pre-eminence of equality claims especially over religious liberty claims. Campbell J, for example, expressed his concerns in *Trinity Western University v. Nova Scotia Barristers' Society* ([2015] NSCC 25 at para 271) that if the test for human rights compliance 'becomes, "What does it say about equality if …?", then a hierarchy of rights has been established, with religious liberty relegated to vastly diminished status'. Of particular assistance to the Court was an article by Rex Ahdar that provided a detailed and contemporary account of some of the conceptual difficulties related to equality when it conflicts with a religious liberty claim, and even explicitly discussed the relevance of these issues to the denial of TWU's accreditation (2016, 172–78).

Some kind of response by the Court to these important issues was required in order for the public to be satisfied that the Court was relying on an intelligible meaning of equality and justly applying its understanding in resolving the dispute. Instead, the Court in its judgement does not address any of the concerns raised about the concept of equality. Further, a search on the Court's online database of cases revealed no cases where a justice has considered any of these authors' arguments about equality. A criminal law article by Westen was referenced, but his article on equality – published in 1982 and widely regarded as a work of central importance in equality jurisprudence – never appears to have been considered by the Court. Considering the gravity of the criticisms made about equality, this lack of engagement is a profound failure by the Court to takes its judicial role seriously, especially in light of the substantial reliance that it and so many other courts place on equality in resolving legal disputes.

Côté and Brown JJ similarly avoided engaging with the philosophical complexities involved with the concept of equality. However, they did demonstrate the flexible nature of the concept by proposing an approach to equality that includes toleration of difference that could be used to support TWU. In support of their proposed approach, the justices referred to Justice Sachs who declared that 'equality means equal concern and respect across difference. It does not presuppose the elimination or suppression of difference […] Equality therefore does not imply a levelling or homogenisation of behaviour but an acknowledgment and acceptance of difference' (*National Coalition for Gay and Lesbian Equality v. Minister of Justice* 1998, 6, para 132, qtd in *Law Society of B.C.*, para 310). Such an understanding of equality could support, rather than undermine, TWU's use of the Covenant, directly contradicting the majority's claim that the denial of accreditation was justified by equality concerns.

B The Religious Dimension of Equality Claims

The Court also failed to account for the breadth of protection typically offered by the right to equality, instead proceeding on an unjustifiably limited approach that only considered how the right to equality could protect the LGBT community. However, the right to equality has a broad scope covering a range of attributes, including that of religion.

Article 26 of the International Covenant on Civil and Political Rights, for example, states that 'all persons are equal before the law and are entitled without any discrimination to the equal protection of the law [...] the law shall prohibit any discrimination and guarantee to all persons equal and effective protection against discrimination on any ground such as race, colour, sex, language, religion [...] or other status'. Similarly, under Article 2 of the International Covenant on Economic, Social and Cultural Rights an obligation is imposed on states to protect rights contained in the Covenant 'without discrimination of any kind as to race, colour, sex, language, religion [...] or other status'. Section 15 of the Charter similarly declares that 'every individual is equal before and under the law and has the right to the equal protection and equal benefit of the law without discrimination and, in particular, without discrimination based on race, national or ethnic origin, colour, religion, sex, age or mental or physical disability'.

The protection that the right to equality affords to religion has been affirmed by Thomas C. Berg who notes that

> equality interests appear on the religious objectors' side too. Gay-rights laws (in marriage or other contexts) may be facially neutral and generally applicable, but like other generally applicable laws their effects fall disproportionately on those religious individuals and groups – in this case, religious traditionalists – whose practices conflict with them. (2010, 225)

Similarly, Iain Benson argues that as religion is protected by the right to equality, 'placing equality and non-discrimination over against religion or placing some forms of non-discrimination (say, sexual orientation) as things more important than the religious person's freedom against non-discrimination is an error – though an all too common one' (2010, 31). The importance of this point is emphasized by Barry W. Bussey who warns that 'if the liberal democratic project is to be successful, there needs to be a recognition that rights of sexuality and the right of religious freedom are both rights of equality' (2017, 202, internal citations removed).

Although the religious liberty claim was central to TWU's claim, they also supported their position by appealing to the right to equality. As the decision to deny them accreditation caused TWU to suffer harm due to their religious commitments it would seem that they had a legitimate claim that their equality rights were violated. Indeed, the gravity of this violation of equality is arguably greater than that experienced by students who might have been adversely affected by the Covenant. These students could still have attended the TWU law school or alternatively decided to study at another law school. However, the denial of accreditation prevents the TWU law school from operating or at least from operating in a manner that TWU considers most appropriate due to its religious commitments. This outcome deprived students, teachers, administrators, other religious adherents and the public of the unique educational, character-forming, cultural and spiritual benefits that could be provided by TWU's proposed law school – benefits that could not be obtained by these individuals attending alternative, non-religious law schools.

Further, the alternative law schools should not be regarded as operating according to a neutral worldview. As TWU's denial of accreditation and subsequent litigation revealed, there is intense hostility among law professors and lawyers against those who adhere to traditional positions on sexuality and marriage, which could be expected to extend to other traditional positions on ethical issues and perhaps even religious belief itself. As Bussey noted, 'A primary source of opposition to TWU's law school proposal was the legal academy. It was the law deans who first voiced opposition […] and every common law faculty in the country passed resolutions condemning TWU' (2019, 197, internal citations removed; see also Bussey 2017, 217–53). To put it mildly, the environment within these law schools is unlikely to be supportive of students, professors and other employees with traditional religious convictions who would have preferred to have joined the TWU law school. The existence of a hostile environment within law schools was supported by Roderick A. Macdonald, a law professor at McGill University, who revealed that

> over the years [he has] heard dozens of conservative Christians lament their sense of exclusion at McGill and the hostility they feel from their classmates and even professors. In language very similar to the well-understood claims of silencing advanced by women, people of colour, and the LGBTQ communities, these students with sincerely held religious beliefs feel that they are being deprived of the right to participate fully in the life of the law school. (Macdonald and McMorrow 2014, 733 n. 54)

Many students and employees with traditional beliefs will likely either pursue an alternative career path or conceal their identity while at these schools. The harm likely to be suffered by these individuals would seem to be very similar to the harm that TWU's Covenant was predicted to have on LGBT students. It may even be worse considering that LGBT students could have attended other law schools.

The Court, however, rejected the attempted equality claim by TWU. The majority recognized that TWU could potentially rely on equality to support their position but ultimately held that whether TWU's claim was based in religious liberty, equality or some other ground, denying accreditation was a proportionate limitation considering the objectives pursued by the LSBC (*Law Society of B.C.*, paras 77–78). The failure of the majority to assess the alternative arguments proposed by TWU led McLachlin CJC to succinctly observe about the merits of TWU's equality claim that the 'majority does not decide this question' (para 123).

McLachlin CJC did address the equality claim but held that even 'if members of the TWU community could show that the LSBC's decision creates a distinction on the enumerated ground of religion, it does not arise from any prejudice or stereotype and effects no discrimination on religious grounds but, rather, ensures equal access to all prospective law students' (para 123). The absence of 'prejudice or stereotype' is disputable but particularly remarkable is the former Chief Justice's emphatic claim that the denial of accreditation 'effects no discrimination on religious grounds'. Denying a religious organization the ability to effectively operate because of its religious commitments would seem to be a clear example of religious discrimination. Such an adverse effect could be justifiable in light of other considerations but to dismiss in a few words the legitimacy of TWU's claim that their equality rights were violated seems untenable.

Rowe J similarly recognized that there could potentially be some basis to an equality claim by TWU but considered such an argument was not available on the material before the Court. TWU 'provided little to go on regarding these subsidiary arguments [which included the equality claim]', in the opinion of Rowe J, nor 'were these claims argued extensively before the courts below or before this Court' (para 252). Such a position is difficult to understand considering the equality claim by TWU is evident on the facts of the case.

There was also a failure by the Court to adequately account for the fact that the Covenant was not targeted at LGBT students. As Côté and Brown JJ recognized, the purpose of the Covenant was 'not to exclude LGBTQ persons, or anybody else, but to establish a code of conduct which ensures the vitality of its religious community. No one group is singled out, and many others (notably unmarried heterosexual persons) would be bound by it' (para 335). A lack of intention to discriminate is not fatal to a legitimate claim that unjust discrimination has occurred, but the failure of the Court to sufficiently respect that the aim of the Covenant was to build an authentic religious community faithful to the community's theological and moral principles and not to discriminate against LGBT students undermines the merits of their judgement.

The gravity of the failure by the Court to take seriously the meaning of equality and the legitimacy of TWU's equality claim should not be underestimated. It was a profound failure to take seriously some of the strongest counters to the claim that TWU's conduct unjustifiably violated the right to equality, which was *the* central argument that the Court relied upon to decide the appeal in favour of the LSBC. Not only was this a major error in reasoning, it also had an important tactical effect by denying TWU the ability to claim that they suffered harm from the discriminatory conduct of the LSBC. This failure led the Chief Justice, for example, to start her judgement with the following question: 'Can a law society deny students from a religious-based law school the right to practise law, on the basis that the school discriminates against same-sex LGBTQ couples?' (para 107). An approach that would have showed appropriate respect to the equality claims of both parties would have replaced 'can a law society *deny* students' with 'can a law society *discriminate* against students (and TWU)'. Such an approach would have been respectful of the equality claims of both sides and would have avoided accusing only one side of 'discriminating' at the very beginning of the judgement before the Chief Justice had even begun to provide the reasons for her decision.

III Dignity

The need to protect the dignity of LGBT students was another central argument the Court relied upon in affirming the reasonableness of the decision to deny accreditation to TWU. McLachlin CJC held that the 'Covenant singles out LGBTQ people as less worthy of respect and dignity than heterosexual people, and reinforces negative stereotypes against them' (*Law Society of B.C.*, para 138). The majority similarly claimed that 'LGBTQ students enrolled at TWU's law school may suffer harm to their dignity' (para 98). They also referred with approval to the dissenting judgement of L'Heureux-Dubé J in *Trinity Western University v. British Columbia College of Teachers* [2001] 1 SCR 772 2001 SCC 31 (hereinafter: *Trinity Western University* 2001), an earlier decision by the Court that upheld an order requiring the accreditation of an education program proposed by TWU despite its critical views of homosexual behaviour. In her judgement L'Heureux-Dubé J affirmed that it was not possible 'to condemn a practice so central to the identity of a protected and vulnerable minority without thereby discriminating against its members and affronting their human dignity and personhood' (para 69, quoted in *Law Society of B.C.*, para 97). Yet, nowhere in the Court's reasoning did any of the justices define how they understood dignity, which is essential to any determination of whether a dignitary violation has occurred.

A The Limited Meaning of Dignity

Relying on the concept of dignity to help resolve disputes is an approach favoured by many judges, not just those who ruled against TWU. Such is its popularity that it has been used by the Supreme Court of Canada in at least 452 decisions (according to a search for 'dignity' on the Court's online case database) and by the US Supreme Court justices in over 900 opinions (Henry 2011, 178). Despite its popularity, the concept is criticized on many of the same grounds as equality, including that it is ambiguous, if not meaningless, and therefore unsuitable as a tool for resolving legal disputes.

Ruth Macklin, after reviewing the use of dignity in bioethical debates, concluded that 'appeals to dignity are either vague restatements of other, more precise, notions or mere slogans that add nothing [...] dignity is a useless concept' (2003, 1419–20). Dennis Davis described dignity as 'a piece of a jurisprudential Legoland – to be used in whatever form and shape is required by the demands of the judicial designer' (1999, 413). Similarly, John Harris writes, 'Appeals to human dignity are, of course, universally attractive; they are also comprehensively vague' (1998, 163) – a point amplified by Steven Pinker (2008) in an article entitled 'The Stupidity of Dignity' declaring that the concept is 'slippery and ambiguous [...] [and] spawns outright contradictions at every turn'.

Criticisms of dignity have also been expressed by the judiciary. Sachs J, for example, in *Christian Education South Africa v. Minister of Education* 2000 (4) SA 757 (Constitutional Court) observed:

The overlap and tension between the different clusters of rights reflect themselves in contra-dictory assessments of how the central constitutional value of dignity is implicated. On the one hand, the dignity of the parents may be negatively affected when the state tells them how to bring up and discipline their children and limits the manner in which they may express their religious beliefs. The child who has grown up in the particular faith may regard the punishment, although hurtful, as designed to strengthen his character. On the other hand, the child is being subjected to what an outsider might regard as the indignity of suffering a painful and humiliating hiding deliberately inflicted on him in an institutional setting. (14–15)

The Court itself has also previously expressed concerns about the utility of dignity in resolving disputes. In *R. v. Kapp* [2008] 2 SCR 483 it declared that although dignity was the guiding principle for all rights, not just the right to equality, the concept was so ambiguous that it had no practical value in determining when differential treatment was inappropriate. The Court affirmed that

human dignity is an essential value underlying the s. 15 equality guarantee. In fact, the protec-tion of all of the rights guaranteed by the *Charter* has as its lodestar the promotion of human dignity [...] But as critics have pointed out, human dignity is an abstract and subjective notion that [...] cannot only become confusing and difficult to apply; it has also proven to be an additional burden on equality claimants, rather than the philosophical enhancement it was intended to be. (Paras 21–22)

Despite these concerns, previous justices of the Court have at least attempted to define the concept before relying upon it in their judgement. Iacobucci J in *Law v. Canada (Minister of Employment and Immigration)* [1999] 1 SCR 497 at para 53, for example, provides the following account:

What is human dignity? There can be different conceptions of what human dignity means. For the purpose of analysis under s. 15(1) of the *Charter*, however, the jurisprudence of this Court reflects a specific, albeit non-exhaustive, definition [...] Human dignity means that an individual or group feels self-respect and self-worth. It is concerned with physical and psycho-logical integrity and empowerment. Human dignity is harmed by unfair treatment premised upon personal traits or circumstances which do not relate to individual needs, capacities, or merits. It is enhanced by laws which are sensitive to the needs, capacities, and merits of different individuals, taking into account the context underlying their differences. Human dignity is harmed when individuals and groups are marginalized, ignored, or devalued, and is enhanced when laws recognize the full place of all individuals and groups.

There has also been extensive work undertaken by academics into how dignity should be defined. Christopher McCrudden undertook a detailed study into how different cultures and legal systems understood 'dignity' and concluded that only a few core concepts could be discerned among the different approaches:

A basic minimum content of the meaning of human dignity can be discerned: that each human being possesses an intrinsic worth that should be respected, that some forms of conduct are inconsistent with respect for this intrinsic worth, and that the state exists for the individual not vice versa. The fault lines lie in disagreement on what that intrinsic worth consists in, what forms of treatment are inconsistent with that worth, and what the implications are for the role of the state. (2008, 723)

Patrick Lee and Robert P. George similarly considered a range of definitions for dignity and argued that the most important sense of the term was the view that 'all human beings have a special type of dignity which is the basis for (1) the obligation all of us have not to kill them, (2) the obligation to take their well-being into account when we act, and (3) even the obligation to treat them as we would have them treat us' and that this dignity means that 'there is no class of human beings to which other human beings should be subordinated when considering their interests or their well-being, and when devising laws and social policies' (2008, 173–75). John Corvino et al. proposed that dignity is harmed when people are treated as 'having less than equal moral standing' (2017, 73). An alternative approach was taken by Leslie Henry who reviewed how the term had been used especially by US Supreme Court justices and argued that dignity could be defined as 'institutional status', 'equality', 'liberty', 'personal integrity' and 'collective virtue' (2011, 189–229).

The proposed definitions by these scholars are only a very small sample of the voluminous work that has been undertaken in an attempt to determine the proper meaning that should be given to dignity. This work is admittedly expansive and complex, but that can hardly be a justification for judges to neglect the task of determining for themselves whether they consider dignity a meaningless concept and, if not, what definition they have decided to adopt. Instead, the Court in *Law Society of B.C.* avoided explaining what it meant by dignity and simply proceeded to claim that one of the key reasons why the LSBC was justified in denying accreditation was that the Covenant violated the dignity of LGBT people. Such an approach is even more remarkable considering that L'Heureux-Dubé J in her dissenting opinion in *Trinity Western University* 2001 at paras 103–10 actually did affirm the definition of dignity adopted by the Court in *Law v. Canada (Minister of Employment and Immigration)* and provided a reasoned decision why she rejected the individual respondent's claim that her dignity had been harmed by the decision not to approve TWU's education program.

B The Difficulties in Claiming Dignity Violations without Defining the Concept

As the Court provided no account of its conception of dignity, it encountered significant difficulty in adequately responding to claims that TWU and its Covenant actually did respect the dignity of LGBT individuals. The Covenant, for example, required staff members and students to 'cultivate Christian virtues, such as love, joy, peace, patience, kindness, goodness, faithfulness, gentleness, self-control, compassion, humility, forgiveness, peacemaking, mercy and justice' and to 'treat all persons with respect and dignity' (2). These commitments by TWU indicate that the legal community that it would have created would have been respectful of all its members, which undermines claims that LGBT students would have been harmed by such a community.

The Court responded to TWU's claim that they were able to respect the dignity of the LGBT community by simply asserting that it is not possible to condemn all sexual activity of individuals who are not in a heterosexual marriage without 'affronting their human dignity' (*Law Society of B.C.*, para 97). However, without the Court providing a definition of how it understands dignity, it was left simply to affirm this proposition as correct without being able to provide any further justification for its position. This meant it was unable to engage with the claim made by TWU that it could both require adherence to the Covenant and respect the dignity of LGBT students and the wider community especially considering the caring environment that TWU was dedicated to creating.

C Defending TWU on the Grounds of Dignity

The ambiguous meaning of dignity means that TWU could also have relied on this ground to claim that accreditation was necessary to protect those committed to joining and supporting TWU's proposed law school whose dignity had been and would continue to be harmed by the refusal to grant accreditation. All the points that Iacobucci J makes about the harm caused when dignity is not adequately protected can occur when the operation of religious organizations is impaired, including harm to self-respect and self-worth, and an undermining of physical and psychological well-being. As mentioned in the section on equality, the extent of this harm was particularly grave since the accreditation decision prevented the law school from operating (at least in a way that complied with TWU's religious commitments) and forced professors, teachers and other employees to either abandon their preferred careers or seek admission to other law schools where they would likely confront hostility towards a range of their religious convictions.

On the significance of the failure to adequately protect the dignity of religious persons Richard Moon argues that when a 'religious community is marginalized by the state in some way, the individual adherent may experience this not simply as a rejection of her/his views and values but as a denial of her/his equal worth or desert – as unequal treatment that affects her/his dignity' (2012, 324). This approach was adopted by Côté and Brown JJ who, in support of TWU, held that 'accommodating diverse beliefs and values is [...] necessary to ensure that the dignity of all members of society is protected' (*Law Society of B.C.*, para 334).

The Court, however, did not respond in any way to the possibility that TWU could legitimately make their own dignitary claim that would need to be considered with the dignitary claim made by those adversely affected by the Covenant. Instead, the Court proceeded to use dignity merely as a rhetorical device to defend their position and provided no further reasons why the concept could only support their decision affirming the reasonableness of denying TWU accreditation.

IV Diversity

The need to protect diversity within the legal profession was another key justification relied upon by the Court. McLachlin CJC held that the LSBC could not 'condone a practice that discriminates by imposing burdens on LGBTQ people on the basis of sexual orientation, with negative consequences for the LGBTQ community, diversity and the enhancement of equality in the profession' (*Law Society of B.C.*, para 146). Similarly, Rowe J affirmed that 'supporting diversity within the bar' (para 258) was a valid reason to deny TWU accreditation. The majority also declared that the LSBC was 'entitled to be concerned that inequitable barriers on entry to law schools would effectively impose inequitable barriers on entry to the profession and risk decreasing diversity within the bar', emphasizing that access to law schools should be 'based on merit and diversity, not exclusionary religious practices' (para 103). The majority expanded on the importance of diversity, arguing that LSBC was

> entitled to interpret the public interest in the administration of justice as being furthered by promoting diversity in the legal profession – or, more accurately, by avoiding the imposition of additional impediments to diversity in the profession in the form of inequitable barriers to entry. A bar that reflects the diversity of the public it serves undeniably promotes the administration of justice and the public's confidence in the same. A diverse bar is more responsive to the needs of the public it serves. A diverse bar is a more competent bar. (Para 43)

A The Contribution of TWU to Social Diversity

As with equality and dignity, the Court failed to explain the meaning and scope of the concept of diversity which it relied upon to affirm that the denial of accreditation would make a valuable contribution to social diversity. The Court's limited engagement with the concept of diversity makes it difficult to understand why TWU could not legitimately claim that its law school would have promoted, rather than undermined, diversity.

Such a claim is not difficult to support. Out of the 21 law schools in Canada in 2019, none of them was religiously affiliated. The proposed TWU law school would have been Canada's first religious law school offering a distinctive legal environment for its students, professors, other staff members and the wider community. The plan for the law school was for it to specialize in areas such as 'non-profit charity law and small-business law, which are not available to Canadian law students today' (Trinity Western University 2012, 7–12; 2018). Its unique Christian environment would also likely have produced distinctive law graduates who would have increased both the diversity of the legal profession and Canadian society. To address concerns that its graduates might offer their legal services in a discriminatory manner, TWU emphasized that it was dedicated to graduating 'caring and trustworthy lawyers ready to represent and advocate for all Canadians, regardless of race, gender, religion or sexual identification' (Trinity Western University 2018). TWU was also committed to establishing and operating the law school without relying on any government funding (Trinity Western University 2012, 37–38).

The contribution of religion to diversity was recognized by the European Court of Human Rights in *Kokkinakis v. Greece* (1994) 17 EHRR 397 at para 31, which affirmed that freedom of religion is 'one of the most vital elements that go to make up the identity of believers and of their conception of life, but it is also a precious asset for atheists, agnostics, sceptics and the unconcerned. The pluralism indissociable from a democratic society, which has been dearly won over the centuries, depends on it'. This point was emphasized by Côté and Brown JJ in their judgement where they stressed that

> accommodating diverse beliefs and values is a pre-condition to the secularism and the pluralism that are needed to protect and promote the *Charter* rights of all Canadians. State neutrality requires that the state neither favour nor hinder any particular belief, and the same holds true for non-belief. Either way, state neutrality must prevail [...] Tolerance and accommodation of difference serve the public interest and foster pluralism. Acceptance by the LSBC of the unequal access effected by the Covenant would signify the accommodation of difference and of the TWU community's right to religious freedom, and not condonation of discrimination against LGBTQ persons. Approval of the proposed law school is, therefore, not inconsistent with 'public interest' objectives of maintaining equal access and diversity in the legal profession, and indeed, it promotes those objectives. (*Law Society of B.C.*, para 269)

Concerns should also have been raised about the possibility that the LSBC's denial of accreditation might cause TWU and other religious organizations to become even more restrictive in their policies. In justifying the LSBC's decision, the majority held that 'being required by someone else's religious beliefs to behave contrary to one's sexual identity is degrading and disrespectful' (para 298). Such views indicate that TWU undermined its position by being willing to include individuals with different worldviews. If TWU had instead restricted admission only to those who were of the same faith, its claim for protection under the Charter may have been more likely to succeed. Such a view is supported by the approach of Rowe J who, in holding that the LSBC's denial of accreditation did not violate the right to religious liberty, made much of TWU's willingness to admit students of any worldview (paras 240–42). The pressure for religious organizations to only employ and admit faithful religious adherents would likely lead to further social fragmentation and undermine the promotion of tolerance and diversity that was central to the Court's reasoning.

Another way in which diversity is threatened by the Court's decision is the pressure it may place on religious communities to close religious educational institutions and other religious organizations or simply not establish them. It should not be underestimated how important many religious communities view their convictions on marriage and sexuality. Attempts to require religious adoption agencies in the United States to provide their services to same-sex couples led to these agencies closing rather than compromising on their beliefs (United States Conference of Catholic Bishops 2018). Similar outcomes for other religious organizations can be expected if lawmakers require them to contradict their religious convictions. As Bussey warns, 'If the religious organization cannot be what it was set up to be, it will not exist. A religious community will not permit its time, money, and effort to go toward a project that is not in keeping with the community's strongly held views. It has no interest in its institution being like the public institutions' (2016, 1196).

B *TWU's Convictions and the Limits of Diversity*

Critics may respond by arguing that not all convictions should be regarded as making a worthwhile contribution to social diversity. Such a position is not controversial. The Court in *Loyola High School v. Quebec (Attorney General)* (2015 SCC 12 at para 43), for example, affirmed that a 'secular state does not – and cannot – interfere with the beliefs or practices of a religious group unless they conflict with or harm overriding public interests'. As the Court's judgement against TWU makes clear, many consider that the conviction that sexual activity should be reserved for heterosexual marriages does 'harm overriding public interests' especially due to its adverse impact on the LGBT community. Indeed, some argue that TWU's views should be treated with the same contempt with which society treats racist convictions. Such was the position adopted by Elaine Craig, who argued that there is 'no principled foundation upon which to approve a law school program delivered by a private institution with religiously based homophobic policies and practices but not one delivered by a private institution with religiously based racist policies and practices' (2013, 159).

The claim that TWU's convictions are too extreme to be regarded as making a positive contribution to social diversity is undermined by the substantial legislative, judicial and community affirmation of the legitimacy of this view, even if it is now held only by a minority of people in Canada and culturally similar countries. Côté and Brown JJ, for example, affirmed that 'the holding and expression of the moral views of marriage which underpin the portions of TWU's Covenant that are at issue here have been expressly recognized by Parliament as being not inconsistent with the public interest and worthy of accommodation' (*Law Society of B.C.*, para 336). The dissenting justices supported their position by referring to the preamble and section 3.1 of the *Civil Marriage Act*, S.C. 2005, which declared that

> it is not against the public interest to hold and publicly express diverse views on marriage [...] no person or organization shall be deprived of any benefit, or be subject to any obligation or sanction, under any law of the Parliament of Canada solely by reason of their exercise, in respect of marriage between persons of the same sex, of the freedom of conscience and religion guaranteed under the Canadian Charter of Rights and Freedoms or the expression of their beliefs in respect of marriage as the union of a man and woman to the exclusion of all others based on that guaranteed freedom.

Additional support for TWU's convictions and their valuable contribution to diversity is provided by Iacobucci and Bastarache JJ in *Trinity Western University* 2001. After reflecting on the legitimacy of accommodating TWU's convictions, they assert that 'the diversity of Canadian society is partly reflected in the multiple religious organizations that mark the societal landscape and this diversity of views should be respected' (para 33). TWU's traditional views (at least in regards to marriage) were also affirmed in *Obergefell v. Hodges*, 576 US ___ (2015) where the majority of the US Supreme Court Justices (who ruled in favour of same-sex marriage) held that 'many who deem same-sex marriage to be wrong reach that conclusion based on decent and honorable religious or philosophical premises, and neither they nor their beliefs are disparaged here' (19). The traditional view is further endorsed by the substantial community support it receives throughout Western countries. In Australia, for example, a ballot held in 2017 by the federal government to determine the views of citizens on whether same-sex marriage should be introduced revealed that 61.6 per cent were in support of same-sex marriage with a still substantial minority of 38.4 per cent supporting the traditional definition of marriage (Australian Bureau of Statistics 2017).

Further, TWU's position needs to be understood in the context of its Christian commitments, especially the Covenant's requirement that members of TWU must 'treat all persons with respect and dignity'. An attempt to isolate its convictions on sexuality and marriage from the rest of its commitments in assessing whether TWU makes a valuable contribution to social diversity would be unjust. TWU's commitment to respecting all people, including LGBT people, is a key feature that distinguishes the university from many other institutions that disadvantage people on characteristics such as gender identity, sexuality, sex and race. A further relevant difference is the rational basis on which marriage can be understood as a heterosexual institution in contrast to the irrational view that interracial couples could not form a marriage. Chief Justice Roberts in *Obergefell v. Hodges*, for example, declared that marriage did not arise 'as a result of a prehistoric decision to exclude gays and lesbians. It arose in the nature of things to meet a vital need: ensuring that children are conceived by a mother and father committed to raising them in the stable conditions of a lifelong relationship' (4–5). Considering these reasons, the claim that TWU's convictions place it beyond what a tolerant society can reasonably accommodate should be rejected.

V Conclusion

The Court substantially justified its decision to affirm the reasonableness of LSBC's refusal to accredit TWU through a superficial reliance on equality, dignity and diversity that failed to engage with the many complexities raised by these concepts. Côté and Brown JJ expressed this criticism appropriately in their judgement when, after they had discussed a range of ways that equality could be defined, they observed that

> none of these (or innumerable other) meanings of 'equality' as an abstraction are relied on by the majority or are evident in its reasons. Rather, by relying on a sweeping abstraction, the majority avoids actually making explicit its moral judgment, its premises and the legal authority on which it rests. A 'value' of 'equality' is, therefore, a questionable notion against which to balance the exercise by the TWU community of its *Charter*-protected rights. (*Law Society of B.C.*, para 311)

This criticism of the Court's approach to its use of equality could similarly apply to its reliance on dignity and diversity. As the highest judicial body in an advanced legal system that takes seriously its commitments to human rights, the Court should not be attempting to resolve disputes in a manner that fails to engage at even a basic level with the philosophical complexities surrounding these concepts.

Such an approach would be unjustified in any matter before the Court, but this decision was one of profound importance. The Court has now clearly affirmed that accrediting organizations may effectively prevent religious universities from operating if they hold to traditional views on marriage and sexuality and expect their staff members and students to do the same.

What impact will this decision have on the future of religious education providers and other religious organizations in Canada? Will accreditation bodies allow religious schools, charities and other organizations to continue operating in the same manner, if at all, if they require their members to adhere to traditional religious beliefs on marriage and sexuality? Will other government and quasi-government bodies consider that they can now legitimately use whatever power they have over such organizations to penalize them for holding to these convictions? Why should bodies with such power limit their focus only to religious organizations with traditional beliefs on marriage and sexuality considering that these organizations might have other controversial beliefs concerning religious practice, religious belief, sex or gender identity? This concern was expressed by Côté and Brown JJ who noted that even if the restrictions on sexual activity outside of traditional marriage were removed 'on the Chief Justice's reasoning the LSBC could not approve the proposed law school, since the admissions policy would still exclude persons who could not agree to live by the tenets of the evangelical Christian faith as expressed by the Covenant' (para 311).

The Court's use of equality, dignity and diversity to rule against TWU raises concerns that future measures against conservative religious organizations will be similarly supported by the Court through a superficial reliance on these concepts that fails to recognize that these very concepts may actually support the targeted religious organizations. Such an approach undermines public confidence in the competency of judicial authorities and the legitimacy of granting courts the role of assessing laws, policies and practices on the basis of their compliance with human rights principles.

References

Ahdar, Rex. 2016. 'The Empty Idea of Equality Meets the Unbearable Fullness of Religion'. *Journal of Law, Religion & State* 4: 146–78.

Australian Bureau of Statistics. 2017. '1800.0 – Australian Marriage Law Postal Survey, 2017 – National Results'. Updated 20 January 2018. https://www.abs.gov.au/ausstats/abs@.nsf/mf/1800.0.

Benson, Iain. 2010. 'Taking Pluralism and Liberalism Seriously: The Need to Re-understand Faith, Beliefs, Religion and Diversity in the Public Sphere'. *Journal of the Study of Religion* 23: 17–41.

Berg, Thomas C. 2010. 'What Same-Sex-Marriage and Religious-Liberty Claims Have in Common'. *Northwestern Journal of Law and Social Policy* 5, no. 2: 206–35.

Bussey, Barry W. 2016. 'The Legal Revolution against the Place of Religion'. *Brigham Young University Law Review* 4: 1127–214.

———. 2017. 'Rights Inflation: Attempts to Redefine Marriage and the Freedom of Religion – the Case of Trinity Western University School of Law'. *Regent University Law Review* 29, no. 2: 197–257.

————. 2019. 'The Legal Revolution against the Accommodation of Religion: The Secular Age versus the Sexular Age'. PhD diss., University of Leiden. https://openaccess.leidenuniv.nl/handle/1887/74476.

Christian Education South Africa v Minister of Education [2000] ZACC 11, 2000 (4) SA 757 (Constitutional Court).

Civil Marriage Act, S.C. 2005, c. 33.

'Community Covenant Agreement'. Trinity Western University. Updated 25 June 2019. https://www.twu.ca/sites/default/files/community_covenant_june_25_2019.pdf.

Corvino, John, Ryan T. Anderson and Sherif Girgis. 2017. *Debating Religious Liberty and Discrimination*, Kindle ed. New York: Oxford University Press.

Craig, Elaine. 2013. 'The Case for the Federation of Law Societies Rejecting Trinity Western University's Proposed Law Degree Program'. *Canadian Journal of Women and the Law and Justice Journal* 25, no. 1: 148–70.

Davis, Dennis. 1999. 'Equality: The Majesty of Legoland Jurisprudence'. *South African Law Journal* 116: 398–414.

Girgis, Sherif. 2014. 'Equality and Moral Worth in Natural Law Ethics and Beyond'. *American Journal of Jurisprudence* 59, no. 2: 143–62.

Harris, John. 1998. 'Cloning and Human Dignity'. *Cambridge Quarterly of Healthcare Ethics* 7: 163.

Henry, Leslie Meltzer. 2011. 'The Jurisprudence of Dignity'. *University of Pennsylvania Law Review* 160: 169.

International Covenant on Civil and Political Rights. Opened for signature 16 December 1966, 999 UNTS 171. Entered into force 23 March 1976.

International Covenant on Economic Social and Cultural Rights. Opened for signature 16 December 1966, 999 UNTS 3. Entered into force 3 January 1976.

Kokkinakis v. Greece (1994) 17 EHRR 397.

Law v. Canada (Minister of Employment and Immigration), [1999] 1 SCR 497.

Law Society of British Columbia v. Trinity Western University and Brayden Volkenant, [2018] 2 SCR 293.

Lee, Patrick, and Robert George. 2008. 'The Nature and Basis of Human Dignity'. *Ratio Juris* 21, no. 2: 173–93.

Loyola High School v. Quebec (Attorney General), 2015 SCC 12.

Macdonald, Roderick A., and Thomas B. McMorrow. 2014. 'Decolonizing Law School'. *Alberta Law Review* 51, no. 4: 717–38.

Macklin, Ruth. 2003. 'Dignity Is a Useless Concept'. *British Medical Journal* 327: 1419–20.

McCrudden, Christopher. 2008. 'Human Dignity and Judicial Interpretation of Human Rights'. *European Journal of International Law* 19, no. 4: 655–724.

Moon, Richard. 2012. 'The Supreme Court of Canada's Attempt to Reconcile Freedom of Religion and Sexual Orientation Equality in the Public Schools'. In *Faith, Politics, and Sexual Diversity in Canada and the United States*, edited by David Rayside and Clyde Wilcox, 321–38. Vancouver: UBC.

National Coalition for Gay and Lesbian Equality v. Minister of Justice [1998] ZACC 15, 1999 (1) S.A. 6.

Obergefell v. Hodges, 576 US ___ (2015).

Pinker, Steven. 2008. 'The Stupidity of Dignity'. *New Republic*, 28 May. https://newrepublic.com/article/64674/the-stupidity-dignity.

R. v. Kapp, [2008] 2 SCR 483.

Trinity Western University. 2012. 'Proposal for a School of Law at Trinity Western University'. June. https://www.twu.ca/sites/default/files/assets/proposal-for-a-school-of-law-at-twu.pdf.

————. 2018. 'Trinity Western University Disappointed with Supreme Court Decision Signalling Loss of Support for Diversity in Canada'. Updated 15 June 2018. https://www.twu.ca/news-events/news/trinity-western-university-disappointed-supreme-court-decision-signalling-loss.

————. N.d. 'Frequently Asked Questions'. Accessed 3 January 2020. https://www.twu.ca/frequently-asked-questions.

Trinity Western University and Brayden Volkenant v. Law Society of Upper Canada, [2018] 2 SCR 453.

Trinity Western University v. British Columbia College of Teachers, [2001] 1 SCR 772.

Trinity Western University v. Nova Scotia Barristers' Society, [2015] NSCC 25.

United States Conference of Catholic Bishops. 2018. 'Discrimination against Catholic Adoption Services'. Accessed 4 January 2020. http://www.usccb.org/issues-and-action/religious-liberty/discrimination-against-catholic-adoption-services.cfm.

Westen, Peter. 1982. 'The Empty Idea of Equality'. *Harvard Law Review* 95: 537–96.

Chapter Twelve

SACRIFICING DIGNITY TO PROTECT DIGNITY: HUMAN DIGNITY AND EXCLUSION ZONES IN AUSTRALIA

Michael Quinlan

A disciple is not above his teacher, nor a servant above his master.

– Mt. 10:24, ESV

Introduction

Most Australian states and territories have introduced exclusion zones around clinics which terminate pregnancies (Access to Terminations Act 2013 (Tas) s. 9(2); Wellbeing Act 2008 (Vic) s. 185D; Pregnancy Law Reform Act 2017 (NT); Safe Access Act 2018 (NSW); Termination of Pregnancy Act 2018 (Qld)). The remaining states are considering doing so (The Greens, 2017; Government of Western Australia Department of Health, 2019). These laws make a range of activities illegal if they take place near a clinic. Many of the proscribed activities such as harassment, intimidation, besetting, threatening, hindering, obstructing or filming anyone attempting to access such places would already have been unlawful in most places under other general laws (New South Wales (NSW) 2018a; Queensland Law Reform Commission 2017, para 248). No prosecutions for breach of exclusion zone laws to date have involved these behaviours, and they are not the subject of this chapter. All prosecutions to date have instead been for peaceful communications about abortion in the excluded zone (*Police v. Preston* 2016; *Edwards v. Clubb* 2017; *Bluett v. Popplewell* 2018; Lynch 2018; Pierre 2019). It is this aspect of these laws and specifically the criminalization of prayer and sidewalk counselling which is the subject of this chapter. Sidewalk counsellors for the purposes of this chapter are people who seek to provide information near abortion clinics about alternatives to the termination of pregnancy and about practical assistance which is available to those who choose to continue their pregnancies to term (*McCullen v. Coakley* 2014).

While this chapter does not address any potential bases on which such laws might be challenged under Australian or international law, it is necessary background to note that the Victorian and Tasmanian exclusion zone laws have been found to be valid by Australia's highest court, the High Court of Australia (*Clubb v. Edwards; Preston v. Avery* 2019). Although s. 116 of the Australian Constitution includes a prohibition on the Commonwealth legislating to prevent 'the free exercise of any religion', it has been read narrowly by the High Court such that no religious believer has succeeded in such a case. The provision only applies to the Commonwealth and not to state laws. Given the High Court's interpretation of s. 116 and the fact that the Australian Constitution does not have any other specific protection of freedom of speech, assembly, conscience or religion, the challenges to exclusion zone laws in the High Court relied only on alleged breaches of the implied freedom of political communication. This freedom has been created by that court. The challenges failed essentially because the communications in question were found not to be relevantly political.

In justifying exclusion zones, legislatures have relied heavily on arguments grounded on the protection of the dignity of women seeking the services provided at clinics that perform abortions and of workers at clinics.

This chapter considers that ground as a foundation for criminalizing prayer and side-walk counselling within such a zone. Section I provides some background to abortion in Australia and briefly considers what the laws prohibit and who has been prosecuted under them. Section II considers the justifications for such laws, the meaning of dignity and what appears to have been meant by dignity when used by proponents of such laws. Section III considers the impact of such laws on the dignity of women within exclusion zones whereas Section IV considers their impact on the dignity of religious believers seeking to manifest their faith through prayer or sidewalk counselling. On the basis of this review the chapter contends that arguments grounded on dignity are a poor justifi-cation for such laws. It argues that, using Adam Schulman's terminology, the term 'dig-nity' in the context of exclusion zones has been used as 'a mere slogan that camouflages unconvincing arguments and unarticulated biases' (Schulman, cited in Glendon 2011). As a result, the chapter argues for the reversal of the exclusion zone trend and for the amendment of existing exclusion zone laws to narrow the scope of the proscribed con-duct. If the protection of dignity is a grounding for the laws, that protection should extend to the protection of the dignity of those adversely impacted by such laws.

I. Background

Abortion in Australia

Abortion has been decriminalized in Tasmania, Victoria, Western Australia, Queensland, the Australian Capital Territory (ACT), New South Wales (NSW) and the Northern Territory. The procedure has been widely used and widely available for many years now, including in South Australia, which is the only state not to have formally decriminalized the procedure in all circumstances (Fleming and Tonti-Filippini 2007). There are demands for full decriminalization there as well (Chapman 2019). It has been estimated that a minimum of 83,000 women access a termination each year in Australia (Hanrahan 2019). The procedure is widely accepted; 81 per cent of those surveyed in the 2003 Australian Survey of Social Attitudes agreed that a woman should have the right to choose whether or not to terminate a pregnancy (Children by Choice 2018). This study also found that 77 per cent of religious respondents shared that view (Children by Choice 2018). Widespread support for the procedure is confirmed by a Vote Compass poll of over 300,000 respondents undertaken in April 2019 in which more than 71 per cent of voters wanted the procedure to be more available (Hanrahan 2019). Support for expanded access was strong among religious groups with 56 per cent of Catholics, 53 per cent of Protestants and 54 per cent of those of other religious faiths supporting an increase in the accessibility of abortion services (Hanrahan 2019). However, as the European Court of Human Rights has observed, 'there can be no doubt as to the acute sensitivity of the moral and ethical questions raised by the issue of abortion or as to the importance of the public interest at stake' (*Annen v. Germany* 2015, paras 65, 74). It is, as the then Acting Chief Justice Kirby of NSW observed in 1995, 'a subject that is prone to engender very strong feelings' (*CES v. Superclinics* 1995, 70). Analyzing the arguments about abortion, including dignity claims for the human foetus or embryo, are beyond the scope of this chapter (Fisher 2012, 157). It is sufficient for present purposes to recognize that such arguments exist.

What the Exclusion Zone Laws Prohibit and Who Has Been Prosecuted

The laws criminalize communications about abortion within the zone. In NSW to be unlawful, the communication must be 'reasonably likely to cause distress or anxiety' (Safe Access Act 2018 (NSW), s. 98D). Given the nature of abortion, virtually any communication or protest about the topic is likely to have this effect (*Clubb v. Edwards; Preston v. Avery* 2019, para 303). The exclusion zone in most jurisdictions covers 70,000 square metres around every clinic in the jurisdiction (para 508). The laws impose significant penalties for breach (Safe Access Act 2018 (NSW), s. 98D). For example, in NSW a first offence attracts a maximum penalty of a $5,500 fine or 6 months of imprisonment, and a subsequent offence twice that penalty (ibid.). Only Christians motivated by their faith to engage in peaceful, non-violent behaviour have been prosecuted in Australia for breaching exclusion zone laws to date (*Police v. Preston* 2016; Minear 2016; Pierre 2019; Bevin 2015; *Edwards v. Clubb* 2017; *Bluett v. Popplewell* 2018; Lynch 2018). All but one prosecution has been successful (*Bluett v. Popplewell* 2018).

Do the Laws Prohibit Prayer?

The High Court has recognized that the laws prohibit even silent prayer vigils (*Clubb v. Edwards; Preston v. Avery* 2019, paras 164, 171, 475). The intended proscription of prayer seems clear from the parliamentary debates. For example, in the second reading speech, in support of the exclusion zone law in Tasmania, Minister Michelle O'Byrne observed that 'it will stop the silent protests outside termination clinics that purport to be a vigil of sorts or a peaceful protest but which, by their very location, are undoubtedly an expression of disapproval' (Walsh 2018). Another example is the second reading debate on the NSW law where Jenny Aitchison, the member for Maitland, said:

> I understand that there are people in this place of all faiths. I grew up in the Catholic Church. However, if someone approached me and told me that they were praying for me in a way that suggested I was doing the wrong thing and in an attempt to persuade me to change my

mind, I would see it as an appalling affront and assault. It is not physical, sexual or emotional assault: it is an assault on my faith. And it is completely wrong. (NSW 2018a, 3)

The view that the laws prohibit prayer is not contradicted by the fact that the sole prosecution for praying to date was unsuccessful. That case did not involve a prayer vigil or a group gathered together in prayer and the location was not typical. It failed as the court concluded that the defendants' behaviour would not have been identifiable by observers, drew no attention and was not therefore a communication (*Bluett v. Popplewell* 2018, paras 80–82, 84–86). The facts were unusual as the three Christians each prayed in silence whilst walking (and in one case sitting) alone near an office block where a clinic operated (paras 80–82, 84–86).

Do the Laws Prohibit Sidewalk Counselling?

The parliamentary debates also make the intention to prohibit sidewalk counselling clear. For example, in the second reading speech on the NSW law, Leslie Williams, the member for Port Macquarie, described sidewalk counselling as abhorrent behaviour to which the legislation would put an end. In her view, while sidewalk counsellors may believe that they are acting in the best interests of the women they engage with, they are all untrained, unqualified and ignorant of the background and circumstances of the woman they intimidate (NSW 2018a, 1).

In debates on the same legislation it is clear that several parliamentarians have even more adverse views regarding sidewalk counsellors. For example, Jenny Aitchison, the member for Maitland, asserted that

these sidewalk counsellors are not protesting. They are not exercising free speech. They are harassing and targeting a group of the most vulnerable women in our community at what is probably the most vulnerable time in their lives. (NSW 2018a, 5)

In her second reading speech in the Legislative Council of NSW Penny Sharpe claimed that

those sidewalk counsellors do not know [who the women accessing clinics are or why they are there] and they do not care. They do not care about those women, their actions do nothing to change the laws and they certainly help nobody. That is why women need safe access zones. (NSW 2018b, 3)

Jodie Harrison, the member for Charleston, recommended other activities to sidewalk counsellors:

I have no doubt that some who protest and provide 'sidewalk counselling' have the best intentions to help women and children. However there are other real means to help people in need. I urge those people to help precious infants who have been born on our streets; they can help in our schools and in our hospitals. They can help through a number of charities aimed at improving the lives of babies, children and women. These are the ways in which a child's life can truly be changed for the better by well-meaning people. (NSW 2018a, 23)

Religious Motivations to Communicate in Exclusion Zones

It is not necessary to consider the specific religious motivations which prompt Christians to communicate in exclusion zones. A Tasmanian case provides some examples. Here the religious motivations of the accused were relevant because the constitution of that state provides protection for religious freedom (Constitution Act 1934 (Tas) s. 46(1)). It is unique in Australia in that regard. Although those protections were read narrowly in the manner of s. 116 of the Australian Constitution and found not to apply, the magistrate recorded the religious motivations of the accused:

> [Mr Preston] has been a Christian since he was 14 and he believes that human life has been created in the image of God uniquely and that human life is of absolute importance as referred to in the Scriptures. That God knows us even when we are growing in our mother's womb and in particular he believes in the incarnation of Jesus as God coming into the world born in his mother's womb and that that validates human life at every stage.

> Mr Preston explained that the Bible teaches people to care for one another and in particular to help those who are most vulnerable or defenceless. He considers that a child in the womb would be probably the most vulnerable category of human beings and that they are completely defenceless. He believes that it is right and necessary that people come to the aid of those who are vulnerable and defenceless which includes unborn children.

> Essentially as I understood Mrs Stallard's evidence she regards herself as a practicing Christian, and as part of her Christian beliefs she believes that every life is sacred. [Mrs Stallard believes] that an unborn life does not have a voice, and that as part of her Christian beliefs she needs to stand up for people without a voice which led her to protest with Mr Preston. (*Police v. Preston* 2016, para 65)

II. Dignity as a Justification for Exclusion Zones

In all jurisdictions, the protection of dignity has been a justification for these laws. For example, the Explanatory Memorandum to the Victorian legislation describes the law's purpose as being

> to provide for safe access zones around premises at which abortions are provided to protect the safety and wellbeing and respect the privacy *and dignity* of both people accessing the services provided at the premises, and employees and other persons accessing the premises in the course of their duties and responsibilities. (Explanatory Memoranda, Safe Access Zones Bill 2015, 2, emphasis added)

Similarly Gabrielle Williams, the member for Dandenong, speaking in support of that law, argued:

This bill will help ensure that women and staff accessing medical facilities that provide abortions can do so safely and with their privacy *and dignity* maintained and most of all it will ensure that respect is maintained for the lawful decision of a woman to do whatever she chooses to do with her own body. (Victoria 2015, 4387, emphasis added)

In the same debates, Ellen Sanell, the member for Melbourne, observed that 'everyone in our community has a right to access lawful health services without interference and in a manner that protects their safety, their wellbeing, their privacy and of course *their dignity*' (ibid., emphasis added).

In arguing for the NSW law, Jenny Aitchison, the member for Maitland, said:

We must respect the right of a woman to make a decision without someone who has no knowledge of her personal circumstances judging her, showing her terrible images, photographing her or even acting in a way that would make her feel even worse about the choice she has made. To assume that any women would even consider going to an abortion clinic without thinking deeply about it is appallingly disrespectful to women. It undermines women's power over ourselves, our agency, our thoughtfulness and our intel- ligence. It is disrespectful and *it robs us of our dignity*. We must ensure that women, their partners and the clinic staff who are there to support them are safe and *have dignified access* to clinics where abortions and other reproductive services are provided. (NSW 2018a, 4, emphasis added)

What Is 'Dignity'?

The word 'dignity' has many meanings (Kurti 2018, 61). It has its critics. Some argue that it is used in vague and inconsistent ways and that it is regularly the subject of emotive appeals (Black 1999, 209). It is 'an odd and ambiguous concept' (Waldron 2010, cited in Durham and Scharffs 2010, 559). It is 'an abstract and subjective notion that [can be] confusing and difficult to apply' (*R. v. Kapp* 2008, para 28). It can be deployed in 'mere slogans that add nothing to an understanding of a topic' (Macklin 2003, 1419). Justice Scalia described it as an empty term which merely '[decorates] a value judgment and conceal[s] a political choice' (*Planned Parenthood of Southeastern Pennsylvania v. Casey* 1992, 983). Despite these criticisms, dignity is regularly used, although not defined, in Australian parliamentary debates, in constitutions and in United Nations' documents (Liu 2014; Glendon 2011). Luban (2009) describes its usage as 'a kind of placeholder – an uncontroversial, neutral-sounding term for the unknown "X" that anchors human rights'. These criticisms are not without merit, but the term is so entrenched in political, international, religious and ethical discourse that it is difficult to imagine it disappearing, so it needs to be addressed. As Schroeder observes:

Dignity is a slippery idea, but it is also a very powerful one and the demand to purge it from ethical discourse amounts to whistling in the wind. It is better to try and eliminate some of its slipperiness than to ignore its supremacy in everyday morality and national and international law. (2008, 233)

Schroeder gives the term four meanings which she calls Kantian, Aristocratic, Comportment and Meritorious Dignity. Aristocratic Dignity is not relevant for present purposes (233). While Killmister argues that these definitions can be further distilled into two (2010, 160) and all would not accept Schroeder's definitions, this chapter will adopt them to guide its discussion.

Schroeder (2008) defines Kantian Dignity or, to give it her fuller description, 'the modern Kantian-inspired definition of dignity' as 'an inviolable property of all human beings, which gives the possessor the right never to be treated simply as a means but always at the same time as an end' (233). In this formulation, dignity is an intrinsic characteristic of human beings which cannot be lost or diminished (ibid.; Kurti 2018, 61). All human beings share in this dignity equally because they are human, and it does not fluctuate due to social circumstances (Somerville 2001, 257). In this understanding a person experiencing anxiety, pain or embarrassment is no less or more dignified as a consequence (Schroeder 2008, 233).

Schroeder defines Comportment Dignity as 'the outwardly displayed quality of a human being who acts in accordance with society's expectations of well-mannered demeanor and bearing' (2008, 234). This might encapsulate what Somerville calls 'social dignity' (2001, 257). As she describes it, this 'is a cultural, largely aesthetic sense of dignity that imbues persons with dignity/worth according to their demonstrations of grace, composure, upright carriage, good manners, modesty, personal hygiene and self-sufficiency' (ibid.). This is a form of dignity which can be gained or lost depending on how the community considers another person's attributes or behaviours and it fluctuates depending on local standards (ibid.).

Finally, Schroeder defines Meritorious Dignity as a dignity which is earned or deserved as a consequence of acting in a 'morally praiseworthy, principled, respectable, upright [or] admirable' way (234). People like Mother Theresa, Father Damien of Molokai, the single student standing in front of a tank in Tiananmen Square, Nelson Mandela or fictional characters like Antigone might be seen as exemplars of this form of dignity (231; Killmister 2010, 161). It may be equated with Comportment Dignity, but to do so would be to lose some of the content and meaning behind the tradition upon which it relies and which gives it a more objective and substantive base. Schroeder equates this form of dignity with living in accordance with the four cardinal virtues and so argues that those who 'possess temperance, courage and justice and are guided by wisdom display dignity in its most perfect instantiation'. She defines this form of dignity as 'a virtue which subsumes the four cardinal virtues and one's sense of worth' (Schroeder 2008, 235).

What Do the Parliamentarians Mean by 'Dignity'?

Despite the usefulness of these definitions, parliamentarians do not generally define 'dignity' when they use the term. Hence, it is difficult to be conclusive about the specific form of dignity which they seek to protect. Indeed, parliamentarians themselves may not have a shared understanding of dignity. They argue essentially that women approaching an abortion clinic should not be exposed to any communication which would not support their proceeding to obtain an abortion and that workers at abortion clinics should similarly not be exposed to any such communications near their workplace. When supporting exclusion zones they seem to use dignity in the sense ascribed to it by the Supreme Court of Canada in *R. v. Law* (2002, para 53): 'Human dignity means that an individual or group feels self-respect and self-worth. It is concerned with physical and psychological integrity and empowerment'.

Some might argue that Kantian Dignity extends so far as to encompass this feeling of 'self-respect and self-worth' and that seeing or hearing people praying or offering alternatives to abortion is an affront to the Kantian Dignity of those near a clinic. They may argue that those who communicate with women in exclusion zones fail to treat each woman as an autonomous person. For example, in the NSW debates, Penny Sharpe, the member for the North Shore, asserted that women visiting abortion clinics have already made up their mind to terminate their pregnancies after carefully considering all of the alternatives (NSW 2018b). As a consequence, any discussions aimed at changing their minds could 'only be seen as harassment and a reflection of the personal views of the so-called "sidewalk counsellors" on abortion, rather than the individual circumstances and needs of the woman' (Felicity Wilson in NSW 2018a, 16). According to this view, sidewalk counsellors might be seen as treating women as selfish, immoral or somehow 'unnatural', adopting an archetypal construct which sees 'female sexuality as solely for procreation' (Kumar et al. 2009, 625, 628, 633) and treating pregnant women 'simply as a means' (Schroeder 2008, 233). Proponents of exclusion zone laws may consider people praying or offering alternatives to abortion to be attacking the Comportment Dignity of women and exposure to differing viewpoint or decisions on abortion as an affront to their human dignity.

Before considering the strengths of these arguments, it is valuable to study some empirical evidence. While empirical evidence cannot measure dignity, it can collate information about the attitudes and views of women who access abortion clinics. Information of this kind can assist in considering the impact of exclusion zones on women and in assessing whether or not woman accessing abortion clinics might all consider that communications with people inside those zones are an affront to their dignity, however defined.

III. The Impact of Such Laws on the Dignity of Women

Broad longitudinal empirical evidence on what happens outside Australian abortion clinics and on the reactions of women to communicating with people outside such clinics is not available. In passing these laws Australian parliaments relied on one unpublished Australian study, hearsay, anecdotal material and submissions from organizations and individuals (e.g. see NSW 2018a). As a result, the laws were introduced without knowledge of what was actually taking place outside abortion clinics across any jurisdiction. The one Australian study relied upon examined the impact on women of being 'confronted by anti-abortion protesters' outside one clinic in Melbourne (the Humphries Study) (Humphries 2011). The Humphries Study is a small unpublished study undertaken by a worker at that clinic for a master's degree. It claims that its findings support initiatives to ensure that 'women are not exposed to picketers when accessing abortion' (Humphries 2011, 45). The study has been criticized by Turner et al. (2018), including for its use of judgemental language. In the Humphries Study, 158 women, 135 of whom 'were exposed' to 'the picketers', completed a survey just prior to undergoing a termination at less than 12 weeks' gestation and just before leaving the clinic afterwards (Humphries 2011, 20–21). The Humphries Study did not show a uniformity of responses by women. A majority reported that abortion was 'very much' stigmatized by 'the picketers' (78 per cent) and that 'allowing anti-abortion picketers to protest outside the front of the clinic stigmatizes abortion "very much"' (71 per cent) (35). While dignity may not be measurable, an assault to a person's dignity might be expected to result in an increase in that person's anxiety. This was not found by the Humphries Study. It found a small correlation between more exposure to 'anti-abortion picketers' and higher levels of pre-abortion anxiety and concluded that exposure to 'picketers' was not a significant predictor of pre-abortion anxiety (34–35).

Multiple US studies demonstrate the variability of women's reactions to communications within the vicinity of abortion clinics even more clearly. Like the Humphries Study, many used judgemental language which may have skewed the results. Cozzarelli and Major reported on 291 women who had first-trimester abortions at a large, private abortion clinic in Buffalo, New York, in 1990. In this survey, while 66 per cent of women who encountered 'antiabortion demonstrators' were upset to some degree, 34 per cent were not upset at all. The authors published a further study in 1994. This study found that demonstrations outside the clinic had no significant impact on depression levels three weeks after the abortion (Cozzarelli and Major 1994, 421). In 2000, Cozzarelli et al. reported on a study of 442 women having first-trimester abortions in Buffalo. It considered the long-term impacts on women interacting with 'prolife picketers' when entering a clinic within an hour of an abortion and after two years. It concluded that those interactions did not appear to pose any significant long-term mental health risks (274). Again the responses of women to 'picketers' varied. Whilst a majority (66 per cent) agreed or strongly agreed that 'prolife picketers' caused psychological harm and should be prohibited (69 per cent), a significant minority (21 per cent) supported the 'picketers'. These women agreed or strongly agreed that the 'picketers' 'help women by making them think twice about abortion' (270). Moreover, 8 per cent of women agreed or strongly agreed that the picketers were 'doing a good thing by trying to discourage abortion' (ibid.). These responses demonstrate that some women who are opposed in principle to abortion may themselves access the procedure. Those women might claim that exclusion zones are patronizing and even infantilizing to them and as such an affront to their dignity. Even those who are strong supporters of abortion rights may be equally strong supporters of freedom of speech, freedom of assembly and freedom of religion and may consider that exclusion zone laws assume women are not strong enough to see people who do not support abortion as they approach a clinic. Some may feel their dignity compromised by laws which assume that all women approaching an abortion clinic in such circumstances support abortion when that is not the case.

A large study conducted across 30 clinics in 21 US states involved interviews of 956 women seeking an abortion between 2008 and 2010. This study found even larger variations in the responses by women who saw, heard or were stopped by 'protesters'

(Foster et al. 2013, 85). In their study 48 per cent of women were not upset at all by the protesters, a quarter were a little upset, 12 per cent moderately upset, 9 per cent quite upset and 7 per cent extremely upset (ibid.). Whilst these studies do not measure the impact on the dignity of women of seeing people who do not support abortion, when approaching an abortion clinic, they do show that women in that environment do not have a consistent reaction to such interaction. Some are not bothered at all by such interactions, and some even consider that the people they encounter are 'doing a good thing' (Cozzarelli et al. 2000, 265). The empirical evidence suggests that not all women who engage in discussions with people outside an abortion clinic find that experience to be an affront to their dignity, unwanted or damaging. The dignity of at least some women seems, if anything, to be undermined by exclusion zone laws.

While the majority of women approaching a clinic may well have determined that abortion is the alternative which they wish to pursue, having been provided with and considered all relevant information, this is not true of all women. The fact that some women decide against a termination on their way to the clinic demonstrates this. Whilst there is no empirical evidence of the number of women who accept offers of assistance from sidewalk counsellors, courts in Australia and in the United States have received evidence that some women decide against a termination as a consequence of such interactions. Evidence was presented in a Victorian court that 300 women had been assisted to continue their pregnancies after such communications outside a Melbourne clinic (*Fertility Control Clinic v. Melbourne City Council* 2015, para 34; Walsh 2018, 1124). In *McCullen*, one sidewalk counsellor said that she had helped 80 and another 100 women who chose to continue with their pregnancies after talking with them (*McCullen v. Coakley* 2014, 4–5). After the creation of a 35-foot exclusion zone in Massachusetts, one said she had been unable to help any women in those circumstances and another that she had helped far fewer (ibid.).

Some women may seek 'a consented but unwanted abortion'. Medeira argues that women who consent to an abortion that they really do not want might continue the pregnancy to term if they had, for example, better financial support, more flexible employment or education opportunities or stronger social support (2014, 52, cited in Coleman et al. 2017). Communicating with sidewalk counsellors may provide such women with these alternatives and not in the confrontational manner assumed by proponents of exclusion zones. Turner et al. describe people who respectfully offer 'aid or alternatives to women who may be considering an abortion for reasons such as limited finances, insecure accommodation and lack of social support' (2018, 105). Similarly, Chief Justice Roberts describes sidewalk counsellors who are committed to maintaining a calm tone of voice, direct eye contact and a caring demeanour and who only speak with women who are receptive to their approach; these individuals completely reject confrontation in their communications (*McCullen v. Coakley* 2014, 4–5). These sidewalk counsellors would not consider their actions to be an attack on the dignity of women approaching abortion clinics, nor would they consider that they act in a manner which seeks to impose anything on anyone. Contrary to the view espoused by proponents of exclusion zones, not everyone who seeks to enter those areas aims to engage in confrontation or protest. Instead, these sidewalk counsellors offer assistance to women who choose to continue their pregnancies. Ambivalence about the decision to terminate is a recognized predicator of possible future mental ill health and psychological distress which some women experience as a result of abortion (Coleman et al. 2017, 113–14; Cozzarelli et al. 2000, 267; Cozarelli 1993, 1224). These women are a particularly vulnerable minority. They may well benefit from further discussion about the alternatives before going through with the procedure even at the clinic doorstep. This is the view espoused by Turner, Garratt and McCaffrey(2018). McCaffrey, who is an Australian obstetrician and gynaecologist, describes treating more than 20 women who had been referred to him after gratefully accepting assistance from people outside an abortion clinic (105).

Exclusion zones may well have the result that women approaching an abortion clinic will not see or interact with people who would prefer that they not go ahead with a planned termination. The majority of women may consider this to be a desirable outcome. If such interactions are properly characterized as an assault on a women's Kantian or Comportment Dignity, exclusion zone laws may reduce some women's immediate feelings of distress or anxiety and help them avoid feelings of stigma which they may consider to be an affront to their dignity (Major and Gramzow 1999, 735). In this way they may protect the dignity of the majority of women accessing such clinics. An express assumption of the approach adopted by parliamentarians supportive of exclusion zones is the assumption that every woman who is booked in for a termination and is approaching an abortion clinic for that appointment is fully committed to completing the procedure and will benefit from it. It is a further express assumption that every person approaching or working at a clinic would feel that seeing or hearing any message which is not completely supportive of abortion is a challenge to their dignity. These assumptions similarly form part of the reasoning of the High Court in its recent rejection of the challenge to the Victorian and Tasmanian laws (*Clubb v. Edwards*; *Preston v. Avery* 2019). In that case the plurality observed that

> Aharon Barak, a former President of the Supreme Court of Israel writing extra-judicially said: 'Most central of all human rights is the right to dignity. It is the source from which all other human rights are derived. Dignity unites the other human rights as a whole.' Generally speaking, to force upon another person a political message is inconsistent with the human dignity of that person. As Barak said, 'human dignity regards a human being as an end, not as a means to achieve the ends of others.' (Paras 50–51)

The clear assumption in this passage is that those within the exclusion zones would force their message on others who do not wish to receive it rather than offering assistance to those who seek or desire it. Exclusion zone laws do not distinguish between those behaviours nor do they distinguish between the behaviours of qualified or unqualified counsellors, psychologists or other medical practitioners. All are criminal. These laws prevent a wide range of communications, including communications which might be welcomed by some recipients, for example, those women who are ambivalent about their decision and in the highest category of risk of harm should they proceed with a termination. By curtailing a final opportunity for such vulnerable women to make a fully informed choice, exclusion zone laws fail to respect their dignity. Some might argue that depriving such women of these interactions is an affront to their Kantian Dignity through the failure to treat each as an autonomous person capable of making her own decisions. In doing so, it might be argued, the state treats all pregnant women approaching a clinic as vehicles on which an abortion procedure will be performed and as persons incapable of deciding not to terminate their pregnancy. Therefore, they may be said to treat this vulnerable minority of women 'simply as a means', thus undermining their Kantian Dignity (Schroeder 2008, 233).

IV. The Impact of Such Laws on the Dignity of Those Engaged in Prayer and Sidewalk Counselling

While the parliamentary debates and the studies considered in this chapter typically describe those near abortion clinics in negative terms such as 'confronting', 'anti-abortion protesters', 'picketers' or 'anti-abortion demonstrators', these terms may not be descriptive of prayer groups and sidewalk counsellors. Dignity is not used in any of the Australian parliamentary debates to describe those whose religious beliefs motivate them to pray or provide sidewalk counselling outside abortion clinics. This might be considered to be surprising given that some, like Tore Lindholm, consider that dignity is broad and basic enough to capture most and perhaps all justifications for religious freedom (Durham and Scharffs 2010, 66). Given that prayer and side-walk counselling are made criminal offences by these laws, their impact on the dignity of those exposed to prosecution by them warrants consideration. At least, the Comportment Dignity of a person is harmed by their arrest and prosecution as a criminal and by the imposition of fines or imprisonment by the state. Even if the penalty imposed for breach of an exclusion zone is restricted to a fine, a criminal penalty has many significant repercussions which can impact on a person's life. A criminal record can impact a person's employability as many employers request information in relation to any criminal record from potential employees. A criminal record is relevant to establishing whether a person is trustworthy, of 'good fame and character' or 'fit and proper', which can be relevant to their ability to join some professions or obtain a firearms license. Criminal records must also be disclosed when seeking a visa to enter certain countries. A criminal conviction can also be relevant to bail applications, for example, under s. 18(1) of the Bail Act 2013 (NSW). Additionally, a record of previous convictions can be relevant to sentencing, for instance, under s. 21A(1)(d) of the Crimes (Sentencing Procedure) Act 1999 (NSW) (hereinafter: Sentencing Act). Having a conviction is a factor police can take into account when deciding whether or not to charge a person with another offence and can reduce the possibility of being able to have a later charge dismissed under s. 10 of the Sentencing Act. So for those people who continue to manifest their religious convictions by prayer or sidewalk counselling in exclusion zones, the potential consequences – deprivation of liberty by imprisonment or the imposition of a financial penalty with a criminal conviction – are serious. While those opposed to abortion may consider that a person arrested for breach of exclusion zone laws is demonstrating Meritorious Dignity by their actions, the consequences of a criminal conviction are at a minimum an affront to a person's Comportment Dignity.

Exclusion zone laws, of course, are designed to discourage the proscribed behaviours and assume that most religious believers will abide by the law. While those who are able to comply with the law may not suffer the indignity of a criminal conviction, incarceration or fines, the laws may nevertheless have a significant impact on their dignity, since they are prevented from fully manifesting their religious faith. For those who believe that human life begins at conception, and that women may suffer harm if they pursue an unwanted termination, prayer and sidewalk counselling may save lives and prevent harm. From this perspective, exclusion zone laws restrict the ability of religious adherents to intervene in matters of life and death. Such laws prevent believers from expressing their convictions in ways they consider compassionate and helpful. The ability of a person to manifest his or her religious beliefs, for example, to pray and offer help to others, is a well-recognized aspect of a person's dignity (International Covenant on Civil and Political Rights 1966, Article 18). As Gonthier and Bastarache JJ of the Supreme Court of Canada observed in dissent in *Chamberlain*, quoting from Dickson J's reasons in *R. v. Big M Drug Mart Ltd* (1985, cited in *Chamberlain v. Surrey School District No. 36* 2002, para 35):

> A truly free society is one which can accommodate a wide variety of beliefs, diversity of tastes and pursuits, customs and codes of conduct. A free society is one which aims at equality with respect to the enjoyment of fundamental freedoms [...] Freedom must surely be founded in respect for the inherent dignity and the inviolable rights of the human person. The essence of the concept of freedom of religion is the right to entertain such religious beliefs as a person chooses, the right to declare religious beliefs openly and without fear of hindrance or reprisal, and the right to manifest religious belief by worship and practice or by teaching and dissemination. But the concept means more than that. Freedom can primarily be characterized by the absence of coercion or constraint. If a person is compelled by the state or the will of another to a course of action or inaction which he would not otherwise have chosen, he is not acting of his own volition and he cannot be said to be truly free. (336–37)

Christian prayer is clearly a manifestation of religion (*Catechism of the Catholic Church* 1994, paras 2742–45, 2692, 1674–79). While it may be possible to pray anywhere, place can be a very important element of prayer (ibid.). This is clear from the traditions of pilgrimage and the common response of prayer gatherings outside sites of tragedy such as that of the Lindt Café siege, the Parramatta police headquarters after the murder of Curtis Cheng or the Christchurch massacre (Cave 2019). Silent action including prayer can also be – and has long been – 'a powerful form or protest and political communication' (*Clubb v. Edwards; Preston v. Avery* 2019). This was recognized by Justice Kirby in *Levy v. Victoria* where he noted the power of silent actions including 'lifting a flag in battle, raising a hand against advancing tanks, wearing symbols of dissent, participating in a silent vigil, public prayer and meditation' (1997, 638, cited in *Clubb v. Edwards; Preston v. Avery* 2019, para 475).

Conclusion

However dignity is defined, it seems a poor justification for exclusion zone laws. These laws treat the dignity of the majority preferentially and disregard entirely the dignity of others impacted by exclusion zone laws, including vulnerable pregnant women. If grounded on protecting the Comportment Dignity of the majority of women near abortion clinics, they adopt a position at variance with current community attitudes. To favour the dignity of the majority, exclusion zone laws grounded in Comportment Dignity must assume that there is community disapproval of abortions. But Comportment Dignity varies with societal attitudes and there is now widespread acceptance of abortion in Australia (Hanrahan 2019). Given those attitudes, it is those seeking to pray or to provide sidewalk counselling who, by their actions, risk their own Comportment Dignity by failing to act 'in accordance with society's expectations of well-mannered demeanor and bearing' (Schroeder 2008, 234). Exclusion zone laws intrude into what would otherwise be a 'collision of dignities', to use the phrase adopted by Gonthier and Bastarache JJ in *Chamberlain* (2002). There, those dissenting judges argued that the inherent dignity of the individual survives moral disapproval – an interpretation consistent with Kantian Dignity. They further argued that a contrary finding would involve treating some persons inconsistently with their human dignity by obliterating their right to express their moral position (para 132). As they observed:

> Language appealing to 'respect', 'tolerance', 'recognition' or 'dignity' […] must reflect a two-way street in the context of conflicting beliefs, as to do otherwise fails to appreciate and respect the dignity of each person involved in any disagreement, and runs the risk of escaping the collision of dignities by saying 'pick one'. But this cannot be the answer. In my view […] a truly free society, must permit persons who respect the fundamental and inherent dignity of others and who do not discriminate, to still disagree with others and even disapprove of the conduct or beliefs of others. Otherwise, claims for 'respect' or 'recognition' or 'tolerance', where such language becomes a constitutionally mandated proxy for 'acceptance', tend to obliterate disagreement. (Para 134)

While the judges were there speaking of laws proscribing moral disapproval of same-sex relationships or behaviours, their reasoning applies equally to exclusion zone laws which preclude those communications which they make criminal. These laws impact adversely on the dignity of religious believers who feel called to manifest their faith by praying in proximity to abortion clinics or by offering information and support as sidewalk counsellors. These manifestations of religious faith are made criminal. The zones also have an adverse effect on that minority of women who are untroubled by seeing opponents of abortion near clinics and, most importantly, on those who would benefit from interacting with sidewalk counsellors. In doing so the laws promote the dignity of the majority to the detriment of these minorities. By adopting this approach they fail to treat the dignity of each person as being worthy of protection at law. The treatment of all women as sharing the same ideological position on abortion is an affront to the dignity of that minority of women who, while choosing abortion for themselves in their particular situation, still consider the activities of those opposing it in a positive light. It is also an affront to the dignity of those women – a vulnerable minority – who would benefit from interacting with sidewalk counsellors and continuing with their pregnancy. In the context of exclusion zones the term 'dignity' has been used to support one ideological position in relation to abortion over another. It has been used as 'a mere slogan that camouflages unconvincing arguments and unarticulated biases' (Schulman, cited in Glendon 2011). Rather than recognizing that interaction outside abortion clinics involves a 'collision of dignities' (*Chamberlain v. Surrey School District No. 36* 2002) necessitating consideration and respect for the dignity of all, the laws favour the majority and act inconsistently with the human dignity of others by obliterating their right to interact with sidewalk counsellors and denying the right of religious believers to express their moral position (para 132). As a result, the trend towards the introduction of broad exclusion zone laws should be reversed and existing exclusion zone laws amended to narrow the scope of the proscribed conduct and give greater recognition to the dignity of those adversely impacted by such laws.

References

Access to Terminations Act. 2013. (Tas). https://www.legislation.tas.gov.au/view/html/inforce/current/act-2013-072.

Annen v. Germany (App no. 3690/10) ECHR 2015.

Bevin, E. 2015. 'Anti-Abortion Campaigner Graeme Preston Arrested Again for Protesting outside Clinic'. *ABC News*. http://www.abc.net.au/news/2015-04-14/anti-abortion-campaigner-graeme-preston-arrested/6392214.

Black, V. 1999. 'Dignity'. In *The Philosophy of Law: An Encyclopedia*, vol. 1, edited by C. B. Gray, 208–10. Bosca Roca, United States: Taylor and Francis.

Bluett v. Popplewell [2018] ACTMC 2.

Catechism of the Catholic Church. 1994. Libreria Editrice Vaticana. https://www.vatican.va/archive/ccc_css/archive/catechism/ccc_toc.htm

Cave, D. 2019. 'Mourners Honor the Dead with Call to Prayer in Christchurch, New Zealand'. *New York Times*. https://www.nytimes.com/2019/03/22/world/asia/new-zealand-vigil.html.

CES v. Superclinics (Australia) Pty Ltd (1995) 38 NSWLR 47.

Chamberlain v. Surrey School District No. 36, [2002] 4 SCR 710. https://scc-csc.lexum.com/scc-csc/scc-csc/en/item/2030/index.do.

Chapman, V. 2019. 'Law Reform Institute to Consider Abortion Law Reform'. https://premier.sa.gov.au/news/law-reform-institute-to-consider-abortion-law-reform.

Children by Choice. 2018. 'Attitudes to Abortion'. https://www.childrenbychoice.org.au/factsandfigures/attitudestoabortion.

Clubb v. Edwards; Preston v. Avery [2019] HCA 11. http://eresources.hcourt.gov.au/showCase/2019/HCA/11.

Coleman, P. K., K. Boswell, K. Etzkorn and B. S. Turnwald. 2017. 'Women Who Suffered Emotionally from Abortion: A Qualitative Synthesis of Their Experiences'. *Journal of American Physicians and Surgeons* 22, no. 4: 113–18. https://www.jpands.org/jpands2204.htm.

Constitution Act. 1934. (Tas). https://www.legislation.tas.gov.au/view/html/inforce/current/act-1934-094.

Cozzarelli, C. 1993. 'Personality and Self-Efficacy as Predictors of Coping with Abortion'. *Journal of Personality and Social Psychology* 65, no. 6: 1224–36. https://www.ncbi.nlm.nih.gov/pubmed/8295119.

Cozzarelli, C., and B. Major. 1994. 'The Effects of Anti-Abortion Demonstrators and Pro-Choice Escorts on Women's Psychological Responses to Abortion'. *Journal of Social and Clinical Psychology* 13, no. 4: 404–27. doi:10.1521/jscp.1994.13.4.404.

Cozzarelli, C., B. Major, A. Karrasch and K. Fuegen. 2000. 'Women's Experiences of and Reactions to Antiabortion Picketing'. *Basic and Applied Social Psychology* 22, no. 4: 265–75. doi:10.1207/15324830051035974.

Durham Jr, W. C., and B. G. Scharffs. 2010. *Law and Religion: National, International, and Comparative Perspectives*. The Netherlands: Wolters Kluwer.

Edwards v. Clubb (2017) MCV (23 December 2017).

Explanatory Memoranda, Safe Access Zones Bill. 2015. (Vic).

Fertility Control Clinic v. Melbourne City Council (2015) 47 VR 368.

Fisher, A. 2012. *Catholic Bioethics for a New Millennium*. Cambridge: Cambridge University Press.

Fleming, J., and N. Tonti-Filippini. 2007. *Common Ground?* Strathfield, Australia: St Paul's.

Foster, D. G., K. Kimport, H. Gould, S. C. Roberts and T. A. Weitz. 2013. 'Effect of Abortion Protesters on Women's Emotional Response to Abortion'. *Contraception* 87, no. 1: 81–87. doi:10.1016/j.contraception.2012.09.005.

Glendon, M. A. 2011. 'The Bearable Lightness of Dignity'. *First Things*. https://www.firstthings.com/article/2011/05/the-bearable-lightness-of-dignity.

Government of Western Australia Department of Health. 2019. 'Safe Access Zone Reform Proposal'. https://consultation.health.wa.gov.au/department-of-health-training/safe-access-zones-reform-proposal-1/.

The Greens. 2017. 'Safe Zone Call for Abortion Clinics'. https://greens.org.au/news/wa/safe-zone-call-abortion-clinics.

Hanrahan, C. 2019. 'Federal Election: Australian Women Want Action on These Three Issues – but Men Not So Sure'. *ABC News*. https://www.abc.net.au/news/2019-05-01/vote-compass-election-women-quotas/11053956.

Humphries, A. 2011. 'Stigma, Secrecy and Anxiety in Women Attending for an Early Abortion'. Unpublished master's thesis, the University of Melbourne, Australia.

International Covenant on Civil and Political Rights. 1966. GA Res 2200A (XXI), UN GAOR, 21st Sess, Supp no. 16, UN Doc A/6316, 16 December.

Killmister, S. 2010. 'Dignity: Not Such a Useless Concept'. *Journal of Medical Ethics* 36: 160–64. doi:10.1136/jme.2009.031393.

Kumar, A., L. Hessini and E. M. H. Mitchell. 2009. 'Conceptualising Abortion Stigma'. *Culture Health Sexuality* 11, no. 6: 625–39. doi:10.1080/13691050902842741.

Kurti, P. 2018. 'Why Dignity Is a Poor Reason to Legalise Assisted Suicide'. *Griffith Journal of Law and Human Dignity* 6, no. 2: 55–69. https://griffithlawjournal.org/index.php/gjlhd/article/view/1127/983.

Liu, S. 2014. 'Human Dignity in a Comparative Legal Context'. Unpublished paper submitted for JD degree, University of Western Ontario, Canada.

Luban, D. 2009. 'Human Dignity, Humiliation and Torture'. *Kennedy Institute of Ethics Journal* 19, no. 3: 211–30. https://pdfs.semanticscholar.org/e2eb/9fd5e9e36a3dbfc0b38c9df172e0dd4b0f0a.pdf.

Lynch, L. 2018. ' "The Law Itself Is a Crime": Abortion Protesters Refuse to Plead Guilty'. *Brisbane Times*. https://www.brisbanetimes.com.au/national/queensland/the-law-itself-is-a-crime-abortion-protesters-refuse-to-plead-guilty-20181228-p50oo8.html.

Macklin, R. 2003. 'Dignity Is a Useless Concept: It Means No More Than Respect for Persons or Their Autonomy'. *British Medical Journal* 237, no. 7429: 1419–20. doi:10.1136/bmj.327.7429.1419.

Major, B., and R. H. Gramzow. 1999. 'Abortion as Stigma: Cognitive and Emotional Implications of Concealment'. *Journal of Personality and Social Psychology* 77, no. 4: 735–45. https://www.ncbi.nlm.nih.gov/pubmed/10531670.

McCullen v. Coakley, 573 U.S. 464 (2014). https://www.oyez.org/cases/2013/12-1168.

Medeira, J. L. 2014. 'Abortion Emotions Regret, Relationality and Regulation'. *Michigan Journal of Gender and Law* 21, no. 1: 1–66. https://repository.law.umich.edu/cgi/viewcontent.cgi?article=1039andcontext=mjgl.

Minear, T. 2016. 'Mother of 13 Arrested in East Melbourne Clinic Protest'. *Herald Sun.* https://www.heraldsun.com.au/news/law-order/mother-of-13-arrested-in-east-melbourne-clinic-protest/news-story/a90d71765491cd1189348579a4f98a0b.

New South Wales (NSW) 2018a. *Parliamentary Debates.* Legislative Assembly, 7 June, 1–29.

———. 2018b. *Parliamentary Debates.* Legislative Council, 17 May, 11.

Pierre, N. 2019. 'Magistrate Chides Serial Anti-Abortion Protester'. *Courier Mail*, 14 March.

Planned Parenthood of Southeastern Pennsylvania v. Casey (1992) 505 US 833. https://www.law.cornell.edu/supct/html/91–744.ZS.html.

Police v. Preston [2016] TASMC.

Pregnancy Law Reform Act. 2017. (NT). https://legislation.nt.gov.au/en/Legislation/TERMINATION-OF-PREGNANCY-LAW-REFORM-ACT-2017.

Queensland Law Reform Commission. 2017. 'Review of Termination of Pregnancy Laws Consultation Paper'. https://www.qlrc.qld.gov.au/__data/assets/pdf_file/0004/576166/qlrc-report-76-2018-final.pdf.

R. v. Big M Drug Mart Ltd, [1985] 1 SCR 295. https://scc-csc.lexum.com/scc-csc/scc-csc/en/item/43/index.do.

R. v. Kapp, [2008] 2 SCR 483. https://scc-csc.lexum.com/scc-csc/scc-csc/en/item/5696/index.do.

R. v. Law, [2002] 1 SCR 227. https://scc-csc.lexum.com/scc-csc/scc-csc/en/item/1947/index.do.

Safe Access Act. 2018. (NSW). https://legislation.nsw.gov.au/#/view/act/2010/127.

Schroeder, D. 2008. 'Dignity: Two Riddles and Four Concepts'. *Cambridge Quarterly of Healthcare Ethics* 17: 230–38. doi:10.1017/S0963180108080262.

Somerville, M. 2001. *Death Talk.* Montreal: McGill-Queen's University Press.

Termination of Pregnancy Act. 2018. (Qld). https://www.legislation.qld.gov.au/view/html/asmade/act-2018–023.

Turner, J., D. Garratt and S. McCaffrey. 2018. 'The High Court, Abortion Clinic Speech restrictions and the Assessment of Harm'. *Western Australian Legal Theory Association.* https://walta.net.au/2018/10/01/the-high-court-abortion-clinic-speech-restrictions-and-the-assessment-of-harm/.

Victoria, *Parliamentary Debates.* 2015. Legislative Assembly, 12 November, 4387–99.

Walsh, G. 2018. 'The Constitutionality of Communication Prohibitions around Abortion Clinics'. *Western Australian Jurist* 9: 80–101. Retrieved from: https://walta.net.au/wajurist/vol9/the-constitutionality-of-communication-prohibitions-around-abortion-clinics/.

Wellbeing Act. 2008. (Vic). http://www.legislation.vic.gov.au/Domino/Web_Notes/LDMS/PubStatbook.nsf/f932b66241ecf1b7ca256e92000e23be/8B1B293B576FE6B1CA2574B8001FDEB7/$FILE/08-46a.pdf.

Chapter Thirteen

RESPECTING THE DIGNITY OF RELIGIOUS ORGANIZATIONS: WHEN IS IT APPROPRIATE FOR COURTS TO DECIDE RELIGIOUS DOCTRINE?

Neil Foster

1. Introduction

It is not uncommon to find wide-ranging statements along the lines that 'courts do not determine religious doctrine' (Hale 2015, 179; *Kumar v. Satsang* 2019, para 21; *Shergill v. Khaira* 2015, para 45: 'the courts do not adjudicate on the truth of religious beliefs or on the validity of particular rites'). But there are other cases where the court finds itself bound to determine at least some religious issues.[1] Are the courts simply being inconsistent? Or is there a rational and workable distinction between cases where religious beliefs ought not to be the subject of 'secular' judicial rulings, and those where the courts have to offer their interpretations of doctrine? The aim of this chapter is to demonstrate that the latter is true and to provide a clearer understanding of the difference between these two situations.

These issues matter for many reasons, including the fundamental idea of human dignity. A basic aspect of the protection of human dignity is respect for the fundamental religious beliefs that may underlie human actions. Freedom of religion is protected in crucial international agreements and is a basic part of the presuppositions of Western societies. A key feature of religious freedom, however, is that it protects not only the rights of an individual in their own autonomy, but also the rights of groups of persons who join together to live out their shared religious commitments.[2] Article 18(1) of the 1966 International Covenant on Civil and Political Rights (ICCPR), for example, refers to the

---

[1] See, for example, *Shergill v. Khaira* (2015, para 45), where the court opined, first, that 'the courts do not adjudicate on the truth of religious beliefs or on the validity of particular rites', then conceded, 'But where a claimant asks the court to enforce private rights and obligations which depend on religious issues, the judge may have to determine such religious issues as are capable of objective ascertainment'. See also *Bruker v. Marcovitz* (2007).

[2] For detailed analysis of the religious freedom rights of groups, see Rivers (2010) and Aroney (2014).

right 'either *individually or in community with others* and in public or private, to manifest his religion or belief in worship, observance, practice and teaching' (emphasis added).

Part of the respect that should be offered to a religious group, then, is that it be left to order its life in accordance with its own understanding of the religious doctrines that shape its existence. Of course, there are some circumstances where the living out of those doctrines may need to be controlled in the interests of the fundamental rights of members of the group or members of the public where a religious group, for example, inflicts physical or sexual abuse on children or other vulnerable persons. There are well-recognised limits to religious freedom. For instance, Article 18(3) of the ICCPR provides that impairment of the right to manifest religion is justified by 'such limitations as are prescribed by law and are necessary to protect public safety, order, health, or morals or the fundamental rights and freedoms of others'. But even in those cases, there are significant questions to be raised as to whether the state should be interpreting, or 'reinterpreting', doctrine, or rather simply saying that 'whatever your doctrine means, we cannot allow this behaviour'. The latter response is more consistent with the dignity of the members of a religious group, or possibly of the group itself,[3] which is not undermined but actually affirmed when the members are held accountable for the lived consequences of their doctrines.

Western societies in general usually assume a separation between 'church' and 'state', and one aspect of that is that secular judges do not typically make definitive rulings on the content of religious doctrine. But while there are good reasons in most cases to be wary of judicial involvement in determining the content of doctrine, a blanket, inflexible policy of this sort may create problems where private parties have entered into arrangements with a shared understanding of religious beliefs.

In any event a blanket 'hands-off' policy is not consistent with the actual history of how courts have made decisions in some areas (for this terminology, see Greenawalt 1998). Judges have regularly asserted that they will not make rulings on theological doctrines; but, historically, courts have just as regularly been called on to determine, in property disputes involving religious trusts, what is an acceptable use of property in accordance with the trust. To decline to make a ruling there will often leave one party at the mercy of another who has behaved in bad faith.[4]

Requiring parties who have entered into legal relations with others on the basis of a shared religious understanding to keep their prior commitment is an aspect of respecting their human dignity. Affording dignity to a person includes treating them as an agent who can be held accountable for their voluntarily assumed obligations. As Schachter puts it:

---

[3] Dwight Newman's chapter in this volume offers a critical assessment of the notion of group dignity.

[4] While the situations are not identical, there are similarities here with the case of a Jewish wife whose husband refuses to grant her a divorce under Jewish law – if a court will not enforce an otherwise binding prior agreement to grant such a divorce, the wife will be left without a remedy for the harm caused by that agreement being broken. See *Bruker v. Marcovitz* (2007).

Our emphasis on respect for individuals and their choices also implies proper regard for the responsibility of individuals. The idea that people are generally responsible for their conduct is a recognition of their distinct identity and their capacity to make choices. (1983, 850)

Requiring such accountability also recognises the dignity of those *to* whom the promise was made.

Some consideration has been given to these issues in the United States, where the First Amendment has led to a long history of debate on these matters. A review by Helfand (2018) surveys the different approaches there, which have often been driven by an assumption based on a particular reading of the First Amendment to the US Constitution that 'religious questions' are not able to be answered. He notes, however, a number of cases where in the past courts have been prepared to review such questions where private rights are at stake, and offers suggestions as to a more nuanced test.

In the United Kingdom there has also been increased impetus for commentary on this question since the decision of the UK Supreme Court in *Shergill v. Khaira* (2015), holding that questions of doctrine are not always 'non-justiciable', as had been suggested in some previous recent decisions.

But there has been little detailed discussion on a principled basis concerning *how* judges in the United Kingdom decide when it is appropriate to determine these matters, and almost none in Australia. The issues are likely to arise more regularly in the future. For example, in *Christian Youth Camps Ltd v. Cobaw Community Health Services Ltd* (2014) (hereinafter: *CYC v. Cobaw* 2014) the court had to determine whether views on appropriate sexual behaviour fell within the broad description of 'doctrines' of the Christian Brethren church. In the end the majority agreed with the holding of a lower tribunal that these views were not 'doctrines' of the church.[5] In dissent in that decision, Redlich JA commented:

Neither human rights law nor the terms of the exemption required a secular tribunal to attempt to assess theological propriety (*Catch the Fire Ministries Inc v Islamic Council of Victoria Inc* (2006) 15 VR 207, 220 [36] (Nettle JA)). The Tribunal was neither equipped nor required to evaluate the applicants' moral calculus. (*CYC v. Cobaw* 2014, para 526)

The aim of this chapter is to consider the framework within which these differing approaches to the question of whether courts should rule on religious doctrines are being applied, discuss whether they can be reconciled and outline guidelines that are consistent with legal principles and past authority which a judicial officer might be expected to follow in dealing with the question.

---

[5] Maxwell P. affirmed the holding of the tribunal, accepting the views of an expert called on behalf of Cobaw that 'the absence of any reference to marriage, sexual relationships or homosexuality in the creeds or declarations of faith which Christians including the Christian Brethren are asked to affirm as a fundamental article of their faith demonstrates the Christian Brethren beliefs about marriage, sexual relationships or homosexuality are not fundamental doctrines of the religion' (*CYC v. Cobaw* 2014, para 276).

There are good reasons to be cautious about courts making pronouncements on religious questions. But it is argued here that an exception to the bar on courts making religious findings should be recognised in circumstances where the private rights of the parties to a dispute are at stake, and the parties themselves have chosen to accept benefits on the basis that they will be bound by certain religious principles. While there should be a presumption that courts will usually have a 'hands-off' approach to religious doctrine, this presumption may be rebutted where there is a civil dispute involving private parties who have agreed to subject themselves to a specific religious regime. In those circumstances, the court has an obligation to resolve the dispute between the parties, even if that resolution may incidentally involve a consideration of religious doctrine. Apart from these circumstances, however, the freedom of an organization or person to determine the meaning of their own religious commitments should be respected.

This approach is one which respects the dignity, autonomy and religious freedom of religious persons and organizations where the community seeks to impose external obligations, but allows the courts to intervene where private parties have decided to subject themselves to a particular religious regime.

2. The Nature of the Problem

The question as to when it is appropriate for a court to make an authoritative ruling on the content of a religious doctrine has been approached in different ways in different contexts.

It might in some cases be framed as an issue as to whether certain matters are 'justiciable', that is, within the formal competence of a court to decide. (For example, one area which has traditionally been held to not be 'justiciable' is a ruling on the actions of a foreign government.) Or, more straightforwardly, it might be expressed simply as an issue as to whether it is 'appropriate' for a court to make such a decision.

a. Related but Different Issues

It is important to distinguish this issue from a similar but different one, which is whether a particular belief or doctrine system is classified as 'religious' (the *truly religious* issue). We should also distinguish this issue from the question whether a particular belief is 'central' or 'foundational' for a particular religion (the *centrality* issue); and also from the question whether a person sincerely or genuinely believes the relevant doctrine (the *sincerity* issue).

The courts have developed a number of doctrines over the years to deal with the 'truly religious' issue[6] and are well able to exclude a 'sham' (a purported religion made

---

6   The decisions most commonly referred to in the common law world for a definition of 'religion' are those of the High Court of Australia in *Church of the New Faith v. Commissioner of Pay-Roll Tax* (1983) and more recently the decision of the UK Supreme Court in *Hodkin* (2013).

up for ulterior purposes) from being given protection as 'religious'. Courts all over the world, for example, have had no problem concluding that the so-called Church of the Flying Spaghetti Monster is a parody invented for argument, rather than being a true religion (see, e.g., *Cavanaugh v. Bartelt* 2016). In the United Kingdom, the Charity Commission has similarly ruled that the Jedi Order (based on beliefs from the fictional Star Wars universe) is not a genuine religion (Holmes 2018; Cheung 2019; Cranmer 2020).

b. The Content of Doctrine Issue

But if we conclude that we are dealing with a genuine 'religion', the question remains: is it appropriate for a court to provide a ruling on the content of the religion (the *content of doctrine* issue)?

Some examples of situations where this question may arise are as follows.

One situation is where a *statute may provide an exemption* from obligations which would otherwise apply, where a religious group is behaving in accordance with its religious beliefs. Here it may be suggested that the court will need to determine whether those beliefs do in fact justify the way that the group is behaving.

Another area which presents the question is where a court has to rule on some action which is taken in relation to real property which is governed by a *trust for religious purposes*. The law has long recognised the category of 'charitable trust', and one valid type of such trust in common law nations like Australia is a trust 'for the advancement of religion' (Ridge 2011). An issue may then arise where property or funds derived from the sale of a property are to be used for certain purposes, as to whether those purposes are consistent with the religious purposes for which the trust was established. To make a decision here the court may be presented with the question of the interpretation of religious doctrine.

Another example may be taken from the literature on *religious freedom* in the United States. The Federal Religious Freedom Restoration Act (1993), introduced after a decision of the US Supreme Court limiting the scope of the constitutional First Amendment free exercise protections (*Employment Division v. Smith* 1990), requires that free exercise of religion be protected such that government may not 'substantially burden religious exercise', unless those burdens satisfy strict scrutiny. But what is a 'substantial burden'? On one view, in determining how 'substantial' a burden on religion is, the courts will need to interpret religious doctrine (Helfand 2016a, 2016b).

Helfand notes that this issue has been discussed in the context of US Supreme Court decisions relating to the 'contraception mandate' under the Affordable Care Act, where some religious bodies argued that being required to fund the provision of contraception (and in particular abortifacient drugs) made them 'complicit' in these actions contrary to their deeply held religious beliefs. The extent to which involvement in a chain of events leading to a specific outcome makes a person complicit under religious doctrines can be said to be a matter of interpreting religious doctrine (Helfand 2018, 274–76).

3. Possible Framework to Distinguish Appropriate from Inappropriate Cases

Given the range of different approaches noted, then, can we formulate a principle to explain and justify circumstances when it is appropriate for courts to make theological judgements, and when it is not?

a. Private v. Public

One formulation of the line between appropriate and inappropriate religious adjudication is Helfand's 'private' as opposed to 'public' suggestion. In his article, Helfand (2018) suggests that an appropriate distinction can be drawn between cases where 'private rights' are in issue – contractual claims, for example – and those where 'public rights' are concerned. In particular, while a court imposing obligations onto parties in accordance with its understanding of a theological doctrine would seem to raise the problems of 'excessive entanglement' with religion, and a 'preferencing' of some theological options might raise 'establishment' issues (in the US context, at least), he argues that in the sphere of private law arrangements a 'contextual' approach may avoid such concerns. Such an approach would involve considering not the 'objective' meaning of religious propositions, but the meaning that the specific parties involved would give to them.

In particular Helfand refers to cases involving 'co-religionists', people from the same theological tradition who enter into contractual arrangements. In many of these cases it seems that a court would endorse an injustice by refusing to provide a remedy should promises not be fulfilled; and if the court is prepared to accept evidence of the shared understanding of the parties about particular terms, it may avoid many of the problems of undue 'entanglement' or 'establishment' (Helfand 2018, 278).

Helfand suggests, for example, that where parties enter into a contract for the supply of 'kosher' food, it would not usually be difficult to identify the specific religious tradition in which they were contracting, and holding them to a bargain would involve the court reading their contract in the context of their shared understanding.

b. 'Hands off unless…'

Another possible formulation with a stronger emphasis on protection of the religious freedom of religious groups might be as follows: that the court should decline to decide a theological question *except* where it is a private law issue *and* the parties have chosen to subject themselves to a specific religious regime (a 'hands off unless' approach). Is this consistent with the way that courts have approached these issues? In the rest of this chapter I aim to show that this is the best approach and is also generally consistent with the current approach of the courts.

4. Underlying Policy Reasons

Before examining the course of judicial authority in more detail, it is important to discuss the theoretical framework within which these decisions are made. What sort of reasons are put forward for a court to determine, or on the other hand not to determine, these matters?

a. *Reasons Why a Secular Court Ought Not to Be Determining Theological Questions*

What reasons are put forward to justify a blanket 'hands-off' policy under which a court would refuse to determine any or all theological questions?

One set of reasons may be called *competency* arguments. Judges are trained in the mainstream 'secular' legal system. With rare exceptions, few will have a deep knowledge of the internal debates within religious traditions or the competence to resolve those debates (Lupu and Tuttle 2007, 119, 138).

Another reason that has sometimes been put forward is all religious doctrine is *subjective*, and hence cannot be discussed in a rational way. For example, in *CYC v. Cobaw* 2014 (para 417) Neave JA cited the decision of the English and Welsh Court of Appeal in *Khaira v. Shergill* (2012) that because religious beliefs are 'subjective inward matters' they are incapable of proof and not justiciable as a legal question.[7] This echoes comments about the 'irrationality' of religious beliefs made by Laws LJ in an earlier English case (*McFarlane v. Relate Avon Ltd* 2010).[8] Holzer has drawn attention to a strain of judicial reasoning in First Amendment decisions in the United States which treats all religious reasons as 'irrational, divisive, and dangerous' (Holzer 2015, 449).

Perhaps it may be briefly noted that to characterise all religious reasons as 'subjective' and 'irrational' is itself to take a broadly 'religious' stance on metaphysical questions and ignore the fact that many religious bodies will offer what they see as good and logical reasons for the truth of their worldview.

Other, more persuasive, reasons for a blanket 'hands-off' approach by courts may be characterised as reasonable *religious freedom* arguments. The view may be put that

---

[7]   As noted earlier, that 2012 decision was later overturned in 2015 by the UK Supreme Court on precisely this point, the Supreme Court holding that it was not true that religious questions were 'not justiciable'.

[8]   See:

> In the eye of everyone save the believer *religious faith is necessarily subjective, being incommunicable by any kind of proof or evidence*. It may of course be *true* [emphasis original]; but the ascertainment of such a truth lies beyond the means by which laws are made in a reasonable society. Therefore it lies only in the heart of the believer, who is alone bound by it. No one else is or can be so bound, unless by his own free choice he accepts its claims. The promulgation of law for the protection of a position held purely on religious grounds cannot therefore be justified. It is *irrational, as preferring the subjective over the objective*. (*McFarlane v. Relate Avon Ltd* 2010, per Laws LJ, para 23–24, emphases added)

recognising the freedom of believers to adopt religious views and to live them out implies that they, and the religious groups they are a part of, should always be given the autonomy and respect for their dignity to resolve issues of what the doctrines of their faith are and how they interrelate. As Schachter observes, 'A high priority should be accorded in political, social and legal arrangements to individual choices in such matters as beliefs, way of life, attitudes and the conduct of public affairs' (1983, 849).

As well as comments from Western countries, similar arguments have been put forward in India, where the Supreme Court has sometimes declined to recognise religious doctrines on the ground that they were not 'essential' to a particular religious tradition (Mustafa and Sohi 2017). Criticising this approach of Indian courts to protect only the 'essential' doctrines of a religion (931), Mustafa and Sohi note: 'The essentiality test impinges on this autonomy [i.e. freedom of religion] because the judiciary assumes the power to decide what the essential or non-essential parts of religious practices are' (937).

Another example from the common law world of a public decision-maker deferring to the internal interpretation of doctrine by a religious group can be found in the decision of the New Zealand Human Rights Review Tribunal in *The Gay and Lesbian Clergy Anti-Discrimination Society Inc. v. Bishop of Auckland* (2013) (hereinafter: *Anti-Discrimination Society* 2013).

Even after New Zealand had passed legislation allowing same-sex marriage, the Human Rights Act 1993 (NZ) s. 39 exempted 'qualifying bodies' from being liable for breaching discrimination law where those bodies were determining admission to a religious organization. In those cases, the relevant bodies were allowed to apply 'the doctrines or rules or established customs of that religion'. The tribunal made it clear that it would not itself take on the task of determining the content of the relevant doctrine (*Anti-Discrimination Society* 2013, 10).

Another reason that has been offered in the past for a court not to decide these issues is the fear that deciding the issues may privilege one religion over another. Helfand refers to these 'establishment' arguments in the United States: 'judicial resolution of such questions will be interpreted as endorsement of one religious view over another – a form of, so to speak, prohibited denominational preference' (2018, 272). But this does not seem a very strong argument: the decision of a court to decide a theological question does not of itself entrench or privilege the religious body whose doctrine is being interpreted.

Yet to some extent it seems that the desire to avoid 'entanglement' with religious issues, referred to in the US First Amendment jurisprudence, may be connected to 'establishment' fears (ibid.).

Finally, we may note that on occasion the concept of 'lack of justiciability' has been put forward either as a separate criterion, or by way of summing up other concerns. See, for example, the Canadian Supreme Court decision in *Highwood Congregation v. Wall* (2018):

> This Court has considered the relevance of religion to the question of justiciability. In *Bruker* v. *Marcovitz*, 2007 SCC 54 (CanLII), [2007] 3 S.C.R. 607, at para. 41, Justice Abella stated: 'The fact that a dispute has a religious aspect does not by itself make it non-justiciable.' That being said, courts should not decide matters of religious dogma. As this Court noted in

Syndicat Northcrest v. Amselem, 2004 SCC 47 (CanLII), [2004] 2 S.C.R. 551, at para. 50, 'Secular judicial determinations of theological or religious disputes, or of contentious matters of religious doctrine, unjustifiably entangle the court in the affairs of religion.' The courts have neither legitimacy nor institutional capacity to deal with such issues, and have repeatedly declined to consider them [...] In the end, religious groups are free to determine their own membership and rules; courts will not intervene in such matters save where it is necessary to resolve an underlying legal dispute. (Paras 36–39)

In this interesting passage, we see the reflection of a number of the reasons noted earlier: the discussion on 'entanglement', 'legitimacy' and 'institutional capacity' (a reference to what we have called 'competence') and a general reliance on the value of autonomy.

b. *Situations in Which a Secular Court Has to Consider Theological Questions*

Despite the above, however, cases arise where the courts have apparently no choice but to make a decision on the interpretation of a religious doctrine: where property is held on trust for religious purposes, or where the parties have entered into a contract agreeing to be bound by a religious framework. If a court declines to rule in these cases, then one party may get a 'windfall' decision in their favour, based on the status quo at the time of the dispute arising, and the other party will not have their case properly heard.

To a large extent these cases depend on the prior consent of the parties to have any disputes resolved within a particular framework. This consent may arise explicitly, under the terms of a contract; or implicitly, under the general principle of property law that a party cannot accept the benefit of property ownership without at the same time agreeing to shoulder the 'burden' of any obligations attaching to the property (e.g. *Halsall v. Brizell* 1957). While this principle is most directly applied in cases dealing with easements or restrictive covenants, it also operates where someone assumes control or ownership of property to which 'charitable trust' obligations have been attached by a previous owner. By becoming owner of such property, the new owner also assumes the obligations attaching to the property under the pre-existing trust.[9]

Of course, by the time a matter reaches the courts, one of the parties will usually no longer prefer that the asserted religious constraints be enforced. But in general terms,

---

9   A similar principle was applied in the NSW Supreme Court decision of *Anglican Development Fund Diocese of Bathurst v. Palmer* (2015), where the court ruled that members of a management board, when they accepted office on the board, impliedly accepted personal responsibility to meet obligations entered into by the board as previously constituted. The court noted, 'Acceptance alone of appointment to a standing committee designated and regulated by comprehensive ordinances plainly intended, amongst others, to ensure continuity and the proper discharge of obligations, is sufficient outward expression of agreement to be bound by contractual obligations undertaken by that standing committee, and which are still on foot' (para 325).

courts have seen it as their duty to apply the legal constraints which have been previously accepted, and in doing so will sometimes need to offer a view on religious doctrine.

An example of a case of this sort is the NSW decision of *Re South Head & District Synagogue* (2017), a contractual dispute. There the contract between a rabbi and the synagogue he served (which was an incorporated body) stipulated that the rabbi could only be dismissed if done so after an order of the Beth Din (a Jewish religious tribunal) applying Jewish law, and this was upheld by the court as a valid clause of the contract. Brereton J commented, 'The parties to a contract governed by Australian law can incorporate into the contract, as terms of the contract, provisions of another system of law, including Jewish law' (para 29; see also *Engel v. Adelaide* 2007, para 36; *Shamil Bank of Bahrain EC v. Beximco Pharmaceuticals* 2004). There was no uncertainty about the content of the relevant law (*Re South Head & District Synagogue* 2017, para 32).

In *Mohamed v. Mohamed* (2012) a question arose as to whether a prenuptial agreement between Muslim parties, requiring payment of an amount under Islamic law should the husband terminate the relationship, was enforceable. It was held that it was enforceable as a contract. The judge considered cases from other common law jurisdictions where a 'dowry' of this sort had been enforced. However, he noted that enforcing the payment did not require interpreting the provisions of Sharia law, it simply involved treating the agreement as a contract under Australian law, so there was no sense in which the court needed to decline jurisdiction (para 62).

5. US Cases

Helfand (2018) discusses a number of US cases where courts have, and have not, ruled on religious doctrines. His comments may be summarised as shown in Table 13.1.

A number of the examples offered by Helfand come from cases where the US courts have had to deal with the aftermath of a 'split' or schism within a church, or a group of churches. Important issues are then raised as to how property being occupied by a 'dissenting' group should be dealt with, if the formal title deeds are held by (or held on trust for) an opposing party. These are precisely the sort of cases where UK and Australian courts have been willing, where necessary, to examine religious doctrines.

6. UK Cases

A pattern of decisions similar to that identified in the US courts may be seen in the United Kingdom. In some cases, courts have declined to decide theological questions. In other cases, it has been necessary for them to enter on the task.

a. Cases in the United Kingdom Where Courts Have Refused to Decide Theological Questions

The best way to analyse the recent UK cases on this topic may be to see the jurisprudence as undergoing a fundamental shift after the 2012 decision of the Court of Appeal in *Khaira v. Shergill*.

Table 13.1 Summary of US decisions discussed by Helfand

Court Should Decline to Decide Theological Issue	Basis for Declining	Court Agrees to Decide Theological Issue	Type of Issue
Wallace v. ConAgra Foods, Inc., 19HA-CV-12–3237 (Minn First Judicial District, 6 Oct 2014)	Court cannot decide a 'purely religious question' (meaning of 'kosher' food) – **First Amendment** analysis	*Bouldin v. Alexander,* 82 US (15 Wall) 131 (1872)	Whether terms of a **property trust** were complied with – 'the majority of a congregational church is considered to represent the church only if [it] adhere[s] to the organization and the doctrines'
Cases noted in Lupu and Tuttle (2007)	'Claims would require courts to answer questions that the state is **not competent** to address'	*Gonzalez v. Roman Catholic Archbishop,* 280 US 1 (1929)	Again, property trust conditions: 'Canon Law in force at the time of the presentation governs'
Cases noted in Eisgruber and Sager (2009)	'If government were to endorse some interpretations of religious doctrine at the expense of others, it would thereby **favor** some religious persons, sects, and groups over others'		
Watson v. Jones, 80 US 679 (1871)	'**Freedom for religious organizations**', which entailed 'an independence from secular control or manipulation' in adjudicating 'matters of church government as well as those of faith and doctrine'		

Note: The cases and comments by academics are illustrative and may not all currently be authoritative due to their subsequent treatment by appellate courts.

This was a dispute within the Sikh faith over the holding of two Sikh places of worship (gurdwaras). Trust deeds over the property required that they be held by the legitimate 'successor' to the original holder, called the First Holy Saint; one side claimed that Sant Baba Jeet Singh Ji Maharaj was the legitimate successor, the other claimed that he was not.

The Court of Appeal ruled that the issue could not be decided without the court making a judgement based on 'religious' issues as to how the claimed successor had been appointed and struck out the claim as, in its view, not 'justiciable' (*Khaira v. Shergill* 2012, per Mummery LJ, para 77).

The decision was, with respect, very unsatisfactory, and indeed it is interesting that the court itself refers to previous decisions where the courts of England did exactly what they refused to do here, deciding 'doctrinal' points which had property implications. A classic example was *General Assembly of Free Church of Scotland v. Lord Overtoun* (1904), where the question was whether trusts set up for the support of the Free Church before the formation of a later denomination could be used for the benefit of the later church.

b. Cases in the United Kingdom Where Courts Have Decided Theology

But the decision of the UK Supreme Court on appeal from *Khaira v. Shergill* has proven to be a significant turning point in the willingness of UK courts, in a carefully circumscribed class of appropriate cases, to consider religious doctrines. In *Shergill v. Khaira* (2015) the unanimous decision of the court (Lords Neuberger, Sumption and Hodge wrote the main judgement, Lords Mance and Clarke agreeing) dealt with some issues of trust law which the Court of Appeal should have ruled on, but then turned to the question of the 'justiciability' of the religious issues.

The view of Mummery LJ in the Court of Appeal that there were no 'judicial or manageable standards' (*Khaira v. Shergill* 2012) which could be used was rejected as being based on decisions to do with behaviour of foreign countries. Non-justiciable issues were said to fall into only two categories: matters beyond the constitutional competence of the courts to do with some transactions of foreign states or the proceedings of Parliament (none of these relevant here) (*Shergill v. Khaira* 2015, para 42); or matters which could be said not to be based on private legal rights or obligations (such as, for example, domestic agreements not intended to be binding); but in these cases they sometimes would be resolved by the courts 'if their resolution is necessary in order to decide some other issue which is in itself justiciable' (para 43).

But the court 'cannot shirk its duty to determine a matter of civil right' if such must be resolved (para 56). There is a long history of courts being perfectly prepared to examine the details of religious doctrine if it is necessary to do so either to enforce a contract or to ensure that a trust is observed (para 45). Where a religious body is a voluntary association, there may still be contractual or other obligations which need to be adjudicated upon, for example, if a party loses a remunerated office (para 46).[10]

---

[10] We will see later that Australian courts have also been willing in some cases to consider doctrinal issues where a minister is dismissed from stipendiary work.

Where a trust has been set up for the purposes of a religious body, the courts have often been prepared to examine the doctrines of the current body to see if it is consistent with the purposes for which the trust was established (para 50).

Cases such as *Overtoun* (1904) were clear authority for this; there was even a more recent Scottish decision in *Smith v. Morrison* (2011, cited in *Shergill v. Khaira* 2015, para 52) where these principles were applied. Other cases involving disputes within the Muslim and Hindu communities were also cited (*Shergill v. Khaira* 2015, paras 54–55).

The Supreme Court held that a case where the court had refused to consider religious doctrine, when needed to deal with a defamation action, was wrongly decided (see *Blake v. Associated Newspapers Ltd* 2003), about which the court in *Shergill v. Khaira* (2015) commented:

> We do not think that the court was correct to refuse to adjudicate on that issue on the ground that it was non-justiciable. The claim was a civil claim in tort and the court will enter into questions of disputed doctrine if it is necessary to do so in reference to civil interests. See also *Forbes v Eden* (1867) LR 1 Sc & Div 568 HL, Lord Cranworth (at pp 581–582), Lord Colonsay (at p 588). (Para 57)

Hence the matter in *Khaira* was sent back from the Supreme Court to the trial judge, who would, if the parties could not agree, have to resolve the issue of what the 'fundamental tenets' of the religious group were, and whether or not the current 'Third Holy Saint' had been validly appointed in accordance with those tenets.

In the aftermath of the appeal, the trial of the substantive issues took place, and in *Shergill v. Khaira* (2017) the judge held that the 'Third Holy Saint' had been validly appointed as a successor to the previous office holders and was to be regarded as in control of the properties.[11]

Following the decision of the Supreme Court in *Khaira*, cases in the United Kingdom where the courts deal with internal disputes within religious groups continue to be resolved under these principles. *Trustees of the Celestial Church of Christ, Edward Street Parish (a charity) v. Lawson* (2017), for example, provides a helpful summary of the circumstances in which a court will intervene in an internal dispute within a church or other religious organization (para 20). On the one hand, the court will not decline jurisdiction simply because a matter of theology or church government has given rise to a dispute. On the other hand, they will not themselves purport to resolve that dispute over theology where that is not necessary, but instead will usually concern themselves with the question whether the decision-making processes agreed upon between the parties have been properly carried out.[12]

In *Otuo v. Watch Tower Bible and Tract Society of Britain* (2019a) the judge allowed a claim to proceed based on the statement made at a Jehovah's Witnesses religious meeting that the complainant was 'not a Jehovah's Witness'. He ruled that while the court would not

---

[11] A later decision in *Khaira v. Shergill* (2017) involved a dispute over costs, which by then had become fairly substantial.

[12] As noted later, in Australia there has been some debate about what civil rights will have to be in issue in an internal, religiously connected dispute, before a court assumes the jurisdiction to resolve the dispute.

be able to adjudicate on the truth of religious beliefs, it would be able to deal with many other issues. In this case it was held that allegations of financial fraud were conveyed by the excommunication, as all members of the congregation present knew that this was what had led to investigations of the congregation member's conduct. These allegations, insofar as they implied dishonest behaviour with money, were 'justiciable'. Presumably it would have been different if the statement made relied heavily on interpretation of a theological context.[13]

At the ultimate trial of the matter, however, the announcement of 'disfellowshipping' was held not to cause any harm to the plaintiff's reputation, as all those present already knew of the allegations (*Otuo v. Watch Tower* 2019b).

7. Australian Authority

As with the other common law jurisdictions considered earlier, there have been some decisions in Australia refusing to decide theological issues and others where the courts have been willing to do so.

a. Australian Cases Declining to Decide Religious Issues

In considering the Australian courts' attitude to this issue, we may start with comments from Latham CJ in *Adelaide Company of Jehovah's Witnesses Inc. v. Commonwealth* (1943), where he referred to the need for the courts to protect religions of all sorts, noting that 'what is religion to one is superstition to another' (at 123). The implication here seems to be that courts should not usually be ruling on the content of doctrines.

A few years after this decision, the High Court of Australia was asked to decide another case involving religion. In *Wylde v. Attorney-General for NSW* (hereinafter: *Wylde* 1948; usually known as the '*Red Book case*'), the Bishop of Bathurst had started using an alternative 'order of service' for Holy Communion, and his decision to do so was challenged by some members of the church in the diocese. It was alleged that the trusts on which the property of the church was held obliged those who celebrated services in those churches only to follow the 1662 Book of Common Prayer and that the additions to those services made in the Bishop of Bathurst's preferred book (the 'Red Book') were unlawful.

Unfortunately, there were only four members of the court hearing the case (five was the more usual number).[14] As it turned out the court was split in two. Latham CJ and

---

[13] In the final trial of the matter, Judge Spearman noted that there was a possibly wider sense of 'Scriptural fraud' spoken of in some JW documents (relating to the holding of 'false doctrine'), and implied that if this had been the issue the court may have declined to hear the matter. But in the context it was allegations of financial fraud that had been at issue, and the court was well placed to decide on issues around that type of fraud; see, for example, 'Although there may be circumstances in which references to "Scriptural fraud" would fall outside the concept of "fraud" as used in the criminal law [...], those circumstances do not arise on the facts of these particular Claims' (*Otuo v. Watch Tower* 2019b, para 17).

[14] The only full academic analysis of the decision seems to be Galbraith (1998). He notes that 'Starke J had been the intended fifth member of the bench for the appeal, but he had fallen ill

Williams J accepted the view that had been taken by the NSW Supreme Court (Roper CJ in Eq) that there was indeed a departure from the law of the Church of England, that the property trusts required adherence to those doctrines and hence that the bishop could be ordered to not use three specific parts of the Red Book which were shown to be unorthodox.

However, the other two members of the court, Dixon J and Rich J, disagreed. Their view was that the property trusts could not be used to enforce doctrinal matters. Rich J set the tone for his comments with his opening sentences: 'The subject of this unhappy controversy is only fit for a domestic forum and not for a civil court. Unfortunately it is not an example of "charity" in the New Testament sense or of the command to love one another' (*Wylde* 1948, 273).

These two members of the court in effect held that the purposes of the property trusts did not extend to governing the form of liturgy used in the churches. The result of this even division of opinion in the court was that, in accordance with the procedure set out in the Judiciary Act 1903 (Cth) s 23(2)(b), the decision of the lower court being appealed from (itself being a superior court of record) was affirmed. While the decision of Latham CJ and Williams J was hence only that of a 'statutory majority', subsequent cases in Australia have indicated that this majority decision represents the formal *ratio* of the case.[15]

An example of a court clearly declining to decide theological issues can be seen in the later decision of *Scandrett v. Dowling* (1992). In that case the NSW Court of Appeal declined to intervene when it was claimed that the Bishop of Canberra and Goulburn was about to ordain a number of women as priests.

The claim was made that only the General Synod of the Anglican Church had authority to allow this to happen, and that the General Synod had not yet approved the change of practice. Priestley JA and Hope AJA, the majority, held that the provisions of the relevant legislation, the Anglican Church in Australia Constitution Act 1961 (NSW), meant that the courts could only be involved in issuing orders in relation to Anglican practice and theology when there was an issue of property rights at stake. Otherwise the Constitution of the Anglican Church was simply a 'consensual compact', the terms of which would not usually be enforced by the secular courts. Hence where, as here, property issues were not directly involved, the courts would not intervene.

Priestley JA commented:

> The consensual compact is thus based on religious, spiritual and mystical ideas, not on common law contract. It has the same *effect* as a common law contract when matters of church property become involved with the other matters dealt with by the consensual compact. I do not think the claims made in this case get out of the area of the consensual compact which does not have the legally binding effect here relied on. (*Scandrett v. Dowling* 1992, 513, emphasis original)

---

a few days before the appeal was due to begin' (242, n. 1). Of the other two members of the court, McTiernan J had been ill for some time, and Webb J was overseas in Japan as part of post-war work.

[15] See, for example, Young CJ in Eq in *Metropolitan Petar v. Mitreski* (2009, para 490).

Mahoney JA also held that the court should not intervene, although his reasons were slightly different. In particular, he took the view that there may be circumstances where a secular court *would* need to resolve issues of doctrinal difference:

> If it be alleged and proved in a case within the jurisdiction of a civil court that there has been a breach of trust, the civil court may not refuse to decide such a question or to give relief even if the determination of the proceedings involves the forming of a conclusion upon religious matters. (499)

Still, in these proceedings, he took the view that no property issues were at stake, no trust involved and the rules in question were not intended to be enforceable. *Wylde* (1948) was different, because there were clearly property issues at stake in that case.

b. Australian Cases Deciding Theological Questions

The *Red Book case*, then, provides one example of courts of Australia deciding theological issues. In particular, the decision of Roper CJ in Eq and the decision of the 'statutory majority' in the High Court, Latham CJ and Williams J, was to the effect that the use of certain rituals in the Red Book was contrary to the official theology of the Church of England as spelled out in the Book of Common Prayer. It is hard to imagine a more clearly 'theological' question, yet these judges held that, in giving effect to trust arrangements over property, it was their duty to consider these matters and come to a decision.

In *Metropolitan Petar v. Mitreski* (2003) Barrett J discussed the fact that religious doctrines may need to be interpreted for the purposes of charitable trusts:

> The circumstance that property is held upon a charitable trust for religious purposes will, of course, introduce elements of justiciability into certain matters affecting such trust property. Use of the property in a way that does not accord with the relevant religious purposes may, for example, be restrained by injunction. (Para 26)

The two cases just discussed illustrate the principle that, in a private law context or where trusts are involved, rulings on theological issues may be necessary in order to give effect to the intentions of those who set up the trusts. Those who agree to hold property on trust impliedly agree to abide by the terms of the trust.

But the next case is an example of a court imposing its views on religious doctrine onto a religious body for the purposes of enforcing a 'public law' (discrimination) obligation, in a completely different context.

Cobaw Community Health Services Ltd v. Christian Youth Camps Ltd & Rowe (2010) (hereinafter: *Cobaw v. CYC* 2010) involved a complaint of discrimination on the basis of sexuality. The complainant, Cobaw, ran a project called WayOut, designed to provide support and suicide prevention services to 'same-sex attracted young people'. The co-ordinator of the project approached Christian Youth Camps Ltd (CYC), a camping organization connected with the Christian Brethren denomination, to inquire about making a booking at a Phillip Island campsite that was generally made available to community groups. Rowe, to whom Cobaw spoke, informed her that the organization would not be happy about making a booking for a group that encouraged a homosexual 'lifestyle', as he later put it.

The CYC's refusal to proceed with a booking was connected with CYC's convictions regarding homosexuality which were based, in their view, on the teachings of Scripture.

Despite these things, the tribunal at first instance (constituted by Judge Hampel from the Victorian County Court) ruled against the CYC, ordered that they had unlawfully discriminated and that they should pay a fine of AUD 5,000.

The primary liability was under ss. 42(1)(a) and (c), and s. 49, of the Equal Opportunity Act 1995 (Vic) (EO Act 1995). These provisions prohibited discrimination on certain grounds (among which were same-sex sexual orientation and personal association with persons of same-sex sexual orientation), in the areas of 'services', in 'other detriments' and in accommodation.[16]

The EO Act 1995 contained two exemptions based on religion. Section 75(2), which applied to religious groups, provided:

> (2) Nothing in Part 3 applies to anything done by a body established for religious purposes that
>
>   (a)   conforms with the doctrines of the religion; or
>   (b)   is necessary to avoid injury to the religious sensitivities of people of the religion.

Section 77, which applied to 'persons' generally, not only groups, provided:

> Nothing in Part 3 applies to discrimination by a person against another person if the discrimination is necessary for the first person to comply with the person's genuine religious beliefs or principles.

One of the issues that came up in the litigation was whether the view that sexual activity should be reserved for marriage between a man and a woman was a part of Christian 'doctrine'. When Judge Hampel came to decide what the content of the relevant 'doctrines' were, she ended up effectively holding that all that could be considered in this area were pronouncements of 'ecclesiastical authorities' similar to the Nicene Creed.[17]

That a County Court judge in Victoria felt obliged to decide what constitutes the core doctrines of Christianity should surely give some pause as to whether this is the way the legislation is meant to work.

---

[16]   The previous legislation has now been replaced by the Equal Opportunity Act (2010) (Vic), which contains provisions to similar effect, most of which came into operation on 1 August 2011.

[17]   A major statement of Christian theology formulated in 325 AD by a church council and since accepted almost universally within Christianity as orthodox belief.

What Judge Hampel did, of course, was to accept the evidence of one scholar over that of another. The Rev. Dr Rufus Black, clearly a representative of the 'liberal' wing of Christendom, was accepted when he ruled out of the category of 'doctrine', beliefs about sexuality. The Rev. Canon Dr Peter Adam, a highly regarded evangelical scholar, gave evidence that beliefs about sexuality were a core part of Christian doctrine. His views were rejected on what was arguably a quite spurious basis (see Foster 2011, 26–27).

In the end, Judge Hampel ruled that 'beliefs about marriage, sexual relationships or homosexuality are not fundamental doctrines of the [Christian Brethren] religion' (*Cobaw v. CYC* 2010, para 305). This ruling was made in spite of the fact that the legislation does not use the word 'fundamental'. A judge of a secular court had decided to come to a theological judgement.

Judge Hampel then also went on to hold that even if a view that homosexuality was sinful could be regarded as a 'doctrine' of the Christian Brethren, refusing to give the support of the CYC camping site to a group formed to promote the view that homosexuality was a normal and ordinary part of human identity could not possibly be something that 'conformed' to the doctrine.

For Judge Hampel the 'narrow' interpretation given to the religious freedom protections under the legislation meant that this fairly general word must indicate that the action was 'required' or 'obligatory' or 'dictated' by the doctrine (*Cobaw v. CYC* 2010, para 317). The fact that no general enquiry was made of campers about their sexual activities was said to mean that the refusal of a booking in these cases was not 'required' by doctrine.

A similar approach was taken by the Supreme Court of Canada in a case involving Trinity Western University, where the court argued that denying accreditation to a Christian law school was justified since 'the limitation [on religious freedom] in this case is of minor significance because a mandatory covenant is, on the record before us, *not absolutely required* for the religious practice at issue: namely, to study law in a Christian learning environment in which people follow certain religious rules of conduct' concerning sexuality (*Law Society of British Columbia v. Trinity Western University* 2018, emphasis added).[18]

On appeal in *CYC v. Cobaw* 2014, the Victorian Court of Appeal agreed with the tribunal and narrowed the scope of what could be accepted as religious doctrine to exclude views on human sexuality. Maxwell P, who gave the leading judgement for the majority, quoted this passage from the judgement of Judge Hampel:

> I am satisfied that Mr Rowe believes that homosexuality, or homosexual activity is prohibited by the scriptures, and so is against God's will. I am satisfied that his belief is based on the manner in which he interprets or applies the doctrine of plenary inspiration. I am satisfied Mr Rowe, Ms Mustafa, Mr Buchanan and Mr Keep's evidence is representative of the range of beliefs held by members of the Christian Brethren in Victoria about marriage, sexual relationships and homosexuality. However, I am not satisfied those beliefs constitute a doctrine of the religion of the Christian Brethren, as I have defined that term. (Para 276)

---

[18] Thanks to Amy Ross for drawing my attention to this parallel.

It is arguable this is the narrow sort of view that is not appropriate in dealing with a broad, internationally recognised human right like 'freedom of religion' (see Foster 2014a; Towers 2014).[19] Even commentators fully supportive of the court's finding here have queried whether it is appropriate for the court to make such a ruling (Murphy 2016, 616).

This Victorian decision may be contrasted with the approach of the equivalent NSW tribunal and appeal court in litigation culminating in 2010 in the decision of *OW & OV v. Members of the Board of the Wesley Mission Council*. The basis of the claim was that OW and OV, a same-sex couple, had applied to the Wesley Mission to become foster carers for children in need. The mission advised them that they were not eligible under its guidelines, which on religious grounds did not regard homosexual couples as suitable foster parents. The mission relied on the traditional Christian view of marriage as the best environment for the raising of children.

In turning down the application, the mission relied on s. 56 of the Anti-Discrimination Act 1977 (NSW) (ADA), which states:

> 56 Religious bodies
>
> Nothing in this Act affects: […]
>
> (c) the appointment of any […] person in any capacity by a body established to propagate religion, or
> (d) any other act or practice of a body established to propagate religion that conforms to the doctrines of that religion or is necessary to avoid injury to the religious susceptibilities of the adherents of that religion.

The provision was relevant because the ADA provides that it is unlawful to discriminate against a person on the basis of their homosexuality, and it was conceded correctly by the mission that unless s. 56 applied, they had done just that.

At first instance the Administrative Decisions Tribunal found that there had been discrimination and ruled that s. 56 did not apply (*OV and anor v. QZ and anor* 2008). A key part of their reasoning was that a preference for 'traditional marriage' (i.e. 'monogamous heterosexual partnership') was not a 'doctrine' of the Christian church as a whole.

This was partly established by the leading of evidence from ministers from within the Uniting Church that there was disagreement among theologians on the point. (The Uniting Church is the 'umbrella' body within which the Wesley Mission operates. However, the Wesley Mission represents what might be fairly called the 'evangelical' or biblically conservative wing of the church and is not uncommonly at odds with the broader leadership of the church.)

This decision was then set aside on appeal to the Administrative Decisions Tribunal Appeal Panel, which held that the original tribunal had misdirected itself by requiring that a doctrine be uniformly accepted across the whole of 'Christendom' before it could 'count' for the purposes of s. 56 (*Wesley Mission Council v. OV & OW (No 2)* 2009).

---

[19] An application for special leave to appeal was refused; see Foster (2014b).

This decision itself was appealed to the NSW Court of Appeal, which in effect affirmed the Appeal Panel's ruling (*OV & OW v. Wesley Mission Council* 2010a).

The matter then came back to the Appeal Panel in the 2010b proceedings. The Appeal Panel reviewed the evidence that had previously been presented to the tribunal by representatives of the Wesley Mission and concluded that the word 'doctrine' was broad enough to encompass not just 'formal doctrinal pronouncements' such as the Nicene Creed, but effectively whatever was commonly taught or advocated by a body, and included 'moral' as well as 'religious' principles (*OV & OW v. Wesley Mission Council* 2010b, para 32–33). The evidence of Rev. Garner, who spoke of the doctrinal issues, was accepted as showing that the provision of foster care services by a homosexual couple would be contrary to a fundamental commitment of the organization to biblical values. Hence the defence under s. 56(d) was established.

Here, then, the decision-maker was prepared to accept evidence focused on the specific religious commitments of the organization involved, the Wesley Mission, rather than coming to a broader (and inevitably controversial) decision about the relevant approach of the whole Christian tradition.

It is of some interest that the Australian government has recently released an 'exposure draft' of federal legislation dealing with religious discrimination, which also adopts the approach (seen in the NSW litigation) of deferring to the decisions of members of a faith tradition about the interpretation of the religious tenets of the body. The second draft of the Religious Discrimination Bill released in 2019, at various points where the content of religious belief held by a religious body is relevant, uses the formula: 'conduct that a person of the same religion as the religious body could reasonably consider to be in accordance with the doctrines, (c) tenets, beliefs or teachings of that religion' (clause 11(1)).[20]

8. Considering Theological Questions in Internal Disputes

A particular area where issues around courts deciding theological questions can become controversial is where such questions are presented by internal disciplinary proceedings, or other disputes between members of the same religious group.

Suppose a minister of religion has been the subject of disciplinary proceedings by their superiors. A question may arise as to whether a court should intervene in such proceedings if there is alleged to be some irregularity (such as denial of natural justice). But another issue which may be presented is whether a secular court should make a ruling on an issue of doctrine, if that has been involved in the decision to discipline.

The question of whether an obligation of 'natural justice' applies such that a court may intervene in the dismissal of a member of the clergy on these grounds has been discussed

---

[20] For use of a similar form of words, see also clauses 5(1) (definition of 'conscientiously object'; definition of 'statement of belief'; para (a)(iii)), 32(8)(b) and 33(2)(b)). For an overview of the second draft, see Foster (2019c).

in a number of recent Australian cases (*Sturt v. the Right Reverend Dr Brian Farran Bishop of Newcastle* 2012; *Harrington v. Coote* 2013; *DEF v. Trappett* 2015 and 2016, leave to appeal denied in 2017; *Live Group Pty Ltd v. Rabbi Ulman* 2017; *Ulman v. Live Group Pty Ltd* 2018). It is relevant to this chapter to note briefly that the general reluctance of courts to intervene in the affairs of 'voluntary organizations' is reinforced when religious groups are involved.[21] One reason offered for the even more heightened reluctance of courts to intervene in the affairs of religious groups is the fact that it is inappropriate for secular judges to rule on theological issues unless the parties have chosen to subject themselves to a shared religious regime. In the appeal in *Ulman v. Live Group Pty Ltd* (2018),[22] McColl JA commented:

> Furthermore, it should be recognised as Murphy J explained in *Grant* that, '[j]udicial determination of religious doctrine and practice is as much state interference in religious affairs as legislative and administrative measures are'. That does not mean that churches (using that expression broadly) are immune from judicial scrutiny, but, generally 'only marginal inquiry into church government is permissible'. In particular, as recognised in a body of United States jurisprudence, 'the decisions of the governing body of the church should be accepted on issues of practice and procedure of ecclesiastical government, as well as issues of doctrine' and 'controversial questions of doctrine (or departure from doctrine) or practice or procedure in ecclesiastical government ... however forceful ... arguments [on these issues] appear to be ... are outside the judicial sphere[']. As Kirby P recognised in *Uniting Church in Australia Property Trust (NSW) v Vincent*, judges' 'competence to determine disputed issues of religious belief is highly doubtful'. (Para 248, internal citations removed)

The position that seems to have been reached in NSW on the question of intervention in disciplinary proceedings in religious groups, since the decision of the NSW Court of Appeal in *Agricultural Societies Council of NSW v. Christie* (2016), is that the mere 'receipt of income' will not give jurisdiction to a court to interfere in the internal arrangements of a 'voluntary association'. Nor would an impact on 'reputation' alone give such jurisdiction (para 35). Instead, what must be shown is a breach of a contractual or property right.

Even where intervention may be justified on such a basis, a court will be very reluctant to decide 'theological' issues in such proceedings and will mainly consider the 'neutral' issues of whether natural justice has been afforded.[23]

Keith Mason (2018), in his comment on these issues, notes that another possible ground for intervention may be found if a 'statutory right' of some sort were given to the cleric. He refers to the decision in *Baker v. Gough* (1963), where it was held that the School Chapels and Chaplains Ordinance (1954) (NSW), cl. 10(a), conferred personal rights on

---

[21] See *Sturt v. the Right Reverend Dr Brian Farran Bishop of Newcastle* (2012, para 46): 'It should also be acknowledged that courts have routinely not interfered in the internal workings of voluntary associations especially religious organisations: *Attorney-General (NSW) v Grant* [1976] HCA 38; (1976) 135 CLR 587 at 613 per Murphy J'.

[22] It should be noted that McColl JA was in dissent on the outcome of the appeal, but her comments on these issues seem to be an uncontroversial restatement of general principles.

[23] See earlier for a similar distinction between religious and secular principles in the *Otuo* case.

a chaplain whom a school council has purported to dismiss without giving him a proper opportunity to show cause.

9. Distinguishing the Circumstances

It was suggested earlier that the approach which best protects the freedom of religious groups to determine the doctrines of their own religion, and the dignity of religious believers to order their lives in accordance with their fundamental beliefs, while protecting the legitimate expectations of private parties who have entered into arrangements on the basis of a particular understanding of doctrine, is what was called the 'hands off unless' approach. This will involve courts not imposing their own interpretations of doctrine on parties from an 'external' point of view, but being prepared to examine doctrine where necessary to enforce private law obligations that parties have voluntarily accepted.

Is this distinction workable and useful? Does the approach deal with the possible issues raised earlier?

On the one hand, it will provide an avenue for parties to have legitimate private law questions resolved. The 'lack of competence' issue will still remain to some extent, but courts can accept expert evidence as to the meaning of particular concepts. While the danger remains that a court will accept the evidence of whichever expert it favours, hopefully the scope for this problem can be reduced when the question becomes not 'what does this doctrine actually mean?', but rather 'what would these parties have thought the doctrine meant?' Courts should be willing to examine the subjective understanding of the parties concerned, as they have to do in other cases, and not 'shy away' from issues simply because religion is involved.

But the courts should be reluctant to enforce their own understanding of doctrine where this would be imposed on a religious group by a public law rule.

The 'hands off unless' aspect of the suggested approach will, then, preserve to the maximum extent possible the religious freedom of persons and organizations to determine their own religious commitments in most cases and afford them the dignity of living out their religious commitments, especially where the imposition of the power of the state is invoked without the consent of the parties involved.

There remains a danger, of course, that this approach would allow a particularly objectionable religious group to claim the freedom to hold a view which is only shared by a minority of their religion – for example, an Aryan or apartheid group claiming that black people are lesser beings based on their idiosyncratic view of the Bible.

One check on this may be that the courts should decline to accept a religious view that is a 'sham' (similar to the way that courts will reject as a 'religion' something that is a made-up religion with ulterior motives). The sincerity of a belief may be tested through a range of the usual sort of evidence that is used in cases of this type, such as whether there is any evidence from other parties that the observed behaviour of a person evidences such a belief.

The other thing to note is that even accepting that a particular view is 'genuinely religious' does not automatically mean that religious freedom will be accepted as a justification for behaviour. It is important to note that this question (as to the extent to which courts should expound religious doctrine) is *not* one where all the problems of religious freedom are resolved. There has to be a separate discussion about the 'limits' of religious freedom. So, acts of physical violence or child abuse should clearly not be exempted on religious grounds, even if such actions are sanctioned by religious teaching. Whether we allow religious freedom to justify the expression of views opposing homosexuality is a broader issue that still continues to be debated in the wider community.[24]

10. Conclusion

This chapter has considered the extent to which courts should be involved in making decisions about the content of religious doctrines. We have seen that, while it has often been said that courts will not involve themselves in resolving these questions, there are important exceptions to this general principle, and we have been attempting to determine whether there are broad reasons which guide when courts will, and will not, determine these matters.

There are good reasons to be cautious about courts making pronouncements on religious questions. While these questions are not always as 'irrational' as has sometimes been suggested (*McFarlane* 2010, paras 23–24), it is certainly true that most secular judges are not really competent to make detailed findings about the content and interpretation of theological truths. This competence argument is all the stronger when we consider the strong principles favouring religious freedom, an aspect of which has always been seen as the dignity and right of religious bodies, and religious persons, to determine for themselves which views they hold on these matters.

However, it has been argued here that an exception to the bar on courts making religious findings should be recognised in circumstances where the private rights of the parties to a dispute are at stake, and the parties themselves have chosen to accept benefits on the basis that they will be bound by certain religious principles. So, it seems appropriate for a person who agrees to do work for a religious organization and to be bound by the religious doctrines of the organization, to be kept to their word and for the organization to be able to rely on them keeping their promises. Where a dispute arises, it may be necessary for a court, in resolving a private dispute, to make findings about the preferable meaning of certain doctrines. In many cases this will be made easier because coreligionists themselves will have a common agreement on the meaning of the doctrines, which can be shown from their prior dealings.

To take another example, where a person or organization assumes control of real property which is known to be subject to a charitable religious trust, a court cannot

---

[24]   Recently in Australia, these debates were sparked by the decision of Rugby Australia to dismiss high-profile player Israel Folau on account of a 'meme' shared on social media suggesting that a range of sinners, including homosexuals, were destined for hell unless they repented. See Foster (2019a, 2019b).

ignore its responsibility to see that the trust is carried out, by declining to decide religious questions. The *Red Book case* (1948) and *Shergill v. Khaira* (2015) illustrate this fact.

This chapter has tried to show that broad assertions that courts should never consider religious issues are not justified, in Australia or the United Kingdom, just as Helfand has shown that they are not justified in the United States. It does make the case, however, for a slightly more nuanced test to be adopted than that put forward by Helfand, of simply asking whether the question is one of private or public rights. Instead, it is suggested that there should be a presumption that courts will usually have a hands-off approach to religious doctrine, but that this presumption may be rebutted where there is a civil dispute involving private parties, who have chosen to subject themselves to a specific religious regime. In those circumstances, the court has an obligation to resolve the dispute between the parties, even if that resolution may incidentally involve a consideration of religious doctrine.

It is hoped that the test put forward here will be of assistance to decision-makers and those advising parties in disputes involving religious persons or bodies, preserving to the maximum extent possible their religious freedom, but allowing decisions to be made which respect the choice of parties to contract or hold property under religious principles. As noted earlier, of course, this chapter's scope does not extend to a resolution of all the complexities of determining the limits of acceptable religious freedom. Even if the freedom of an organization or person to determine their religious commitment is respected, there are some broad areas where the community has to determine that religious rights cannot override other fundamental rights. But hopefully these suggestions will make the issues around determination of the content of religious doctrine clearer.

References

Adelaide Company of Jehovah's Witnesses Inc. v. Commonwealth (1943) 67 CLR 116.

Agricultural Societies Council of NSW v. Christie [2016] NSWCA 331.

Anglican Development Fund Diocese of Bathurst v. Palmer [2015] NSWSC 1856.

Aroney, Nicholas. 2014. 'Freedom of Religion as an Associational Right'. *University of Queensland Law Journal* 33, no. 1: 153–86.

Attorney-General (NSW) v. Grant [1976] HCA 38; (1976) 135 CLR 587.

Baker v. Gough [1963] NSWR 1345.

Blake v. Associated Newspapers Ltd [2003] EWHC 1960.

Bruker v. Marcovitz, 2007 SCC 54 (CanLII), [2007] 3 SCR 607. http://canlii.ca/t/1v5zk.

Cavanaugh v. Bartelt. 12 April 2016. USDC for Nebraska, 4:14-CV-3183.

Cheung, T. 2019. 'Jediism: Religion at Law?' *Oxford Journal of Law and Religion* 8, no. 2: 350–77.

Christian Youth Camps Limited v. Cobaw Community Health Services Limited (2014) 50 VR 256, [2014] VSCA 75.

Church of the New Faith v. Commissioner of Pay-Roll Tax (Vic) [1983] HCA 40; (1983) 154 CLR 120 (the *Scientology Case*).

Cobaw Community Health Services Ltd v. Christian Youth Camps Ltd & Rowe [2010] VCAT 1613.

Cranmer, Frank. 2020. 'Religion and Public Benefit in United Kingdom Charity Law'. In *The Status of Religion and the Public Benefit in Charity Law*, edited by Barry W. Bussey, 81–100. London: Anthem.

DEF v. Trappett [2015] NSWSC 1840.

DEF v. Trappett [2016] NSWSC 1698.

DEF v. Trappett [2017] NSWCA 163.

Eisgruber, Christopher L., and Lawrence G. Sager. 2009. 'Does It Matter What Religion Is?' *Notre Dame Law Review* 84, no. 2: 807–36.

Employment Division v. Smith, 494 U.S. 872 (1990).

Engel v. Adelaide Hebrew Congregation Inc. (2007) 98 SASR 402.

Equal Opportunity Act. 2010. (Vic), 1 August 2011.

Foster, Neil. 2011. 'Freedom of Religion in Practice: Exemptions under Anti-Discrimination Laws on the Basis of Religion'. Paper presented at Law and Religion: Legal Regulation of Religious Groups, Organisations and Communities, July. Melbourne Law School, University of Melbourne. http://works.bepress.com/neil_foster/46.

———. 2014a. 'Christian Youth Camp Liable for Declining Booking from Homosexual Support Group'. 21 April. http://works.bepress.com/neil_foster/78.

———. 2014b. 'High Court of Australia Declines Leave to Appeal CYC v Cobaw'. 18 December. http://works.bepress.com/neil_foster/89/.

———. 2019a. 'Reflections on the Israel Folau Affair'. *Law and Religion Australia* (blog). https://lawandreligionaustralia.blog/2019/04/14/reflections-on-the-israel-folau-affair/

———. 2019b. 'Further Reflections on the Israel Folau Affair'. *Law and Religion Australia* (blog). https://lawandreligionaustralia.blog/2019/06/02/further-reflections-on-the-israel-folau-affair/.

———. 2019c. 'Second Draft of Religious Discrimination Package Released'. *Law and Religion Australia* (blog). https://lawandreligionaustralia.blog/2019/12/10/second-draft-of-religious-discrimination-package-released/.

Galbraith, D. 1998. 'Just Enough Religion to Make Us Hate: An Historico-Legal Study of the Red Book Case'. PhD diss., University of NSW.

The Gay and Lesbian Clergy Anti-Discrimination Society Inc. v. Bishop of Auckland [2013] NZHRRT 36.

General Assembly of Free Church of Scotland v. Lord Overtoun [1904] AC 515.

Greenawalt, Kent. 1998. 'Hands Off! Civil Court Involvement in Conflicts over Religious Property'. *Columbia Law Review* 98, no. 8: 1843–907.

Hale, Hon. Baroness. 2015. 'Secular Judges and Christian Law'. *Ecclesiastical Law Journal* 17, no. 2: 170–81.

Halsall v. Brizell [1957] Ch 169.

Harrington v. Coote (2013) 119 SASR 152, [2013] SASCFC 154.

Helfand, Michael A. 2016a. 'Identifying Substantial Burdens'. *University of Illinois Law Review*, no. 4: 1771–808.

———. 2016b. 'How to Limit Accommodations: Wrong Answers and Rights Answers'. *Journal of Law, Religion and State* 5, no. 1: 1–24.

———. 2018. 'When Judges Are Theologians: Adjudicating Religious Questions'. In *Research Handbook on Law & Religion*, edited by Rex Ahdar, 262–85. Cheltenham: Edward Elgar; Pepperdine University Legal Studies Research Paper No. 2017/12.

Highwood Congregation of Jehovah's Witnesses (Judicial Committee) v. Wall, 2018 SCC 26 [2018] 1 SCR 750.

Holmes, Rachel. 2018. 'Charity Commission Decision: The Temple of the Jedi Order'. *Farrer & Co LLP* (blog). https://www.farrer.co.uk/news-and-insights/charity-commission-decision-the-temple-of-the-jedi-order/.

Holzer, S. 2015. 'Religious Reasoning and Due Process of the Law: Why Religious Citizens Have the Burden to Prove the Innocence of Their Reasoning in the Public Square'. *Journal of Church and State* 57, no. 3: 419–49.

In the matter of South Head & District Synagogue (Sydney) (Administrators appointed) [2017] NSWSC 823.

International Covenant on Civil and Political Rights. 1966. United Nations General Assembly Resolution 2200A (XXI), 21 U.N. GAOR Supp. (No. 16) at 52, U.N. Doc. A/6316 (1966), 999 U.N.T.S. 171. Entered into force 23 March 1976.

Khaira v. Shergill [2012] EWCA Civ 983.

Khaira v. Shergill [2017] EWCA Civ 1687.

Kumar v. Satsang Hindu Maha Sabha of NSW Incorporated (No 2) [2019] NSWSC 325.

Law Society of British Columbia v. Trinity Western University, 2018 SCC 32, [2018] 2 SCR 293.

Live Group Pty Ltd v. Rabbi Ulman [2017] NSWSC 1759.

Lupu, Ira C., and Robert W. Tuttle. 2007. 'Courts, Clergy, and Congregations: Disputes between Religious Institutions and Their Leaders'. *Georgetown Journal of Law & Public Policy* 7, no. 1: 119–64.

Mason, Hon. Keith. 2018. 'Clergy Status in the Age of the Royal Commission'. Robin Sharwood Lecture in Church Law, University of Melbourne, March. https://www.trinity.unimelb.edu.au/getattachment/about/news-media/news/Trinity-host-Robin-Sharwood-Lecture-series/CLERGY-STATUS-IN-THE-AGE-OF-THE-ROYAL-COMMISSION.pdf.aspx?lang=en-AU.

McFarlane v. Relate Avon Ltd [2010] EWCA Civ 880.

Metropolitan Petar v. Mitreski [2003] NSWSC 1007.

Metropolitan Petar v. Mitreski [2009] NSWSC 106 (4 March).

Mohamed v. Mohamed [2012] NSWSC 852 (31 July).

Murphy, B. 2016. 'Balancing Religious Freedom and Anti-Discrimination: *Christian Youth Camps Ltd v Cobaw Community Health Services Ltd*'. *Melbourne University Law Review* 40, no. 2: 594–625.

Mustafa, Faizan, and Jagteshwar Singh Sohi. 2017. 'Freedom of Religion in India: Current Issues and Supreme Court Acting as Clergy'. *BYU Law Review*, no. 4: 915–56. https://digitalcommons.law.byu.edu/lawreview/vol2017/iss4/9.

Otuo v. Watch Tower Bible and Tract Society of Britain [2019] EWHC 344 (QB) (2019a).

Otuo v. Watch Tower Bible and Tract Society of Britain [2019] EWHC 1349 (QB) (2019b).

OV and anor v. QZ and anor (No 2) [2008] NSWADT 115.

OV & OW v. Members of the Board of the Wesley Mission Council [2010] NSWCA 155 (2010a).

OW & OV v. Members of the Board of the Wesley Mission Council [2010] NSWADT 293 (2010b).

R (on the application of Hodkin and another) v. Registrar-General of Births, Deaths and Marriages [2013] UKSC 77.

Religious Freedom Restoration Act. Pub. L. No. 103–141, 107 Stat. 1488 (16 November 1993). Codified at 42 U.S.C. § 2000bb through 42 U.S.C. § 2000bb-4.

Ridge, Pauline. 2011. 'Religious Charitable Status and Public Benefit in Australia'. *Melbourne University Law Review* 35, no. 3: 1071–98.

Rivers, J. 2010. *The Law of Organized Religions*. Oxford: Oxford University Press.

Scandrett v. Dowling (1992) 27 NSWLR 483.

Schachter, O. 1983. 'Human Dignity as a Normative Concept'. *American Journal of International Law* 77, no. 4: 848–54.

School Chapels and Chaplains Ordinance 1954 (NSW), cl 10(a).

Second exposure draft, Religious Discrimination Bill 2019 (Cth), cl 11(1); cl 5(1) para (a)(iii)), 32(8)(b) and 33(2)(b).

Shamil Bank of Bahrain EC v. Beximco Pharmaceuticals [2004] 1 WLR 1784.

Shergill v Khaira [2015] AC 359.

Shergill v. Khaira [2017] EWHC 883 (Ch).

Smith v. Morrison (2011) SLT 1213.

Sturt v. the Right Reverend Dr Brian Farran Bishop of Newcastle [2012] NSWSC 400.

Towers, Katherine. 2014. 'New Anti-Discrimination Laws "Erode Religious Freedom"'. *Australian*, 9 May. https://works.bepress.com/neil_foster/81/.

Trustees of the Celestial Church of Christ, Edward Street Parish (a charity) v. Lawson [2017] EWHC 97 (Ch).

Ulman v. Live Group Pty Ltd [2018] NSWCA 338.

UN General Assembly. 1966. *International Covenant on Civil and Political Rights*, 16 December. United Nations, Treaty Series, vol. 999, p. 171. Accessed 29 October 2020. https://www.refworld.org/docid/3ae6b3aa0.html.

Wesley Mission Council v. OV & OW (No 2) [2009] NSWADTAP 57.

Wylde v. Attorney-General for NSW (1948) 78 CLR 224 ('the *Red Book case*').

NOTES ON CONTRIBUTORS

Iain T. Benson, PhD (Wits), MA (Cambridge), JD (Windsor), BA (Hons) (Queens), was born in Edinburgh, Scotland, raised in Canada and now lives in France and Australia. He is called to the Bars of British Columbia and Ontario, Professor of Law, University of Notre Dame Australia, Sydney (since 2016). Iain is Professor Extraordinary, University of the Free State, Bloemfontein, South Africa (2009, ongoing). His central research areas are theories of pluralism and subsidiarity, the jurisdiction of law, religious liberty and 'the language of values'. He is author of *Living Together with Disagreement: Pluralism, the Secular and the Fair Treatment of Beliefs by Law* (2012) and co-editor of *Religion, Liberty and the Jurisdiction of Law* (2017) and *The Cambridge Handbook of Human Rights and Natural Law* (forthcoming).

Heiner Bielefeldt, PhD (Tübingen), Post-Doctoral Habilitation degree (University of Bremen), was born in 1958 in the school building of a small village near Aachen. After his school education, he studied philosophy, theology and history at the Universities of Bonn and Tübingen. In 1989, he completed his PhD thesis on social contract theories and their impact on contemporary constitutional theory. In 2000, he finished his Habilitation (Post-Doctoral) degree at the University of Bremen with a thesis on the philosophy of human rights. Bielefeldt held teaching positions in different faculties at the Universities of Mannheim, Heidelberg, Toronto, Bremen, Bielefeld and Erlangen-Nuremberg. Between 2003 and 2009 he served as Director of the German Institute for Human Rights (based in Berlin). In 2009, he took the newly established chair of human rights and human rights politics at the university of Erlangen-Nuremberg. From 2016 to 2019, he also held the position of a Professor 2 at the Human Rights Centre of the University of Oslo. Bielefeldt's research interests include different interdisciplinary facets of human rights theory and practice, with a particular focus on freedom of religion or belief. He has published numerous articles, reports and books in different languages.

From 2010 to 2016, Heiner Bielefeldt served as the UN Special Rapporteur on Freedom of Religion or Belief, which is a worldwide mandate, originally established in 1986. In discharging his mandate, he undertook country inspections and presented reports to various UN forums (all available at the website of the Office of the High Commissioner for Human Rights: www.ohchr.org).

Bielefeldt has been Honorary Professor at the law faculty of the University of Bielefeld since 2007. He received an honorary doctorate from the theological faculty of the University of Lucerne, Switzerland (2014), the annual religious freedom service award of the Brigham Young University in Provo, United States (2016) and the Alfons-Auer

Ethics Award of the Catholic theological faculty of the University of Tübingen (2017). The OUP Commentary on 'Freedom of Religion or Belief', co-authored with Nazila Ghanea and Michael Wiener, received the 2018 Guiseppe Alberigo Award (Category A) from the European Academy of Religion in Bologna. In October 2017, the German President Frank-Walter Steinmeier awarded Bielefeldt with the Order of Merits (Bundesverdienstkreuz Erster Klasse).

Vito Breda, PhD, is the research leader of the International and Comparative Law Group at the University of Southern Queensland and Visiting Professor of Comparative Public Law at the Universities of Deusto and Brescia. Previously he held a tenured position at the University of Cardiff. He is currently researching 'constitutional loyalty' for a forthcoming Oxford University Press volume. Vito recently published monographs and edited collections on legal philosophy and comparative constitutional law. The list of his publications includes: *Legal Transplants in East Asia and Oceania* (2019), *Constitutional Law and Regionalism* (2018) and *The Objectivity of Judicial Decisions* (2017).

Barry W. Bussey, PhD, is Director of Legal Affairs at the Canadian Centre for Christian Charities and Adjunct Associate Professor, University of Notre Dame Australia (Sydney). Barry has advocated for religious freedom throughout his career in court and writing. He served as Intervener Counsel in several Canadian cases arguing in favour of religious freedom. He holds degrees in theology, political science, peace and conflict studies, and law. He holds a PhD in law from the University of Leiden. He is currently writing a volume on conscience which is being scheduled for publication in late 2021. He is the editor of *The Status of Religion and the Public Benefit in Charity Law* (2020) and co-editor, with Iain T. Benson, of the LexisNexis publication *Religion, Liberty and the Jurisdictional Limits of Law* (2017); in 2012 he was a recipient of the Diamond Jubilee Medal for religious freedom work in Canada and abroad; during 2009–11 he represented the Seventh-day Adventist Church and the International Religious Liberty Association in Washington, DC, at the United Nations in New York and Geneva.

Clint Curle, PhD, is Vice-President: Exhibitions, Curation and Partnerships at the Canadian Museum for Human Rights. His research interests include the history of human rights, Holocaust and genocide studies, and international human rights and humanitarian law. He holds a Law degree, Master's degrees in theology and legal studies, and a PhD in political science. He is the author of *Humanité: John Humphrey's Alternative Account of Human Rights* (2007). His most recent publication, with Dr Jeremy Maron, is 'Balancing the Particular and the Universal: Examining the Holocaust in the Canadian Museum for Human Rights' (*Holocaust Studies* 24, no. 4 (2018): 418–44).

Neil Foster is an Associate Professor in Newcastle Law School at the University of Newcastle, NSW, Australia. He has a combined Arts/Law degree from the University of NSW, a degree in theology from the Australian College of Theology and a research Master of Laws degree from the University of Newcastle. He teaches torts, workplace health and safety law and an elective in 'law and religion'. He is a co-author of textbooks on torts and property law, published by LexisNexis Australia, and the sole author of *Workplace Health and Safety Law in Australia* (2016), published by the same company; he also runs a blog on law and religion issues (lawandreligionaustralia.blog).

Matteo Frau, PhD, is tenured researcher in Comparative Public Law at the University of Brescia. He holds a PhD in Italian and European Constitutional Law from the University of Verona. He is currently researching on the implications of the modern doctrine of separation of power. Among his latest publications are: 'PESCO and the Prospect of a European Army: The "Constitutional Need" to Provide for a Power of Control of the European Parliament on Military Interventions' (with Elisa Tira; *European Journal of Legal Studies*, 2019); *La sfiducia costruttiva* (2017); 'L'equilibrio originario dei poteri di guerra nella Costituzione americana' (*Journal of Constitutional History*, 2017); 'La pluridimensionalità del diritto all'oblio e il problema del bilanciamento con la libertà di informazione' (*La democrazia costituzionale tra nuovi diritti e deriva mediale*, edited by G. Ferri, 2015).

Robert P. George is McCormick Professorship of Jurisprudence and Director of the James Madison Program in American Ideals and Institutions at Princeton University. He has served as Chairman of the US Commission on International Religious Freedom and on the US Commission on Civil Rights and the President's Council on Bioethics. He was a Judicial Fellow at the Supreme Court of the United States, where he received the Justice Tom C. Clark Award. A Phi Beta Kappa graduate of Swarthmore, he holds JD and MTS degrees from Harvard University and the degrees of DPhil, BCL, DCL and DLitt from Oxford University, in addition to 21 honorary doctorates. He is a recipient of the US Presidential Citizens Medal, the Honorific Medal for the Defense of Human Rights of the Republic of Poland and the Canterbury Medal of the Becket Fund for Religious Freedom.

Katya Kozicki holds a PhD in juridical science from the Federal University of Santa Catarina. She is currently Full Professor of Law at Pontifical Catholic University of Parana and Federal University of Parana – undergraduate and graduate program. She was a Visiting Researcher Associate at the Centre for the Study of Democracy, University of Westminster, London, United Kingdom, from 1998 to 1999, and a Visiting Research Scholar at Benjamin N. Cardozo School of Law, New York, United States, from 2012 to 2013. She is also a Research Fellow – CNPq, National Council for Research, Brazil.

Angus J. L. Menuge is Chair of the Philosophy Department, and Co-Chair of the Classical Education program at Concordia University Wisconsin. He was raised in England and became an American citizen in 2005. He holds a BA in philosophy from Warwick University and a PhD in philosophy from the University of Wisconsin-Madison. He is author of *Agents Under Fire* (2004) and many articles on the philosophy of mind, philosophy of science and Christian apologetics, and editor of several collections, including *Reading God's World* (2004), *Legitimizing Human Rights* (2013; 2016), *Religious Liberty and the Law* (2017) and, with Jonathan Loose and J. P. Moreland, *The Blackwell Companion* *to Substance Dualism* (2018). He is past president of the Evangelical Philosophical Society (2012–18).

Dallas K. Miller has served as a federally appointed trial judge for almost 15 years. In addition to his JD degree (United States, 1984), Justice Miller has degrees in history and theology. He has studied theology and human rights in Strasbourg, France, and holds the *Certificat* from the International Institute of Human Rights. He is a Fellow of the Society of Advanced Legal Studies in London and teaches human rights and judicial/rule of law training in Bolivia with a human rights organization (www.ijm.ca). He has lectured on justice issues at many international venues. Recent publications include contributions to *Legitimizing Human Rights* (2013), *Religious Liberty and the Law* (2017), *The Commonwealth Magistrates and Judges Association Journal* and a recent article on residential schools in the *Dalhousie Law Review*.

Dwight Newman, QC, is Professor of Law and Canada Research Chair in Indigenous Rights in Constitutional and International Law at the University of Saskatchewan. He has been a Visiting Fellow in recent years at Cambridge, Montréal, Oxford and Princeton. He completed his BA and JD in Canada and his BCL and DPhil from Oxford University, with his DPhil focused on legal philosophy. He has also studied at the Hague Academy of International Law and completed his Graduate Diploma in Christian Studies from Regent College. He has published widely, with some of his recent books being *Religious Freedom and Communities: The Law of the Canadian Constitution* (co-authored) and *Mining Law of Canada*. His long-standing philosophical interests in collective rights led to his older book *Community and Collective Rights: A Theoretical Framework for Rights Held by Groups* and will be a renewed focus in some of his upcoming work.

Andrea Pin is Associate Professor of Comparative Public Law at the University of Padua; Senior Fellow at the Center for the Study of Law and Religion, Emory University; and member of the Scientific Committee of Oasis International Foundation. A former clerk for the Italian Constitutional Court, Andrea Pin has taught in Italy, the United States and Ireland. He has authored four books, including *The Legal Treatment of Muslim Minorities in Italy* (2016), and published in Italian, American, British, German, French and Spanish academic journals, with articles such as 'Arab Constitutionalism and Human Dignity' (*George Washington International Law Review* 2017). His main fields of research are religious freedom, Middle Eastern constitutionalism, comparative legal systems, and constitutional law and AI.

Michael Quinlan holds an LLM from the University of New South Wales, an MA in theological studies from the University of Notre Dame Australia, and has completed the Practical Legal Training Course. He is currently Professor of Law and Dean at the University of Notre Dame Australia, School of Law. Prior to assuming this role in 2013, Professor Quinlan had a distinguished career of over 23 years at the commercial law firm Allens. He is deeply interested in the relationships between law, morality and religion. His research focuses on religious freedom, marriage, euthanasia and exclusion zones. Professor Quinlan is Junior Vice President of the St Thomas More Society, a Board Member of Freedom for Faith and a Committee Member of the Sydney Catholic Archdiocese Anti-Slavery Taskforce Advisory. He is co-editor of *Religious Freedom in Australia – a New Terra Nullius?* (2019) and author of numerous scholarly articles.

William Soares Pugliese holds a PhD and an LLM from the Universidade Federal do Paraná, Brazil. He is a Visiting Scholar at the Max-Planck Institut für Ausländisches Öffentliches Recht und Völkerrecht and a Substitute Professor of constitutional law, state theory and political science at Universidade Federal do Paraná, Brazil. Dr Pugliese is Coordinator of the Civil Procedural Law Specialization Program at Academia Brasileira de Direito Constitucional (ABDCONST, Brazil). He is a researcher of the Constitutionalism and Democracy Research Group and of the Comparative Civil Procedural Law Research Group (UFPR) and also an attorney at law.

Greg Walsh completed his Bachelor of Laws/Science degree from the Australian National University, a Master of Laws degree from the University of Sydney and PhD on the regulation of religious schools under anti-discrimination legislation from Curtin University. He is currently working as a law lecturer at the University of Notre Dame Australia and has previously lectured at Western Sydney University and the University of New South Wales. Dr Walsh has worked in various legal roles in Australia and overseas, including as a prosecutor in New South Wales, a medical negligence lawyer and a legal officer for the Office of the United Nations High Commissioner for Human Rights. His research interests include medical law, human rights law and the intersection between law and religion.

INDEX

www.ingramcontent.com/pod-product-compliance
Lightning Source LLC
Chambersburg PA
CBHW022351280326
41935CB00007B/148